Reinhold Würth
The Entrepreneur and His Company

Ute Grau and Barbara Guttmann

REINHOLD WÜRTH

The Entrepreneur and His Company

Swiridoff Verlag
Künzelsau

CONTENTS

7   "Knowing history is a prerequisite for understanding the present"
Business History at Würth

16   1 | **How everything started** | 1945 to 1954
A "Nine Days' Wonder"? – Foundation of the Würth Company in 1945 | Difficult Start in the Postwar Era | From Economic Control to the Reconstruction Boom | Adolf Würth Bets on the Automotive Industry | Reinhold Würth Accepts the Challenge

27   2 | **Family Roots** | Reinhold Würth and His Family

34   3 | **Reinhold Würth takes over the Company** | 1954 to 1960
The "Silver" 1950s | Reinhold Würth's Start as Entrepreneur | The First Employees | A Decisive Step: Building up a Sales Force | A Company Culture Develops | Success Factor Multiplication – the Growing Company

45   4 | **Würth and the Region** | A Baden-Württemberg Success Story
Hohenlohe – What Does the Name Stand for? | Hohenlohe – an Agricultural Region Formerly the Granary of Württemberg | People and Mentalities | From Poorhouse to Model Region – the Development of Hohenlohe after World War II | Heilbronn-Franconia – the Growth Region | The Würth Group – Global Player from Hohenlohe | Advantages and Disadvantages of Being Located in a Rural Area | Würth Expands and Diversifies in the Region | Würth Points the Way to the Future in Regional Gastronomy | Freemen of the City of Künzelsau: Carmen Würth and Reinhold Würth | Hermersberg – a Castle as Domicile of an Entrepreneur | Reinhold Würth– Global Entrepreneur from Baden-Württemberg | Citizens' Action Group Pro Region Heilbronn-Franken

70   5 | **Expansion Head-on** | The 1960s
Between the Economic Miracle and the Recession | Stepping beyond Borders | From Survival Tactics to Strategic Business Planning | Internal Management and External Consultants | Selling – Development of the Sales Force in the 1960s | Prices, Commissions, and Sample Boards – Stories from the Sales Side | Expansion of Corporate Headquarters

89   6 | **Fifty per cent of Success** | Würth and the World
Beginning Internationalization | The First Companies to be Founded – The Netherlands, Austria, and Switzerland | The Star among the New Companies – Italy | France | Successes in the North – Würth in Scandinavia | Spain and Portugal | "A Network of Selling Companies" – the Opening of the East | Go West – Würth in the USA | South America and South East Asia | Africa – and the Rest of the World | Coordination of the International Activities | Founders' Rules | The Würth Group and Adolf Würth GmbH & Co. KG

112   7 | **Growth requires a certain Structure** | The 1970s
The 'Oil Crisis' Environmental Awareness, and a Policy of Détente | Würth Braves the Economic Crisis | "As Much Organization as Necessary" – Reinhold Würth Points the Way for a Group Structure | An "Efficient Regulating Mechanism" – Corporate Advisory Board, Corporate Philosophy, and Sets of Rules | Management, FÜKO, and Coordinating Conference – Development of a Management Structure | New Forces in Management | The "Guardians of Progress" – New Structures in the Sales Force | A New Pricing and Commission System | Information and Incentives – Staff Motivation | Another Milestone on the Way to Success: Divisionalization | Logistics, EDP, and Marketing – Expansion of Administration and Sales | The New Distribution Center | "Würth Creates Connections" – Marketing Concepts and Product Policy | "Profit Lies in the Purchasing of Goods" | Successes and New Visions

8 | Computers, Networks and Phoenix | The History of EDP at Würth — 139

"Countdown to a New Era" | A Difficult Start | Logistics and New Leadership | The New EDP Manager | Computer-Aided Purchasing and Selling | Sales Representatives with Laptops | "War for Ten Days" | World Wide Würth | Using the Company's Own Resources – Würth Software | Würth Phoenix | "As Much EDP as Necessary, but Not One Tiny Bit More!"

9 | The Würth Idea for the 80s: Satisfied Employees! | The 80s — 160

The Opening of the Wall and Continuity – Economy and Politics in the 80s | The Company | "The Fast Ones Eat Up the Slow" | "Happy Days" | Products and Customers | Focus on Staff – Satisfied Employees | Growth through Diversification | Schraubenwerk Gaisbach | Würth Elektronik | Management with Visions | Degrees of Freedom | Marketing Prize Awarded to Würth | Succession Settled in Time – the Family Foundations

10 | The Human Being – The Focus of Attention | Working at Würth — 185

Personnel Development from 1955 to 2005 | The Sales Force – the Foundation of the Business | Good Sales Representatives Require Good Leadership | Good Pay in Exchange for Good Work | Structures in the Sales Force | Sales, Administration, Distribution – Order Processing at Würth | Corporate Culture and Employee Participation | Working for the Colleagues – the Members of the Council of Trustees | Life-Long-Learning – Further Education and Training at Würth | Synergy Effects between Schools and the Business | Qualification and Career | An In-House Campus – the Würth Academy

11 | He's still the Boss, You Know | The 1990s — 210

Reunification Boom and Social Change – Germany in the 1990s | A Slow Start and a Record Finish – the 1990s at Würth | The New Länder – Würth Goes East | Expansion and Customer Commitment | Competent and Professional – the Würth Service | The Transparent Company – the Würth Information System | A Family-Owned Business Approaches the Capital Market | Consulting by McKinsey – Structures in a State of Flux | Divisionalization of the Würth Group | Reinhold Würth Becomes Chairman of the Advisory Board | New Projects for Reinhold Würth

12 | Reinhold Würth | The Entrepreneur and His Contributions to Society — 235

The Businessman as Art Collector | The Collector in His Role as Businessman | Open to the Public – the Würth Collection | The Würth Museum in Künzelsau | Kunsthalle Würth in Schwäbisch Hall | The Hirschwirtscheuer in Künzelsau | The Museum of Screws and Threads | The Würth Collection in International Würth Subsidiaries | The Würth Collection on the Road | Patronage of the Arts within the Framework of the Würth Foundation | Swiridoff Publishing Company | "The Most Public Form of Art" – Architecture at Würth | Entrepreneurship in Theory and Practice – the Entrepreneur on His Way to Professorship | Honorary Senator of the University of Tübingen | Honorary Doctor of the University of Tübingen | Professor of Entrepreneurship at the University of Karlsruhe | An Entrepreneur's Curriculum | Stimulus for Self-Employment

13 | Conquering New Territory | Würth in the New Millennium — 270

Turbulent Times – the First Few Years of the New Century | The Vision Becomes a Reality – the New Millennium at Würth | The Chairman of the Advisory Board at Grass Roots Level | New Structures in the Group | Risk Management | New Ways of Selling – Regionalization and Customer Segmentation | Conquering New Territory: Würth Diversifies | Good or Bad? Diversification at Würth | Würth – Where to Now?

"I always wanted to be in front, get ahead, move up …"
Interview with Reinhold Würth — 287

Footnotes — 307

Index of Persons — 321

"Knowing history is a prerequisite for understanding the present" (Reinhold Würth)

BUSINESS HISTORY AT WÜRTH

In the year 2005, the Würth Group can look back on 60 years of business history and Reinhold Würth, who took over management of the company 50 years ago, will celebrate his 70th birthday. This is ample reason for researching the success story of the entrepreneur and his company, with its development from small screw wholesaling to worldwide operating group, and to present it in a new form.

"Information about the present becomes valuable only when backed by events from the past. Predictions of the future and the creation of strategic competitive advantages are only conceivable against the backdrop of the uninterrupted sequence of past, present, and future", stated Reinhold Würth 1986 in his thoughts about the development of the company up to the turn of the millennium. As the head of a relatively young company, he developed a very clear sense of history at quite an early point in time. By the middle of the 1980s, the establishment of central corporate archives had already been initiated parallel to the setting up of a corporate library, and the book "Nach oben geschraubt", published for the first time in 1991, documented the development of the company from its inception in 1945 until the beginning of the 1990s. In the autobiographical publication "Management Culture: the Secret of Success" (1994), Reinhold Würth described the success story of his company from the point of view of the active entrepreneur.

Whereas in the Würth story "Nach oben geschraubt" Karlheinz Schönherr preferred the narrative style of a more journalistic publication, the present corporate biography seeks to comply with modern scientific standards while remaining a good read. The difference in the autobiographical publication "Management Culture: the Secret of Success" is its objective perspective. The two original books end in the first half of the 1990s, while the present publication also describes developments in the 1990s and the new century as well as Reinhold Würth's activities since then, both inside and outside the Würth Group. The objective is to identify the specifics of the "Würth success story": the development of a small company located in a provincial, rural region into a globally operating group of companies and of the entrepreneur from sales representative in his own, two-man business to head of the group and finally Chairman of the Advisory Board, collector of art and university professor. The authors seek to make this development understandable, not primarily for the experts hailing from the different disciplines of economics, social history, and the history of economics, but rather for every interested reader – without at the same time ignoring basic scholarly standards.

"Companies are complex social and historical entities in which […] past experiences also shape and influence the type of behavior in the present and the assessment of the future", wrote the historian Paul Erker in 1997, in the magazine "Archiv für Sozialgeschichte". [1]

In recent years, business history has gradually been coming into fashion. The ever-increasing importance of companies for the economy, society, and politics since the middle of the 19th century turns their analysis into a central aspect of recent history. [2] In Germany, however, business history does not exist as an independent discipline as it does, for example, in the USA, where a chair in Business History was established at the Harvard Business School in 1926. Independent, modern business historiography has yet to be established and developed here. [3] Since the foundation of the Society for Business History in 1976 and the publication of "Zeitschrift für Unternehmensgeschichte" a more intensive reflection on methods has resulted in the development of a large number of different approaches. [4] In the most recent discussion about objectives and methods of business historiography, which since 1999 has featured mainly in "Zeitschrift für Unternehmensgeschichte", two principal points of view have begun to emerge. On the one hand, the focus of business historical research on the economic logic and internal structure of the organization has been advocated. [5] This standpoint is countered by the argument that, for one, the internal logic of entrepreneurial activity can perhaps never be "completely deciphered", and that this endeavor harbors the risk of losing sight of the complexity of the company and the interrelation of economics, culture, politics, and history and therefore also of doing injustice to the deep-rooted social importance of companies: "All in all it must be stated regarding business history that the analysis of a company's balance sheets, the development of accounting and controlling, the interplay of capital spending and funding plans, the establishment and expansion of organizational structures are very interesting. However, it is doubtful that this looks at the history of businesses from every possible angle." [6] In view of the fact that businesses are integrated in their time and context, they cannot only be "explained and described by themselves." [7] They are closely connected with their environment through markets, cultures, and a global framework of operation. Business history must therefore cover cultural, political and social history, the history of thought and technology and many other historical factors, in order properly to understand the object of research: the business.

The concept of social history formulated by Hans-Ulrich Wehler that, following Max Weber, assumes four equally fundamental categories – economy, social structure, politics, and culture – lays claim to a multi-dimensional analysis of historical processes. These factors also exist in businesses. As Wehler observes: "Of course, a factory is a production and market-oriented enterprise, but at the same time an organization of domination and a place of popular cultural traditions, behavior patterns, and value orientations". [8]

For the formulation and strategic orientation of corporate goals, the personality of the entrepreneur is of decisive importance. Up till now, the history of many businesses has mainly been derived from the dominant personality of their CEO or general manager. [9] Therefore, business history is often inextricably linked with the biography of the entrepreneur, at least in cases of businesses run by their owners.

Honoring entrepreneurs with a biography on the occasion of a company anniversary started to become popular at the beginning of the 20th century. After 1900, however, a number of important biographies of entrepreneurs were written that, rather than focus on their business activities, concentrated on their social standing and political significance. Among the numerous biographical works of the first half of the 20th century are some written by important personalities, e.g., the biography of Georg von Siemens, founder of Deutsche Bank, written by the scientist, banker, and statesman Karl Helfferich.[10] Theodor Heuss, who wrote a number of biographies of important politicians and scientists after having been dismissed as lecturer at the College of Politics by the National Socialists in 1933, started working on the biography of the entrepreneur Robert Bosch in 1943, which was published in 1946 and reprinted in 2002.[11]

The development of the theoretical-methodical "entrepreneurship approach" in economics led to the rediscovery of the dynamic inventor-entrepreneur as defined by Schumpeter.[12] A number of more recent biographies now deal with pioneers such as Henry Nestlé, August Oetker and Emanuel Merck.[13] An excellent example of a more recent biography of a German entrepreneur is the study of Hugo Stinnes.[14] Its author, the historian Gerald D. Feldman, sees the biographical representation as a chance to test generalizations by reality and fill structures with live content.

Whereas Feldman analyzed the life and work of the entrepreneur and politician Hugo Stinnes more than 70 years after his death, the authors of the biography of Würth dealt with a relatively young company and a highly active entrepreneur. However, the historical assessment and evaluation of processes and developments in a business as well as the work of a personality is made easier if a certain period of time has elapsed. If there is no such interval, objective representation and location in an economic and social context is naturally more difficult. This was already an issue in Theodor Heuss' preface to his biography on Bosch. He pointed out that, owing to the "closeness of time" and the "closeness of people", it was not altogether easy to write the biography: "Some events and decisions of both a business-related and general nature cannot yet be evaluated from the more simplifying perspective of distance; it is absolutely clear that a business cannot disclose anything and everything even though I was generously granted access to the confidential resolutions and agreements." It is true that the authors of the present study also had unlimited access to the documents stored in the corporate archives. However, the statement made by Theodor Heuss is valid here, too: if this

"KNOWING HISTORY IS A PREREQUISITE FOR UNDERSTANDING THE PRESENT"
BUSINESS HISTORY AT WÜRTH

biography were written thirty or forty years later it would be easier " … to talk more freely about one or the other problem whereas today a certain restraint is a natural requirement." [15]

On the other hand, it is certainly an advantage and a big asset well appreciated by the authors of the present book to have got to know personally the entrepreneur who built a worldwide trading corporation enjoying international acclaim from a small screw wholesale business in Hohenlohe and to have had the opportunity to talk to him as well as to many people who accompanied him through life or are still doing so – be it in friendship, from a critical distance, or even in conflict.

The many conversations and interviews with active and former members of the management – a "highly qualified management team with its rare degree of continuity and coherence" as Reinhold Würth describes the people who stayed with him on the way out of the "rampant conglomeration of medium-sized businesses that made up the Würth Group at the beginning of the 1960s into a streamlined corporation operating on a worldwide basis" [16] – yielded a wealth of information and also conveyed an impression of living business history. Whereas historians mainly deal with written records, minutes, process sequences, and descriptions of the situations of businesses, the rare opportunity existed here to let the "decision-makers" have their say. The authors also talked to Reinhold Würth's companions from the world of politics, the fine arts, and society. These interviews with "contemporary witnesses", without whom the present biography could not manage, supplement the information gleaned from written sources and publications.

The most important source, though, was the documents filed in the central archives of Adolf Würth GmbH & Co. KG, of which a central, Würth-specific collection is to be specifically emphasized: the "company histories" that have been updated annually ever since the mid-1980s by the Würth Companies and the Allied Companies, the members of the Board of Management, the managing directors, the authorized signatories and the regional sales managers of Adolf Würth GmbH & Co. KG. Meanwhile, the collection comprises nearly 1,000 reports that contain a wealth of information about the foundation and development of individual companies as well as the career of individual employees. These company histories make it possible to look at business history from different angles. It must, however, be taken into consideration that these reports are not primary sources in the proper sense of the word in that they reflect the subjective point of view of their respective authors.

Objective data on corporate development was available from annual reports, minutes, and business correspondence. Another important element was the company publications, filed in the central archives, including business magazines, external documents, and Reinhold Würth's manuscripts of speeches and lectures.

The authors were able to use scientific papers dealing with Adolf Würth GmbH & Co. KG for specific issues. In some cases, they offer profound analyses of the different aspects of both business management and business development as well as the arts and cultural sponsorship.

These sources and publications proffer an inside view of the company, while the collection of press releases compiled over more than thirty years gives an impression of how the business and the entrepreneur Reinhold Würth are perceived from the outside.

"Business history must make an effort to represent comprehensive connections that focus on the human being as entrepreneur, manager, worker and employee, decision-maker, patron, citizen, or politician."[17] The present biography of the business and the entrepreneur tries to put into practice the claim formulated by Manfred Pohl, director of the Historical Institute of Deutsche Bank and co-founder of the Society for Business History. The study has both a chronological and a thematic perspective. The most important developments, the activities of the entrepreneur as well as his respective positioning in the business, are traced through the individual decades from the 1950s into the new millennium, always against the backdrop of the general economic and social development.

Thematically structured chapters shed light on areas and developments that in past publications about Reinhold Würth and his business have only been touched upon briefly. These chapters begin at the starting point of developments and trace these to the present.

The respective chapters – be they structured chronologically or thematically – can also be read individually. As such, certain repetitions could not be avoided altogether, as they enable the reader to comprehend certain developments without having to read the entire book.

The book starts with a chronology of the first 15 years of business history, covering the foundation of the company by Adolf Würth as well as the first years of Reinhold Würth's entrepreneurial activity. A brief, thematic insertion is dedicated to the family of Reinhold Würth. This is followed by the chapter "Würth and the Region – a Baden-Württemberg Success Story". It deals with the geographic, economic, and historical prerequisites of the domicile of the company in Hohenlohe, a rural region characterized by small towns on the edge of Baden-Württemberg. The chapter explores the interrelationship of location, region, and company.

At a very early stage, Reinhold Würth ventured outside the rural Hohenlohe region into the world, establishing his first foreign-based companies at the beginning of the 1960s. The chapter "50 Per Cent of Success – Würth and the World" follows the chronology of the 1960s, discusses the global development of the business, and takes a closer look at some of the foreign-based companies.

The development of such a large direct selling company as Würth would have been inconceivable without the electronic data processing of the last 30 years. Adolf Würth KG purchased its first IBM computer in 1970. The history of the further computerization of the business since the 1970s is illustrated in a chapter entitled "Computers, Networks, and Phoenix". With "The Würth idea for the 80s: Satisfied Employees", Reinhold Würth directed his management team's attention to questions of staff management and staff motivation[18], since a company can only be successful if it has committed and qualified employees. Therefore, a chapter focusing on "Working at Würth" follows the discussion of business development in the 1980s. Taking the example of Adolf Würth GmbH & Co. KG, the sales force as the "foundation" of the company as well as other departments are highlighted. In addition, the chapter deals with corporate culture, employee participation, and the issue of further education and training at Würth.

Reinhold Würth's transfer from operative management of Adolf Würth GmbH & Co.

KG to Chairman of the Advisory Board of the Würth Group at the beginning of 1994 went hand in hand with increasing public interest in the entrepreneur and his business. The last thematic chapter following the illustration of the 1990s therefore diverts the reader's glance from the inside of the company to Reinhold Würth's manifold social activities. The chapter primarily concentrates on his commitment to cultural and arts sponsorship, as well as his activities as Professor of Entrepreneurship at the University of Karlsruhe (TH).

Apart from the chapters sketched, quotes by employees, friends, and companions of Reinhold Würth interspersed among the text convey subjective opinions about the entrepreneur and the history of his business.

Reinhold Würth himself wrote the closing words. In an interview conducted by the authors, he recapitulates important decisions and developments of his business's history, explains the current situation of the Würth Group, and gives his outlook on the future of the business.

The writing of the present business biography in roughly one year, a relatively short period of time for such a project, was made possible by the friendly support of the staff of Adolf Würth GmbH & Co. KG. We would like to thank everybody involved, especially Mr. Ludger Drüeke, director of the Würth central archives, Mr. Norbert Bamberger, personal consultant to Reinhold Würth, Mrs. C. Sylvia Weber, art director at Würth, and everybody else not mentioned by name who provided us with information and gave us an insight into the company. We would also like to thank our numerous interview partners who took the time to share their experiences and impressions with us.

Last, but not least, we want to thank Prof. Reinhold Würth for entrusting us with this project. His unconventional, swift decision-making impressed us just as much as his life's work, which manifests itself in the development of the Würth Group as described in this book.

"KNOWING HISTORY IS A PREREQUISITE FOR UNDERSTANDING THE PRESENT"
BUSINESS HISTORY AT WÜRTH

1   HOW EVERYTHING STARTED

1954 to 1960

The history of the largest worldwide direct sales business in the field of assembly and fastening technology officially started on July 16, 1945. It was on a Monday that Adolf Würth, whose name the German parent company of the Würth Group still bears today, opened up his screw wholesale business in the Schlossmühle in Künzelsau. This was by no means an easy venture in the first months after the end of World War II, since a number of obstacles had to be overcome first.

A "Nine Days' Wonder"? – Foundation of the Würth Company in 1945

On the morning of April 11, 1945, troops of the 7th US Army occupied Künzelsau. After the Western Allies had succeeded in crossing the River Rhine on several locations in March, they had started a large-scale advance into the center of Germany. Künzelsau became a conflict area in the second week of April. Reinhold Würth remembers: "For weeks, we 10 year olds had watched how the German Wehrmacht built defense positions on the slopes over the Kocher valley, how the USAF fighter bombers attacked railway facilities and how the two bridges over the Kocher River were blown up by the retreating German Wehrmacht." [2] The US occupying forces also confiscated the apartment of the Würth family to accommodate their officers. Together with his wife Alma and his sons Reinhold and barely one-year-old Klaus-Frieder, Adolf Würth found shelter with friends, the Krätzer family and his parents in Ilsfeld south of Heilbronn. After the apartment had been evacuated in July 1945, the family returned to Künzelsau, covering the distance of roughly 45 miles (70 km) on foot.

Immediately after their return, Adolf Würth began his preparations for establishing a company. Such an endeavor, though, was impossible without approval by the local US military government. And yet this was not the only obstacle to be overcome. The main problem was the procurement of goods. This is what Adolf Würth concentrated on while waiting for permission to do business to be granted. Having worked as authorized signatory at the old-established screw wholesale business,

Reisser, he knew all the important suppliers and was well known to all of them. However, the majority of manufacturers of screws and nuts were located in the zone occupied by the British and it was impossible to get in touch with them in July 1945, since every occupying power treated its zone as autonomous and a closed-off economic area. It would furthermore have been very difficult to transport the goods, since many roads were destroyed. One screw manufacturer, though, was accessible: the screw factory L & C Arnold in Ernsbach close by started production again in the first days of July 1945 and the military government granted Adolf Würth approval to purchase screws there. Another problem was the procurement of rooms for the company, since every square foot available was occupied by soldiers and refugees. Finally, Adolf Würth succeeded in renting a room of about 1,800 ft² (170 m²) in an annex to the old Schlossmühle. An evacuated joiner by the name of Auth from the Rhineland built the shelves required for storing the merchandise – supported by the ten-year-old Reinhold Würth.

View of the Schlossmühle and its annex in Künzelsau. This group of buildings, since demolished, was the true cradle of the Würth Group

In the Schlossmühle in Künzelsau, the newly founded business had good company. In 1944, the large, Stuttgart-based – but bombed-out – bookbinder's, Sigloch, had transferred its production there. Sigloch was followed by another Stuttgart-based company, Stahl, which specialized in the manufacture of elevators and switchgear. After the end of the war, the electric motor works, Ziehl-Abegg, which was formerly located in Berlin, ventured a new start in one hall of the Schlossmühle. All these businesses enjoy an international reputation today. And Würth? "A nine days' wonder!" That's what one of the town councilors of Künzelsau remarked at the time.³ However, business went well for the screw wholesale company, screws being hard to come by in postwar years.

Difficult Start in the Postwar Era

The economy of postwar years suffered from a lack of raw materials and energy: destruction caused by the war, requisitions, and dismantling had weakened production potential enormously. The logical consequence was a massive drop in industrial sector output. This situation

Abschrift

Wirtschaftsministerium
Württemberg-Baden

(14a) Stuttgart-O, den 25. April 1947.
Neckarstraße 195
Fernsprecher Nr. 90057/59

Aktenzeichen: II W 456/11 (F) Wei/Ho.
(Aktenzeichen im Schriftverkehr stets angeben)

Dem Antrag des **Adolf Würth** in Künzelsau, Austr. 13.

auf Erteilung der Erlaubnis zur Errichtung eines **Grosshandelsunternehmens in Künzelsau für Holz- und Gewindeschrauben**

entspreche ich gemäß §.1 Abs. 1, § 3 des Gesetzes Nr. 64 über die Errichtung gewerblicher Unternehmungen vom 5. November 1946 (Reg. Bl. d. Regierung Württemberg-Baden 1946 Nr. 21) unter folgenden Bedingungen und Auflagen:

1. Die Genehmigung gilt nur, solange der Antragsteller seinen Sitz in der amerikanischen Zone von Württemberg-Baden hat.

2. Die Genehmigung gilt nur zum Grosshandel mit den oben genannten Waren. Andere Waren dürfen nur mit meiner besonderen Genehmigung hinzugenommen werden

3. Für die Erteilung der Erlaubnis setze ich gemäß Nr. 7 Gebührenverzeichnis zur Landesgebührenordnung eine an die Kasse des Landrats in **Künzelsau** zu entrichtende Gebühr von 200.— RM an.

Gebühr 200.— RM
gem. Nr. 7 Geb. Verz. z. LGO.

Im Auftrag
(gez.) Kessler

The document that approves the business of the Würth screw wholesale company for the first time. It was issued in April 1947 by the Württemberg-Baden economics ministry

HOW EVERYTHING STARTED
DIFFICULT START IN THE POSTWAR ERA

Excerpt from the "register of business advertisements submitted to the representative of the local authority, 1934–1959" of the city of Künzelsau. The screw wholesale business established in July 1945 is officially registered in December 1945.

was aggravated by transport and traffic problems as well as production bans imposed by the Allies. Minimum supply was faced by enormous demand and finally by an abundance of money. Agricultural production, too, had gone down considerably owing to the decline in stock farming as a consequence of the war, a scarcity of seeds, and a permanent lack of concentrated feed. Consumer durables were not available on the free market, but were subject to economic control as exercised by the occupying powers. Foodstuffs were only available through the food ration cards issued by the military government – with the exception of the quickly emerging "black market" – but even the daily ration of 1,550 calories could very often not be achieved. Therefore, the problems governing life were hunger and malnutrition and, at the same time, an abundance of cash until the currency reform of June 1948.

It was in this difficult situation that Adolf Würth made his first business transactions as screw wholesaler. Wood screws, in particular, were very much in demand. Expanding the business beyond the limits of the town of Künzelsau, however, was problematic because of the transport situation. The railroad line to Schwäbisch Hall was opened up again first and, in October 1945, trains started going to Heilbronn. Places located in the district of Künzelsau could not be reached again by the post-office bus until November 1945. Transporting goods across even the shortest distances was very difficult. In the beginning, the screws manufactured by Arnold had to be taken from Ernsbach to Künzelsau by bullock cart.

The transport situation improved somewhat in the course of the year 1946, thus enabling Adolf Würth to expand his business. New purchasing possibilities opened up in 1947 after the US and British military governments had merged their occupied zones into the "United Economic Area," so-called "Bizonia". His first journey brought Adolf Würth to Lüdenscheid and Plettenberg in western Sauerland, where a number of screw manufacturers were situated. Even though traffic obstruction and zone-related obstacles had been removed, unrestricted purchases were still not possible since screws continued to be subject to economic control. Screws could only be purchased with iron coupons that were issued by the local economic agencies. Adolf Würth succeeded in expanding his field of activities step by step in the first postwar years with a great deal of optimism and perseverance, but only modest growth was possible owing to the difficult economic situation characterized by restrictions, rationing and pricing rules, and a shattered currency.

From Economic Control to the Reconstruction Boom

The currency reform in June 1948 changed the conditions of business operation overnight. On June 18, 1948, the military governments of the Western Zones announced the abolition of the worthless Reichsmark that was replaced by the Deutsche Mark. Every citizen received "head money" amounting to 40 DM as a start from the agency issuing the food rationing cards and, two months later, an additional 20 DM. Old money and bank deposits were exchanged in a ratio of 100 Reichsmark : 6.50 DM. The currency reform eliminated the money surplus resulting from the National Socialist economic and war funding policy and created the basis of a new economic life.

Doing away with the traditional, instruction-based economy, however, was not so swift. The elimination of the rationed consumer goods market was only a gradual process. Until February 1950, sugar was not available on the free market, and carburetor fuel only in March 1951. Even after economic control of consumer goods had been lifted, the economy was still subject to other restrictions, such as government-bureaucratized capital transactions and foreign trade. It was only in 1958 that the convertibility of the DM was announced, with the banking business finally unblocked in 1968.

As a reply to the currency reform of the Western Zones, the USSR ordered a complete blockade of Berlin's Western Zone in June 1948, which was countered by the Western Powers organizing an airlift for the provision of West Berlin. The military governors of the Western Powers urged the prime ministers of the Länder to convene a constituent National Assembly to prepare the founding of a state. Initial misgivings on the part of the countries of the Western Zone that this measure would seal the division of Germany were countered by Berlin's mayor, Ernst Reuter, saying that the division had already taken place. At the end of July 1948 the prime ministers of the Länder decided to summon a parliamentary council to draw up a constitution. The Basic Law of the Federal Republic of Germany was passed on May 8, 1949. On October 7, the German Democratic Republic (DDR) was founded in the part of Germany occupied by the Soviets.

In the elections for the first Federal Diet in August 1949, the SPD (Social Democratic Party) garnered 29.2 per cent of the votes and the CDU (Christian Democratic Union) 31 per cent, creating a government coalition together with the FDP (Free Democratic Party) (11.9 per cent) and the German Party (4 per cent). On September 12, 1949, Theodor

Heuss was elected first German President. In his policy statement, German Chancellor Konrad Adenauer, elected by the Federal Diet on September 15, announced the free market economy proclaimed before by the CDU convention. The economic process was supposed to be based on the private initiative of both producers and consumers, with economic growth now the principal objective of the national economic policy.

The foundation of the Federal Republic of Germany was accompanied by an economic boom. Condemned in the past to roughly a decade of thriftiness, the Germans now gave free rein to their urge to spend. It started with a "food craze" – in 1952, German Federal men were overweight by an average of 3lbs (1.5 kilos) – followed by a "cleaning craze" and then a "construction craze." In the beginning, though, the purchasing power created by the currency reform was faced by a scarce supply of consumer goods. The consequence was an unnaturally high velocity of circulation of the new money, with prices soaring. The trade sector made exceptional profits from the "unrestrained" consumer. Between 1949 and 1953, the sales volume of department stores and consumers' cooperatives doubled. [4]

Adolf Würth Bets on the Automotive Industry

The prerequisites for further developing the trade business had considerably improved since the summer of 1948. This, however, was accompanied by ever-increasing competition in the screw trade. In the vicinity of Künzelsau there were other screw wholesalers apart from Würth, and it became increasingly difficult to make money with wood screws. In this situation, Adolf Würth made his most important and far-reaching business decision: he decided to open up a new market. Since the currency reform, people had been able to buy cars again, with the automotive industry consequently reporting a clear upward trend. So Würth bet on "the" growth industry of German postwar economy. Demand for cars became the pacemaker of economic growth. Between 1950 and 1980, a new consumption structure emerged thanks to the private car: after foodstuffs and semi-luxuries as well as rent, the category "traffic and news" leapt from last to third position in the rankings of private consumption. [5]

Vehicles in Running Order in Baden-Württemberg [6]

	MOTORCYCLES	PASSENGER CARS	TRUCKS
1938	131.058	106.669	26.296
1950	165.451	88.834	45.459
1954	398.710	222.604	71.936
1957	418.759	361.896	76.662
1966	427.809	1.550.506	124.388

The Würth Company broadened its offer for the new customer target group: sheet metal screws, brass-chromium Plated threaded screws, license-Plate screws and brass Plates. Consequently, the first order obtained by young Reinhold Würth in January 1951 was placed by Düsseldorf's largest VW-dealer. This was also the first year that the Daimler-Benz Company was supplied with brass-chromium Plated threaded screws. At the beginning of the fifties, the number of customers rose steadily; sales went up to 350,000 DM in 1951 [7] and the Würth Company purchased its first car that same year.

The room in the annex of the Schlossmühle had become too small, so in 1952 Adolf Würth decided to erect a new building. At the railroad station in Künzelsau he found a suitable location with favorable traffic connections. A one-and-a-half story building was constructed that offered about double the space of the former domicile, with a total area of 4,200 ft² (388 m²). The basement of the new building as well as the largest part of the ground floor served as storage room, and on the side a small office was set up. The screw wholesale business Würth was prepared for the future. The rising trend continued in the years to come, if not rapidly at least consistently.

However, all of this was jeopardized suddenly: on December 14, 1954, completely unexpectedly, Adolf Würth died of a heart attack at the age of 45. The small, upcoming business was left without a leader. Liabilities from the construction of the company building to stocking the inventory had to be honored; the family's livelihood needed to be safeguarded.

Reinhold Würth Accepts the Challenge

In this situation, Reinhold Würth at 19 years of age decided to follow in his father's footsteps and take over the management of the business – in the beginning, together with his mother Alma, and by himself after

1956. He had certainly never imagined having to shoulder such an enormous responsibility, since the sons of businessmen usually only enter the business once their fathers retire and they have already acquired considerable know-how and experience.

It is true that Reinhold Würth was very young at the time, but he was familiar with the business, having actually grown up in it. When Adolf Würth had founded the screw business after the end of the war, Reinhold Würth – "sometimes because I was forced to," [8] as he himself remarks – was with him from the start. The ten-year-old soon became interested in the business and helped his father zealously. He often sat on the bullock carts bringing the screws from Ernsbach or accompanied his father on customer visits by railroad to Schwäbisch Hall. When the Kocher River flowing through Künzelsau flooded the business premises in the annex of the Schlossmühle in the winter of 1946/47, he helped his father to salvage the packages of screws from the flood and to clear the rooms of the thick layer of sludge. Reinhold Würth put together deliveries to customers and brought them to the railroad station in Künzelsau on a hand-drawn barrow. When there were no other means of transport available he even delivered to customers by barrow, as far afield as Ingelfingen and Niedernhall six miles (ten kilometers) from Künzelsau.

Since he was familiar with the screw business from childhood, it seemed natural to Reinhold Würth to look for his professional future in this field. At the age of 14 he therefore left the Künzelsau boys' high school to begin a commercial apprenticeship in his father's company. He attended the commercial vocational school in Künzelsau and took his final examination in 1952. In the year before, at the age of 16, he had traveled to Düsseldorf by himself for the first time. Very soon he stopped being nervous during conversations with customers because his know-how boosted his self-assurance. The result of his first week in the field: sales of 2,000 DM.

Reinhold Würth was assigned yet another responsibility when the first company car was purchased in 1951: he was supposed to drive it. Although the legal age for driving a car was 18 years, he was granted special permission and passed his driving test on his 16th birthday. As his "father's private chauffeur" [9] he not only became a good

"Reinhold Würth is a natural entrepreneur. That's something you can't really learn, he was endowed with it from birth."

Georg Krupp, former member of the managing board of Deutsche Bank AG; deputy chairman of the Würth Advisory Board for a number of years and still a member of the Foundation Supervisory Board of the Würth KG driver, but also an excellent salesman. He learned a great many things about the sales business accompanying his father on customer visits, and his self-confidence grew with his experience. He started having fun visiting customers himself.

Reinhold Würth was by no means a newcomer to the screw business in December 1954 and, six days after his father's death, still before Christmas, he went on a sales tour to the Rhineland: "I was able to continue the company thanks to the knowledge conveyed to me by my father in the first years of my employment with the company." [10]

Conversation between father and son during a walk through the forest: one of the few pictures showing Adolf Würth with his son, Reinhold

Everybody smile, please: Reinhold, Klaus-Frieder, Alma and Adolf Würth

FAMILY ROOTS   2

Reinhold Würth and His Family

Reinhold Würth, born in Öhringen on April 20, 1935, describes his ancestors as "predictable, respectable and reliable people."[11] His father, Adolf Würth, was the son of farmer Friedrich Würth, who produced his own wine in Ilsfeld south of Heilbronn, owned a restaurant, and also ran the local payments office of the Württemberg provincial bank. At the age of 13, Adolf Würth became an apprentice with the screw wholesale business, Reisser Brothers, at that time located in Kupferzell – a company that his son Reinhold would bring into the Würth Group about 30 years later. Adolf Würth, being motivated and reliable, soon made a career for himself, becoming his boss's right-hand man and being granted general power of attorney. Coming from a strictly Lutheran family, he was won over to the New Apostolic faith by his boss, Gotthilf Reisser, and converted. His father, Friedrich Würth, was certainly not in favor of it, but patient enough to tolerate his son's change of beliefs. "Do what is right and fear nobody" – this is how Reinhold Würth characterizes his family's motto in questions of faith.[12]

Adolf Würth met his future wife during a visit to a New Apostolic church. In 1932, on the occasion of a business trip to Hamburg, he started a conversation with Alma Schott. She sang in the choir and came from a market-gardening family in Uetersen near Hamburg. They got married and, by the time their first son, Reinhold, was born in 1935, Adolf Würth was running the Öhringen subsidiary of the Reisser Company. In 1937, the screw wholesale business moved its corporate headquarters to Künzelsau, and so the small town at the Kocher became the home of the Würth family. During World War II, Adolf Würth was called up and charged with running a subsidiary of the German Zinser Company in France, producing goods for the armaments industry. Reinhold Würth and his mother stayed behind in Künzelsau, only seeing Adolf when he returned home from Alsace on vacation. In the spring of 1944, the second son,

Adolf and Alma Würth during a Sunday walk

FAMILY ROOTS
REINHOLD WÜRTH AND HIS FAMILY

1 Creative from a young age: Reinhold Würth playing with his "train set" (1938)
2 Klaus-Frieder and Reinhold Würth with their father, Adolf, taking a walk through the woods
3 Having fun: Klaus-Frieder, Reinhold and Adolf Würth at the Baltic Sea
4 Adolf and Alma Würth with their son, Reinhold, during a visit to Schönbrunn Castle in 1943
5 Alma Würth, née Schott, as a young lady
6 Alma and Reinhold Würth
7 Alma Würth with her sons, Klaus-Frieder and Reinhold

Reinhold Würth and his brother Klaus-Frieder Würth on the occasion of their mother's 90th birthday in May 2003

Klaus-Frieder, was born. A few months later, in late fall of 1944 when the French and US forces recaptured Alsace, Adolf Würth returned to Künzelsau where he started his screw wholesale business in the summer of 1945. Reinhold Würth helped his father from the very beginning and, from 1948 to 1952, undertook a commercial apprenticeship in the business. When Adolf Würth died completely unexpectedly on December 14, 1954 at the age of 45, Reinhold Würth carried on with the business, supported by his mother, Alma, who had secretly hoped her first-born would become a teacher. She helped with the company in the beginning and contributed to the further development of the business from 1969 until 1974 as limited partner of Adolf Würth KG [13] and then from 1975 until 1998 as member of the corporate advisory board. A former member of the Board of Management described her as the "true mother of her son," who took in both facts and trends very precisely and judged "unemotionally correctly." [14] Reinhold Würth's younger brother, Klaus-Frieder, also worked in the company for a while. He acted as limited partner of Adolf Würth KG, formed in 1969, and after 1978 of Adolf Würth GmbH & Co. KG, whose corporate name had been changed accordingly. In 1971, he was granted general power of attorney for the Munich subsidiary of the business, and in December 1974 was appointed general manager of Würth Verwaltungsgesellschaft GmbH joining Reinhold Würth, Rolf Bauer, Otto Beilharz and Hans Hügel. At the beginning of 1981, Klaus-Frieder Würth left the company. In his function as limited partner of Adolf Würth GmbH & Co. KG he was replaced by Reinhold Würth's wife, Carmen Würth. [15]

Just like his father, Reinhold Würth met his future wife for the first time during a visit to the New Apostolic church. During a business trip to Friedrichshafen at Lake Constance he attended evening service. During a conversation with community members he got to know Carmen Linhardt, who worked as a secretary in the Friedrichshafen gear drive fac-

FAMILY ROOTS
REINHOLD WÜRTH AND HIS FAMILY

tory. On December 9, 1956 – as the first business year that Reinhold Würth had managed the company on his own drew to its successful end – they were married. Carmen Würth therefore accompanied her husband's business career almost from the start.

Carmen Würth, characterized by the photographer and long-time friend of the family, Paul Swiridoff, as "very reserved, but extremely friendly, kind, […] of almost noble reservation mixed with outstanding modesty," [16] has been her husband's mainstay. "I was the hostess, I was the cook […] I was everything;" this is how Carmen Würth describes her role as wife of the entrepreneur who, as she says, always focused on his long-term goal with great perseverance. [17] She looked after the family: their two daughters, Marion and Bettina, and particularly their son Markus, who has been handicapped from childhood owing to a vaccination accident.

After the Würths had purchased Hermersberg Castle in 1971 and extended it as their family home, Carmen Würth, in her role as the hostess who "cultivates an excellent cuisine" (not just her husband's opinion), made sure that the historic building became a place in which guests from all over the world, company members as well as artists, politicians, and top executives from the world of business and the economy like to spend some time. [18] "Hermersberg is enlivened by my presence," says Carmen Würth.

In the business, too, she was present, if – as was the case with the starting up of the new high-bay warehouse in 1978 – the staff had to work on the weekends. "Often, Carmen Würth helped out and always provided us with coffee and cake," remembers one employee. [19]

Carmen Würth is not particularly fond of public commitments, yet she considers her representation of the company as "paying her respects to the staff," since in such cases she always feels a part of the company and the staff: "I try to be an ambassadress at all times."

Reinhold and Carmen Würth
at the Vienna opera ball (1995)

While for her the years characterized by the growth and consolidation of the business were always filled with many commitments as wife of the entrepreneur, mother, and hostess, Carmen Würth at the beginning of the new millennium finally found some time and opportunity to put a long-cherished plan into action. Owing to her experience as the mother of a handicapped child, she has long debated the question of how it may be possible to give meaning and fulfilment to the life of handicapped people, how one can create opportunities for them to meet others, and how understanding for the handicapped can be awakened in people.[20] When Reinhold Würth bought an old house in the center of Künzelsau a few years ago, she took the opportunity to implement a project aimed at awakening people's understanding of the handicapped, on the one hand, and giving the handicapped meaningful projects to do, on the other. After careful consideration and travels to integrative projects in Germany, the decision was made to set up a restaurant in which both handicapped and non-handicapped people can work together. On March 14, 2003, the hotel and restaurant "Anne-Sophie" was officially opened. Carmen Würth hopes that the guests will come "with open hearts, open eyes, and open ears."[21] Reaching out to people open-mindedly and touching their hearts with small gestures was a gift of Anne-Sophie, Carmen and Reinhold Würth's granddaughter who was killed in an accident at the age of nine.

"Reinhold Würth embodies a mixture of acumen and conciliation, of precision in the field of business and generous patronage, of sportsmanlike behavior and reliability, of rootedness to his native soil and a sense of ethical and moral dimensions."

Prof. Dr. Hans Küng, Professor of Theology at the University of Tübingen

Reinhold and Carmen Würth live in Hermersberg together with their family, which now includes six grandchildren. Daughter Marion Würth, who often accompanies her father on business trips, runs a farm there. Bettina Würth and her husband, Markus Würth, work in the company. Markus Würth is a member of the management team of

Adolf Würth GmbH & Co. KG and, since 2001, Bettina Würth has been a member of the Board of Directors of the Würth Group. With increasing age, the family gains importance for Reinhold Würth: "The older I get, the more important my family becomes to me, each and every member of it – both those who are alive and those who are no longer with us. I see myself as being one link in a chain that reaches from my ancestors to my grandchildren, as part of a tree whose roots are hidden in the past. I draw my life from these roots, from my parents, grandparents, and great-grandparents." [22]

The proud grandfather with his grandson, Nikolaus (1994)

3 REINHOLD WÜRTH TAKES OVER THE COMPANY

1954 to 1960

Reinhold Würth's first business trip shortly after his father's death in December 1954 was a disappointment. Right before Christmas most of the customers did not want to place any orders. The Würth Company finally managed to close the year 1954 with sales of 146,000 DM. However, the conditions for further development of the company were favorable. Reinhold Würth took over the business in times of economic upswing; the wartime days of need were over. By the end of the decade, the young entrepreneur had created important foundations for successful further development of the company.

The "Silver" 1950s

Thanks to the Marshall Plan, a program developed by the USA to support and coordinate economic activities in European countries and the introduction of a free market economy, West Germany experienced a turn toward prosperity. In June 1950, the Korean War caused an explosive boom on the raw commodity markets, in whose wake the Federal Republic slid into a balance of payments crisis. This had an impact on the liquidity of companies, as the Bank Deutscher Länder now adopted a restrictive credit policy. Economic growth, though, was not seriously impaired, owing to enormous demand in this era of economic recovery.

In 1952, the German Treaty between the Federal Republic and the Western Allies ended the occupation, with the new West German state being granted full sovereignty in 1955. The treaty on the foundation of the European Coal and Steel Community in 1952 created the prerequisites for economic cooperation between the Western European countries. The re-integration of the Federal Republic into international economic and monetary transactions was facilitated by the "London Debts Agreement" that settled the pre-war debts from the Dawes and Young Plan as well as Germany's post-war debts. In 1956, the Deutsche Bundesbank was founded as successor institute to the Bank Deutscher Länder that had still been established by the occupying powers. With the instruments of Bundesbank, it was now also possible to enforce regulatory restrictions on monetary policy.

Hohenlohe, the home region of the Würth Company, was now part of the new southwestern state of Baden-Württemberg that emerged in 1952 from Württemberg-Baden, formerly occupied by US forces, as well as from Länder Baden and Württemberg-Hohenzollern, which were occupied by the French. Mechanical engineering and vehicle construction as well as electrical engineering and precision mechanics belonged to Baden-Württemberg's growth industries. [23]

In the mid-1950s, the West Germans' attitude toward life changed from a feeling of inferiority as the "losers" of World War II to a self-confident "we are back in the race" – the Germans had after all won the world championship in soccer on July 4, 1954. Millions had listened to the match on the radio; listening to the radio was actually the most popular hobby of the German population during those years. Television was not that widespread, even though programs were broadcast again after 1949. People went to the movies where, in 1950, the film "Schwarzwaldmädel" ushered in a whole series of sentimental movies with a regional background. In terms of music, the Germans were somewhere between the "Caprifischer" and rock 'n roll made popular by Elvis Presley; the most successful singer was Freddy Quinn.

The "economic miracle" was reflected in fashion and design, with the symbol of economic recovery being the car. On August 5, 1955, the one-millionth beetle left the assembly line in Wolfsburg. The automotive boom had a down side to it, too, however: every day, about five people were killed on the roads of Baden-Württemberg and fifty were seriously injured. In 1957, the ratio of inhabitants to cars was 22:1, whereas it had still been 73:1 seven years earlier. [24] The reconstruction boom with accelerated economic growth continued until the end of the 1950s. Industrial growth was supported by a multiplication of jobs and increase in working hours.

Reinhold Würth's Start as Entrepreneur

Reinhold Würth began the year 1955 with the objective to safeguard the company's survival. It was most important to make money and maintain the business's ability to pay. At that time, strategic plans, not to mention vision, were very far from his mind. "To begin with, I continued in a quite mechanical way what my father had started nine years earlier," he remembers. [25] It had been Adolf Würth's motivation when founding the screw wholesale business to be self-employed, to be independent, and to ensure that his family always had a good income. Since he had quite a strong need for security he had not planned on expanding the business. Reinhold Würth combined determination and curiosity. One of his first employees, Hans Hügel, had noticed during his recruitment that his new boss was "very single-minded and determined, character traits that stayed with him during his entire professional career. If he had something in mind he very quickly put it into practice. In my opinion, this is one of the reasons for his success." [26] Reinhold Würth's joy of discovery, nurtured when he was still a child, also manifested itself in business after he found that he was much more successful in running the company than he had originally anticipated. In the business year 1955, his first year in charge, he greatly exceeded his target of maintaining the previous year's sales volume, increasing sales by 21.5 per cent. [27] While still in the 1950s, he initiated a five-year strategic plan combined with a five-year forecast.

After the successful start in 1955, Reinhold Würth and his mother Alma decided to change the legal structure of the company. After the death of her husband, Alma Würth had at first been the sole owner of the company, with Reinhold Würth an employee. On January 1, 1956, the former sole proprietorship was changed into a general commercial partnership, with Alma Würth and Reinhold Würth as partners. Reinhold Würth was now in a legal position to represent the business independently.

The First Employees

Reinhold Würth congratulates Hans Hügel on his 40th company anniversary, at the honors ceremony organized in Waldenburg for all employees celebrating an anniversary (November 1995)

In the beginning, Reinhold Würth went on business trips across the entire Federal Republic. In the meantime, his mother took care of business at home in the small warehouse and office building at the Künzelsau railroad station. At the time, the company had one clerk as well as Albert Berner, who had begun his apprenticeship with Adolf Würth and still managed the payroll. [28]

REINHOLD WÜRTH TAKES OVER THE COMPANY
THE FIRST EMPLOYEES

The first clerk of the Würth Company gave notice in March 1955, however, probably because he had doubts about the future of a business run by a boss who had not yet come of age. Albert Berner left the company in 1958 to establish his own screw wholesale business, which became for a time the biggest competitor of the Würth Group. The first apprentice hired by Reinhold Würth, Hans Hügel, remembers the stir caused by Albert Berner's leaving: "The business he founded became our first competitor since it targeted the same customers and tried everything to copy us wherever possible. And yet our sales went up and up and we realized the truth behind the saying that "competition raises the level of business." [29]

> "Reinhold Würth was always going at some speed. If he had something in mind he usually put it into practice very quickly."
>
> Hans Hügel, former Würth sales manager and authorized signatory

Hans Hügel was hired by Reinhold Würth in December 1955. The son of a farmer from Amrichshausen, he was originally supposed to carry on with his parent's business, but after having a heart defect diagnosed a job less physically strenuous seemed more advisable, so he started a one-year clerkship course at the commercial school. It was there that he learned from a friend that "a widow and her son" were looking for an apprentice for their small business. Hügel did not hesitate in applying for the job, since apprenticeships were hard to come by in Hohenlohe at that time: "Even though the company was still in its infancy, it appealed to me somehow." [30] After he had reached an agreement with Reinhold Würth – who paid the 100 DM fine that Hügel incurred for dropping out of the training course at the commercial school – a career started that would become typical of the Würth Company. After completing his apprenticeship and working as a sales representative, Hans Hügel became a top salesman and in 1961 took over the management of the automotive, repair and body shops division. In 1963, he was granted general power of attorney, and in 1973 was appointed member of the management team of Würth Verwaltungsgesellschaft. After he had resigned from the position of sales manager in 1976 for health reasons, from that time on acting as substitute sales manager, he maintained a successful relationship with the business until his retirement in 1998.

In February 1956, Reinhold Würth hired Hans Rapp for order processing and corresponding with the customers. Rapp, who would soon make his influence felt on the warehouse and accounting systems and would work as authorized signatory for many years, was the undisputed authority during the boss's absence.

This proved to be an advantage, since Reinhold Würth extended his business trips and was on the road a lot. It was therefore Hans Rapp and Albert Berner who had their first interview with Hermann Leiser in June 1956; he joined the company as second apprentice and is still working for Würth at the time of writing (2004) as pricing manager in the Auto/Cargo Division. At first, Alma Würth was concerned for him, considering him rather "short and delicate" for handling the heavy boxes of screws. Albert Berner thought him suitable, however, since he at least knew what a wood screw was. On the following Monday, Hermann Leiser started his apprenticeship. In his company history, he remembers how the "head apprentice" Hans Hügel introduced him to his new job:

"1. Sweep the office with a broom without raising a lot of dust. This was not that easy since the parquet floor had millimeter-wide cracks and dirt accumulated there.

2. If necessary, start a fire in the winter months. For starting a fire I had to go down to the basement, smash a wooden crate in which merchandise had been received, go and get coals and then light the fire.

3. Dust the desks (we had three) and roll-front cabinet and cover the office machines." [31]

> "Reinhold Würth and I are completely different. He is the No. 1 in our industry, and I am certainly the No. 2. It would be stupid if we gave each other a hard time. I cannot say anything negative about him. I admire him. It is definitely remarkable that we, being competitors and located in the same town to boot, like each other and can look each other in the eye."
>
> Albert Berner, competitor

And then work began. Every morning, the apprentices Hügel and Leiser took the hand-drawn barrow to the station and to the post office to pick up incoming merchandise. The heavy crates took their toll on the means of transport. In the first and second year of his apprenticeship Hermann Leiser wore out three barrows; in his third year, the company bought an automotive electrical cart. The three apprentices – Hubert Dehnelt had in the meantime been hired, too – unpacked the crates and, if necessary, weighed the content on a pair of old kitchen scales. Small quantities were counted manually.

Apart from Reinhold Würth, Albert Berner also went on business trips. On Thursday evenings, they returned with their orders, and on Friday and Saturday mornings the shipments for the customers were prepared: "We counted screws, labeled boxes, wrote delivery slips (everything manually) and packed parcels. Hans Hügel was a true artist when it came to assembling parcels out of individual cardboard boxes and cartons. [...] At the same time, we were requested to write the necessary invoices. All the invoice amounts were calculated with a small crank handle and the invoices were written on the typewriter." [32] In Hermann Leiser's first year as apprentice, the range of products was still very limited and now and then the incoming orders granted the apprentices some time for "unofficial practical jokes." This changed very soon, however, as sales went up month by month.

Competition stimulates business: Reinhold Würth and Albert Berner on the latter's 60th birthday (July 1995)

A Decisive Step: Building up a Sales Force

Reinhold Würth expanded his sales territory across the borders of the Federal Republic to nearby Austria and Switzerland. He covered more than 55,000 miles (90,000 km) in his Mercedes Diesel in 1956, an effort that soon paid off: sales increased by more than 100,000 DM compared to the previous year. Only three years later, the company succeeded in generating 100,000 DM in sales one month alone.

Sales of the Würth Company 1954–1959

1954	146.000 DM	75.000 EUR
1955	170.000 DM	86.000 EUR
1956	276.000 DM	141.000 EUR
1957	354.000 DM	181.000 EUR
1958	619.000 DM	316.000 EUR
1959	1.115.000 DM	570.000 EUR

Reinhold Würth took a decisive step: he realized that he would not be able to increase sales indefinitely by himself and therefore needed sales representatives. His first attempt at hiring a sales representative for a part of southern Germany, however, was not crowned with success.

A young, energetic businessman responded to the ad in the Stuttgarter Zeitung and was given a VW by Würth that had been purchased by the company specifically for his sales trips. But orders did not come in, and nobody heard anything from the new employee. Reinhold Würth decided to check that everything was alright in Bad Cannstatt. He took with him the apprentice Hans Hügel, who had taken his driving test just two days before so that he could drive the VW back to Künzelsau. They arrived just in time to keep the idle sales representative from going on vacation in the company car. Hans Hügel still has vivid memories of the drive back. Being a beginner behind the steering wheel, he had to grapple with the double clutch and find his way out of Bad Cannstatt to Künzelsau. Not only that, although the boss wanted him to return the car, he also expected Hügel to use the return trip as his first sales exercise.[33] This practice of making staff members – including in-house employees – familiar with sales as early as possible has remained typical of the Würth Company.

The negative experience with the sales representative from Bad Cannstatt remained an exception, though the question of recruiting new and qualified sales representatives remains significant today. Reinhold Würth had the right touch in hiring new employees after that. In Otto Hempel from Hanover, he found a competent and reliable traveling salesman for northern Germany. Hempel's recruitment marked another important step in the development of the company. In the spring of 1958, sales could also be stepped up in southern Germany with the help of Artur Herold from Murrhardt, a former insurance agent. Hans Hügel, who had concluded his apprenticeship in April 1958 by passing his commercial exam, extended the company's sales force. Hempel, Herold, and Hügel were the "men of the first hour" in the field. In 1959, they were joined by Gerhard Kühn, and at the beginning of the new decade the number of sales representatives had risen to six, thanks to Ernst Knoch. Their customers were automotive repair shops, car body pressing companies, automotive accessory shops, industrial and craft businesses, as well as construction firms.

"I was handed a sample case with four boards full of screws and off I went," remembers Artur Herold about his first sales trip.[34] When the storeman of an automotive dealership in Ansbach wanted to order 8mm lock washers, Herold was of the opinion that the company did not carry these as he only had samples of screws with him. The customer set him right. He also had a hard time remembering the DIN-names. Karl

REINHOLD WÜRTH TAKES OVER THE COMPANY
A DECISIVE STEP: BUILDING UP A SALES FORCE

Specht, who started his career with Würth in September 1961, had to learn – even though he was convinced that selling was his strong point – that the job was not all that easy without proper training, because of the wide variety of products. When he started on his first sales trip, he did not really know which products Würth carried in the range. "Being all by myself on the road I was often pretty desperate," he recalled when talking about his beginning in sales. [35]

Reinhold Würth, the young boss, (second from left) with his first three sales representatives Otto Hempel, Hans Hügel and Artur Herold

"Learning by doing" was the motto of the new sales representatives in the early years of the company. One was still very far away from the induction programs for new sales representatives developed at a later date. The first salesmen were highly motivated, just like their boss, and very enthusiastic about selling. "Travel is life, life is travel [...]. Getting on with people, exchanging thoughts, opinions and ideas, and experiencing different scenes and situations are really the big advantages of being involved in sales," said Reinhold Würth almost 40 years later. [36] Hearing him relate his most recent sales trips in the spring of 2004, one can still see enthusiasm in is eyes. Hans Hügel, too, is still of the opinion today that "being a sales representative is the best job in the world." [37]

To reward commitment to the job and to stimulate further performance increases, Reinhold Würth introduced a new commission system in 1958. Commission amounted to five per cent of sales. If the monthly sales volume of a sales representative exceeded 10,000 DM, he received an additional five per cent on the amount exceeding this mark. Hans Hügel, whose salary came up to 270 DM in the beginning plus the five per cent commission on sales, reached the 10,000 DM mark for the first time in June 1958. In July 1959, commission of almost 1,600 DM was added to the basic salary of 400 DM that resulted in a monthly salary of roughly 2,000 DM – an above-average income at the time. [38]

Reinhold Würth's motto "performance must pay off" was also reflected in the reputation that Würth employees enjoyed outside the company. Christoph Walther, who worked as detail design engineer at the Stahl Company in Künzelsau at the beginning of the 1960s, remembers: "For some time I had been noticing a couple of young gentlemen in the "Café Frick" who seemed to be quite well off. Neatly dressed, generous, driving a 190 SL [...]. I asked my younger brother who moved in those circles and was told that the two were Mr. Hügel and Mr. Dehnelt and that they worked as sales representatives for the small screw wholesale business at the station in Künzelsau." [39] Walther wanted to work for such a company, too. In April 1962, he made his wish come true and started his career at Würth as the company's [40]th sales representative.

A Company Culture Develops

It was, however, not solely the financial aspects that contributed to the motivation of the young business. Even if not called by that name, corporate culture developed at that time under the management of Reinhold Würth. The young boss, only two years older than his apprentice, Hans Hügel, was very determined, a character trait that the latter had already noticed in his first job interview. He knew very well what to expect from his employees. When Christoph Walther was hired in 1962, Reinhold Würth requested him to have his hair cut. "That's something he did quite often!", remembers Walther.18 In the company standards drawn up later, Reinhold Würth stipulated a dress code for the sales representatives so that they would leave a positive impression with the customers.

Good performance on the part of the employees and successes of the company were not only rewarded from the onset, but also celebrated. When Herrmann Leiser and Hubert Dehnelt passed their commercial exams in the summer of 1959, their boss acted as chauffeur and invited them to dinner. In 1957, they took their first company outing, which Hermann Leiser remembers vividly: "The whole group consisted of five people. Mr. Würth rode in his new yellow Mercedes 190. Our outing took us to Baden-Baden, the Black Forest scenic route, Schwarzenbach Dam, and the Mummelsee. For Hans Hügel and me it was a big adventure, since this was the first time we had traveled further than Stuttgart. The second company outing took place exactly one year later: we visited the zoo in Nuremberg. At that time we already had two company cars." [41] In 1959, the staff needed a bus to accommodate everybody. The number of staff had gone up to 14, and Reinhold Würth also invited their spouses to come along. It was then, and still is, very important to him to involve the families of staff members. He wants the family members to get an impression of the company, the people working there, and the working climate.

Success Factor Multiplication – the Growing Company

At the end of the 1950s and beginning of the 1960s, the Würth Company had entered into a new phase of its development with the establishment and further expansion of its sales force. An important basic principle of corporate success emerged: sales growth by way of multiplication. Reinhold Würth realized that it was indispensable to reduce the size of the sales territories to exploit the existing sales opportunities more efficiently. A sales representative can only call on a limited number of customers during his day in the field. If the area is too big, a considerable proportion of his time will be spent driving around. It was Reinhold Würth's objective to create territories that enabled the sales representative to work intensively and build up a customer base as large and as stable as possible. In 1960, this was still a long way off, but Reinhold Würth got increasingly closer to this target with each new sales representative.

> "Reinhold Würth's principle is to set new targets every day. Whatever is good today must be better tomorrow."
>
> Hermann Leiser, long-time employee and former chairman of the Council of Trustees

Even today, the sales representatives are worried that their sales volume and consequently their income will drop if sales territories are reduced in size. Artur Herold felt the same: "In 1960, Mr. Würth repeatedly informed me that my territory was way too big. He thought it impossible for me to intensively work my customer base. Deep down inside I agreed with him, but for quite a long time I opposed my having to give up part of my territory. However, Mr. Würth insisted." [42] Finally, Mr. Herold realized that his boss was right: despite a reduction in his territory, he achieved considerable sales increases. Hans Hügel's worries about losing out on sales by having his territory split turned out to be unfounded.

Increasing sales required a higher inventory level and therefore also more storage space. In the first years of tempestuous growth, the space available would always lag behind the sales development. "Sales went up month after month, we admitted new products in the range all the time, and the existing storage capacity was totally insufficient so that the entire warehouse was filled to the brim with crates and boxes. To reach certain products, we always had to scramble over packages of screws." [43]

In 1958, an extension of the warehouse and office building erected only six years earlier in Künzelsau's Bahnhofstrasse was absolutely inevitable. Reinhold Würth used the enlargement of the company premises for putting into practice a plan he had been considering for quite some time: to start his own screw production. At the end of 1958, the first screws and nuts were produced with three machines located in the basement of the enlarged building. For the first time, in 1959, the name "Schraubenfabrik" (bolt and screw manufacture) was emblazoned across the price list of Adolf Würth OHG. In March of that year, screw production was in full swing. The company manufactured brass threaded screws according to DIN 84 and DIN 86 as well as brass nuts. It thus lessened its dependence on suppliers in parts of the range and also enhanced the company's prestige. From conversations with customers, Hans Hügel learned that the new company name had a positive effect.

Apart from more storage space, increasing sales also required more in-house personnel. "Our company had grown to a size that in-house departments needed to be set up. I worked in purchasing and sales and was also in charge of our Kardex warehouse card index," relates Hermann Leiser, who was furthermore assigned projects such as "selling by phone and telex machine, and planning the supply of goods in cooperation with suppliers, as well as overseeing the entire warehouse card index with incoming and outgoing shipments." [44] In 1959, the Würth Company had 14 employees on the payroll: nine men and five women. This was also the year that the employee joined the company who – in her function as personal secretary – has accompanied Reinhold Würth's business career to this day. After attending the commercial school, Hermine Künast started her apprenticeship with Würth on April 1, 1959. On her very first day in the job, Reinhold Würth said: "You can stenograph and know how to work the typewriter" and employed her as his secretary. [45]

"When the boss said something you could count on its being valid."

Hermine Künast, Reinhold Würth's personal secretary

Despite the extensions, the building housing the Würth Company still looked rather modest at the end of the 1950s: "From the outside it looked like a larger apartment building with a ramp. Up the stairs, to the right Hermine's office, […] then on to Reinhold Würth. Both offices had only about 150 ft^2 (14 m^2) The boss's office was sparsely furnished – a desk, a chair, a cabinet, and a chair for visitors." [46] Behind the façade, though, the establishment of the sales force and the reduction in size of sales territories had created the basis of the company's successful expansion.

WÜRTH AND THE REGION 4

A Baden-Württemberg Success Story

"Our integration into the Hohenlohe region has contributed a great deal to the growth of the Würth Group; and, vice versa, our growth has also contributed, right down to the present, toward keeping down the unemployment rate in Künzelsau and the area round about." [47] With these words Reinhold Würth characterizes the interrelationship between his company and its location.

As at spring 2004, the Würth Group is represented in 80 countries of the world with 294 companies, while remaining loyal to its regional roots. Reinhold Würth still lives in the Hohenlohe region today, and the company's location remains in Künzelsau where Adolf Würth founded the business in 1945.

The name "Würth" is widely known, yet Künzelsau is not that well known outside of Baden-Württemberg. One would expect to find the corporate headquarters of worldwide operating businesses in big cities yet, since 1945, a number of global companies apart from the Würth Group have settled in the Hohenlohe region. The Schlossmühle in Künzelsau can therefore rightfully be considered the cradle of both nationally and internationally important companies. It is not only the Würth Company that started here, but during and after World War II the large bookbinders Sigloch – one of the largest bookbinders in Europe today –, the Stahl Company, which manufactures cranes, elevators, and switchgear, and the electric-motor producers, Ziehl-Abegg, all grew their businesses here.

This might come as a surprise, since Hohenlohe is a region that until World War II stayed very much in the background in Baden-Württemberg and down to the present day often feels neglected by politicians, e.g., regarding the region's opening for traffic.

Hohenlohe – What Does the Name Stand for?

Today, the term "Hohenlohe region" is the geographical name of an historical area in the northeast of the Federal Land of Baden-Württemberg. [48] Initially, Hohenlohe was not a geographical place, but a dynastic name that derives from a former castle, Hochenloch or Holach. The noblemen of Hohenlohe are then to be found in Weikersheim and Pfitzingen and, in 1250, the name appears in Öhringen. The noble family whose members were later named counts and princes have managed to sustain two main lines until today, despite all the historical turmoil, divisions of estates, gifts of land, and denominational separations, and subjection to sovereignty, revolution, and the emergence of a republic.

In the beginning, Hohenlohe stood for the former territories of the different lines of the House of Hohenlohe. These were complemented by the estates of the former burgrave of Nuremberg and later margrave of Ansbach, the knights of Limpurg, and the Teutonic Order, as well as territories belonging to the free imperial cities, clergy, and knights. The area called Hohenlohe today was neither a politically nor a religiously unified whole. "Common interests were imposed on the region from the outside. It was the state of Württemberg that called the newly acquired territories "Württembergisch Franken". [49]

1806 marked a decisive year in the history of Hohenlohe and all southwest Germany. The large south German states of Württemberg, Baden, and Bavaria benefited from their alliance with Napoleon in the Rheinbund against Prussia in the form of considerable territorial gains. When the Princes of Hohenlohe by a majority opposed voluntary submission to the Duke of Württemberg, first Prince Elector and later made king, French and Württemberg troops marched into Öhringen on October 13, 1806, and Württemberg formally assumed sovereignty.

In the years following, the term "Hohenlohe" was banned from everyday usage before it acquired a new significance as a geographical term in the middle of the 19th century: maps now showed the names "Hohenloher Ebene" (Hohenlohe Plains) and "Hohenloher Land." After World War I, Hohenlohe was advertised as tourist region.

Today's district of Hohenlohe, though, only covers part of the historical area, and was developed in the wake of the Baden-Württemberg regional and administrative reform in the year 1973 by the union of the former districts of Öhringen and Künzelsau. The area called Hohenloher Land also covers today's district of Schwäbisch Hall as well as the Main-Tauber district.

Hohenlohe – an Agricultural Region Formerly the Granary of Württemberg

Down to the present day, Hohenlohe has remained a region characterized by agriculture. At the beginning of the 1990s, a total of 89 per cent of the area of Hohenlohe were used for agriculture and forestry. The pioneer of Württemberg's promotion of small and medium-sized enterprises, Ferdinand Steinbeis, assigned Hohenlohe the function of granary for the kingdom of Württemberg in the 19th century and consequently did not believe in the region's commercial and industrial promotion.

During the 18th century, agriculture made considerable progress on the fertile soil of the Hohenlohe Plains. In Hohenlohe, people dismissed the medieval threefield system earlier than in other parts of Germany and cultivated forage plants on the former fallow thirds. The advocate of the Enlightenment, Johann Friedrich Mayer, a priest in Kupferzell who as early as 1740 started growing potatoes, contributed greatly to this development.

Highly successful cattle farming developed, particularly in the eastern part of the Plains between Kupferzell and Blaufelden. The Hohenlohe beef oxen became known by the name of "Boeuf de Hohenlohe." In 1780/81, two cattle dealers alone from Künzelsau and Kupferzell drove more than 3,000 head of cattle from Hohenlohe to Mannheim, Strasbourg, and Paris. Up to 15,000 head of cattle were sold every year. The affiliation with Württemberg was not altogether positive for the rich cattle farmers and cattle dealers from Hohenlohe, however. During the Napoleonic wars, business with beef oxen was almost brought to a standstill. In the first half of the 19th century, farmers had to change from ox fattening to cattle breeding and hog-raising.

In contrast to the fertile Plateau where usually the oldest son inherited the entire farm, the principle of division into equal parts prevailed in the valleys along the Kocher and Jagst Rivers. Here, farms were split up among the heirs. As a consequence, the estates were getting smaller in the 19th century and, being located along the rivers where it was warmer than on the Plateau and where wine was grown on the slopes, could no longer support the people, with the result that many emigrated.

Industrialization, which began in Württemberg and safeguarded the survival of many on the Swabian Jura, did not take place in Hohenlohe and was not actively promoted by the state. Owing to the availability of the necessary water, as well as in reaction to the lack of income from agriculture, trades such as tanners, dyers, and cobblers had begun to settle along the rivers since the 18th century, with a number of shoe factories emerging in the 19th century.

People and Mentalities

At the beginning of the 19th century, Hohenlohe became a part of Württemberg, but even though since then the Swabian dialect has spread and the Franconian-Hohenlohe dialect is less evident, there is one thing that cannot be denied: Hohenlohe is Franconian. Even today the boundary between Franconian and Swabian-Alemannic is defined by the border between the Franconian bishopric of Würzburg and the Alemannic bishopric of Augsburg, a border that is fifteen hundred years old. Differences in mentality between the inhabitants of Hohenlohe and the Swabians provide material for innumerable anecdotes.[50] One of the most widely known is about two guys, one from Swabia and one from Hohenlohe, who work on a farm. Every evening, they receive two eggs from the farmer's wife. When this does not happen one evening, the Swabian says: "You haven't given me my eggs," whereas the guy from Hohenlohe says: "Don't your chickens lay eggs anymore?" This illustrates the difference between the blunt Swabian and the more ironic person from Hohenlohe. Apart from their diplomacy, the people from Hohenlohe are also said to be proud and somewhat cosmopolitan.

    Such differences in mentality can be explained historically to a certain degree. Until 1806, the Hohenlohe region was characterized by boundaries often running between individual villages – complete with new competences and hierarchies of power. It was a matter of survival to get along with everybody and not lay oneself open to attack. Bluntness could jeopardize people's existence, so irony and diplomatic behavior were cultivated and refined. A type of "polite business partnership" developed between farmers and princes, owing to the particular vested rights. As a consequence of the right of succession, a certain prosperity had spread that might have served as basis for the proud attitude that the Swabians liked to interpret as arrogance. After all, the farmers and cattle dealers in Hohenlohe sold their cattle way beyond the border into France, a circumstance that contributed to their cosmopolitan outlook.

Under Württemberg reign, however, the region was marginalized economically due to its location on the edge of Württemberg and the unfavorable road links, thus becoming the kingdom's poorhouse. Whereas the population increased in Württemberg as a whole, it continuously decreased in Hohenlohe. In 1933, Künzelsau had almost 900 inhabitants less than in 1880. In 1939, a total of 246,000 people lived in Hohenlohe, almost 40,000 fewer than in 1871. [51] Many tried to make a living in the industrial regions and migrated. Even today, population density at roughly 180 inhabitants per square kilometer is way below the average of 290 in Baden-Württemberg. [52]

From Poorhouse to Model Region – the Development of Hohenlohe after World War II

After the end of World War II, the population in Hohenlohe went up again. Despite the many war victims, the number of inhabitants initially increased by almost 100,000. The area of Baden-Württemberg as we know it today reported [21] per cent migration gain until 1961 and therefore the highest percentage in West Germany due to the fact that many refugees and displaced persons found a new home here.21 A large number of refugees and displaced persons were directed to Hohenlohe, too, where many residential buildings had remained intact. The district of Künzelsau numbered 32,421 inhabitants in September 1964 and had thus almost doubled its population compared to 1939. Almost one quarter of the inhabitants of Künzelsau were refugees and displaced persons at the time. They needed jobs, but some of them also founded their own businesses and contributed to economic growth. In Künzelsau, Richard Hofmann – who had fled from the Ore Mountains – established the stocking factory RIHO. [54]

Whereas the former district of Künzelsau had 1,624 jobs in industry in 1950, this figure had increased to 6,500 in 1964. [55] At that time the town was connected with the highway network only through a major road called the B 19. People placed their hopes in the planned construction of the highways Heilbronn–Nuremberg and Heilbronn–Würzburg. However, it was some years before the highway Heilbronn–Nuremberg was completed, in 1979. The enormous economic upswing of the region cannot only be explained by the improved road network. In contrast to the 19th century, the region has been receiving government funds aimed at structural development. A number of support programs have contributed to Hohenlohe's experiencing major progress in respect of industrialization.

In 1950, the state government declared the greater part of Hohenlohe as deserving promotion, and in 1956 the state promotion program Hohenlohe-Härtsfeld was established to "support this economically somewhat backward region by selective measures initiated by the state." [56] Among others, measures aimed at the promotion of small and medium-sized enterprises and the development of industrial sites were supported. These were followed in 1958 by regional promotion programs of the Federal Government and, in 1969, the grand coalition passed the law on joint projects that, among other things, intended the improvement of the regional economic structure and became the most important government subsidy for economically weak regions. The entire area of Hohenlohe was admitted to the program and remained in it until 1981. [57] Recently, Hohenlohe has benefited from the Baden-Württemberg structural development program for rural areas. At the time of writing, Künzelsau is at the top of this development program with a subsidy of 369,100 Euro. [58] In the meantime, new residential buildings and industrial parks have developed on the edges of most of the towns and cities of the "country of castles."

Heilbronn-Franconia – the Growth Region

Today, Hohenlohe belongs to the region of Heilbronn-Franconia that – apart from the city of Heilbronn – also covers the districts of Heilbronn, Schwäbisch Hall, and Main-Tauber and therefore constitutes the largest region in Baden-Württemberg in terms of surface area. In the 1970s, a state law created a region that was initially called Franconia. In search of a new identity, the four districts as well as the city of Heilbronn finally decided to change the name to Heilbronn-Franconia to avoid future mix-ups with Franconian administrative districts in Bavaria.

Identified as a rural area according to the state development plan of 1983, the region is still one of the most strongly growing areas in the southwest. Its overall economic output increased sixfold between 1970 and 1998. A continuous influx of inhabitants has been witnessed, particularly since the 1980s, together with the region's gain in economic strength. It is especially the medium-sized cities and their surroundings that expanded, rather than the more agricultural communities. A total of 16 communities in Hohenlohe have fewer inhabitants than they did in 1880.

"Even though the region of Heilbronn-Franconia ranks among the regions in the state that are largely rural in character, it is one of the strongly growing regions in Baden-Württemberg. [...] Obviously, both entrepreneurs and employees working in this region have found a way to successfully bring their products and processes in line with demand and at the same time have maintained and permanently increased their competitiveness," said Walter Döring in 1999, at the time Minister for Economic Affairs.[59] Starting at a comparatively low level, the employment figures have increased by nearly 30 per cent since the beginning of the 1970s – unparalleled in comparison with the other regions of the state. The district of Hohenlohe ranked first both in the region and in the entire state, with the district reporting employment growth of 32 per cent from 1983 to 1992.[60] At the same time, considerable sectoral shifts occurred. Whereas in 1939 a total of 64 per cent of all waged and salaried workers in Hohenlohe were employed in the agricultural industry, their share had dropped to 8 per cent by 1987. This development is opposed by a massive increase in waged and salaried workers in both the production and service sectors. In the meantime, Hohenlohe does not differ so much anymore from the Baden-Württemberg average in respect of the distribution of the workforce across individual sectors, and the differences to the general economic development of the state have become smaller.[61]

Contrary to the positive employment development, the number of unemployed has been increasing more strongly in the Heilbronn-Franconia region than in the rest of the state since 1985.⁶² In view of an unemployment rate of 2.9 per cent in the Hohenlohe region in 1986, it was nevertheless difficult for Würth to recruit new employees. At that time, the unemployment rate in Stuttgart was higher by 40 per cent, in Heidelberg by 120 per cent, in Mannheim and Freiburg even by 150 per cent.⁶³

By 2002, the unemployment rate in the district of Hohenlohe had risen to 5.6 per cent, yet it was still below the 6.1 per cent state average and the average of the region of Heilbronn-Franconia of 6.2 per cent, the largest part of which was accounted for by the city and the district of Heilbronn.⁶⁴

In the meantime, the district of Hohenlohe ranks among those with the largest share of industrial workers and employees in Baden-Württemberg. Industry and trade are concentrated in the Kocher valley and the Hohenlohe Plains. "Economic priorities are the electrical engineering industry, the metalworking industry […], automatic control engineering as well as the textile industry and publishing. Highly efficient craft businesses and important trading corporations, particularly in the field of fastening technology, as well as numerous service enterprises complement the diverse mix of industries."⁶⁵

Künzelsau in the center is the location of four internationally operating corporations: Ziehl-Abegg AG, market leader in the field of drive motors for elevators, the well-known German producer of jeans, Mustang, Adolf Würth GmbH & Co. KG, and its competitor, Albert Berner GmbH.

All in all, the inhabitants are very satisfied with the region. This was the result of the largest online survey about socio-political issues in Germany in 2003, carried out by the management consulting company McKinsey, the magazine "Stern," the "Zweites Deutsches Fernsehen" and the Internet provider T-Online. More than 1,600 people from the Heilbronn-Franconia region gave a positive rating, primarily for the "soft location factors" such as nature, peace, and quiet and a beautiful landscape as well as a pleasant social environment. The job market, shopping facilities, and the range of schools and educational opportunities were considered to be good by the persons asked. They saw flaws in the fields of road and rail links, the availability of housing, and child-care.⁶⁶

The Würth Group – Global Player from Hohenlohe

With Adolf Würth GmbH & Co. KG, the Würth Line Companies, and the Allied Companies, the Würth Group provides more than 4,000 jobs in the Heilbronn-Franconia region. [67] The business that started as a small family enterprise in Künzelsau in 1945 has become an important economic factor of the region.

As a group of companies operating on a global basis, Würth brings a piece of the world into the "province." Anybody who visits the Museum Würth at corporate headquarters in Künzelsau-Gaisbach and has a coffee in the company's cafeteria afterwards can – quite unexpectedly in such a rural area – hear scraps of conversation in English, Italian, Spanish, or French, apart from the Hohenlohe dialect. Corporate headquarters with the Museum being open to the general public illustrates the company's cosmopolitan outlook and therefore also a part of Würth's corporate philosophy. For outsiders it might still be quite astonishing to see that an international corporation has its headquarters in this very rural area in the northeast of Baden-Württemberg.

Advantages and Disadvantages of Being Located in a Rural Area

Reinhold Würth quite adamantly says "no" to the question if the location in Künzelsau was a disadvantage for the company's development: "Looking at the map you will see that Künzelsau is situated right in the center of southern Germany and has great road links in all directions thanks to the Heilbronn–Nuremberg highway." The airport in Schwäbisch Hall is of paramount importance to the business. From there you can reach "all locations in Europe non-stop; flight time between Schwäbisch Hall and London is 1 hour and 45 minutes, from Hall to Helsinki 3 hours and 45 minutes, from Hall to Istanbul 4 hours." [68] In view of the permanently increasing volume of traffic on the highway A6, whose further extension is a long time coming, the airport in Schwäbisch Hall has become vitally important for the business. Reinhold Würth says: "If we did not have the opportunity to take off from Hall we would quite soon consider the possibility of moving into the vicinity of a large city with an airport." [69]

The Schwäbisch Hall airport is managed by a limited liability company, 90 per cent of which is owned by the Würth Company and 10 per cent by Bausparkasse Schwäbisch Hall (savings and loan association). To make sure that the airport can also in the future be used for commercial business traffic, it was necessary to extend the runway. To this aim, the Würth-Grundstücks-GmbH, Künzelsau purchased the complex covering 190 acres (77 hectares) in 2003 for 7 million Euro and leased it to Flugplatz Schwäbisch Hall Gmbh. Würth furthermore invested 17.5 million Euro in the extension of the airport with a subsidy of 6 million Euro from the state of Baden-Württemberg.[70]

The traffic issue touches upon a sore spot that always gives rise to heated debate in the region. Apart from the excessively heavy traffic on the highway A6, the business sector sees additional locational disadvantages in the lack of connection with the intercity express-network of the German railroad, the poor communication links to Stuttgart, Frankfurt, and their respective airports, and the lack of an airport with transatlantic connections in Baden-Württemberg.[71]

Another frequently mentioned deficit of the region in connection with the recruitment of a qualified workforce is the lack of universities and colleges offering courses in the field of technology and business. This results in a lack of specialist staff, since young people have to leave the region to study at a university or college and very often do not return after graduation. Economists have come to the conclusion that geographical proximity to educational institutions and research institutes is a significant locational factor, since the exchange of know-how and experience is facilitated by personal communication and cooperation.[72]

Reinhold Würth, too, sees the geographical locational disadvantage in the field of R&D in high tech: "Chemical, electrical, and electronics companies cannot do without cooperation with universities and technical colleges. The

Reinhold Würth in the cockpit of his airplane with co-pilot Christian Riedel (1995)

geographical, but first and foremost the emotional-psychological, distance to universities and scientific institutes has a negative impact on R&D."[73]

Würth has had the experience that is indeed not that easy to hire specialists who are willing to work in a rural area. In 1986, the length of stay of IT-specialists in the company amounted to three years, yet it would be interesting to investigate if the length of stay of this professional group is longer in conurbations. In the 1980s, a "desert allowance" in addition to the salary had frequently to be paid if one wanted to lure away an IT expert to Künzelsau.

In Reinhold Würth's opinion, the assumption that specialists are isolated from progress in the province is more a subjective issue than an actual fact. He points out that, in the age of IT, even Künzelsau offers sufficient opportunities to communicate with the world. After all, the companies that have settled in the district of Hohenlohe from the fields of electrical engineering and electronics have developed very positively: Stahl, Ziehl-Abegg, Elektrobau Mulfingen, and Würth Elektronik in Niedernhall belonging to the Würth Group, to name but a few.

The Würth Company attempts to address the shortfall in specialist staff with qualified university or college training at the company's location. The Würth Academy, situated at corporate headquarters in Künzelsau-Gaisbach is a group-wide facility for staff education. Specialist qualification and developmental programs have been developed for both junior managers and upcoming top managers. Another group-owned educational institution was officially opened in Bad Mergentheim in November 2003: the Würth PHOENIX Academy that primarily offers courses for further qualifications in the field of IT.

Würth also participates in initiatives aimed at the further qualification of specialist staff beyond the company's limits. Within the framework of a joint project with the Heilbronn Chamber of Commerce and Industry, masters and journeymen from the construction, metalworking, electrical, and wood-working industries have the opportunity to be trained in the qualification of "fastening technology specialist."[74] The teachers of this course come from the University of Stuttgart as well as from Adolf Würth GmbH & Co. KG. In addition to this, the Würth Academy offers seminars on business theory and practice to craft customers.

Reinhold Würth and his company contribute to the improvement of the region's educational infrastructure in the field of universities and colleges. In the fall of 1988, Künzelsau became the second location of the Heilbronn University of Applied Sciences. Here, courses on business administration with priority programs on culture and leisure-time management, product and customer management, and media management, as well as building system engineering, electrical engineering, and industrial engineering are offered. The endowment of a chair in sports management enabled Würth to introduce this priority program in the year 2000. In cooperation with the Heilbronn University of Applied Sciences, the University of Louisville, Kentucky (USA), and the Grand Valley State University of Allendale, Michigan (USA), a course of studies accompanying the students' work and finishing with an MBA (Master of Business Administration) was developed for employees of the Würth Group, the degree also being acknowledged in the USA. In November 2003, the first 14 graduates finished this postgraduate course of study that is spent half in the USA and half in Germany. Apart from part-time lecturers of the universities, knowledge is imparted to the students by top managers of the Würth Group and Prof. Reinhold Würth. [75]

Würth furthermore belongs to those corporations in the region that train staff at the Business School of the Mosbach Vocational Academy opened in Bad Mergentheim. This is the first time that the dual course of studies at a vocational academy has been connected with a Master's degree at a British university. In December 2003, 23 young people finished their studies with a Master's in Economics (MA) or a Master's in Business Data Processing (MA) at the Vocational Academy. [76]

The Würth Company contributes to eliminating locational disadvantages in many different ways – for its own benefit, but also for the benefit of the region.

Reinhold Würth noticed one locational advantage in the mentality of the Hohenlohe workforce. The population is characterized by distinct immobility, many employees being either part-time farmers or wine-growers and most of them having a house they either built themselves or inherited. "These people are rather conservative and rooted to their native soil; they have ties with the region and the company. The employees' willingness to perform is higher, the number of staff ill lower than in big cities." [77] Reinhold Würth is convinced that rural locations will also remain attractive for business enterprises in the future, particularly for those businesses that handle a high volume of merchandise in relation to their value and for those with high labor costs: "Industrial sites in conurbations have become so expensive that the interest to be paid for the land cannot be built into the sales price asked for high-volume, low-cost products any more. Sufficient existing industrial areas at reasonable prices pave the way for the construction of highly efficient production and warehousing facilities in rural areas." [78] This applies particularly to a direct selling company such as Würth.

Würth Expands and Diversifies in the Region

The Schlossmühle in Künzelsau soon burst at the seams, so that the Würth Company founded in 1945 moved into a new building at the station in 1952. After only a short while the space available there no longer sufficed either for the quickly expanding business. Nearby Gaisbach offered favorable conditions for a larger corporate building. In 1963, screw production was moved into a new factory building in Gaisbach, the administration and finally the warehouse following suit in 1969. The manufacturing operations that had been carrying on business under the firm of SWG Schraubenwerk Gaisbach since 1967 were experiencing a rather serious lack of space by the mid-1970s, and so rooms were rented from the Schäuffelen Company in Niederhall in August 1976. In the fall of 1986, Würth filed an application with the city of Künzelsau for the construction of a new production and warehousing facility. The procedure dragged on, however, it proving impossible to find an agreement with the municipal authorities about the exact location of the building. It soon became obvious that the Waldenburg location offered much better conditions for SWG. [79] In 1988/89, the business moved to Waldenburg where more than 300 employees were working for SWG in the year 2000. This is only one of many examples of how the company's diversification in the region led to additional locations and therefore also to additional jobs.

In 1971, Reinhold Würth established the department Würth Elektronik that started its own independent development five years later with its entry in the Schwäbisch Hall Commercial Register. Würth Elektronik GmbH & Co. KG settled in Niedernhall, the municipality in which Hermersberg, the family's place of residence purchased in 1971, is also situated. On the occasion of the purchase of this estate the company and the municipality had agreed to the settlement of a business in Niedernhall.[80] This small, medieval town remained almost unchanged within its centuries-old walls well into the 20th century. The inhabitants earned their living as small farmers, wine-growers, and craftsmen. Niedernhall experienced its first economic upswing with the settlement of the Schneider und Kern Company in 1930. However, after World War II, additional infrastructural prerequisites had to be created for further industrial settlements. Most important initially was the regulation of the Kocher River that was completed in 1960. The regulation of the Kocher as well as the completion of the road to Künzelsau – which until then had been no more than a country lane – created the foundations of further industrial settlements at the Kocher.[81] Since then, 100 businesses have settled in Niedernhall, the small town with its roughly 4,000 inhabitants boasting a total of 1,800 jobs.[82] The total number of employees working at Würth Elektronik GmbH & Co. KG increased from 69 in 1984 to 798 in 2000. However, not all the employees work at the Niedernhall location; the Würth Electronics Group has four different divisions with additional locations in Waldenburg (EMC & Inductive Solutions), Öhringen, Pforzheim, Rot am See, Schopfheim, and Marbach (Würth Solergy).[83]

Kupferzell and Bad Mergentheim became additional locations of Würth spinoffs in the region apart from Waldenburg and Niedernhall. The company RECA NORM GmbH & Co. KG that emerged from a merger of various trading corporations taken over in the 1960s and 1970s moved out of the distribution center in Gaisbach in 1986 and settled in Kupferzell. The company had 472 employees in 2000.

WÜRTH AND THE REGION
WÜRTH EXPANDS AND DIVERSIFIES IN THE REGION

Würth Industrie Service GmbH & Co. KG has been represented in Bad Mergentheim as an independent subsidiary of the Würth Group since January 1, 2000. The business developed from the spin-off of the Industry Division from the internal structures of Adolf Würth GmbH & Co. KG. The company purchased the area of the former Teutonic Order barracks from the city of Bad Mergentheim in December 1998. This is another example of how the locational advantage of rural areas – low real estate prices – was used for the benefit of both the company and the municipality. The total area covers 270 acres (110 hectares) and provides ample reserves for the future expansion of the Würth Group. From here, customers of all lines of business belonging to medium-sized and large industry are supplied with the entire range of products carried by the Würth Group for manufacturing operations, maintenance, and repair. Three hundred employees work on a large number of logistical services in Bad Mergentheim. [84]

Jobs were also safeguarded by Würth's taking over companies in the region that were steeped in tradition. Owing to a change in ownership within the group of companies, the screw factory L. & C. Arnold established in Ernsbach in 1898 became an independent company of the Würth Group in 1994 by the name of Arnold Umformtechnik. [85] The company had 400 employees in the year 2000. The Reisser Company, too, founded in 1921, has been part of the Würth Group since 1994. Soon after the brothers Gotthilf, August, and Hermann Reisser had opened up several hardware stores in the region, they also attracted customers from out of state. Before Adolf Würth established his own business in 1945, he worked for Reisser as authorized signatory. In 1952 the company started to manufacture high-quality screws. In the meantime, Reisser has more than 160 employees. [86]

The spin-offs and acquisitions mentioned cover the most important, yet by far not all, of the Würth Group's entrepreneurial activities in the region. Apart from its core business, the corporation also points the way to the future in other areas.

Würth Points the Way to the Future in Regional Gastronomy

In 1987, Adolf Würth GmbH & Co. KG purchased Panoramahotel from the city of Waldenburg right in the heart of Hohenlohe. After renovation and enlargement, the hotel offers its guests an elegant environment with its 69 rooms as well as 9 meeting and banqueting rooms and provides a very attractive panoramic view of Hohenlohe, thanks to its location at an elevation of 1,660ft (505m).

In 1999, Panorama Catering joined Panorama Hotel & Service GmbH Waldenburg. Initially intended as catering for the staff as well as for conferences and guests, Panorama Catering has in the meantime gone beyond in-house services and is very much sought after for smaller and larger events such as the Langenburg Classics in the year 2000, the Unterland Exhibition in Heilbronn, the Open House of Würth Industrie Service GmbH & Co. KG in Bad Mergentheim, and the Open House of Adolf Würth GmbH & Co. KG in Künzelsau.

The hotel and restaurant Altes Amtshaus in Ailringen constitutes a gastronomic highlight in the region, and with it Würth also saved a cultural monument from going to ruin. The former administrative center of the Teutonic Order was built around 1580/1600 as Renaissance building with decorative timber framing, yet its character is also greatly influenced by a Baroque reconstruction phase. In 1992, Reinhold Würth bought the house of the Teutonic Order complete with the parish barn to save it from further decay. After large-scale restoration, one of the most beautiful houses in Ailringen was officially opened as a hotel and restaurant on November 4, 1997. Numerous historical remnants were preserved: plasterwork, colored fittings, stucco, timber framing, massive walls, and vaulted ceilings testify to the house's long history. At the same time, state-of-the-art, comfortable furnishings were integrated that fulfil today's demands on hotels. Altes Amtshaus Ailringen is listed in every noted hotel and restaurant guide. Within a very short period of time managing director Heinz Schiebenes and chef Olaf Pruckner garnered a coveted Michelin star.

WÜRTH AND THE REGION
WÜRTH POINTS THE WAY TO THE FUTURE IN REGIONAL GASTRONOMY

The most recent gastronomic project of the Würth Group, the Sudhaus in Schwäbisch Hall, was officially opened on May 22/23, 2004 adjacent to Kunsthalle Würth. The desolate structural condition of the listed brick building of the early 20th century, as well as the question of how such a building could possibly be used, considerably complicated the decision to purchase it. Finally, Adolf Würth GmbH & Co. KG decided to take the risk. For Reinhold Würth it is clear that this decision was the right one: "Since in today's culture the combination of visits to museums and dinners in first-rate evening events has become rather popular, I suspected that the Sudhaus could be a wonderful completion of the Kunsthalle Würth in that the Sudhaus can be used for gastronomic purposes as well as for conferences and meetings." [87] In the three-year planning and reconstruction phase it was not only the entire façade that was renovated and restored, but also the interior was changed completely. A brewery has been integrated into the ground floor, the floors above house a restaurant and a brasserie as well as conference and seminar rooms, and the whole is capped by a roof terrace that offers a breathtaking, panoramic view of Schwäbisch Hall. Below the Sudhaus, an additional 7000 ft^2 (650 m^2) of exhibition space was created as an extension of the Kunsthalle. "And the city gains another culinary highlight with the Sudhaus – centrally located and with fascinating views of the city. […] the long tradition of breweries in the city is now being continued […]. Thanks to the reconstruction this striking building lending the city its character can be preserved with its unique charm as a brewery and refurbished very elegantly in line with the demands for the protection of historic buildings. Owing to its difficult financial situation the city would not have been in a position to do this. Kunsthalle and Sudhaus, the arts and gastronomy, make the Katharinenvorstadt, which has stayed in the shadows for so long, flourish again," [88] remarked Hermann-Josef Pelgrim, mayor of Schwäbisch Hall, with great joy.

Since the spring of 2003, the Anne-Sophie-Haus, too, has offered modern gastronomy within historic walls. The Anne-Sophie-Haus is the realization of an extraordinary and at the same time unique project of its kind in Germany. Both the restaurant and the hotel are managed jointly by handicapped and non-handicapped people and offer a comfortable and pleasant environment to both handicapped and non-handicapped guests. Carmen Würth, who is behind the entire project, wants to eliminate barriers, awakening understanding for handicapped people on the one hand and assigning meaningful projects to handicapped people on the other.

Freemen of the City of Künzelsau: Carmen Würth and Reinhold Würth

On April 8, 2003, the couple Carmen and Reinhold Würth were given the freedom of the city of Künzelsau for their outstanding services to the promotion of economic, cultural, and social integration. Even though the Würth family lives today in nearby Niedernhall, Reinhold Würth says about himself: "In my heart I have always stayed a citizen of Künzelsau." [89] The Würth Company as one of the largest employers of the region is an integral part of Künzelsau. In his ceremonial address, Volker Lenz, mayor of Künzelsau, focused particularly on Würth's commitment going beyond entrepreneurial activity. The promotion of fine arts and culture – among other things, the art collection and the screw museum, involvement in the Förderverein Künstlerfamilie Sommer, and the Hirschwirtscheuer situated in the heart of Künzelsau and used as museum – constitutes an asset to the city just like the concerts, cultural events, and open-air concerts organized by Akademie Würth.

Würth's many-sided commitment also covers the field of promoting educational institutions. A considerable donation supported the construction of the Reinhold-Würth-School in Künzelsau-Gaisbach and, in addition, the employment of a part-time lecturer at said school is subsidized, enabling work on projects that could not be financed through government funds. The company runs the Akademie Würth, while Würth provides scholarships for outstanding students in the fields of

"Prof. Reinhold Würth is a veritable treasure for the city of Künzelsau. Without the Würth family, both the business scene and the social and cultural landscape would look a lot different."

Volker Lenz, mayor of the city of Künzelsau

natural sciences and languages and supports the Künzelsau location of the Heilbronn University of Applied Sciences with an endowed chair in sports management. Carmen Würth's social involvement is represented particularly well by the Anne-Sophie-Haus, the meeting place for handicapped and non-handicapped people.

Volker Lenz, mayor of Künzelsau, grants the Freedom of the City of Künzelsau to Reinhold Würth and his wife Carmen (2003)

Hermersberg – a Castle as Domicile of an Entrepreneur

In his autobiographical description, Reinhold Würth quotes his home as one of his sources of strength apart from his family and religion: "When my wife and I return from one of our business trips we truly enjoy the peace and quiet of Hohenlohe and the friendliness of the inhabitants. Valleys and forests lend themselves to long walks. I do not see any downsides in the quality of life between the city and the countryside." [90] It is therefore not surprising that he remained loyal to his regional roots when looking for a new family home in 1969. When it became known precisely at that time that the administrative office of the Prince of Hohenlohe-Oehringen planned on selling both Hermersberg Castle and the estate, he immediately contacted the mayor of Niedernhall, Wilhelm Balbach, and the administrative office. Reinhold Würth associated memories of a school outing in 1944 with Hermersberg. Avoiding the low-flying planes of the Allies, the third-graders and their teacher had arrived at Hermersberg: "It was during that outing that I, as a nine-year-old, consciously came in contact with Hermersberg for the first time." [91]

In May 1971, Reinhold and Carmen Würth purchased the castle complete with 9 acres (3.7 hectares) of land. In coordination with the Landesdenkmalamt (state office for the protection of historic buildings and monuments), reconstruction started in 1972. After only a couple of months it became obvious that the costs would exceed the original estimate by double or even triple the amount. In view of the economic slowdown attendant on the first oil crisis of 1973, the new owner of the castle from time to time had his doubts as to whether he had made the right decision. On April 30, 1974 the Würth family finally moved into the newly-renovated, historic building. The initial lack of understanding in Reinhold Würth's surroundings soon changed, as he reports, from a wait-and-see attitude, through watching and being amazed, to "smiling approval". In the Rittersaal of Hermersberg Castle that had to be preserved in its original state upon request of the Landesdenkmalamt, many guests from all over the world have since listened to concerts: business associates from the People's Republic of China, Japan, or Taiwan as well as celebrities from the world of politics, economics, and administration. Comments and compliments confirm the correctness of Reinhold Würth's decision to buy the castle. For him, Hermersberg is "perhaps more than a modest contribution to the preservation of our historic monuments for the coming generations." [92]

Congratulations to Reinhold Würth: students and teachers of Reinhold-Würth-Elementary School congratulate him on his 63rd birthday (1998)

Reinhold Würth – Global Entrepreneur from Baden-Württemberg

Theodor Heuss' characterization of the people from Hohenlohe as "clever, lively, bright, a bit self-opinionated and confident" [93] might also apply to Reinhold Würth. Aware of the independent Hohenlohe tradition, Würth refers to the overall Baden-Württemberg tradition "of tinkerers and thinkers, reflective people and philosophers, forceful people and doers." [94] In his opinion, the most important components of his success are hard work, staying power, tenacity, energy, and the ability ascribed to the Swabian pioneer of modern agricultural technology, Max Eyth, to inspire and guide people.

As a logical consequence, Reinhold Würth, having been awarded the Wirtschaftsmedaille of the state of Baden-Württemberg in 1987 and the Verdienstmedaille of the state of Baden-Württemberg in 1994, was presented as Baden-Württemberg's model entrepreneur in the 2003 image campaign of the state titled "Wir können alles außer Hochdeutsch" (We can do anything – except speak High German). [95]

Being an entrepreneur from Baden-Württemberg, Reinhold Würth sometimes complains about the lack of a shared tradition in the young state in the southwest of Germany: "At a disadvantage to the 800 years of Bavaria's Wittelsbach state tradition and the only slightly younger, deep-rooted structures of Switzerland, the national consciousness of our young state is certainly capable of development." [96] The states of Württemberg and Baden, joined together in the course of history from different secular and clerical territories and finally enlarged in 1806 as a consequence of Napoleon's politics, were split up again in 1945 by the allied occupying powers, France and the USA. Baden in the south, occupied by the French, was governed from Freiburg, southern Württemberg was joined together with Hohenzollern, Prussian until then, to form Württemberg-Hohenzollern, and northern Baden as well as northern Württemberg were merged by the US occupying power to form Württemberg-Baden, with Stuttgart as the state capital. It was only in 1952 that the new southwestern state of Baden-Württemberg emerged from these three states. Traditions and mentalities differing from one region to the next clash here and sometimes have a hard time developing a joint identity. This is not altogether surprising in view of the fact that even smaller regional structures such as the Heilbronn-Franconia region is considered to be an "artificial entity." Stefan Gläser, mayor of Wertheim, remarks that the region "thrown together in terms of administration" in the 1970s has not yet had the opportunity to grow together as closely as is perhaps desirable. [97]

However, it is not like Reinhold Würth to lament a condition; he much rather wants to "set things in motion by inspiring people and advance the region." [98] Thanks to his many initiatives and activities he has helped to change the face of the region in past decades. Reinhold Würth also initiated a number of changes in his dealing with mayors and district administrators. At the end of the 1980s, for example, Reinhold Würth exchanged opinions with Dr. Franz Susset, then administrator of the district of Hohenlohe, about economic issues in rural areas. [99] The two of them discussed how the Würth Company could support the efforts of the state government to create additional educational possibilities in rural areas for farmers leaving the field of agriculture. Reinhold Würth asked Ursula Küblbeck, at the time in charge of in-house further education and training, to think about which qualified jobs could be particularly suitable for farmers. A number of suggestions submitted by district administrator Susset to Lothar Späth, then prime minister, concerning initiatives in the district of Hohenlohe, have since been put into practice, e.g., in the field of further education and training for medium- to higher-qualified employees.

The interests of his company's location and his home always play an important role for Reinhold Würth in his many different functions. Within the framework of his chair of entrepreneurship at the University of Karlsruhe he assigned a Master's thesis that was to test the hypothesis that the Heilbronn-Franconia region is under-represented by the state's administration concerning the allocation of public funds. Another request was to compare the provision of scientific and research institutes with that of other regions.[100]

Citizens' Action Group Pro Region Heilbronn-Franken

Since 1997 Reinhold Würth has been active as first chairman of a union of committed citizens for the interests of the Heilbronn-Franconia region. The idea for this union was born in May 1996 during a forum on "Competition of the Regions – What Are the Chances of Heilbronn-Franconia?" by both Reinhold Würth and Frank Stroh, the authorized representative of the German engineering workers' union. The region was supposed to be led out of the "vale of tears" and a future-oriented profile developed. The motto of the union official Stroh, "action instead of complaints," was very much to the liking of the entrepreneur Reinhold Würth, and

Reinhold Würth with the mayor of Schwäbisch Hall, Hermann-Josef Pelgrim, during the inauguration of the Day of the Region in Schwäbisch Hall (2002)

> "Reinhold Würth is certainly a big asset for the region. He can definitely rub people up the wrong way, but he is very open to new ideas even if they come from people who do not share his political beliefs. On the platform 'pro Region' we leave aside day-to-day politics."
>
> Frank Stroh, deputy chairman of the citizens' action group pro Region Heilbronn-Franken, press spokesman of the German engineering workers' union

so the two soon got together for "concerted action" to find fellow supporters.[101] In April 1997, a total of 34 representatives of different bodies from within the economy, the fine arts, unions, and district administrations were welcomed on the occasion of their first meeting.

Reinhold Würth, elected first chairman at the meeting, finally presented the new citizens' action group to the general public as an association aiming to promote optimism. Together with as many people with the same kind of interest as possible the association's mission was to fight against "the damned whining idleness."[102] It is the objective to strengthen the region's feeling of belonging together, to emphasize the region's strong points in competition with others, to identify its weak spots, and to urge for change. The citizens' action group, whose office is located at Adolf Würth GmbH & Co. KG, produced a video of the region for the first time in 1998, which was reissued in 2003. Regional days are organized on an annual basis and, since 1999, a yearbook of the region has been published. Since September 2000, the magazine "Pro" has been published monthly.

It goes without saying that Reinhold Würth's commitment to the region is also critically regarded. From time to time he is accused of being involved in the region's affairs more or less out of self-interest. However, at the same time people admit that Reinhold Würth lives up to his entrepreneurial responsibility by generous sponsorship of the arts and culture in the region.[103]

Not everybody considers the growth of the Würth Group with its effect on the economy to be entirely positive. One of the long-time top managers of Würth, Karl Specht, remarked that, in the mid-1960s when the company grew extremely quickly, "something akin to envy of the Würth Company getting bigger and bigger" had spread among the companies in the district of Künzelsau. [104]

The readers of the newspaper "Echo am Mittwoch" and "Echo am Sonntag", though, appointed Reinhold Würth "Man of the Year 2000 from the Region Heilbronn-Franconia." This might be an indication that the entrepreneur, the sponsor of fine arts and culture who in the meantime owing to his outstanding commercial success and social commitment is widely known well beyond the region and also beyond Baden-Württemberg, is deeply rooted in the region.

WÜRTH AND THE REGION
CITIZENS' ACTION GROUP PRO REGION HEILBRONN-FRANKEN

Honors and Decorations for Reinhold Würth's Commitment to Baden-Württemberg

1986	Ehrennadel in Silber des Fecht-Clubs Tauberbischofsheim (Silver Pin of Honor by the Fencing Club Tauberbischofsheim)
1987	Fördernadel in Silber vom Württembergischen Betriebssportverband e.V. (Silver Pin by the Sports Association Württemberg e.V.)
1987	Wirtschaftsmedaille des Landes Baden-Württemberg (Medal awarded by the state of Baden-Württemberg)
1993	Goldene Ehrennadel des Baden-Württembergischen Luftfahrtverbandes e.V. (Golden Pin of Honor by the Aviation Association Baden-Württemberg e.V.)
1994	Verdienstmedaille des Landes Baden-Württemberg (Medal of Merit awarded by the state of Baden-Württemberg)
1997	Württembergischer Archäologiepreis der Volksbanken und Raiffeisenbanken (Württemberg Archaeology Prize by People's Banks and Rural Credit Cooperatives)
1999	Staufermedaille des Landes Baden-Württemberg (Staufer Medal awarded by the state of Baden-Württemberg)
1999	Ehrenmedaille der Industrie- und Handelskammer Heilbronn-Franken in Gold (Gold Medal of Honor by the Heilbronn-Franken Chamber of Commerce and Industry)
2002	Medienpreis 2002 des Haller Tagblatts (Media Prize 2002 by Haller Tagblatt)
2002	Reinhold-Maier-Medaille, verliehen durch die FDP/DVP Fraktion im Landtag von Baden-Württemberg (Reinhold-Maier Medal awarded by the FDP/DVP parliamentary party in the Baden-Württemberg state parliament)
2003	Ehrenbürgerwürde der Stadt Künzelsau (Freedom of the city of Künzelsau)
2005	Goldene Ehrennadel der Handwerkskammer Heilbronn-Franken (Golden Honor Pin awarded by the Heilbronn-Franken Chamber of Handicrafts)

5　EXPANSION HEAD-ON

The 1960s

At the end of 1960, the Würth Company had seven sales representatives; one year later, this had risen to seventeen and, by 1966, to thirty-five. The multiplication of the sales force became the driving force behind the business, with intensive servicing of the market in the 1960s leading to rapid development of sales. This inevitably led to a change in Reinhold Würth's field of activities; he set further milestones in the success story of his company by founding the first foreign-based businesses in The Netherlands, Austria, Switzerland, Italy, and France. He used the opportunity offered by Germany's favorable economic development for further business expansion.

Between the Economic Miracle and the Recession

A new and unexpectedly strong economic boom had set in during the summer of 1959 with the third business cycle since currency reform. There was huge demand for both investment goods and consumer goods, while at the same time the country reported high growth rates in the export industry. The German Mark was upvalued and the discount rate reduced to three per cent by the West German Central Bank to stabilize prices and bring down the balance-of-payments surplus criticized abroad. However, these measures did not succeed in putting a stop to the overheating of the economy. In 1962, the Minister for Economic Affairs, Ludwig Erhard, who would replace Konrad Adenauer as German Chancellor the following year, requested trade unions, consumers, and businessmen to use some restraint: "This inferno will continue if excessive wages lead to higher prices and those higher prices in turn to higher wages." [105] In the spring of 1964 the business barometer went up again, with Germany continuing to bring the Federal price and cost level in line with the rest of the world. In May 1964, the Stuttgart Chamber of Commerce and Industry reported that, for the first time after currency reform, orders on the book – predominantly in mechanical engineering – had increased in such a way that suppliers were frequently having to postpone their delivery dates. The economy needed far more employees than were available in West Germany, and so the government decided to recruit workers from southern Europe. By 1964, their number had risen to almost one million.

In trade, too, the upward trend was recognizable, although there was a change in demand. Whatever had been considered a luxury in the past turned into a vital necessity in the 1960s. Buyers identified other commodity markets that were important for their satisfaction of wants. The retail trade for foodstuffs and clothing by far missed the sales growth of the 1950s, yet companies trading in wallpaper and floor coverings, radios, TV sets, and record players as well as businesses trading in automotive parts reported radical sales increases.[106]

Until the mid-1960s, economic growth continued almost uninterruptedly. The aspects stimulating growth were reconstruction, the expansion of new industries and new products, and the rather low energy costs. A number of positive factors had a stabilizing effect on the economy: the level of consumption on the part of the affluent citizens was high, entrepreneurs were willing to invest, and the government developed a network of social services. The parallel economic cycles in Europe further stabilized the economic situation.

In the course of the 1960s, though, the first indications of a change in the growth and business pattern appeared. Labor costs increased while the labor market tightened: at Würth, the wages and salaries increased by 36 per cent in 1966 compared to the previous year even though the number of staff had only gone up by 15.5 per cent.[107] New production technologies intensified competition, with a number of markets showing signs of saturation. The result was a reduction in profit margins.

After 1965 the economic growth rate went down dramatically, signaling the end of the unbounded upswing. Economic growth that had slowed down somewhat finally began to slacken in 1967, with the implications for Baden-Württemberg clearly felt. Daimler-Benz worked shortened shifts. At the latest in this year of recession, 1967, a general change in trend materialized: while the economic growth of the 1950s had been supported by an increase in the number of jobs and man-hours, structural change set in during the 1960s and a new phase of the technical-industrial revolution began. Productivity increases were now a logical consequence of technical-innovative progress. The economy soon recovered from this first post-war crisis, but people's faith in ongoing economic growth was badly shaken.

The economic downswing triggered considerable unrest among the population and in the world of politics since it could not be halted with the traditional instruments used for stabilizing the economy. More and more people started to criticize the system of the liberal, market-directed economy. The elections for the Federal Diet in September of 1965 resulted in the creation of a Christian-Liberal ruling coalition that was increasingly strained by international differences of opinion. Because of differences in opinion regarding budgetary policies, the Liberal Democratic Party broke up the coalition with the CDU/CSU only one year later that in the following entered into a coalition with the SPD. After the election for the Federal Diet in 1969, this grand coalition was replaced by a social-liberal government under German Chancellor Willy Brandt and foreign minister Walter Scheel. On the left wing spectrum an extra-parliamentary opposition (APO) developed. The state visit by the Persian Shah in 1967 caused unrest in numerous cities: in Berlin, the demonstrating student Benno Ohnesorg was shot during police intervention, which resulted in the student movement becoming increasingly radical. The so-called 1968 movement of the extra-parliamentary opposition did not only point the way to the political future, but the sexual revolution propagated in the wake of the student movement and the new women's movement also indicated a change in the code of morals. It was only a small minority of young people who revolted and practiced new forms of life in apartment-sharing communities, forms of life that were radically different from the social mores of the time. The fact, however, that moral standards were changing was reflected in fashion. The British fashion designer Mary Quant started a revolution with the miniskirt in 1965. Her creation was regarded as a symbol of women's sexual liberation and emancipation and would have been inconceivable in the 1950s. A change in role behavior also became apparent in another area: more and more women appeared behind the steering wheels of cars, whose numbers had also increased. After 1963 the number of marriages among the German population decreased, and a drop in the birthrate starting in 1966 initiated the so-called "baby bust." Whereas the average number of children per woman had still been 2.6 in the year 1962, it had dropped to 1.8 ten years later.[108] The decade finally concluded with the first man landing on the moon. Neil Armstrong's legendary first step on the moon on July 21, 1969 secured the USA a lead in the ongoing fierce competition with the USSR in space.

Stepping beyond Borders

In this turbulent decade – between boom and recession in the field of economy, and stagnation and revolt in society – the young Würth Company developed extremely well. In 1964, sales increased by 32 per cent over the previous year, and in October of that year, monthly sales of one million DM were achieved for the first time. Reinhold Würth remarked: "So we have finally left the phase of being an insignificant business behind!"[109] By founding the first sales branches abroad he had initiated in 1962 the development of the small business in the direction of an international corporation. On March 1, 1962 the first foreign-based company was established in s'Hertogenbosch in The Netherlands, with Hendrik J. Lastdrager appointed as managing director. During the first years Belgian customers were also supplied from Holland, but in the spring of 1964 Reinhold Würth set up a company in Belgium itself that was also run by Hendrik J. Lastdrager.

Only about two months after the establishment of the Dutch company, Reinhold Würth founded Schrauben-Würth GmbH in Basel, Switzerland on April 30, 1962, and in the summer of that year he continued his efforts to further internationalize the business in Austria. "Schrauben-Würth Vertriebsges. m.b.H." was founded in Vienna in December 1962 and started doing business in January 1963, with Peter Drexler appointed as managing director.

In the same year, one of today's largest foreign-based companies of the Würth Group was established: Würth Italy. After Belgium and Denmark in 1964, France followed in 1966, Sweden the year after, and at the end of the decade Reinhold Würth took the plunge across the Atlantic to North America in 1969.

Reca Union, later called Würth Holding, was founded in Chur, Switzerland in 1963 as umbrella organization of the foreign-based subsidiaries.

Sales Generated by the Foreign-Based Würth Companies

1966	4.720.000 DM	2.413.000 EUR
1967	6.514.000 DM	3.331.000 EUR
1968	8.363.000 DM	4.276.000 EUR
1969	12.207.000 DM	6.242.000 EUR
1970	18.498.000 DM	9.458.000 EUR
1971	24.745.000 DM	12.652.000 EUR
1972	35.101.000 DM	17.947.000 EUR
1973	47.539.000 DM	24.307.000 EUR
1974	60.943.000 DM	31.160.000 EUR
1975	69.013.000 DM	35.286.000 EUR
1976	76.678.000 DM	39.205.000 EUR

In 1964, the sales share generated abroad of 169,000 DM accounted for 16.9 per cent of the overall sales volume of the Würth Company, and between 1966 and 1970 foreign sales almost quadrupled. The overview of sales development both at home and abroad clearly illustrates the far-reaching implications of Reinhold Würth's decision to establish companies abroad for the future development of the business.

Sales Development of the Würth Group 1960–1969

	TOTAL	ADOLF WÜRTH KG
1960	2.024.000 DM	2.018.000 DM
1961	3.540.000 DM	3.536.000 DM
1962	5.053.000 DM	5.028.000 DM
1963	7.133.000 DM	6.486.000 DM
1964	10.010.000 DM	8.318.000 DM
1965	13.400.000 DM	10.497.000 DM
1966	18.000.000 DM	11.888.000 DM
1967	21.300.000 DM	11.340.000 DM
1968	26.633.000 DM	13.466.000 DM
1969	39.363.000 DM	20.116.000 DM

Despite increasing competition, the Würth Company succeeded in stepping up total sales in 1965 to a so far unparalleled extent. Reinhold Würth considered this an outstanding result, particularly in comparison with the economic development in West Germany that only reported 8 per cent growth whereas Würth achieved more than 26 per cent. And yet, he critically analyzed the sales growth on the occasion of a sales conference of the business in Salzburg in 1964. He pointed out that the price level had gone up by roughly 10 per cent that year and that therefore inflation had to be taken off the sales growth, so merchandise turnover actually amounted to 16 per cent and not to 26 per cent. At the same time the number of registered cars had increased by 20 per cent and indicated as yet untapped market potential. Reinhold Würth appealed to his sales representatives to step up sales. "The number of cars has gone up by 20 per cent this year, but the number of car repair shops has only slightly increased. The logical consequence is that the demand for products from individual businesses has grown by about 20 per cent."[110]

This illustrates another principle adhered to by Reinhold Würth, the entrepreneur, that contributed to the success of the company: successes are acknowledged and celebrated, as will be described later, but resting on one's laurels is not acceptable. Success is always scrutinized and analyzed critically, with the aim of becoming even better, even more successful.

From Survival Tactics to Strategic Business Planning

Reinhold Würth's idea concerning the aggressive expansion of the business developed in an evolutionary fashion. [111] In the first years after taking over the company he concentrated on tiding it over, yet by the 1950s he had already developed the first five-year strategic plan. In the mid-1960s, he focused on more long-term planning targets. On the occasion of the company's Christmas meeting in Berlin in December 1966, he forecast having between 100 and 120 sales representatives by 1974. In doing so, Reinhold Würth had formulated his first entrepreneurial vision. At that time, however, all the sales representatives present "roared with laughter" [112] since economic stagnation was already in the offing with the declining automotive market. And yet, the set target was achieved a lot earlier than originally planned. Hans Hügel, sales manager at the time, remembers: "We learned to be more cautious in the future whenever Reinhold Würth made forecasts, as more often than not they came true." [113]

In the 1960s Würth increasingly developed in the direction of strategic planning. This change took place at a time when business strategies in general experienced a shift, as was described by Reinhold Würth during a managing directors' conference in the spring of 1981.

In the 1950s, the companies' strategies aimed at maximizing profit were mainly geared toward the inside against the backdrop of undersupplied markets and a low level of competition. Key problems of both an operational and an organizational nature had to be solved. In the 1960s, this would change completely. Now, success was the result of a relative competitive position, but not of "trying harder." Companies had to develop and use competitive advantages. "The plant producing at low cost predominates in the competitive situation and achieves more than average profits with a less than average risk […]. For this reason, the competitor who develops and maintains a cost situation more favourable than his competitor will earn more and more money with less of a risk." [114]

In view of the distinct economic growth and technological progress the general development of business strategy in the 1960s was geared toward market leadership. [115] The idea was to increase capacities faster than one's competitors. To facilitate the expansion of capacities it was necessary both to limit withdrawals from profits and raise loans.

Companies were meant to grow faster than was possible by way of their cash flow alone. The best way of doing this was by adopting a "business strategy," which is exactly what Reinhold Würth did, too: while the quikkly-growing companies of a business strove for market leadership they were supported by slowly-developing branches of business. Reinhold Würth pushed his group of companies by establishing subsidiaries abroad and by taking his first steps in the direction of diversification.

During the 1960s and the decade following, a number of costly, future-oriented investments in the fields of sales, distribution, and marketing had to be made if one wanted to conquer additional market segments. However, there was also a limit to the desire of further business expansion since the financial situation at the beginning of the 1960s was rather tight. "This applied particularly to years characterized by extremely high expansion, when we had to fully utilize the suppliers' terms of payment or even overdraw them since too much liquidity was tied up at the customers," [116] remembers Reinhold Würth. An event occurred during that time that he likes to relate even today to underpin the importance of his constant striving for increasing the company's equity share. The director of his bank called him into his office and urgently warned him to comply with his line of credit. [117] He did not want to risk his pension by extending loans to the Würth Company. In the beginning, the banks hesitated to increase the credit lines.

Reinhold Würth was prepared to take risks, but also wanted to create a sound foundation. In the first ten to twenty years of his business activities he adopted a policy of thrift and tried to build up equity capital to safeguard the supply of operating resources. Reinhold Würth not only attached importance to increasing sales, but also to increasing profit, so that a high share of equity capital could be guaranteed for investment projects that were indispensable for future growth.

To limit the risk of financial liability, it was decided in 1965 to change the legal structure of the company. In the general commercial partnership (OHG) the partners carried full and unrestricted liability extending to their personal assets. In 1965, the legal form was changed to a limited commercial partnership by the name of Adolf Würth KG with a limited liability company (GmbH) as general partner.

On July 1, 1966, the screw production facility was spun off from Adolf Würth KG. It now represented an independent company by the name of SWG – Schraubenwerk Gaisbach. "We coined this name because we often ran into problems with our dealers out there. We met up with them time and again under the name of Würth, and they told the screw manufacturing company they would stop buying since we directly supplied the end customer," [118] relates Hans Hügel, sales manager at the time.

The first branch offices were established in 1966. A distribution warehouse was set up in Munich to enable the faster supply of customers in Bavaria , and a room of 860 ft² (80 m²) was rented to serve as a distribution warehouse in West Berlin to improve local customer service. It was here that Würth acquired its first company in June 1966: a company by the name of Schrauben Schmid was purchased and continued to be run as an independent business.

Internal Management and External Consultants

Reinhold Würth's sphere of activity changed with the quickly-growing business. In 1957, he involved a first external consultant, the CPA Dr. Heinz Kleinknecht from the Treuhand-Gesellschaft in Heilbronn, to support him in matters of finance. Until his sudden death in 1984, Dr. Kleinknecht was an important adviser and confidant in the building up of Würth Companies at home and abroad.

The young businessman started to recruit external consultants for certain areas, but also internally it became indispensable to delegate certain management tasks. The company had slowly started to differentiate internally, and the first structures emerged. "Owing to the expansion of our business Mr. Würth is no longer able to accompany our sales representatives on customer visits. Since it has proven to be advantageous that a person visits customers with the different sales representatives from time to time and coordinates the sales activities, we have decided to assign Mr. Hans Hügel management responsibility for the automotive and body repair customers. The management of the company grants Mr. Hügel limited commercial authority." [119]

This circular informed the Würth sales representatives about the appointment of the first sales manager on October 13, 1961. Hans Hügel, who had started his apprenticeship with the company in 1955, was granted general commercial power of attorney at the beginning of 1963 and in OHG was now able to carry out all commercial acts as well as recruit or dismiss both white- and blue-collar workers.

While Hans Hügel went down in the history of the company as its first manager, another three gentlemen took up work with Würth in the 1960s who, in their function as top managers, would decisively shape the history of the business for many years.

Karl Specht started his career at Würth as the company's 16th sales representative in September 1961, at the age of 23. He vividly remembers his job interview with Reinhold Würth: "On the top floor I met a young man, barely older than me, and asked him where I could find Reinhold Würth. He said he would take me there. He went ahead into a sparsely furnished office, took a seat and told me that he was the boss."[120] Specht was surprised; he had not imagined the owner of the company being so young, just three years older than him. The two came to an agreement, but the start was not altogether easy for Karl Specht, who thought selling was his personal strong point. He started working in the warehouse, an experience that Reinhold Würth expected of all new employees. Rolf Bauer, who joined the company in July 1963, remembers: "It was a custom with Würth that all the new employees started in receiving. Only those who 'passed the test' in receiving stood a chance of getting ahead."[121]

Adviser and fatherly friend: Dr. Heinz Kleinknecht, shown here during an award ceremony with Reinhold Würth

However, Karl Specht threatened to leave the company if he were not allowed to travel immediately. Reinhold Würth did not want to lose such a highly motivated sales representative and initially sent him – in Specht's private car – on a sales trip to Franconian Switzerland with the comment that Specht could not really do any harm there. After difficulties in the beginning, Specht achieved the highest sales of all sales representatives in 1963, and the following year his sales soared to such an extent that Reinhold Würth accompanied him on his tours to convince himself that there was not anything fishy about the results.[122] In 1971, Würth appointed the successful sales representative area manager, then district manager in 1975 and, in the following year, deputy sales manager. In 1977, Karl Specht was appointed sales manager responsible for the whole of Germany. In this function he was appointed managing director in 1978 and was a member of the Board of Management of Adolf Würth GmbH & Co. KG until 1996. When in 1979 the Board of Management – internally called FÜKO – was established as the central managing body, he remained a part of it until his retirement in 1996.

Rolf Bauer, who had previously done an apprenticeship with Ziehl-Abegg as electro mechanic, started his commercial apprenticeship with Adolf Würth OHG on July 15, 1963. Bauer, who was friends

EXPANSION HEAD-ON
INTERNAL MANAGEMENT AND EXTERNAL CONSULTANTS

with Reinhold Würth's brother, Klaus-Frieder, was highly motivated: "I wanted to show everybody what I was capable of doing." He, too, went into the warehouse on his first day of work. "A considerable number of steel nuts packed in bags had to be taken off a truck. There were no such aids as high-lift trucks, platform lift-trucks, or pallets. There was not even a loading platform in the receiving department. We pulled the bags from the truck's loading platform with a board and threw them on a big pile." [123]

In the following three months, Rolf Bauer got to know all departments in the warehouse, subsequently taking over order processing from Reinhold Würth and Hans Rapp. When the head of the accounting department, Rudolf Hampel, left the company in 1966, Reinhold Würth offered the post to Rolf Bauer. However, Bauer thought bookkeeping "too dry a matter" and soon asked his boss for another project. After having worked in order processing for some time, Rolf Bauer took the opportunity to take over purchasing. In 1967, he made first contact with suppliers in Japan, and these initial contacts developed into close business relations.

Rolf Bauer never saw his purchasing activities as independent projects. Keeping his eyes and ears open for what went on in other departments such as sales he rather considered himself to be a "link between purchasing and sales." [124] During that time and under Rolf Bauer's direction, a working group for order handling and the inventory was set up in straightforward fashion, without elaborate selection procedures or concrete assignment of responsibilities. Information between purchasing and sales was exchanged on Saturdays. "There was hardly a Saturday without at least 8 to 12 sales representatives in the company. These Saturdays were very exciting." [125]

In fact, all aspects concerning products and customers, purchasing, and warehousing – in short, the in-house flow of commodities – have remained Rolf Bauer's area of responsibility until today, and he is also in the top management body of the Würth Group. [126] Apart from these projects he has always played an important part in the reorganization of companies acquired by Würth and occasional "biggest worries" of the Würth Group. Rolf Bauer, who was granted general commercial power of attorney in 1968, was appointed member of the management team of Adolf Würth KG in 1973 and has been a member of the Group's Board of Management since

> "In my opinion, Reinhold Würth is the typical entrepreneur with particular farsightedness, yet spontaneous decisions."
>
> Rolf Bauer, deputy spokesman of the Board of Directors

1981. He was appointed member of the newly established Board of Directors in 2001 that initially had three, now five, members and holds the position of deputy spokesman of this body.

Since Rolf Bauer had decided against succeeding the accountant Rudolf Hampel, an advertisement for the position of head of the accounting department was published in the "Stuttgarter Zeitung." Among the applicants was Otto Beilharz, who had done an apprenticeship as industrial clerk with the screw wholesaling company Gross in Stuttgart after his intermediate high school certificate and had discovered his love for matters of finance through the head of Gross's accounting department. During an unpaid traineeship with Württembergische Girozentrale – later to become Landesbank Stuttgart – Otto Beilharz gathered additional experience and afterward took up work in the field of accounting and EDP with the Kodak Company in Stuttgart. When he applied for a job advertised by "a bolt and screw manufacture in northern Württemberg," he was working as head of the accounting department of the Protestant Society in Stuttgart – a position that could not fully satisfy the businessman. That is why he had attended courses on the preparation of balance sheets in the evenings and on Saturdays and had taken the related accountancy exams. Otto Beilharz, applying for the job, was an experienced businessman from out of town. It was his wife, however, who, hailing from Langenburg, was very much attracted by the prospect of her husband's finding a job in Künzelsau. She was the one who convinced him to attend the job interview because he had turned on his heels after having inspected the outer appearance of the Würth Company, which at that time was not very attractive. Otto Beilharz was not really impressed either by the modest interior of Reinhold Würth's office. He was finally won over by the balance sheets submitted by Reinhold Würth and positively surprised by the high profit percentages of the company compared to the sales figures. When Dr. Kleinknecht gave his go-ahead – after having thoroughly examined Otto Beilharz' qualifications as accountant – he started his career at Würth as head of the accounting department on October 1, 1966.[127] Until his retirement at the end of 1999, Otto Beilharz accompanied the development of the company first as the person responsible for the field of finance and later also for the Allied Companies. In the 1970s he was a member of the management team of Adolf Würth KG and, from 1979 onward, a member of the Board of Management at the head of the Würth Group.

Selling – Development of the Sales Force in the 1960s

During the 1960s Reinhold Würth concentrated on speedy expansion of the sales force, which also entailed a further reduction in size of the sales territories. A few months after Karl Specht, he recruited an additional sales representative for Bavaria. In the past, Arthur Herold alone had been responsible for Bavaria, but within a period of one-and-a-half years he had had to accept the third reduction in size of his territory. Once again he was afraid of a possible decline of his sales volume. This was an issue that always worried the sales representatives affected by a division in their territory, but it was always without reason. Territory splits were advantageous in that they reduced driving time. Some customers could now be reached without the sales representatives having to stay overnight, and so they were able to spend more time with their families. In 1968, the sales representatives were backed up by so-called sub-agents, who supported them in working their sales territories and marked the beginning of a more sophisticated sales force structure.[128]

The sales representatives were now given monthly sales breakdowns. Reinhold Würth's expectations regarding sales were geared toward the number of registered cars since the most decisive stimulus for growth at the beginning of the 1960s, which originated in the motorization wave. The sales target of a sales district was based on the number of registered cars. Annual sales of 8 DM had to be achieved for every 100 cars. The so-called ranking lists enabled the sales representatives to take a look at the sales figures achieved by their colleagues in the previous month and to make comparisons. This was meant to stimulate competition among the sales representatives. After May 1966, however, the company stopped publishing ranking lists since it had come out that Albert Berner, the largest local competitor, was always very well informed about the performance of the Würth Company, and it was suspected that somebody from within the company had "leaked" the monthly sales figures.[129]

The sales targets for the following year were decided upon and published during the pre-Christmas sales conferences. Hermann Leiser remembers: "Very often, lively discussions developed, but in the end everybody calmed down and tried to achieve the set targets."[130]

In the past, Reinhold Würth had personally surveyed the performance of the sales representatives, but owing to his greater sphere of business activities he was only able to accompany sales representatives occasionally. This was the reason why by October 1961 he had appointed Hans Hügel as sales manager. The appointment of the young man was a logical consequence of his success in sales: he was always on top in the ranking lists. Hügel took on the task of accompanying the individual sales representatives on their trips every quarter and concentrated particularly on those whose sales figures left a lot to be desired. He was supposed to draw up a brief report on the condition of the sales territories he had traveled in and to submit suggestions. By way of sales training he was also expected to help the representatives to achieve higher sales. [131] After 1966 those sales representatives who achieved less than 80 per cent of their targets had to prepare visit reports – one of Hans Hügel's measures that did not meet with overwhelming approval since "red tape is seen as a tiresome task." [132]

When he was appointed sales manager, Hans Hügel ceded a large part of his territory to Hermann Leiser and just kept Reutlingen and Tübingen with a number of important customers for himself. Despite this drastic cut in his territory, the sales volume he generated himself did not decline. Following an initiative by Reinhold Würth, Hermann Leiser had transferred from commercial in-house service to the sales force. After accompanying Hans Hügel for two weeks, he took over his new sales territory, which is sketched briefly below to give the reader an idea of the size of sales territories at the time. Leiser's territory covered the entire Black Forest, an area that in the west and the south was delineated by the Rhine Valley along the French and Swiss borders all the way to Friedrichshafen at Lake Constance, in the east by the Swabian Jura and in the north by the cities of Hechingen, Nagold, Freudenstadt, Gaggenau, and Rastatt. In the course of the years Hermann Leiser's territory was reduced in size, too, yet it was still so big that Leiser had to stay overnight in hotels throughout the week, something he started to dislike in 1968 after having set up house. [133]

Prices, Commissions, and Sample Boards – Stories from the Sales Side

Just like the future top managers Karl Specht and Rolf Bauer, all new sales representatives started their jobs in the warehouse where they got a first, general idea about the product range and packaging sizes when putting away the shipments received from suppliers and making up the orders for delivery. The sample boards were hand-made. Christoph Walther who, in the spring of 1962 at the age of 21, took over part of Arthur Herold's Bavarian territory as the 18th sales representative of the Würth Company remembers: "Equipped with the sample boards, an order form with two carbons, a list of selling prices as well as a list of discounts, I feverishly awaited my turn in the field." [134]

The induction period for new sales representatives at the time was a mere two weeks; afterward, they were on their own in their respective territories. Hans Hügel remembers how Karl Specht – to name just one – returned from his sales trips without a clue about the product samples that purchasing agents wanted to buy from him. "He did not really have any product knowledge and was quite helpless concerning many of the items." [135] Christoph Walther's start as sales representative was rather rough, too, due to a lack of proper instruction. He had learned quite a bit from Arthur Herold in his first week of accompanying him in the field, but Walter did not have sufficient information about the company's pricing policy. This led to a delicate situation with an annoyed customer during his very first week of traveling by himself. "My confidence at having been employed by the 'top company' in the industry was badly shaken. Nobody had taken the time to explain the pricing situation in comparison with our competitors to me […]. I had started my job rather ill prepared." [136] He was furious, called Reinhold Würth the same evening, and gave notice. Würth showed some understanding for his situation, tried to calm him down, and asked him to continue the sales trip until the end of the week, which in fact ended rather successfully. Walther managed to sign up 28 new customers and, upon return to the company on Saturday, said: "Let's forget about it" when asked by Reinhold Würth about his notice.

That Walther had been insufficiently informed about prices for products and commission rates after his short induction period was also due to the fact that Arthur Herold had sent his orders to Murrhardt at night where his father-in-law managed his customer files for him and filled in the prices. In many other cases, this task was carried out by the wives of the sales representatives. Karl Specht's wife, too, took care of all administrative tasks, made sure her husband had all the necessary background information about his customers available, kept track of developments, ran statistics, and did clerical work so that her husband could fully concentrate on his work in the field. [137]

Reinhold Würth soon realized how immensely important the wives of the sales representatives were for their success or failure in sales and therefore also for the success of the company. That is why Reinhold Würth called them "behind the scenes employees." [138] Since the company outing in 1959 all the wives and spouses have always been involved in the Würth family, last but not least also in incentive trips and company meetings.

The issue of pricing has played an important role in the history of the Würth Company down to the present day and in part gave rise to highly controversial discussions between the sales representatives and company management. During the sales conference in 1964, sales representatives reported that customers complained about prices being too high for products sold by Würth. They said that competitors also used this argument in their dealing with customers. On the list of selling prices that was given to Christoph Walther in 1962, prices were on average 40 per cent higher than on the association price list that gave sales representatives the opportunity to grant 40–50 per cent discount. This discount, however, influenced their commission. Reinhold Würth always put quality first and remarked that quality had its price. High service, good quality, reasonable price – this has always been the motto of Rolf Bauer, who also had very good experience with this concept in different Allied Companies.[139]

In December 1962, all the sales representatives received employment contracts featuring six months' notice and a non-competition clause along with compensation. Reinhold Würth decided on this step after Hubert Dehnelt, a sales representative, had left the company at rather short notice to start up his own business. This caused quite a stir since Würth was afraid of Dehnelt luring away other sales representatives. Christoph Walther, who had been approached by Dehnelt's new business partner in this matter, decided to stay on board. He was happy about his new company car, "a brand-new Opel-Rekord S with a steel sliding roof, radio Becker Mexico, two-colored, four doors and complete with whitewall tires," that had been ordered for the disloyal sales representative Dehnelt.[140]

During those years it became a tradition for the sales representatives from Künzelsau to meet in the company on Saturday mornings. Rolf Bauer, the purchasing manager, was always there and very often also Reinhold Würth. The men not only exchanged information about their work, but also told many stories about their experiences in the field.

What is meant by Reinhold Würth's remark that at the time "we sometimes quite casually fought our way into the market"[141] is perhaps illustrated by an incident that Christoph Walther remembers.[142] In December 1967 it was cold and wet and Christoph Walther did not want to travel by himself, so he went on the road together with a colleague – totally inconceivable today. They visited a body shop in Esslingen and learned that the owner's son was just in the process of setting up his own car repair shop in Plochingen. He wanted to sell a car to the two Würth sales representatives who in turn hoped for a large order from the young businessman. They finally reached an agreement. The Würth sales representatives received an order and – exceeding their powers – ordered a small car in return. When they came back to corporate headquarters in Künzelsau on Saturday morning, they had to justify their actions vis-à-vis Reinhold Würth, who showed some leniency. "In contrast to today where everything is very tightly organized and has to be organized, it was pretty relaxed with us those days," [143] says Christoph Walther.

Karl Specht remembers: "Since we were so successful in sales we, the traveling salesmen, loved to party when we were on the road." [144] From personal experience Reinhold Würth knew that selling is an exciting, yet also tough, job and so he had no qualms celebrating the enormous successes of the 1960s in style together with the sales representatives. "We have worked so hard, the company can foot the bill now," Hans Hügel recalls hearing Reinhold Würth say on the occasion of a lavish dinner during the Frankfurt trade show. [145] Specht, too, has fond memories of the first few times in particular that the Würth Company had an exhibition stand during trade shows. "Our boss almost took offense if we did not spend enough money." [146] The Würth Company had its first appearance in a trade show at the 1967 Frankfurt Auto Show (IAA) in Frankfurt/Main. Rolf Bauer had put together the first Würth customer catalog. "I had spent hours and hours in the evenings pasting together individual catalog pages. As a cover I used the green plastic files that had been kept in the attic for years." Reinhold Würth helped to put up the exhibition stand until long after midnight. Rolf Bauer was in charge of the electrical installation and, in his function as purchasing manager, negotiated the introduction of the first chemical product ever sold by Würth, "Rost off," with the management of the NIGRIN Company during this trade show. [147]

> "We were a wild bunch then – and we were very young. We sold like crazy and sometimes we also partied like crazy."
>
> Karl Specht, formerly sales manager at Würth and FÜKO-member

Expansion of Corporate Headquarters

The speedy growth of both the sales force and order volume required a corresponding expansion of both warehousing and in-house service capacities that could not be organized as quickly as expected at all times. Customer deliveries were sometimes complicated by bottlenecks and from time to time orders could not be handled quickly enough, which led to customer complaints. The company building at the Künzelsau station that had only been expanded in 1958 was bursting at the seams. Rolf Bauer had his place of work in Hermine Künast's office. "I was sitting almost right under the door leading to Reinhold Würth's office." Negotiations with suppliers had to be carried out standing in the hallway, with one of the boxes lying around serving as a desk.[148] In this situation Reinhold Würth decided to put a plan into action that he had already had for quite some time, namely to move the screw production from the basement of the building to nearby Gaisbach to gain more storage space in Künzelsau. As early as 1960 he had purchased a site covering 1 acre in Gaisbach on which a manufacturing hall for screw production was erected in 1962. However, this did not alleviate the lack of space in Künzelsau's Bahnhofstrasse. Inventory continued to go up, and the increasing business volume required the recruitment of more and more in-house staff. At this time, the company had 102 in-house employees on the payroll.[149]

"In the warehouse, the conditions were almost as bad as in the offices. In 1966 the places of work had still been normal, but by 1967 almost all available space had been used up. Nuts were stored on the radiators, and the burner was partly blocked," remembers Otto Beilharz. The situation concerning lack of space would soon improve for the new head of the accounting department, however, as in March 1968 he and his staff would move to a private building the company had rented in Gaisbach.[150] The physical separation of individual departments of the company did not make work any easier, though, and the additional space for warehousing in Künzelsau that resulted from the move was very soon used up again.

Today's administrative building B,
a lonely edifice against the Gaisbach skies (around 1970)

Therefore, construction of a new administrative building in Gaisbach started in 1968. In March of 1969, when the craftsmen were still at work, Reinhold Würth moved into his new office on the top floor of the four-story building. The official opening ceremony of the new corporate headquarters took place in June 1969. The architect, Hans-Peter Sperling, had created a simple office building whose "technically cool aluminum façade and far-reaching porch roof over the main entrance" set itself at a clear distance from the monotonous banality that was customary at that time in the cuboid office blocks of that size.[151] The interior design of the "elegantly furnished entrance hall" – so described in the "Hohenloher Zeitung" on the occasion of the official opening ceremony – came from Prof. Hundhausen from Staatliche Kunstakademie Stuttgart. The Würth employees now had a state-of-the-art company restaurant at their disposal, which could seat 100 people and was located on the fourth floor above the offices. The company quite proudly wrote in a letter to the Schwäbisch Hall employment office: "Just to give you an example of our modern company management, we would like to point out that the office building is equipped with a loudspeaker system for music and that the staff can listen to three hours of music every day during working hours." [152] To make sure that all employees and all apprentices, too, could reach their new place of work in Gaisbach without any problems, transport was laid on from Künzelsau and Kupferzell, with a special bus of the Federal Post Office running from Künzelsau.

> "The atmosphere at Würth was always good – in our initial years we experienced a "go west" effect. Everybody did everything for everybody else."
>
> Karl Specht, formerly sales manager at Würth and FÜKO-member

For the time being, the warehouse remained in Künzelsau, which complicated the work of both the purchasing and the sales staff. "A vehicle was on the road all the time taking invoices and delivery slips to Künzelsau." [153] This problem could only be solved with the move of the warehouse during the 1969 summer holidays. Now, all departments were together again in corporate headquarters in Gaisbach. With the new office building and warehouse, the expansion of the sales force, and the in-house staff the Würth Company had made a number of expensive investments in the future by the end of the 1960s.

The development of the company during this decade was not only dynamic, but downright breathtaking. Highly motivated, the young boss Reinhold Würth – in 1965 he was still only 30 years old – and his equally young staff – Rolf Bauer, Karl Specht, and Hans Hügel were all in their mid to late twenties – had even braved the recession in 1967. The decline in the automotive industry that year had had an effect on the company, yet Würth still achieved 8 per cent sales growth. The general economic situation had changed since the mid-1960s, but this did not obstruct the growth of the Würth Company. In May 1969, Würth proudly announced: "Today, our company has 430 predominantly commercial employees on the payroll at home and abroad. This year we will achieve more than 35 million DM in external sales and maintain independent sales companies in eight European countries and in the USA" [154]

The building of Würth USA in Ramsey, New Jersey

FIFTY PER CENT OF SUCCESS

6

Würth and the World

At quite an early point in time the company started to reach out beyond the borders of Germany. Reinhold Würth explains at least 50 per cent of his success with this fact. [155] This chapter outlines the start-up and development of a number of exemplary foreign-based Würth Companies.

Occasional start-up difficulties and ultimate success in most of the cases, together with the negotiation of cultural differences, characterize the path of the Würth Group around the globe, set against the backdrop of the respective national situations and international developments. New challenges developing with the emergence of new markets, as illustrated by the situation in the former Soviet Union, are just as fascinating as the pioneering feats in both the old and the new world.

Beginning Internationalization

At the beginning of the 1960s Reinhold Würth ventured outside Germany, which was unusually early for a company of the size that the Künzelsau-based screw dealership had at the time. Reinhold Würth himself says that he really did not think too much about it at the time. The internationalization of Würth KG was by no means a strategically planned step – at least not at the start, according to a lecture he gave in the summer of 2002 to his Karlsruhe students at the Interdisciplinary Institute for Entrepreneurship. Würth had always tried to transfer the successful German strategies to the foreign-based companies. "The multiplication of successes and the division of errors turned the internationalization of the Würth Group into a huge success." [156]

Reinhold Würth says that his father had already done business in Switzerland and Austria. [157] Even before World War II, Adolf Würth had sold screws in Switzerland for the Reisser Company and, after starting his own company, the automotive bodywork firm Ramseier + Jenzer in Switzerland became an important customer. [158] In the 1950s, Reinhold Würth continued this strategy, being the sole sales representative of the company and selling his products in Austria and Switzerland.

At the beginning of the 1960s Europe was covered by a network of Würth Companies – a trend that continued way into the 1970s. In 1969, Reinhold Würth took the plunge into the American continent: first the USA and afterward South America. Ever since the 1980s, Würth has also been represented in the Far East. The 1990s – characterized by the fall of the Berlin Wall and the ensuing opening of the former Eastern bloc – offered new markets and huge expansion possibilities for the business.

The histories of the foreign-based companies are in part very similar. In the beginning, there was usually a person who Reinhold Würth considered capable of sounding out the local market; this special person might well be the owner of a local ice-cream parlor, for example. Equipped with a certain amount of products and capital, the new managing director was expected to set up the new company. In most cases, this implied that the first managing director of the new Würth Company would also be the sole sales representative, warehouse worker, and bookkeeper of the fledgling company. Very often, the warehouse of this latest Würth initiative would be located in the managing director's living room or bedroom for months.

     Most of the founding managing directors of Würth's foreign-based companies were unique personalities: Hendrik Lastdrager, who built up the subsidiaries in The Netherlands and in Belgium; Ernst Clausen, who conquered Scandinavia starting from Denmark; and José Viana, who laid the foundations for the setting up of the companies in Spain and Portugal. Viana, a banking expert, also helped to drive forward Würth Finance in Zurich. He was appointed a member of Würth's Board of Management in 1992, the first foreign manager to be so.

     The success story of the first foreign-based Würth Companies is closely linked with the names of those gentlemen who invested their energy and know-how in the foundation and further development of the subsidiaries. To name but a few: Klaus Hendriksen (Brazil); Anton Seebacher, Engelbert Sandrini, and Helmut Gschnell (Italy); Hans Sigrist (Switzerland); Josef Laister (Austria); and Pentti Rantanen (Finland).

The First Companies to be Founded – The Netherlands, Austria, and Switzerland

The first company abroad was founded in s'Hertogenbosch in The Netherlands. The reason for this foundation was that it had turned out to be too difficult to supply foreign customers from Künzelsau.[159] In particular, the customs formalities that the customers had to deal with complicated their business relations with Würth. The foundation of the company in Holland in March 1962 developed from an existing business relationship with the former employer of Hendrik J. Lastdrager, who was appointed first managing director of the Dutch subsidiary. Reinhold Würth managed to contract him away and win him over for the establishment of his first foreign-based company. In the course of the years, Lastdrager built up a highly profitable company in The Netherlands for Reinhold Würth. Lastdrager, who ranks among the most impressive personalities in the group of managing directors, always put profit first in his business plans.

Even though Würth was a relatively small enterprise at the time, Lastdrager realized the dynamic outlook of both the business and the entrepreneur Reinhold Würth and left his old position – a phenomenon that would repeat itself with a number of other managing directors of Würth Companies. Lastdrager, who started selling Würth products and items purchased in Holland at the end of 1961 even before the official establishment of the company, like most of the early managing directors held a small percentage interest in the new Würth Company. His beginnings are typical of all the foreign-based companies that were founded in later years. At start-up, he and his wife used their own apartment as warehouse and office, Mrs. Lastdrager helping her husband with the administrative tasks. This is something that, down to the present day, characterizes almost all newly-developed companies and many sales representatives: without this help and support, the success of the newly-founded companies would have been inconceivable. Be it in the function of switchboard operator or bookkeeper, all the wives of the managing directors helped with the building up of the companies, at least during the initial years.

After Mr. and Mrs. Lastdrager had found a big enough warehouse in August 1962, they were once again able to take possession of their private apartment. The customers were happy about shorter delivery periods, since now a number of products could be stocked locally, and Hendrik J. Lastdrager was able to recruit two additional sales representatives in his first year of business. In the following year, two warehouse workers and an office worker joined the small team – the company Würth Nederland N.V. had experienced a successful start.

Due to the fact that Lastdrager had also supplied customers in Belgium from Holland, Reinhold Würth founded Würth Belgie PVBA together with him in June 1964. The young company developed by leaps and bounds. In the summer of 1967, Würth Nederland's first company building was officially opened in s'Hertogenbosch. The Netherlands and Belgium taken together reported more than ten times the annual sales volume than only three years previously: 4.63 million DM. [160] A field of industry slowly started to emerge apart from the automotive sector and the company was soon facing a lack of space. The building in s'Hertogenbosch had to be extended in 1970.

By the 15th anniversary of the Dutch subsidiary in 1977, the company had 7,000 customers, with roughly 15,000 items permanently kept in stock. In these first 15 years, the company generated total sales of 64 million Dutch guilders and net profits of roughly 8 million Dutch guilders. [161] At the end of the 1970s, the automotive sector was achieving the highest sales in the Dutch company, followed by industry and trade.

The work of the subsidiary was drastically interrupted by a fire on November 16, 1980 that burned all offices and storage rooms to the ground. All of a sudden, Würth Netherlands had no building left, and almost overnight new premises were rented, crates and boards were made into desks, and the company bought and installed a new EDP-system. Within five days, the first pallets with products ready for delivery were received from Germany so that work could be continued, albeit under adverse conditions.

Hendrik Lastdrager retired in 1990, with management of the company being taken over by Pieter Bak and Sjifong Djotirto.

Reinhold Würth established Würth Switzerland in Basel in the same year as Würth Netherlands – 1962. Here, too, business started in the apartment of the first managing director, Max Schneebeli. However, Schneebeli left the company just one year later, and was replaced by his colleague, Peter Wyss. [162] Hans Sigrist from Zurich joined the compa-

FIFTY PER CENT OF SUCCESS
THE FIRST COMPANIES TO BE FOUNDED ...

Key player for commercial success in Eastern Europe: Josef Laister, managing director of Würth Austria between 1983 and 2001, with Reinhold Würth during a visit to Vienna's Chamber of Commerce (1997)

ny in January 1964 as the first and highly successful sales representative and later succeeded Peter Wyss in his position as managing director.

The start of the business in Switzerland was a bit slower than in The Netherlands because of the highly active and numerous local competitors. Würth's principle of territory splits combined with the search for customers in both the craft and the construction industry, however, soon led to sales increases. The company exceeded the million-DM sales level in 1966, but, compared to Holland, the profit generated by the company was still not satisfactory. As late as ten years after its foundation, in 1972, Schrauben-Würth GmbH in Switzerland officially opened its first warehouse and office building in Münchenstein, near Basel. In 2003, Würth Switzerland achieved sales of 121.3 million Swiss francs with almost 500 employees. On January 1, 2004, Hans Sigrist handed over his position of managing director to Pius Müller and Christian Stöckli.[163]

The managing director of the third company to be founded in 1962, Würth Austria, was recruited by way of a newspaper advertisement.[164] Peter Drexler, who started doing business from home in January 1963, also held a percentage interest in the company. Mrs. Drexler was responsible for bookkeeping and office organization. In contrast to the two other Würth Companies founded abroad, Würth Austria got off to a very slow start and even reported a loss in the first year. The reasons were customs formalities and problems, high import levies, and the refusal on the part of Austrian suppliers to supply the company with merchandise. For a number of years, Würth was not accepted as wholesaler, so that the company had to pay higher purchasing prices. Construction work in Austria was also very complicated. Official requirements and lengthy procedures aimed at obtaining building permits slowed down construction of planned buildings.

After Peter Drexler's death, the company's financial manager, Josef Laister, took over management of the company. Thanks to his very good contacts with Eastern Europe, the company gradually conquered this market in accordance with the tried and tested principle of "cell division."

Alfred Wurmbrand started to support Josef Laister in 2002 [165] and succeeded him in office at the end of 2003 when Laister retired.

The Star among the New Companies – Italy

The foreign-based Würth Company with the highest sales volume so far was founded in 1963: Würth Italy. Reinhold Würth had sounded out the Italian market in 1962 when he had sent the owner of an ice-cream parlor in Künzelsau, Onorino Soccol, to South Tyrol to find out if there was a ready market for Würth products there. The answer was positive, an ad was placed in the paper for the position of managing director of Würth Italy GmbH, and Anton Seebacher was recruited. Onorino Soccol became Anton Seebacher's first sales representative and, in October 1963, Helmut Gschnell joined them as office and warehouse assistant. [166] Three years later he started working as sales representative and today he is the managing director of Würth Italy – a typical Würth career. The start of the new company, though, was also rather difficult because of the economic crisis in Italy at the time; the positive development of the business could not be foreseen. It was particularly the "payment behavior of the Italian customers" that left a lot to be desired. [167] In 1976, Reinhold Würth decided to appoint a second manager apart from Anton Seebacher, and chose Engelbert Sandrini. [168] At the end of 1968, however, the balance sheet of the company showed a loss of 1.8 million lira. [169]

Würth Italy only started to see light at the end of the tunnel in 1969, in which year sales went up by 79 per cent. [170] The company now also cooperated with Italian screw manufacturers, and Helmut Gschnell opened a branch office in Rome in 1973. [171] Würth Italy continued to grow in the mid-1970s despite the worldwide oil crisis and other problems. Würth Italy was the first company abroad that generated monthly sales exceeding one million DM, in 1974.

In the wake of the company's expansion, the problem of lack of space became more and more pressing. In 1979 the staff – now numbering more than 250 – moved into a new building in Siebeneich, close to Bolzano,[172] but only three years later the warehouse ran into space-related problems again.[173]

At the beginning of the 1980s, the divisionalization into automotive and craft proved to be very successful for Würth Italy, too. Furthermore, an additional five trading companies from the field of assembly technology were acquired. In 1982, Würth Italy was on the point of becoming a "really big" company. People worked up the areas of logistics and informatics for the transition to these future dimensions.[174] The 1980s have so far been the most successful decade in the history of Würth Italy, with the number of staff multiplying by a factor of 2.5 and sales increasing ninefold.[175]

The Würth Company was the market leader in Italy in 1990, with an annual sales volume of 269 million DM achieved by 1,134 employees, of which 754 worked as sales representatives. By 1994, Würth Italy was the biggest foreign-based company and it is not surprising to note that the company achieved a new monthly sales record, at roughly 42 million euro, in July 2003.[176] In 2003, Würth Italy's total sales amounted to 437.7 million euro, with a staff of almost 4,000 of which 75 per cent work in the field.[177]

France

S.à.r.l. Würth France, the French subsidiary of Würth, was founded in Erstein on October 24, 1966.[178] The founder and managing director was Jean-Paul Meyer, who obtained the first orders in his function as sole sales representative of the company. In November 1966 the first shipments arrived from Künzelsau. The first sales representative recruited by the company caused severe problems. He submitted high expenses claims before obtaining so much as one customer order.

The company had a rough start, just like the other companies abroad. In the course of 1967, Meyer together with the slowly growing staff of the company assembled the office furniture in the evenings. At the end of 1968, Würth France had 11 people on the payroll, and sales continued to increase with the growth of the company: from roughly 670,000 francs in 1968 to 1.1 million francs in 1969 and 6.3 million francs in 1972.[179]

Richard Burgstahler, who had stood in for Meyer during his absence through illness at the end of 1974, was appointed co-managing director by Reinhold Würth in 1975 and sole managing director one year later.

In November 1977, an EDP-system was installed in the French company that caused considerable problems. However, this was not the only difficulty the business had to deal with; there was also friction in human relations, though this was eventually eliminated.[180]

Both the company building and the warehouse were enlarged, with pre-tax sales amounting to 80 million francs in 1981. A branch office was opened in Lyon in 1989 and, in the same year, the company opened up agencies in the overseas départements of Réunion, Martinique, Guadeloupe, and French Guiana. One year later, New Caledonia and Guinea were added to the group.[181]

However, at the beginning of the 1990s, management in Künzelsau was no longer satisfied with the results in France, as the sales representatives were not being directed according to Würth principles and philosophy. The employees were poorly trained and did not receive performance-oriented salaries.[182] It became indispensable to dismiss Richard Burgstahler, the managing director, Dieter Krämer and Walter Jaeger were sent to France to restructure the company and, for a while, Würth's Board of Management took care of running the company. It was only under the direction of the new managing director, Pierre Hugel, that the company became a success, generating sales of 347 million euro with 2,500 employees in 2003.[183]

Successes in the North – Würth in Scandinavia

Ernst Clausen, the founding managing director of Würth Denmark, like so many of his fellow managing directors came to Würth by way of a newspaper advertisement. As an employee of a forwarding agency he had not seen any future prospects for himself and decided to join Würth, even though he had thought the Künzelsau-based company a bit small during his job interview. However, when he saw upon his return that the money for the foundation of the new company had already been transferred to the bank, he was duly impressed. Ernst Clausen received equity capital of 100,000 Danish kroner from

Adolf Würth KG, acquired a five-percent interest in the business, sold his car to the company, and bought a house in a strategically favorable location.

In the beginning, Ernst Clausen was not given any sales targets, but together with Hendrik Lastdrager's Würth Nederland the Danish Würth Company was one of the few businesses that was profitable from start-up. He remembers "having sneaked" into the market, as initially the competition was not supposed to notice him. [184] However, customers could very quickly be convinced of both the quality and the wide range of the products. Mrs. Clausen also worked in the business: she was in charge of bookkeeping for which an old accounting machine had been purchased. A secretary was only hired after a number of years.

Very often Ernst Clausen put his own ideas into practice, one example of this being the prices for products that Reinhold Würth occasionally called the "Danish" or the "Scandinavian illness," yet accepted because of their profitable results. Clausen explains the success of Würth Denmark with a good logistics system and uncompromising service orientation. It was perfectly natural for him to visit customers on a Sunday if they needed something urgently.

In the middle of the 1990s, all the Scandinavian companies that Ernst Clausen was also responsible for reported highly positive figures. In Denmark, he was succeeded in 1994 by his son, Otto Clausen, who was assigned the position of managing director at Reinhold Würth's behest.

In 1973, Reinhold Würth and Ernst Clausen opted for Ole Molland as managing director of Würth Norway. He turned the company into one of the most successful foreign subsidiaries. In the 1990s, Reinhold Würth admitted: "In our Scandinavian companies,

> "What I always liked about Reinhold Würth is his directness – he never swept anything under the carpet. He also accepted differences in opinion even though this was usually hard work. I could always be certain with him that when he said 'yes' he really meant it."
>
> Ernst Clausen,
> former managing director of Würth Denmark

Highly successful and very relaxed: Pentti Rantanen, managing director of Würth Finland, in conversation with Reinhold Würth (1988)

8.5 orders per sales staff member per day are the rule – more than in our German Adolf Würth GmbH & Co. KG!" [185]

The company Würth Oy founded in Finland in 1976 achieves the highest sales volume compared to its market potential: here, the most items are sold per capita of the entire population. Almost since its inception, the managing director of the business has been Pentti Rantanen, an engineer who started selling as the sole sales representative from Hyvinkää, about 30 miles (50km) from Helsinki, and worked in the office at weekends. He hired two additional sales representatives only in the second year of business and since 1979 has been concentrating mainly on his projects as managing director. Würth Finland is the secret favorite of the Würth Group. It was Rantanen who was able to attend a trade show in Tallinn in the former Soviet Union in 1988 for the first time and who helped to prepare the establishment of Würth Russia in 1993, thanks to his contacts. Rantanen's recipe for success was certainly both his curiosity and his creativity. Ernst Clausen remembers that he always asked many questions and wanted to know all the details. [186] Ultimately, though, he did everything differently. Something he definitely organized differently was his sales force – Rantanen's sales representatives achieve their extremely high results at much lower cost than in other Würth Companies.

Spain and Portugal

Spain and Portugal belong to the businesses founded in the 1970s and in terms of sales development the two companies are – just like Italy and France – the stars among the European Würth Companies.

The start-up work of the founding years was carried out by José Carlos Viana, a native Portuguese, who became the first managing director of both Würth Portugal and

Würth Spain. His wife, too, "from the onset a Würth woman," [187] was a big help in her function as accountant, secretary, and chauffeur.

José Viana had gotten to know Reinhold Würth in 1972 on a private occasion and was very impressed by him. Yet he spent a long time thinking about the suggestion put forward by the entrepreneur from Künzelsau that he should take responsibility for starting up a Würth Company either in Spain or Portugal, since for this he would have to give up his secure and profitable position as a banker in Switzerland – and the Würth Group was really not as impressive in the 1970s as it is today. Viana recalls that, in the end, it was Reinhold Würth's personality that decided the matter for him. This marked the start of an important career at Würth that would finally result in José Viana's joining the Board of Management of the company in 1992 as the first foreign managing director of a Würth Company to be so appointed.

When he started his job in 1974, José Viana had only received an oral contract and 100,000 DM from from Reinhold Würth to set up a company in Portugal. He had neither proper training nor any idea about the industry and could only base his work on the minimal amount of training he had been given in Künzelsau – one day in the field and one day in the business. Therefore, Viana asked Hans Hügel for advice regarding his first attempts at selling in Portugal. Würth Germany was always very interested in receiving large initial orders from foreign subsidiaries as these increased the local company's success in sales, but it also left José Viana with hardly any working capital. He asked himself what he was supposed to live on in the future and immediately started selling the merchandise. Despite the Revolution of the Carnations and the economic crisis, business in Portugal developed extremely well at the end of the 1970s. For two years, Viana was more or less by himself in the field. Today, Nuno Dias manages the company with great success.

"Reinhold Würth impressed me greatly. I realized that this man was a fighter and a brilliant businessman. Reinhold Würth is a man who sticks by his word."

José C. Viana, former FÜKO member;
Würth Spain and Portugal; Würth Finance

In 1977, José Viana embarked on his second pioneering feat: Würth Spain. After Reinhold Würth had founded the company Würth Tornillos de España S.A. in Barcelona, which was quite an achievement since it was actually only Spaniards who were allowed to establish a company, the first order was obtained in January 1978.

Reinhold Würth talking to José C. Viana (1989)

At the beginning, Viana was rather uncertain about the potential of the new company. Many of his employees started their own firms with a similar business idea and frequently took other good sales representatives along with them. In 1989, however, the Spanish Würth Company – established as a one-man business – hired its 100th employee and, in August 1990, the staff moved into a new company building. Viana was satisfied with his successes, first as managing director of Würth Spain and later as area manager: that is, as the person assigned by the Board of Management of the Würth Group to monitor the development of the company on site and to intervene, if necessary.

And yet, as soon as he had given up this function, sales went down and in 1994 Spain even incurred a loss. In the end it was suspected that bizarre esoterics had influenced the man running the business and he was therefore replaced by Juan Ramírez, who has been doing an excellent job down to the present day. From that moment on, José Viana in his function as member of the Coordinating Conference resumed his responsibility for Spain, which since then has not only been reporting increasing sales, but also outstanding profits. In 1997, the 20th company anniversary was celebrated in Barcelona, with annual sales volume in 2003 amounting to 282 million euro.[188]

"A Network of Selling Companies" – the Opening of the East

"From the Elbe River upstream we practically covered the entire former Eastern bloc with a network of selling companies, including Russia and other follow-up states of the former Soviet Union such as Kazakstan and Uzbekistan,"[189] Reinhold Würth told his students

FIFTY PER CENT OF SUCCESS
"A NETWORK OF SELLING COMPANIES" – THE OPENING OF THE EAST

in Karlsruhe in 2002. It all started in the 1980s when Josef Laister, managing director of Würth Austria, had persistently forged ahead to Eastern Europe. Würth had been represented at trade shows and automotive fairs in Hungary since the 1970s, yet could not do any major business there because of the foreign exchange problem. This changed at the end of the 1980s when Würth succeeded in organizing a joint venture with Würth Austria and two Hungarian companies and took up work in Budapest with the first ten employees. In May 1989, this interim solution was abandoned, and Würth Szerelestechnika KFT was instead set up as a straight Würth Company, with the staff predominantly servicing the automotive sector. In 1989, the 22 employees achieved a sales volume of 2.2 million DM.

The relatively quick start-up of Würth Companies in Eastern Europe after the fall of the Iron Curtain is due to the Eastern contacts of both Laister and Pentti Rantanen. First contact with Poland was made by Würth Austria as early as the fall of 1989, and in the following spring Würth Polska – with the first female managing director, Anna Bombala – was founded as the 34th foreign subsidiary of Würth in Warsaw. Number 35 followed in Czechoslovakia, where Würth Cesko-Slovensko started doing business in Bratislava, the later Slovakian capital, on July 19, 1990. This was followed by a company in the Czech Republic in 1992 and attendance at the trade fair Autoindustrija Moscow. Together with Rolf Bauer, Peter Zürn founded the company Würth Russia in 1993 after only two visits there, which proved a rather strange and exotic matter as Zürn recalls. They experienced a number of surprises and had to get used to the Russian mentality first.[190]

In the same year, Würth Croatia, Würth Ukraine, Würth Romania, Würth Slovenia, and Würth Bulgaria were established, followed by Belarus in 1994, Estonia in 1995, Kazakstan, Lithuania, Russia North Caucasus, Russia Ural, and Uzbekistan in 1996. A total of 19 new foreign subsidiaries were founded in 1997, with the focus once again on Eastern Europe: Würth Latvia, Georgia, Armenia, Kyrgyzstan, and, in 1998, Azerbaijan. Paul Thon, who passed away in the year 2000, rendered outstanding services to business start-ups in the former Eastern bloc.

In line with tradition, the early years were difficult, as Günter Theurer, expert in financial management at Würth, remembers: "With most of our 'eastern companies' we did have problems."[191]

There was not enough time for continuous, detailed checking of the financial statements and the local CPAs had little experience of Würth Group requirements. According to Theurer, many "crossword puzzles" had to be solved. In 1997, accounting was still being done manually in the Ukraine, and finance specialist Theurer was shocked to see that the inventory was done on index cards with a pencil.

Regular seminars on Group accounting principles were organized for finance specialists and CPAs of the eastern companies, with the participants in these seminars proving very eager to learn. "Critical" companies such as Poland, the Czech Republic, Slovakia, and Hungary received on-site support.

At the end of the 1990s, Würth was not really satisfied with development in Russia, not only because of the many organizational problems, but also because the economic situation in the east caused a lot of concern.

Go West – Würth in the USA

In the middle of the 1990s, both profit and sales were developing best in Europe, although Würth was, and is, happy with the successes achieved in other regions of the world. There are two exceptions, however: the USA and Japan. "Our American staff are apparently not used to working in the ways we are familiar with in Europe, and especially in Germany. Their willingness to go in for job hopping is relatively high." [192] On average, the US sales representatives obtain considerably fewer orders per day than their (west) European counterparts. Be it the dimensions – America is almost an entire continent unto itself – be it the different mentality of both the customers and the sales representatives that has caused problems, or be it that until today the company has not succeeded in finding the right management – if you ask Würth managers about the reasons, all the above arguments are stated, though with different priorities. It is a fact that the attempt to lead Würth to the successes achieved in the usual way elsewhere has so far not yielded the expected success in the USA.

Looking back, Reinhold Würth self-critically admits to having made the first mistake. In Spring Valley/New Jersey, he had hired two gentlemen as managing directors with equal rights, who were supposed to supervise each other. They did not get along, though, and each tried to create a separate "power situation." [193] This had a negative impact on the staff of Würth Screw and Fastener Corp., established in 1969, and the anticipated business success was not realized. The company should actually have been a huge success, since metric nuts and bolts for European cars were very hard to come by in the USA during the 1960s. Instead of simply founding a new business, Alan Oakes from Würth England was commissioned to put things right, but he, too, failed. At the beginning of 1972, there were still only nine sales representatives traveling through an enormous territory on the east coast. Reinhold Würth therefore decided to tackle the USA from different sides. Four additional sales representatives were supposed to conquer California. A warehouse was set up in Los Angeles, but both the huge distance to the east coast, where the managing director had to be replaced once again, as well as problems with the customs authorities led to a petering out of this initiative, too.

It was difficult to open up new business and old customers were often dissatisfied with the long delivery periods. Time and again staff problems hampered the Würth USA project, which the company had a hard time coming to grips with given the enormous distances involved and the attendant lack of supervision.

Results achieved on the east coast were not satisfactory either. The business was making some progress – in 1978 the company moved to Allendale/New Jersey – yet it was still extremely difficult to handle staff turnover. No matter whether it was a warehouse worker, sales representative, or managing director – whoever found a more suitable job would leave the company, occasionally with the customer files.

In 1985, Ernst Clausen, managing director of Würth Denmark, was asked to check things out in the USA in his function as general manager. Together with the sales manager, Lee Sarafin, he once again tried to conquer the market. They created a number of areas with independent area managers. In 1990 the holding company Würth Group of North America was set up and initially run by Ernst Clausen.

However, the mentality in the USA seemed to be different from Europe. Personal commitment to a company was an exception and commitment to customers seemed rather weak – according to Dieter Krämer, head of the Coordinating Conference for the foreign Würth Companies since its inception in 1976 until his withdrawal from the company.[194] This is problematic for a company whose strong point is, after all, customer commitment.

Ernst Clausen, too, remembers the years he spent in the USA. People often fought each other there: the in-house staff fought against the sales force and nobody accepted responsibility for mistakes. At first he tried to offer advice, but upon taking a closer look he realized that this was not enough. José Viana, responsible for Würth Florida in the 1990s, in his function as "mentor," also identified a severe problem in the lack of control and supervision. According to Viana, leadership is extremely important; one has to keep at it at all times and check compliance with the Würth rules. Daily contact between the sales representatives and the company is indispensable. It is interesting that the female sales representatives, who were hired in Florida as early as 1991, are particularly successful. José Viana recalls that the top three positions on the ranking list of the sales representatives were mostly occupied by ladies.[195]

In the 1990s, a number of different Würth managers were assigned responsibility for the USA: Ernst Clausen, Helmut Gschnell, and José Viana who, as Ernst Clausen thinks, developed very different management styles all the way through to different pricing and commission systems, so that relatively few synergies resulted from this measure.[196]

There is now only one company left in the USA, Würth USA Inc., with four locations and eleven regions that are situated in the east and in the center of the country, apart from Würth USA West. Inc.[197]

South America and South East Asia

Business in South America developed far better than it did in the north of the continent. Parafusos Wurth do Brasil-Comércio Ltda. was established in São Paulo in 1972. After a difficult start, the company's managing director, Klaus Hendriksen, who was born in Germany and emigrated to Brazil in 1955, achieved the breakthrough. He sold to automotive repair shops instead of industrial businesses that were difficult to satisfy and by 1977 was generating sales of 1.3 million DM. His highly motivated sales representatives had to cover huge distances on the way to their customers. However, Hendriksen offered good working conditions and social benefits unusual for Brazil, something that proved to be very helpful in finding committed staff.

In the start-up years it was mainly the import restrictions that forced Hendriksen to buy as many goods as possible locally, as well as the high inflation rate. And yet, Hendriksen managed successfully to apply the Würth-specific principle of multiplication, with territory splits yielding enormous sales increases. By the beginning of the 1980s, the number of sales representatives had doubled. In 1986, Würth Brazil officially opened a new company building, and in 1990 the company generated almost 80 million DM in sales. There are branch offices all over the country. In 1990, the company had 260 sales representatives. Hendriksen, who later established companies in Argentina, Uruguay, and Chile apart from Würth Brazil, also supported additional company start-ups in Central America.

Ever since the 1980s, Würth has also been represented in South East Asia with a large number of companies, with only Japan not yet reporting satisfactory results. Similar to the USA, different mentalities clash here and the right people had still to be found at the end of the 1990s. Despite many changes in staff in the company's finance department it has proved impossible to get the Japanese staff to accept that financial statements have to be prepared according to Group rules.[198] High personnel costs as a consequence of extremely low productivity, coupled with little acceptance of Würth's business idea on the part of the customers who have different expectations and customs to Europeans, cause Würth Japan to lag behind expectations down to the present day.

Africa – and the Rest of the World

The Würth Group is represented in all continents of the world, yet Africa is for the most part still a blank on the map of Würth, with the exception of South Africa where the company put down roots in 1970. As late as the end of the 1990s, Würth Companies with a total of about 30 employees were founded in Egypt (1999), Morocco (1997) and Kenya (1996).

On the grounds of the commitment in South Africa, both the company and Reinhold Würth were forced to defend themselves several times owing to the system of apartheid, which was eliminated finally in 1994. There was an article on special sales training for colored sales representatives in the first issue of the Würth-report 1971 [199], and the newspaper "Haller Tagblatt" reported on a round-table discussion during which Reinhold Würth had explained his position: in the event that the Federal government imposed sanctions the Würth Company would obey, yet without such measures he did not see the necessity to limit his economic commitment on the continent. [200]

After initial problems, Peter Zürn, today the management spokesman of Adolf Würth GmbH & Co. KG, led Würth Australia to success, the Würth Company on the fifth continent. Before that time and until 1982, it had been looked after by Hans Sigrist from Switzerland. When Zürn arrived in Australia with his family in 1986, the company had a mere five sales representatives. Supported by his wife he had to go out selling, too, something he was not used to. However, he also learned a lot that way. When Zürn had to leave after a few years, he really had to learn to "let go" again. [201] The start-up phase was relatively easy and very pleasant, according to Zürn. High personal commitment leads to great successes, but expanding a foreign subsidiary and turning it into a more impersonal business after having gotten it off the ground successfully had better be carried out by somebody else. He said that in such a case one either "has to leave or stay forever." Today, Würth Australia is a profitable company with roughly 300 employees. Peter Zürn recalls that the market was easy; there are many German-speaking immigrants, so business can be done successfully even without speaking "perfect English." [202] According to Zürn, the subsidiaries in New Zealand and Asia are strong companies, too, after having weathered the crisis in Asia at the end of the 1990s. Since the end of the 1980s, foreign subsidiaries have been set up in Asia, e.g., Thailand, Indonesia, South Korea, and Malaysia.

The market of the future – the People's Republic of China – has been under siege by the Würth Group since 1994. Then, Karl Heinz Winter founded a company in Tianjin, Würth China Tianjin GmbH, and Ken Huang set up Würth Hong Kong. Würth has been represented in Guangzhou since 1996 and in Shanghai since 1997. According to the

Würth Handbook 2002, all these companies taken together have about 100 employees, who primarily service car repair shops and industry customers. [203]

Coordination of the International Activities

The Würth Companies abroad are not, and never were, a homogeneous mass. They are individual entities managed by individuals whose characters differ and whose personalities are very often integral to these companies' secrets of success. In the wake of the creation of a Group structure in the 1970s, the desire developed to better coordinate the international activities. At the same time, though, Reinhold Würth did not want to have rigid structures limiting the initiative and responsibilities of the local managing directors. In 1976, he thought about deploying experienced managing directors as consultants for poorly-performing foreign subsidiaries. The Fall Conference of the foreign-based companies was in the process of creating superior management categories. Dieter Krämer recalls that Reinhold Würth assigned him the task of coordinating the international activities "during the coffee break." A project that was not always easy "in the field of tension between […] Reinhold Würth and autarkic sovereigns, between centralist requirements and decentralized entrepreneurship." [204]

The Coordinating Conference was inaugurated in Künzelsau on August 16, 1976. Initially it had a merely communicative function, but was listed as part of the management of the Würth Group in the 1987 Annual Report. In this report, it states that the Coordinating Conference as managing body is part of the International Division and can be compared to the "Board of Directors" in comparable US American management structures. [205]

The companies are run in decentralized fashion by managing boards and managing directors. Within this framework, every company is fully responsible for the results it achieves. However, the Coordinating Conference was responsible for coordination and consultation between the management of the Würth Group, the worldwide Würth Companies, and the Allied Companies in respect of the "regional, divisional, and functional business units." [206] In 1991, international Coordinating Conferences for divisions were also introduced. [207]

A fundamental reorganization of the management structure on January 1, 2001 took into account the increasing globalization and size of the Group. The Coordinating Conference was replaced by a new board of management that constitutes the second executive management level of the Group after the Board of Directors. [208]

From an organizational and legal point of view, all foreign subsidiaries are united under the umbrella of Würth Holding GmbH, which is located in Chur, Switzerland. This company was founded in 1963 under the name of Reca-Union GmbH and changed its name to Würth Holding Gmbh in 1989. Since that time, the company has also been responsible for coordinating the purchasing activities for the International Division apart from its function as holding company.

Today, more than 230 selling companies worldwide are united under the umbrella of Würth Holding, either under the name of Würth or as Allied Companies that continue to do business under their original name. From 1973 to 1991, the Swiss, Hans Pronk, acted as managing director of the holding company. Today, Michel Kern, Jürg Michel, and Gerd Rössler are in charge of the roughly 200 employees of Würth Holding GmbH. [209]

Reca Union Finanz AG, today called Würth Finance, was set up in Zurich in 1978 with the banking expert José Viana as managing director, for handling corporate financial transactions. In the beginning, the company had a very modest location in two rooms in Zurich, and Gerti Viana, in line with Würth tradition, supported her husband in the start-up phase. [210] The company's initial task was to finance the international Würth Companies through loans and to build up an internal Group factoring system. The foreign subsidiaries have to generate an equity base in their respective countries through net profits. The financial commitment by Adolf Würth GmbH & Co. KG is restricted to the original capital and favorable credit for stock purchasing. Eighty per cent of the money the subsidiary firms earn is reinvested in the domicile country. [211] In 1994, the seat of the Würth bank, now called Würth Finance International B.V., was transferred to Amsterdam; a branch office remains in Zurich. In the meantime, Würth Finance also carries out standard internal banking transactions. [212]

Founders' Rules

In Reinhold Würth's opinion, one of the most important prerequisites for founding a subsidiary is collaboration with a resident business attorney who knows the local conditions. It has furthermore proven worthwhile to fill the position of managing director with people from the respective domicile country.[213] According to Reinhold Würth, success depends on the management, a fact that can be observed throughout the Group. Most of the managing directors of the foreign subsidiaries were found by way of newspaper advertisements, and very often Würth hit the jackpot "Sometimes we were not that lucky."[214]

Würth's principle of canvassing the market is based on the trust and confidence placed in individual managers operating in a decentralized fashion. The respective managing director is responsible for the result achieved by his or her company. However, the overall strategy and targets are determined by the Board of Management, called FÜKO, which is under the direction of Reinhold Würth. During its existence the Coordinating Conference participated in this process. The members of this body, the majority of the foreign subsidiaries' managing directors and also members of Würth's Board of Management, also assumed responsibility for others apart from their own business abroad or field of activities at home, such as Ernst Clausen's co-responsibility for the USA and Scandinavia or José Viana's co-responsibility for Florida and Mexico, Portugal and Spain. The managing directors of the foreign subsidiaries can discuss the plans made by the Group's top management body and submit suggestions themselves. The so-called Commitment Conferences that take place in Künzelsau every fall also serve to coordinate plans with the international companies. These conferences cover a period of several weeks, during which all the managing directors come to Künzelsau. Every other year, the Würth Congress takes place in different locations all over the world. The Würth Group's top management bodies as well as the managing directors of the foreign-based companies and top executives meet there for special conferences and leisure activities.

When the management structures of the Würth Group were reorganized in 2001, the newly incorporated Board of Management with its now 25 members also coming from abroad replaced the Coordinating Conference. The FÜKO members are responsible for Group operations management and each of them is in charge of a strategic business unit. [215] It is within this body that international problems and strategies are discussed. FÜKO replaces an institution initially called into being by Reinhold Würth that, in the opinion of its longstanding member, José Viana, "considerably shaped […] the development of the Würth Group." [216] He describes his cooperation in the Coordinating Conference as "one of the most inspiring experiences of my Würth-life." [217]

The Würth Group and Adolf Würth GmbH & Co. KG

Reinhold Würth's first company, Adolf Würth GmbH & Co. KG, played a leading role in the Würth Group for a long time. However, since the foundation of the first foreign subsidiary in 1962, extremely successful companies have developed far from Künzelsau and for a number of years now the subsidiaries have been catching up with the parent company.

In 1984, the combined sales volume of all foreign Würth Companies exceeded that of Adolf Würth GmbH & Co. KG for the first time. Moreover, there were nine sales representatives more on the payroll of the international companies than in Germany. When the Würth Group exceeded 2,000 sales representatives in February 1984, almost 1,400 of these worked abroad, and in 1997 the figure was 9,355 out of 12,444: thus, more than two-thirds. [218]

In 1994, the total sales volume of the Würth Group amounted to 3.5 billion DM, of which the foreign subsidiaries accounted for 1.87 billion DM. In the business year 2001, Würth generated 56 per cent of total sales abroad, primarily in Central Europe. Today, Würth is the largest business in the industry. It is true that there are bigger local competitors, yet Würth applies its tried and tested principles there, too. Instead of getting involved in price wars, the Würth Group focuses on service outside of Germany, too: Würth is faster, friendlier, more innovative, and more professional than the competition. [219]

The relationship between the foreign Würth Companies and corporate headquarters is still characterized by a decentralized management style, even though the Group as a whole is getting increasingly bigger and more complex and the managing directors are no longer given a share in the companies. However, the development of controlling instruments and risk management has in the meantime considerably increased the effort required in benchmarking and supervision. [220] Rolf Bauer sees a problem, particularly for the smaller foreign subsidiaries, in that they are sometimes sidetracked by the need to "feed" the management information system. [221] Even though structures are necessary and helpful, one of the principal success factors of Reinhold Würth and his business was, in Dieter Krämer's recollection, the "liquidity of power, the openness and delegation of responsibility depending on the respective situation. Würth has always been a growing, moving and changing organism." [222]

Or, letting Reinhold Würth having the final say: "One of the most successful fountains of youth has been […] our internationalization." [223]

7 GROWTH REQUIRES A CERTAIN STRUCTURE

The 1970s

In 1970, the Würth Group had more than 700 employees in Germany and abroad, almost 14 times as many as ten years before. In the same period of time sales had gone up from over two million to more than sixty-four million DM. [224] This development continued in the 1970s. By 1971 the number of staff exceeded 1,000 and between 1970 and 1979 this figure would more than quadruple.

For the time being the development of corporate structures could not keep abreast with this outstanding growth. However, in the second half of the 1970s Würth managed to point the way for a successful further development of the business. Decisive steps in this process were the creation of internal management structures, the reorganization of the sales force, and several future-oriented investments in the fields of marketing and distribution. The subdivision into marketing segments proved a particular milestone in the history of the business. A number of far-reaching business decisions ensured that the first crises of the company and the global economic crisis in the mid-1970s could be overcome, so that by the end of the decade Würth had evolved into an international Group.

The 'Oil Crisis,' Environmental Awareness, and a Policy of Détente

In the fall of 1973, the Arab states for the first time used oil, which had so far been sold to industrialized nations at a relatively favorable price, as a political weapon. Owing to their pro-Israel stance in the Arab-Israeli Yom Kippur War, an embargo was imposed on The Netherlands and the USA, with restricted exports to the remaining western nations that drastically inflated its price. The Federal Republic of Germany was hit hard by this measure, since it impacted on 55 per cent of its energy requirements; in respect of imported crude oil, 75 per cent came from Arab countries. In 1974, Germany had to pay roughly 17 billion DM more than in the previous year for oil imports. Because of the energy shortage, industry had to limit production, and on the part of consumers the extra energy costs resulted in declining demand in other areas. Within a one-year period, the price for a liter of regular gas had escalated by 20 per cent, from 70 to 83 pfennig. The automotive industry and its suppliers were particularly affected by the oil crisis. In Germany, the sale of cars dropped by 24 per cent compared to the year before, and this effect was also felt by Würth. Due to a wave of insolvencies and a considerable decline in the number of orders, in 1975 sales declined for the first time in the short history of the business. Economic slowdown in the construction and automotive industries led to short-time working, mass redundancies, and company mergers. Between 1973 and 1974, the unemployment rate increased from 2.2 to 4.2 per cent. In Baden-Württemberg, too, the number of unemployed exceeded 100,000 for the first time since the end of the war. At 143,000, six times more people were out of work at the end of 1975 than in the recession of 1967.[225]

Anniversary: the 25th anniversary of the business was celebrated in Künzelsau's city hall. The Württemberg Chamber Orchestra inaugurates the celebration

The Federal government tried to control the energy crisis by passing a law on energy conservation that provided for immediate measures aimed at energy saving, including a ban on driving on four Sundays in the months of November and December 1973 and the imposition of a speed limit. All in all, the economy in Baden-Württemberg weathered the 1974/75 crisis relatively unscathed. After the trough in automotive sales, the car once again established itself as a mainstay of private consumption after 1976. At the end of the decade, however, the prices for crude oil rocketed again during the second oil crisis, which was triggered by insecurity and the breakdown of oil production due to the war between Iran and Iraq.

In the wake of the oil crisis, people started to focus on nuclear energy. However, this resulted in massive protest and the emergence of an ecological movement that finally led to the foundation of a Green Party. The population's environmental awareness developed in view of increasing piles of garbage, polluted air, and polluted rivers. Between 1970 and 1975, power plants, industrial smoke stacks, private chimneys, and cars emitted 330,000 tons of sulfur dioxide and 260,000 tons of nitrogen oxide every year in Germany[226], the reserves of the existing landfills were exhausted, and Lake Constance was close to death. The Federal government reacted with a raft of laws and decrees, the Federal Environment Office was established, and a law on environmental statistics was passed in 1974. However, the effects of all these measures would become obvious only many years later.

Federal politics continued to be determined by a socio-liberal coalition under Social Democratic chancellor Willy Brandt and Free Democratic foreign minister Walter Scheel, who initiated a policy of détente with the east. Treaties with the Soviet Union and Poland in 1970 paved the way for relations with the two countries to normalize; in this connection, Willy Brandt was awarded the Nobel Peace Prize in 1971. The following year, the ratification of the so-called Eastern Treaties resulted in confrontation in the Bundestag and the ruling coalition losing its majority. After the chancellor proposed a vote of confidence on his Ostpolitik and failed to gain a majority, the Bundestag was dissolved. The new elections, however, resulted in a continuation of the socio-liberal coalition, and the Basic Treaty became effective in 1973 after heated debate in the Bundestag. However, Willy Brandt announced his resignation in May 1974 after his trusted aide, Günter Guillaume, was unmasked as spy for Eastern Germany. His successor was the Social Democrat, Helmut Schmidt, the former minister of finance and economic affairs. Walter Scheel was elected federal president, his party colleague Hans-Dietrich Genscher being elected foreign minister and vice-chancellor. The 1976 Bundestag elections confirmed the socio-liberal coalition of Schmidt and Genscher.

Würth Braves the Economic Crisis

The Würth Company had made a brilliant start in the 1970s, but the consequences of the oil crisis inevitably left their mark on a company so closely linked to the automotive industry. The market became more difficult, customers placed fewer orders or ordered less, and a wave of insolvencies started. However, despite a decline in the automotive industry and a crisis in the construction and investment goods industries, the Würth Group managed to increase worldwide sales by more than 30 per cent in the years 1973 and 1974 respectively. The plus in sales was mainly due to increasing business abroad. All in all, however, the result was not satisfactory. The aftermath of the first oil shock and the ensuing turbulence in global markets led in 1975 to the first decline in sales in the history of the company, amounting to 7.3 per cent overall and 15.2 per cent in Germany. [227]

GROWTH REQUIRES A CERTAIN STRUCTURE
WÜRTH BRAVES THE ECONOMIC CRISIS

Sales Development of the Würth Group 1970–1979

	ADOLF WÜRTH KG	TOTAL GROUP
1970	30.527.000 DM	64.301.000 DM
1971	42.708.000 DM	83.887.000 DM
1972	60.789.000 DM	119.829.000 DM
1973	75.698.000 DM	164.197.000 DM
1974	104.895.000 DM	217.193.000 DM
1975	90.719.000 DM	201.419.000 DM
1976	112.928.000 DM	241.249.000 DM
1977	135.682.000 DM	285.899.000 DM
1978	147.473.000 DM	333.124.000 DM
1979	179.203.000 DM	429.635.000 DM

During Reinhold Würth's career as an entrepreneur the years between 1973 and 1975 were the most difficult ones. Owing to dropping sales it was no longer possible to cover the ever-increasing costs and considerable monies due were tied up in the foreign subsidiaries. It was in this situation that the costs for renovating Hermersberg Castle, which had been purchased by Reinhold Würth in 1970, skyrocketed. "The result was a pathetic balance sheet for 1974 that indicated a clear setback in our development." In view of the overall economic crisis, banks exercised tighter credit control. "We, too, were requested to keep within our credit limits, and banks started to become insecure in the evaluation of our group of companies," Reinhold Würth recalls.[228] "Every day some bank called to ask if we would soon transfer money since a lot of checks had been issued again and the account was by far overdrawn," remembers Gerhard Knoblauch, who worked in accounts during[229] 3/74.197 The company's liquidity problems were also due to its explosive growth; since there were no exact plans, "the banks' credit limits were occasionally insufficient and overdrafts could not be avoided."[230]

The situation was aggravated in 1973 by credit becoming considerably more expensive, since the German Central Bank was squeezing both the discount and Lombard rates to curb inflation. In June 1973, the head of the accounting department, Otto Beilharz, stated that up to 100 per cent more interest had to be paid compared to the same period in the previous year.[231] The company managed to control the situation, however, not least because of a new way of financing capital assets. Instead of the usual mortgage loans and land charges, the company changed over to leasing in 1973, initially for the company cars, but then also for buildings. The first leased building was a shopping center close to Gaisbach, which the company used as warehouse, and when plans were drawn up for a new distribution center was in 1976, the management negotiated with DAL, the largest German industrial leasing association.

In the field of accounting, Reinhold Würth decided to introduce factoring with the Interfactor Bank, a procedure developed in the USA. With standard factoring, invoicing is taken over by the factoring company. Owing to the large number of customer accounts at Würth, however, this was impossible, so that part of the accounting system was kept within the company. For outgoing payments, however, new accounts were set up with the company's banks. Günter Theurer, appointed to monitor the factoring process, reports: "After the first sale of receivables, we did not really know who the incoming payments from the customers belonged to. The whole process got going properly only after a few days, and incoming payments were used as advance payments for new accounts receivable to be sold." Difficulties in the start-up phase were soon eliminated, and Theurer remarked: "This system new to all of us had the advantage that growth could be financed immediately without any problems." [232] Dr. Walter Jaeger, who worked for Würth in his function as colleague of Dr. Kleinknecht at the time, remembers that Kleinknecht in view of such progressive financing methods was often worried about how he could possibly direct "this 'crazy' Würth Company with the dynamic and always optimistic entrepreneur Reinhold Würth into economically moderate and sound channels." [233]

In 1975 the business tried to cut costs through slimming the workforce and, for the first time in the history of the company, 200 employees were dismissed. However, in the following year almost 200 staff were recruited again, and the upward trend continued after 1977. By the end of the decade Würth had almost 3,000 employees. [234]

"As Much Organization as Necessary" – Reinhold Würth Points the Way for a Group Structure

In the end, the oil crisis served to speed up a structural change in the economy in the direction of labor and energy efficiency. There could be no doubt that the times of seemingly unlimited growth of the economic miracle were over. Structural and economic factors such as the oil price explosion, government regulations, high inflation rates, and marginal growth became increasingly important. Business strategies had to change, too, against this backdrop. Anybody who wanted to remain market leader was forced to improve his performance faster than the competition.²³⁵ To achieve this aim, Reinhold Würth had to make a number of business decisions, particularly in the second half of the 1970s, which pointed the way for the further development of the company.

"At the beginning of 1975 I feel that our group of companies is going through a time of upheaval. We are leaving behind the stage of the medium-sized enterprise and will in the next few years enter the dimension of a large company. To achieve this objective it will become necessary to improve our so far rather rudimentary and shirt-sleeve leadership methods, particularly in the management of our companies, with the help of scientifically substantiated findings." ²³⁶ It was with these words that Reinhold Würth characterized the situation in 1975 in the preamble of the corporate philosophy, formulated for the first time that year. The business that had grown continuously in the last 20 years after being taken over by Reinhold Würth, with the effects of the oil crisis barely overcome, was now faced with another major challenge: the development of appropriate structures.

Demands on the organization of the business went hand-in-hand with its growth and appropriate management and communication systems had to be developed. Professor Tietz, Professor of Business Science at the University of Saarbrücken, played an important role as consultant in this phase. Reinhold Würth had met Tietz for the first time during a seminar in Zurich. From that moment on, the two stayed in touch, and in 1972 the first consultations were held. At the end of 1974, Otto Beilharz and Dieter Krämer, who had joined the company the year before, also attended one of Bruno Tietz' seminars. "I am convinced that our enthusiasm and the feeling of a certain strategic vacuum in our company led to cooperation between Reinhold Würth and Professor Tietz," Dieter Krämer remembers. ²³⁷ In January 1975, Professor Tietz recommended, among other things, the drawing up of a corporate philosophy as well as the appointment of an advisory board.

An "Efficient Regulating Mechanism" –
Corporate Advisory Board, Corporate Philosophy, and Sets of Rules

Reinhold Würth decided to establish a nine-member corporate Advisory Board that, being a body staffed by highly-qualified experts, has been advising the company in matters of critical importance until the present day. The Advisory Board gives advice and recommendations to corporate management. Reinhold Würth sees the corporate Advisory Board as "an extraordinarily efficient regulating mechanism, preventing any escapades that might have been too adventurous." [238] The Advisory Board works according to precise statutes and has rights and authorities that go beyond those of a supervisory board of a stock corporation. "The Advisory Board is the highest supervising and controlling body of the Würth Group. It gives advice in matters of strategy and approves the business planning, use of financial resources, and appointments of both the members of the Board of Directors and the managing directors of the big companies;" this is how the function of the body is described in the 2001 Annual Report of the Würth Group.

The constituent meeting of the Advisory Board took place on April 16, 1975, with the following people appointed members: Director Braun from Interfactor Bank in Mainz, Director Helmut Pfleiderer from Handelsbank Heilbronn AG, Artur Herold as staff representative, and Reinhold Würth's mother, Alma Würth-Kindermann, who fulfilled this role until 1997. [239] Professor Bruno Tietz was appointed first chairman of the Advisory Board being succeeded in 1985 by his deputy, Dr. Alfons Humpert, chief executive of Deutsche Genossenschaftsbanken Frankfurt. Reinhold Würth became chairman of the Advisory Board of the Würth Group in 1993.

In the corporate philosophy drawn up in 1975, Reinhold Würth defined the fundamental objectives, framework of operation, and regulations of the company. The top priority was striving for further growth and higher market share, with greatest importance being attached to improving profitability and achieving higher profits. Reinhold Würth coined his often-quoted, basic principle that has been embodied in the corporate philosophy since 2000: "Growth without profit is fatal."

The ruling principles of business policy for the domestic operations of the Würth Group were stipulated by the management of Adolf Würth KG and those for the foreign subsidiaries by Reca-Union GmbH Chur. Every managing director in Germany and abroad had to gear his or her actions toward the benefit of the overall group. "As is the case in national law, public benefit is to be valued higher than self-interest." [240]

Reinhold Würth and Prof. Bruno Tietz during a meeting of the Advisory Board of the Würth Group in 1981

Organization and planning were identified as two of the most important tasks in the business. Business operations were the subject of a seven-year forward plan, with special emphasis on the planning of sales, personnel, matters of finance, profit, and space requirements. All plans were checked for target attainment at least every quarter. Reinhold Würth made fundamental statements on management and personnel that have remained important elements of corporate culture until today: the human being must be the focus of all decisions. Cooperation between management and staff is based on mutual confidence and mutual respect. "The management of the Würth Group is not geared toward authoritarian management, but toward cooperation […]. For the purpose of explanation and transparency, instructions and orders given to the downstream department or employee must always be accompanied by additional information." However, Reinhold Würth also made the limits of "democratization in the business" clear: it ends where "a decision might have a negative impact on the overall Group." Final decisions were to be made by him in his function as executive partner (until the end of 1993), a principle he has remained true to until today. "The greater the successes, the greater the liberty and freedom granted," states the corporate philosophy at the end of the millennium. Corporate management is basically decentralized and liberal, therefore, with responsibility for success being delegated downward. If success does not follow, however, individual companies or people responsible for the results have to hand over their projects to corporate headquarters, either in part or even entirely.

Dieter Krämer recognized the dynamic between the infinite, decentralized possibilities for development that were yet held in tension by the control mechanism of "final power," referring to these factors as the "ingredients of the recipe for success" of the business. An "almost extreme information and communication policy" was confronted with an authority having the final say, as can only be practiced in companies managed by the owner.[241]

> "In retrospect I must say that I liked my work on Würth's Advisory Board best – and I was a member of a great many advisory boards of large and medium-sized businesses. This is due to Reinhold Würth's charismatic personality, and also to the fact that one really had the opportunity to get to know the company in detail. There was always a sense of belonging."
>
> Georg Krupp, former member of the managing board of Deutsche Bank AG, deputy chairman of the Würth Advisory Board for a number of years

Apart from corporate philosophy, a so-called "Policy and Procedure Manual" – PAP – was developed in the 1970s that is given to every managing director of a Würth Company. Its creation was based on the realization that decisions made during meetings were very often filed away, never to be put into practice. PAP codifies the management techniques that are typical of the Würth Group in the fields of overall management, finance and accounting, personnel, investment, operations, field sales organization, marketing strategy, product strategy, and purchasing. Its character is that of a set of recommendations. The managing directors can also opt for other ways to solve a problems, but are reminded of the PAP "if they ever deviate from the path of virtue," as Reinhold Würth puts it. [242]

At the end of the 1970s, the head of the company also realized the importance of what we today call the "soft skills" in a continuously growing organization. His policy statements and announcements within the company were increasingly devoted to matters of staff motivation and corporate culture. [243] This became an important aspect in the further development of the business.

Management, FÜKO, and Coordinating Conference – Development of a Management Structure

The formulation of the corporate philosophy and the establishment of the Advisory Board constituted significant milestones in the company's organizational development in the mid-1970s, with 1978 marking the birth of Adolf Würth GmbH & Co. KG. In the company name, Adolf Würth KG, the additional designation "GmbH & Co." – for "limited liability company" – had not so far been included because German law then still allowed this designation to be omitted even if a joint-stock company was a full partner in the limited partnership. At the beginning of the 1980s, however, the legal requirements were altered so that limited partnerships that did not have at least one person as a fully liable partner had to indicate this in the company name. [244]

At the time of the name change the company consisted of the parent company, Adolf Würth GmbH & Co. KG in Künzelsau, with ten branch offices in the Federal Republic of Germany, nine wholesalers in Germany specializing in certain fields of assembly technology, and 17 foreign subsidiaries in Europe, North and South America, and South Africa. [245]

The management of Adolf Würth KG and the specialized functions in the Group remained more or less identical until 1977. The first step in the process of staff-related independence of the parent company of the Group was made at the end of 1979, with the establishment of a Board of Management – FÜKO – as the top management level of the overall company and the separate representation of the management of Adolf Würth KG. As the foundation of FÜKO approached, the possible dangers of such a "floating body" placed somewhere between Reinhold Würth, with his full authority, and the managing directors of the subsidiaries were discussed. However, the Board of Management proved a highly successful body at the top of the Würth Group. "The Board of Management constitutes the central management of the Würth Group and determines business policy. Under the chairmanship of Reinhold Würth, the heads of the Group's specialized functions and business segments bear responsibility for the long-term profitable and secure development of the group of companies subsumed under the name of 'Würth Group'," states the company's 1988 Annual Report. Up until the reorganization of central management in 2001, the Board of Management was responsible for central operations management, under the chairmanship of Reinhold Würth until the end of 1993 when he moved on to become chairman of the Advisory Board.

> "Reinhold Würth has an incredibly strong personality; a lot of things in the company are tailored to him."
>
> Hans Hügel, former Würth sales manager and authorized signatory

The so-called "Coordinating Conference" was inaugurated to improve communication with the foreign subsidiaries. It was convened for the first time in Künzelsau in August 1976 and was listed as part of the management of the Würth Group for the first time in the 1987 Annual Report. The body was led by Dieter Krämer until the end of 1998. The history of the Coordinating Conference ends with the introduction of a new Group management structure in 2001.

With the corporate Advisory Board as well as the Board of Management and the Coordinating Conference, a robust management structure had developed in the Würth Group by the end of the 1970s. The business of Adolf Würth GmbH & Co. KG was at that time conducted by Rolf Bauer, Otto Beilharz, Dieter Krämer, and Karl Specht under the chairmanship of Reinhold Würth.

New Forces in Management

While Rolf Bauer, Karl Specht, and Otto Beilharz had been with the company since the 1960s, the continuous growth of the business made the recruitment of additional employees with management functions indispensable. In the 1970s, a number of these joined the business who represent the continuity of the management in terms of personnel; all worked for the company until recently and some are still with Würth today.

Gerhard Knoblauch came to Würth from the People's Bank in the summer of 1970, to support Otto Beilharz in the field of finance and accounting. In the following years, he mainly assisted the changeover of the accounting system to EDP. At the beginning of the 1980s, Knoblauch assumed a leading position in the company. From 1980 to 2002, he was a member of the management of Adolf Würth GmbH & Co. KG in the fields of finance, planning, and personnel. In 1997, he was appointed deputy member of the Board of Management for financial services and special projects. In this function he also belonged to the new and enlarged Board for central operations management, up until 2002.

When Dieter Krämer joined Würth in the fall of 1973, the Group acquired an organizational expert who would decisively shape the development of its organizational structures. Krämer had advanced quickly after completing a commercial apprenticeship with Hornschuch AG and – through his friendship with Rolf Bauer – had applied for the position of organization and EDP manager. His first interview with Reinhold Würth convinced him. Krämer was mainly impressed by Reinhold Würth's way of seeing things as a whole and not getting bogged down in details. The salary was another attraction. His first work-station was in the company restaurant, however, "with the Coke vending machine in the back," [246] since the office building the staff had moved into only a few years ago was again bursting at the seams. Like all other newcomers, Krämer went to the grass-roots level to gather some experience and traveled the district of Schwäbisch Hall together with a sales representative. Remembering those times, he says: "I was not happy during my first months at Würth." However, one evening he met with Hans Hügel to discuss strategic issues such as the acquisition of strongly-growing companies operating in industries other than Würth's or the building up of subsidiaries as specialists for certain products – issues that Krämer considers topical still in retrospect. During the first conference for managing directors of

> "We were a highly motivated army of rebels led by a charismatic leader who broke traditional rules of the market and aggressively marched ahead with incredible motivation."
>
> Dieter Krämer, former FÜKO-Member

the foreign subsidiaries in the spring of 1975, a first strategy seminar under the direction of Professor Tietz was organized, and the conference taking place the following year became a milestone in Krämer's career. In passing, "during the coffee break," Reinhold Würth assigned him the task of coordinating the company's international activities. In 1979 Krämer, who in the meantime had become a member of the management of Adolf Würth GmbH & Co. KG, moved on to the Group's Board of Management. As a member of this body he shaped the development of the business until his withdrawal at the end of 1998. Considering the results, and with reference to his own contribution, Krämer conjectured in 1994 that the success of the Würth Group might be due to the fact that the targets set and methods applied were correct most of the time, but that, on the other hand, the tremendous drive and occasionally also the weaknesses of the people involved ensured that previous achievements never degenerated into inertia or even paralysis.

In the spring of 1975, another new employee began his career with Würth who would play a decisive role in establishing the field of marketing in the business. Gerhard Fried, with a Master's in Business Administration (MBA), started in internal sales after previously working in the warehouse for two weeks, as was traditional within Würth. "The organization of internal sales at the time caused problems and trouble for the customers rather than supporting them," was how Fried described the situation when he joined the company. He therefore introduced "basic organizational structures" in the form of sales groups and "made first modest attempts" at demonstrating what was to be understood by marketing or, as he himself puts it, "very slowly and repeatedly spelled out the strange notion of 'customer support' to his colleagues." In Fried's opinion, the relationship between company and customers was still "alarmingly weak" in the middle of the 1970s and he made sure that this changed completely in the period following. In 1977, issues such as "customer orientation" and "sales force orientation" were discussed for the first time. As the person responsible for marketing, Gerhard Fried was appointed member of the management of Adolf Würth GmbH & Co. KG in 1980; in 1984, he became a member of the Group's Board of Management. In the 1990s he also assumed responsibility for the Wood Division before taking early retirement for health reasons.

Werner Rau, who stepped in for Fried and took over the Wood Division, had joined Würth as a purchasing agent in 1976. On his first day of work he found himself in the warehouse "dressed in a blue workcoat, counting washers in shelf no. 5, taking them out of a small box and putting them into a smaller one. Somewhat frustrated, I had to realize that, during the next four weeks, I would have to work my way through different shelves and that this was the usual period of induction," he recalls.[247] He soon found out, though, that it was quite instructive to work in the warehouse and to "touch the articles" he was later supposed to purchase "with my own hands." He assumed responsibility for organizing the purchasing department.

In view of rising supplier prices in Europe at that time, people came to realize that Asia could be an attractive alternative. In the spring of 1978, Rau together with Rolf Bauer embarked on his first trip to Japan, Hong Kong, Taiwan, and China to sound out the market in the Far East. Innumerable business trips followed that also provided Rau with interesting insights into the cultures of the Far East, which he describes in his company history. In his function as purchasing manager and person responsible for the field of export, Werner Rau has been a member of the management of Adolf Würth GmbH & Co. KG since 1980. In the wake of the reorganization of central management in 2001, Rau was appointed member of the new operations Board of Management of the Würth Group, in which position he also assumed responsibility in 2003 for purchasing and export.

The "Guardians of Progress" – New Structures in the Sales Force

The creation of structures could not be limited solely to the management level; the entire company had to be equipped with appropriate structures in all areas, both in-house and in the sales force. The organizational model of the Würth Group developed in the middle of the 1970s was characterized by the management's attempt to have administration and marketing keep pace with the growth of the sales force.[248] A new infrastructure in the field of logistics and information technology living up to the requirements of the growing business had to be developed, with networks to the subsidiaries in Germany and abroad operating in accordance with specific organizational routines. The sales force had to be developed "from a bunch of sales reps selling screws into a standing army," as Dieter Krämer jokingly remarked in 1976.[249]

The sales force is instrumental in the success or failure of the company. On the occasion of the 1976 Würth Congress, Reinhold Würth said that the sales force constitutes the basis of progress: "Frankly speaking, our sales representatives are the guardians of our group's progress."[250]

GROWTH REQUIRES A CERTAIN STRUCTURE
THE "GUARDIANS OF PROGRESS" – NEW STRUCTURES IN THE SALES FORCE

During the previous year, priority had been given to the organization and future development of the sales force in the corporate philosophy drawn up by Reinhold Würth. He was convinced that all the problems in subordinate departments, such as the administration and product distribution, would be solved almost automatically, provided the sales force worked properly. In the second half of the 1970s, though, a number of difficulties kept the sales force from running smoothly.

The growth of the control and management system could not keep up with the enormously speedy growth of the number of sales representatives and the system they represented in the early 1970s.

The organizational structures had not developed in line with the sales force. There was no office available for the relevant sales manager until 1977 and neither processes nor operations were structured. Karl Specht recalls the period during which he held this management position: "Sometimes we didn't know what was going on any more." In the following period a "department in charge of sales management – sales force" was built up, which worked on administrative issues relating to the entire sales force and guided and supervised the sales representatives, training and promoting them.[251]

Since 1960 there had been so-called "principal sales representatives" who were one step below area managers in the hierarchy. Each was in charge of a group of sales representatives whose sales volume also influenced his commission. It was the task of the principal sales representatives to look after and train new colleagues. At the beginning of the 1970s, however, Karl Specht, who was area manager at the time, suggested having the principal sales representatives, too, spend part of their time selling to increase overall sales. He calculated a sales increase of 9 million DM per year on the basis of 54 principal sales representatives; this convinced the management, with the position of principal sales representative gradually being abolished over time and, the system simply consisting of sales management, area managers, and sales representatives.

In 1975, Germany was divided into five sales districts. The regional sales managers – formerly called district managers – organized the work of the area managers reporting to them and participated in monitoring the market and the development of marketing concepts. The area managers were responsible for both looking after their sales representatives and servicing the key accounts in their area. Sales representatives were subdivided into the categories A, B, or C depending on the sales volume generated and the number of orders obtained every month.[252] Until 1976, Hans Hügel was the sales manager responsible for the whole of

Germany; he then stepped back for health reasons and in his function as deputy supported his successor, Karl Specht.[253]

A New Pricing and Commission System

The new sales management was soon confronted with new problems. Between 1976 and 1978, customers started to become dissatisfied, a development that was reflected in a growing number of complaints. During the Fall Conference of 1979 in Bolzano, Italy, Reinhold Würth remarked that the work of the sales force was characterized by both lack of enthusiasm and dissatisfaction.[254]

What were the reasons? How could this vicious circle – dissatisfied customers leading to dissatisfied sales representatives, dissatisfied sales representatives in turn leading to higher staff turnover and therefore again to dissatisfied customers – be broken? One focus was on the obsolete pricing and commission system. The sales representatives enjoyed great leeway regarding prices and could determine both prices and discounts independently for every customer. The higher the prices and the lower the discounts, the more commission they received. Corporate headquarters in Künzelsau, though, determined certain basic prices. Reinhold Würth himself assumed that, because of repeated price increases, the price lists published by headquarters had become unrealistic, and that the sales representatives no longer relied on them for their pricing. However, if they charged their customers lower prices their commission went down – in short, the salary of the sales representatives had gone askew. In 1976 it was therefore decided to offer fixed salaries to the sales representatives, a measure that proved to make little sense from the point of view of the company, since the sales representatives were no longer motivated to sell as much as possible at the highest possible prices.

In this situation, it became obvious that targets, role models, and guidelines had to be established for the sales representatives and that the idea of performance and achievements required some serious brushing up. Reinhold Würth decided to create a sound basis for this approach, and so a study of the sales force of Adolf Würth KG was commissioned in cooperation with the University of Saarbrücken in 1977. One of the results of the study was a modified pricing and commission system that was tried out first in the spring of 1978 and officially introduced that summer. To avoid further insecurity among the sales representatives, the individual employee had a say in determining when he would to change over to the new system. The new income consisted of a basic salary, commission, and, provided the sales target was achieved, a bonus. After 1979, performance-oriented pay was also introduced for the area managers, their commission being calculated on the basis of the sales volume generated by their sales representatives.

Information and Incentives – Staff Motivation

As Reinhold Würth observes: "Successful staff are contented, contented staff are successful." [255] To promote the idea of performance, a large number of supporting measures were taken in the 1970s. In October 1987, the "Club of the 80,000 DM-Men" was set up, a measure that people smiled at condescendingly at first, but was successfully continued with the "Success Club" and the "Top Club" of the top-performing sales representatives. A performance-oriented rule concerning the award of company cars was also introduced in 1978. The successes of a sales representative were now reflected in the car he used for work. The head of the company was aware of the fact that top-performing sales representatives greatly influence the mood in the sales force, and for this reason he invited the top 100 sales representatives together with their wives to a year-end meeting in Sonthofen in December 1978 and asked them for support in improving the performance level of the sales force. Letters of appreciation as well as bonuses were introduced for high achievers. Supporting measures included special sales campaigns as well as a Würth Points-Rally, which was introduced at the beginning of 1979. Sales points could be collected by the sales representatives, and whoever collected 300 points received the legendary Citroen 2CV. However,

Reinhold Würth congratulating Gerald Tauber, who became the first member of the „Club of the 80,000-DM men." Karl Specht, sales manager at the time, is in the background

Würth had to gather experience with incentives first before the system really bore fruit. At the start, sales manager Karl Specht found out occasionally that sales figures had been dressed up at the customers' expense to collect bonus points, and so the company's complaint rate went up. Overall sales volume, however, increased by 17 per cent in 1979. [256]

Apart from improving the sales representatives' motivation and willingness to perform, the company also tried to improve the flow of information within Adolf Würth KG. In July 1978, the area managers were invited to come to Künzelsau for two weeks to get a comprehensive overview of the complex tasks of corporate headquarters. Furthermore, every manager of Adolf Würth KG was requested specifically to support two or three sales areas, a measure that Reinhold Würth also participated in. Starting in February 1979, the "Intern-Letter," confidential information from the management to the Würth sales representatives, was published on a monthly basis. In the fall of 1978 and spring of 1979, Reinhold Würth and Karl Specht organized district conferences all over Germany to brief the sales representatives on management strategy. Increased presence on the part of top and sales management in the field resulted in heightened activity on the part of the sales force management. Cooperation between managers and sales representatives intensified.

The induction of new sales representatives, which still left a lot to be desired, was also improved. According to Karl Specht, the period of settling in was not structured well enough, a circumstance that contributed to staff turnover. For this reason a three-month induction program was developed for every new sales representative. [257]

All these measures produced the desired results and led to a mood swing in the sales force. Surveys showed that the sales representatives' confidence in the business increased.

Another Milestone on the Way to Success: Divisionalization

Another important component of success was fixed in 1977 that – with its further development in the 1990s – would turn out to be one of the milestones in the history of Würth. Divisionalization started with the subdivision into Automotive (KFZ) on the one hand and Wood and Metal, called CRAFT, on the other. Karl Specht emphasized this innovation, commenting that "such a radical change was so far unheard of in our company." [258] After just a few months, the areas in which divisionalization had been introduced reported "fantastic success", with sales up 70 per cent. Since the total product range had become too comprehensive for individual sales representatives to manage, this separation of the Automotive and Wood/Metal sectors directly improved customer service. Reinhold Würth explained the measure: "The salesman is becoming a specialist in a subsector of our marketing program." [259] The introduction of divisionalization did not go that smoothly, however, and confronted the sales management with a major challenge. Karl Specht recalls: "The entire changeover caused a lot of trouble." The 350 sales representatives on Adolf Würth KG's payroll at the time suddenly had a different customer base, and it was often quite difficult to make the sales force understand decisions taken by the management, e.g. concerning territory cuts. In some cases, decisions were simply not accepted, so that Reinhold Würth had personally to sign orders. Ultimately, the entire management level of the sales force had to be reorganized, with some managers having to be let go. However, the company succeeded in overcoming these obstacles, and the project forged ahead. Reinhold Würth thanked both Karl Specht and Hans Hügel for their outstanding work with a trip to the USA. [260] By January 1979, divisionalization had been completed throughout Germany. After the reorganization of the sales force, the region of an automotive area corresponded to that of two Wood or Metal areas, and each of the two divisions had their own divisional management. Since the separation of the two divisions had proven so successful, it was decided to set up a separate division for the sale of products to industry customers in 1979.

Divisionalization led to an increased demand for managers in the sales force. In this situation, it became obvious that upcoming managers were scarce within Würth. [261] Both top and sales management were forced to think about the issue of training top performers for the sales force. Following an initiative by Reinhold Würth, the Würth Career Model was developed in 1978.

The measures initiated in the period between 1976 and 1979 not only increased the sales force's size and power, but also resulted in a standardization of the sales strategy. Both the product knowledge and motivation of the sales representatives were improved considerably. The successes were reflected in further sales increases.

Logistics, EDP, and Marketing – Expansion of Administration and Sales

The sales force constitutes the foundation of the success enjoyed by a direct sales company such as Würth, so it requires a support network in both administration and distribution that corresponds to its size. As in the previous decade, the administrative and warehousing capabilities had difficulty keeping pace with the quickly growing sales force; Würth was once again "bursting at the seams."

The constantly growing number of employees not only required more space, but also the establishment of a personnel department responsible for supplying the demand for quality staff in all areas as well as fulfilling the requirements of the unions and labor laws. Up to that time, matters of personnel had been attended to by the respective department manager with hiring in most cases being done orally, accompanied by a brief written memo. Jürgen Röhrig was hired as personnel manager on July 1, 1973. He was authorized to prepare employment contracts up to the level of department manager and to consult the management in drafting contracts for principal department managers and staff employees.

By 1974 it had become indispensable to enlarge the administrative building in Gaisbach, officially opened only five years previously, in view of the ever-increasing number of in-house staff, projects, and departments. Reinhold Würth decided to commission one of the most distinguished architects of post-war modern art: Sep Ruf of Munich, who had designed the airy, steel-glass pavilions for the world exposition in Brussels in 1958 together with Egon Eiermann, set the standards for future corporate architecture at Würth. Ruf placed a four-story cube made of glass and steel on the longitudinal axis of the previous building. Surrounded by steel galleries on all four sides, the building could disappear completely behind a sunshade and "mutate into a white cube." An "escape stairway elegantly bent around a slender pillar" juts wide into the open air with its "almost immaterial connecting bridges like an abstract geometrical sculpture. With this architectural monument in the tradition of classical modern art [...] for the first time both architectural and sculptural values have become the focus on the premises of Würth." [262]

During the 1970s, Würth achieved architectural highlights not only with its corporate buildings, but also with a new warehouse: erected only a few years later, it set the modern standard for distribution of merchandise and generated great expert interest among the experts.

The New Distribution Center

In 1976, Reinhold Würth was forced to acknowledge product distribution as the "only weak point in Würth KG." [263] It was only with great effort that the company succeeded in maintaining its capability to deliver, the boom in incoming orders making it necessary considerably to increase stocks. For the time being, the company tried to make do with renting two warehouses in the vicinity of Künzelsau. The staff worked in two shifts, in the warehouse and in shipping, from 5 a.m. to 10 p.m. At the beginning of 1976, Würth started planning a new distribution center. Reinhold Würth explained: "Product flow will be controlled semi-automatically with a lot of technology, conveyor belts, shelf conveyors, process control computers and EDP." [264] The decision had been made in favor of a high-bay warehouse. A distribution center with 7,000 pallet spaces and 32,000 spaces for storage containers was erected on a base area of 34,500 ft² (3,200 m²). The lower part of the building housed goods received and the weighing department. All in all, the construction of the building and the technical facilities took twelve months, with Paul Jakob in charge of project management. Paul Jakob had joined the company in 1974 as production engineer for circuit boards at Würth Elektronik and represented the field of warehousing and distribution in the management of Adolf Würth GmbH & Co. KG from 1980 to 1994. [265]

The costs for the new distribution center amounted to 15 million DM, this major project being realized in accordance with leasing procedure. The high investment expenses were not only justified by the urgently needed expansion of warehouse capacity and safeguarding of a fast delivery service. The objective was also to reduce the costs per ton of goods handled. The company aimed at achieving competitive advantage by rationalizing the workflow. Moving many hundreds of pounds of screws and assembly material no longer required the physical work of the staff, but was to a great extent taken over by technical installations that helped to increase the number of tons handled per employee. Reinhold Würth dissipated misgivings that the new distribution center would abolish jobs through technological advance. "The new distribution center makes your jobs even more secure because it gives us another considerable cost advantage over our competitors […]. The warehouse constitutes an important element in the safeguarding of our Group and the jobs of our employees […] it is our declared aim to double the tonnage sales within a short period of time with the same or only slightly increased number of staff." [266]

In September 1978, the new distribution center started operations "with all the conceivable start-up problems" that such a highly technical, major project entails, as Karl Specht recalls. [267] Thanks to the "nearly superhuman effort" shown by all employees involved during the changeover in shifts, lasting up to 72 hours as Reinhold Würth described on the occasion of the official opening of the distribution center in May 1979 [268], the start-up difficulties were soon overcome. At the beginning of 1979, the company was able to put together more than 2,000 orders every day, and the merchandise was on its way to the customer within 24 hours of receipt of the order. However, capacity utilization of the new distribution center had not yet reached its limits: it was designed for further sales growth so that at a later date up to 4,500 orders daily could be handled.

The warehousing technology of the new distribution center, being state of the art at the end of the 1970s, was run and controlled with the help of EDP. This was nothing new to Würth, since the business had started thinking about electronic data processing a decade before in view of the fact that the ever-increasing amounts of goods, as well as matters of finance and personnel getting more complex all the time, had to be handled as efficiently as possible.

When Otto Beilharz started working for Würth in 1966, the accounting department worked with Taylorix accounting machines, a card index box for accounts payable, and about four to five card index boxes for accounts receivable. Every day, the staff had to pull out the account cards and sort them back into the boxes after posting the transactions. Two apprentices were constantly busy with sending manual reminders to customers. [269] The rapid growth of the business required more efficient methods, however, if it wanted to safeguard its competitive advantage in this respect, too.

In 1970, the first IBM computer was taken into operation and, after a number of start-up problems, the advantages of the new technology soon became obvious: costs were reduced, and profits increased.

The computerization of the business was first managed by Kurt Tag, who left the company in 1976. He was succeeded by Dieter Krämer and, in 1979, by Dr. Harald Unkelbach, who holds a master's degree in mathematics. Harald Unkelbach is another employee who joined the company in the 1970s and still holds office in the top management body today. From 1980 until the end of 2002, he was responsible for the fields of organization and EDP in the management of Adolf Würth GmbH & Co. KG, as well as acting for a certain period as spokesman of the management. He has been a member of the new Board of Management of the Würth Group since January 1, 2003.

"Würth Creates Connections" – Marketing Concepts and Product Policy

The seller's market of the post-war years increasingly changed to a buyer's market. In the 1950s and 1960s people had purchased whatever was available on the market, but now it became more important to satisfy customers and tie them to the company. This was something a direct sales company such as Würth had to react to if it wanted to strengthen its position in the market.

The marketing department created by Gerhard Fried therefore worked on many different projects. [270] Intensive cooperation between the in-house sales department and sales representatives helped to guarantee customer satisfaction. Sales groups were set up with the aim of handling customer requests and complaints more quickly. The network of branch offices was extended to bring them even closer to the customers. Whereas product distribution had been the focus when opening the first warehouses in the 1960s, it was now both the canvassing and consulting of customers that enjoyed top priority. This brought Würth into direct competition with local trading companies in the industry. By the end of 1979, Würth customers were able to supply their immediate wants through a total of 13 branch offices in Munich, Berlin, Karlsruhe, Mannheim, Nuremberg, Stuttgart, Rodgau, Hanover, Aachen, Kassel, Oldenburg, Regensburg and Saarbrücken, the remaining products being shipped from Künzelsau. The customers of a branch office were serviced by three to seven employees, who were additionally assigned so-called "base sales representatives" directly at the location.

In the 1970s, the marketing department also started to research the market, surveying the sales development of individual product groups. The results influenced the set-up of the product range. This finally led to the development of house brands that would become a byword for quality in connection with the Würth name.

The name Karl Weidner is inextricably linked with the company's product development. It was he who designed a system for this. Weidner joined Würth in 1972: "My first working day started in the warehouse, where I began on shelf no. 4 […]. After just a few days I was fed up to the back teeth." [271] And yet, Weidner stayed on, laying the foundations for his profound product knowledge. After his induction period, he moved on to the purchasing department, whose management he took over two years later. With the introduction of the Zebra brand for high-quality products, the development of private label products was forced up. Initially, hose clamps followed by twist drills and cable rolling devices were launched under the new brand name. In the chemical-technical field the company so far only had Würth Rost-Off and Würth Contact Spray in the range as private label products, but in 1977 it was decided to add further private label products to this section of the range.

In the beginning, Karl Weidner tested the products in his workshop at home, trying to find out if the products developed by Würth and manufactured by other companies commissioned to do so actually fulfilled the quality requirements. In 1976, an employee was hired to develop quality control and the first testing devices were purchased. Finally, in 1978, the product development department came into being under the direction of Karl Weidner. "In our field of responsibility there was nothing there at the beginning", he recalled, "[…] we practically had to start from scratch." [272] From 1986 onwards, Karl Weidner belonged to the management of Adolf Würth GmbH & Co. KG. Until his premature death in the summer of 2000, he ran the continuously growing R&D department of the company that, in part in cooperation with scientists from the Fraunhofer-Institute Stuttgart, developed many innovative products such as ergonomically shaped tools or – in the 1980s and 1990s – environment-friendly chemical products.

In 1987, Adolf Würth KG had more than 300,000 different parts in its range, which concentrated on fasteners and assembly technology. The customer base comprised roughly 180,000 businesses, 110,000 of which were abroad. [273] Since 1970, the "Würth-report" had been published by Reinhold Würth as information for the customers. Until 1992, the editor and publisher of this successful company magazine was the photographer Paul Swiridoff, who remembers the beginning of his cooperation with Reinhold Würth. "During a turn of the year we spent together, my new friend came up with yet another idea. An idea that was to change my life, too. As was always the case with Reinhold Würth, this new company magazine was to be published very quickly. We christened this press baby "Würth-report," and the first issue was ready for publication four months later." [274]

More time and energy was now also invested in product information. In 1972, the first product overviews were published in color, and a colored principal catalog was published on the occasion of the Frankfurt Auto Show in 1973.

The Würth-report was one of the first projects in the field of advertising and public-relations work, but in the 1975 corporate philosophy Reinhold Würth announced the creation of a corresponding staff position for the entire Würth Group, since he had in the meantime recognized the importance of image building. The areas of advertising, sales promotion, and PR were added to the marketing department. Reinhold Würth's secretary, Hermine Künast, recalls that, in the 1970s, more and more information about corporate policy was divulged to the public. [275] The first Annual Report of the Würth Group was published in 1978.

"Profit Lies in the Purchasing of Goods"

The introduction of new marketing strategies, the newly structured sales force, and the divisionalization process ensured the continuing success of the business. The growing number of orders, however, could not be handled from the point of view of distribution alone. Before goods could be delivered, they had first to be procured.

Purchasing is another fundamental in the success or failure of a business, and Reinhold Würth was convinced that profit margins also depended on the terms and conditions of purchase of the goods to be sold. In 1975, his first corporate philosophy stated: "The profitability of our Group is decisively influenced by purchase price. An old truism from business life says: 'Profit lies in the purchasing of goods.'" He requested the purchasing department to closely observe the market and fight for the best possible purchasing conditions for the company. "Hard, yet fair" [276] was his motto in negotiating with suppliers.

Particularly in times of a booming economy, as at the beginning of the 1970s, the purchasing department was faced with a number of challenges in its attempt to have 95 per cent of the orders shipped to customers within 24 hours. Quite often, the company had to put off customers who had ordered popular items, since the screw manufacturers had very long delivery periods. The purchasing department was increasingly forced to make long-term plans for procurement, something that was not all that easy to do. The staff had practical schedules to work with, yet one unexpected, large order could lead to fresh bottlenecks. The objective was to keep a balance between maintaining high supply capability on the one hand and not locking up too much capital in inventory on the other. In the beginning, the purchasing department was run by Rolf Bauer, yet his ever-increasing field of activities soon made it necessary to find additional employees who could take over his responsibilities. After Karl Weidner, Werner Rau was put in charge of running the purchasing department.

Sales conferences could already look back on a long tradition at Würth, and in the fall of 1973 the first purchasing conference took place in Künzelsau. In the 1970s, the constantly growing number of staff in the purchasing department concentrated their efforts on finding reasonable and reliable suppliers in Eastern Europe and the Far East. Last but not least the German government's politics under Willy Brandt resulted in a first, albeit cautious, opening in the direction of the Eastern-bloc states, with traveling becoming easier. In 1973, Rolf Bauer attended the Leipzig Fair with the objective of establishing contact with possible suppliers in the Eastern bloc. Steel screws and ironwood screws were purchased from the GDR. Poland, Czechoslovakia, and the former Yugoslavia were countries on the agenda of Karl Weidner's business trips in 1976. Wood screws were already being purchased from Hong Kong and, after 1973, they were also sourced from China.[277] Over the following years, the business succeeded in reducing its dependence on German and West European principal suppliers by placing orders in Japan, China, Taiwan, Hong Kong, and Eastern European countries.

Successes and New Visions

In the 1970s, decisive steps on the company's way to developing into a large Group had been taken through the creation of management structures, the reorganization of the sales force, divisionalization, the building up of a marketing strategy, and the development of a corporate product range, as well as by the construction of a modern, high-tech distribution center. In 1978, Würth had acquired a five-percent share of the market.[278] Between 1970 and 1979, global sales of the Würth Group increased over sixfold. The strategy of establishing foreign subsidiaries, acquiring companies, and diversifying initiated in the 1960s once again proved to be advantageous.

The first half of the 1970s saw Würth acquire a number of companies trading in and producing screws and tools, such as the Frankfurt-based trading company Sonderschrauben Güldner in 1973.[279] The acquisition of the Viennese company Kellner & Kunz AG marked the first time that a company active in the same industry was included in the Würth Group as a foreign-based subsidiary. In 1971, Reinhold Würth turned his attention to the potential of the electronics industry, founding a separate electronics department that five years later started its independent development as Würth Elektronik GmbH & Co. KG with headquarters in Niedernhall. Many acquired businesses had to be reorganized first, however, and it took some time for them to become profitable. Not all of the spinoffs developed smoothly either. In October 1975, Reinhold Würth assigned Rolf Bauer the task of supporting SWG, since the screw manufacturer was "in a real mess."[280] Rolf Bauer initiated the reorganization from a mere production company to one that was also active in the field of trading, and in 1977 the German subsidiaries reported an altogether positive development: "almost all of them" were making a profit or had been able drastically to cut their losses.[281] In 1978, German subsidiaries operating in other fields of industry, such as Würth Elektronik or the car dealer Schubert, made a higher-than-average contribution to the total sales generated by the Würth Group.[282]

In the 1970s, the existing foreign subsidiaries were joined by eight newly established companies: South Africa, Canada, Brazil, England,

Portugal, Norway, Finland, and Spain. Of the more than 2,900 employees of the Würth Group in 1979, almost 1,900 worked in foreign subsidiaries; they accounted for more than 58 per cent of total sales.[283]

Against this backdrop, Reinhold Würth developed long-term objectives. On the occasion of a meeting of the top 100 sales representatives in 1978, he put his entrepreneurial vision into words. By the 40th anniversary of the business in 1985, global sales of his company were to exceed one billion DM. One year later, during the Fall Conference of the foreign subsidiaries in Bolzano, he explained his longer-term perspective: "Ten years are a long time, it is certainly not possible to approve reliable sales targets today. And yet we must not shut our eyes to the future; businessmen are constantly requested to think about the future. Management business games extending all the way to the end of the 1980s are therefore quite practical."[284]

COMPUTERS, NETWORKS AND PHOENIX   8

The History of EDP at Würth

"Countdown to a New Era"

In 1986, Reinhold Würth stated in a presentation [285] that, ever since the beginning of the 1970s, the global economy had been experiencing a "countdown to a new era" and that "computerization and robotization" were "the landmarks of society's change from a production to an information society." In doing so, he summed up a development that was also reflected in the Würth Company.

    At that time Reinhold Würth said that the development of EDP, systems analysis, and business logistics were among the most important factors of the future success of a company apart from corporate culture and a highly developed corporate code. The prerequisite, though, was further development of the EDP systems to accommodate projected growth.

At the time when the head of the company was working on this presentation, Würth could already look back on 16 years of EDP experience, without which the business would never have been able to report such rapid growth and sweeping success since "it is only with full of the EDP systems and best possible administration of information that the forecast volume growth can be handled cost-efficiently and within reasonable limits." [286]

After a number of initial problems, the time had come at the beginning of the 1970s: the successful set-up of the first IBM computer system enabled the staff of Adolf Würth KG to computerize routine work and, soon afterward, certain projects relating to product distribution. If one were to show the annual growth of EDP transactions in a chart – as Reinhold Würth noted in 1986 [287] – this curve would exceed the sales curve by far. Looking back in 1993, he once again emphasized "the incredible revolution and upheaval in business enterprises in general" that had taken place since the introduction of the first computers at the end of the 1960s. [288] This revolutionary increase in the use of EDP, though, also caused stress in the Group from time to time: "The changeover to a new computer, the introduction of a new operating system, the implementation of new EDP processes not only required superhuman effort on the part of the EDP staff, but the users, too, often felt unduly troubled." [289] However, there was no way back. Reinhold Würth forecast that by the end of the millennium the success of the Würth Group would to a far greater extent depend on EDP – simply "to be able to maintain the transparency of the Group, its manageability and controllability."

A Difficult Start

It was not only at Würth that people at a very early stage of this development realized the enormous potential of the new technology. In the 1960s, the EDP boom had resulted in an annual sales increase of 20 per cent and explosive growth of the number of employees at IBM in Sindelfingen, the company that manufactured the first computer used by Würth. [290] In 1955 and with roughly two-and-a-half thousand employees, the company had begun to manufacture the first "really and truly programmable" computer, the IBM 650, which was operated by electron tubes and coupled with a magnetic tape and disk. At the beginning of the 1960s, the IBM 1401, the second-generation computer operating with transistors and printed circuits set out to conquer Germany from Sindelfingen.

The arrival of EDP at Würth, which heralded the company's entry into the IT-era, was interspersed with obstacles. In the beginning, the head of the company was far from happy about the things that were in store for him and his employees. [291]

Following a fact-finding visit to IBM in Sindelfingen, Reinhold Würth had decided to buy a computer system in 1969, after initial hesitation. However, sales had risen to more than 39 million DM annually after the company's move to Gaisbach in that same year, of which 17.8 million DM were generated by Adolf Würth KG. [292] Until that time, the staff at Würth had worked with Taylorix-accounting machines and customer cards that had to be pulled out for every bookkeeping operation. The boss was displeased about the fact that the accounts were often not updated properly. Open items could not be identified immediately and sometimes customers were not reminded of outstanding

COMPUTERS, NETWORKS AND PHOENIX
A DIFFICULT START

> "Reinhold Würth is a true entrepreneur with a quick, analytical mind and high practical intelligence as well as the characteristics of a man of action. He has the power and vitality necessary to put his visions into action."
>
> Dr. Walter Jaeger, spokesman of the Board of Directors of the Würth Group

payments. To improve the situation, the decision was made to rent a first computer from IBM in January of 1970, an IBM 360/20 with 12 kB working memory and an IDM memory disk 2311 with 21.6 MB capacity for the purpose of installing an "open items accounting system" using punch-card technology.

The entrepreneur first decided against hiring a programmer since the assumption at the time was that this programmer would be out of work after installing the programs. Rolf Bauer, the authorized signatory who had been a member of the company since 1963 and purchasing manager at Würth since 1967, was supposed to handle this project in addition to the many others he had. Despite a programming course he attended, however, neither he nor Otto Beilharz – who was assigned the project together with Rolf Bauer – felt up to the task and so Kurt Tag was hired as EDP expert.

Not only Tag, but all the employees of the company were soon involved with the upcoming EDP introduction, through numerous meetings. The Würth sales representatives were trained in the new number system for the items sold by Würth, which had been developed for the new technology. The in-house staff, too, received instruction on how to punch the cards. Erika Jungfer, head of data collection at the time, remembers the first weeks when the staff had to apply the new technology.

She had joined Adolf Würth KG in 1969 and by October of that year Kurt Tag had already started his seminars on EDP. The employees had to familiarize themselves with the new data entry devices since in future all customer and article data were to be recorded on punched cards. Because of the fact that all other projects remained unattended for some time, the computer chaos at Würth was nearly complete – particularly since IBM could not deliver the machines on time because of a strike and therefore the January deadline for EDP introduction could not be met. For this reason, physical stocktaking at the end of 1969 had to be copied onto the warehouse card index again. Finally, at the end of January 1970, all data from the card index were fed into the EDP system. The higher-than-average order volume aggravated the situation so that no invoices could be issued for a number of days.

Reinhold Würth, back from a business trip, threatened to call it all off. "Mr. Würth was desperate because we could not mail any invoices, he wanted to get straight back to the old working method. However, Mr. Tag succeeded in convincing Mr. Würth that the initial problems would soon be eliminated." [293] Rolf Bauer, too, persuaded his boss to let the situation continue for a few more days, and on a Sunday evening he finally managed to generate the first invoices within the new system – the new computer was allowed to stay.

Chaos, however, was to remain for a while longer. "It was the most comprehensive changeover to date and both the in-house staff and sales representatives were confronted with the consequences for months." [294] Entire nights, including weekends, were spent going through checklists. "The level of tension in the company was high – almost unbearable." As a reward for the ladies in the in-house administration who, despite external support, had had to work overtime and do weekend shifts for months, the company organized an outing to Heidelberg in 1970.

EDP soon became an issue that affected everybody. By 1971, apprentice industrial clerks had to deal with EDP within the framework of their professional training. In the card-punching hall, they were taught how to record the orders by the ladies doing the punching. [295] In 1972, the company purchased a residential building in Gaisbach's Gartenstrasse, which is where the EDP department complete with data collection and programming moved to in the summer, recalls Erika Jungfer who organized the smooth and time-saving flow of work in the new domicile. Since the staff felt like "one big family" they also "had one or the other party there." [296] It was only in 1974 when the new administration building was ready that the EDP department moved into an open plan office. At that time, 1,400 orders had to be punched every day.

Economically speaking, 1975 was a bad year, and the announced redundancies at Würth put a further damper on the mood in the EDP department. All this happened at a time when the staff had to work day and night to get the new program off the ground, which had been purchased in 1974 – despite the recession and the oil crisis – together with a new computer, an IBM 370/125 with 96 kB working memory. Furthermore, data were being stored now on tape machines as well, since the company started microfilming customer data in 1973. [297] From 1974 the telephone system with its 600 extensions was also managed by the computer, and in 1975 the company purchased the first four IBM 3277 screens: the era of "online" data collection had begun.

The new EDP system also resulted in career possibilities for many Würth employees. Some of them used their spare time for training and became self-taught programmers. [298] In 1974, there were four employees who worked as operators, three programmers, and eight ladies in charge of data collection.

Logistics and New Leadership

After Kurt Tag left the company, Dieter Krämer temporarily ran the DP department, from 1976 to 1979. Very soon, one of his most important responsibilities apart from collecting customer data was the "reduction of order processing times." [299] In Reinhold Würth's opinion, competitive advantage could only be achieved by increasing the number of stock turns. At the Künzelsau railroad station stockkeeping had already presented a challenge and now, at the end of the 1970s when the business was selling roughly 30,000 different articles, product distribution had turned into a serious problem for the company because of the rapid growth of the number of orders. Without a modern and well-functioning EDP system, the business really did not stand a chance of improving its readiness to deliver. The required storage space threatened to assume alarming proportions and the volume of goods in stock would soon cause liquidity problems. What was more, the field of logistics harbored great potential for saving personnel costs, provided the company succeeded in increasing the "tonnage per employee" [300] – quite an interesting aspect after the difficult years following the first oil crisis.

The business had in the meantime been able to work with more storage space, thanks to renting two large warehouses in the vicinity of Künzelsau, yet despite the warehouse staff working two shifts and having EDP support, the construction of a high-bay warehouse had become a real necessity. [301] Together with the Miebach company, which was responsible for the technical aspects, and the Heyde company, a project titled "handling the movement of goods with the help of a high-bay warehouse" was initiated. Dieter Krämer recalls that this new distribution center was developed under difficult circumstances. [302] "Pioneering work" was undertaken. [303] A completely new software provided for batch processing in the warehouse, using the newly-developed database technology with the newest IBM-technology. Professor Tietz, too, was involved in the development of this 15-million-DM project that was executed on a leasing basis and aimed at both expanding warehouse capacity and speeding up deliveries to the customers.

When the new, high-bay warehouse was officially opened in 1979, the project staff had lived through a number of very strenuous months. They often had to work day and night and occasionally slept at the company in sleeping bags, to be ready on site when needed. During the day, all available employees had to help out in the new warehouse. This pioneering spirit seems to have had a very motivating and inspiring effect, however, not least because it eliminated differences between departments and hierarchical levels. [304] With the introduction of online technology in logistics that same year, the service degree in the fields of inventory management and accounts receivable rose to 90 per cent.

After successful completion of this enormous task, Dieter Krämer, too, wanted to hand over this office, having been temporarily responsible for EDP since 1976, so the company looked for a successor. After intensive in-house discussions, a decision was taken in favor of an outside expert – rather unusual for the company at that time. Dr. Harald Unkelbach [305] was hired away from the Heyde company. Harald Unkelbach took over management of the department "Z-Org. und EDV-Systeme" (organization and EDP systems) of Adolf Würth GmbH & Co. KG on February 1, 1979. The first big event after the successful reorganization of EDP and logistics within the Würth Group was a "paper and cheese party." "After a big cleaning-up session in all the rooms and on all the desks, we feasted on a lavish cheese buffet and later danced in the offices." [306]

The New EDP Manager

With Harald Unkelbach, member of the Board of Management today, the company hit the jackpot for a department that was, and still is, so enormously important for the business. In Dieter Krämer's opinion, it is one of Reinhold Würth's great entrepreneurial feats to have taken the field of EDP seriously from the beginning and to have turned it into an organizational unit that company management took responsibility for. Krämer believes that the competitive advantage of a selling company largely depends on EDP.[307]

The first project of the new EDP manager was the development of a concept for a public customs warehouse in cooperation with the Heilbronn Regional Finance Office and the Heilbronn principal custom-house. Comprehensive tracking of the movement of goods from receipt to shipping was necessary for this. Imports into the Federal Republic of Germany were exempt from customs clearance, provided the goods were exported again to the foreign Würth subsidiaries. Würth expected major savings from this measure.[308]

By 1983, warehouse capacity required further enlargement; a new, high-bay warehouse and warehousing for chemical articles were to be developed. In 1984, storage space was doubled. The new storage building also improved both the goods received and shipping processes, so that customers received their shipments faster. It was still in the 1980s that the company succeeded in stepping up the service degree to 96 per cent.

It goes without saying that start-up problems had to be overcome until these systems ran smoothly. The employees concerned were faced with real challenges for months. In the meantime, Jürgen Häckel, who is today responsible for information systems and on whose detailed records a large part of the present chapter is based, had, among others, joined the team.

Dr. Harald Unkelbach, member of the Board of Directors

In 1984, the EDP department also worked on a communications concept aimed at transmitting data between Group member companies and suppliers. For the time being, however, the foreign subsidiaries were to be enabled to transmit their orders electronically to Künzelsau, to shorten the lead-time for deliveries. Responsibility for this project rested with Peter Drexler, who had already been put in charge of coordinating the EDP issues of the foreign subsidiaries in 1976 [309] since many of these companies quickly reached dimensions that were impossible to handle without the use of computers.

In 1985, the Würth branch offices were integrated into the corporate EDP system, and a project for the branch offices called "automatic supply" [310] was started. Handling of special items was automated in 1986; in 1987, the goods received department was enlarged by a three-story building covering 38,000 ft² (3,500 m²), with an adjacent high-bay warehouse for bulky goods; and after 1988 bulky goods were handled separately. At the end of 1989, the company started thinking about the planned new distribution center north and the consequences for EDP technology. Electronic data exchange between customers and suppliers became increasingly popular, with growing talk of just-in-time production. The management discussed off-the-peg solutions, but these were not suitable, and so on the basis of existing standards at Würth customized company software was developed.

Construction of the new distribution center north started in 1990 and it came on stream in 1992. The costs for the fully automated pallet warehouse and two high-bay warehouses amounted to 60 million DM. On the part of the EDP system, everything went smoothly: four weeks before the deadline, everything was already under control in the new warehouses. The new inventory management systems for customer consignment stock, trunk stock, and branch offices also became operational. However, this solution would not last long: by 1984, the company had already started to think about an expansion of the distribution center north.

In 2004, roughly 620 employees in the field of logistics work in two shifts, achieving a service degree ranging between 97 and 99 per cent. Goods received handles about 350 tons of incoming goods every day, and between 85,000 and 90,000 item requests are processed every day. Orders are transmitted either directly by the customers or by the sales representatives via modem, using either the ADIS-sales force information system, fax machine, or telephone. [311]

Computer-Aided Purchasing and Selling

By the 1970s, price advantages in purchasing could only be achieved through sophisticated forward planning, so this area was gradually computerized, too. The company had started to develop a computer-controlled, automatic, materials-planning program [312] in 1979 that was supposed to identify, plan in advance, and calculate the optimal order quantities. The objective was to record the most favorable conditions of supply, and also alternative sources, orders on hold, and the most important article information. After all, a total of more than 30,000 different articles and almost 2,500 suppliers worldwide had to be handled.

There was no such program on the market at the time and so, as with the customer-supplier software, it had to be developed by Würth, something that constituted a major challenge. The EDP experts needed to understand the processes in purchasing first before being able to transform them into EDP operations. Adolf Würth GmbH & Co. KG was the first user of this system, but the Würth Group gradually started to branch out internationally, with the foreign Würth Companies also needing data processing applications for handling their business. [313]

However, there was more. 1982 marked the year of the introduction of Nixdorf word processing at Würth. Even before IBM had put its personal computer, or PC, on the market, Nixdorf had offered a forerunner, the microcomputer, a comparatively reasonable office computer. Gerhard Bugelnig from Würth Austria developed the necessary software for these Nixdorf-computers, since there were no ready-made programs for accounting available at the time. Developing the software was quite challenging, since the different requirements of the countries in which Würth was represented called for individual solutions. Between 1978 and 1981, Nixdorf systems were installed in France, Italy, The Netherlands, Belgium, Great Britain, and Kellner & Kunz in Austria, despite these problems. In 1984, the first IBM PCs were put on the market. A PC with 256 kB main memory and 2in x 8in disks with 128 kB capacity then cost 10,000 DM; Würth purchased the first DOS-PC with color screen at 8,000 DM in 1986. The advantage over the previous system: considerably higher working speed, fixed-disk storage, IBM compatibility, and a wide range of software such as Wordstar for word processing. From that moment on, the computerization of the offices made rapid progress. In 1989, a new department called "PC user service" was installed, which was responsible for training the staff and for defining standards and guidelines. At that time there were already 20 PCs in the bookkeeping department. One year later, the Nixdorf text system was completely replaced by PC-word processing with WordPerfect. EDP-based time and access control for the staff was introduced in the new administrative building in Künzelsau-Gaisbach in 1992. The employees were requested to wear an admission card everywhere they went, a request that was thought quite strange in the beginning.

Another important task for the EDP experts at Würth was preparing statistics for the top executives of the Group. The data being collected on an ongoing basis could increasingly be evaluated for the company. In 1989, a new dimension in networking was achieved with the Würth Information System, which was developed in cooperation with the University of Constance. Würth headquarters became a "data pool and information hub," [314] and it became possible to make objective comparisons of the individual Group member companies' performance.

Sales Representatives with Laptops

Over time, the number of sales representatives that the company had to look after had steadily increased, so it was decided to redefine and restructure the database to create an information and management system. A database for the collection of master data, key figures, and planning data was developed for the sales management department. It enabled the company to use a computer for drawing up the sales representative's profile, which so far had been prepared manually. Every change in order handling, however, required the generation of new databases and new programs. "The colleagues had to get used to completely new processes." On weekends, the new programs were tried out. [315]

Beginning in 1985, each sales representative was gradually issued with a so-called HHC, the hand-held computer that was the forerunner of today's notebook, for order handling. At the time they cost about 3,700 DM per unit and could only be programmed in a special language. An initial sales district was equipped with the new devices for trial; the data could be transmitted via acoustic coupler and telephone to Künzelsau, thus rendering mailing time and data collection superfluous. The managers in the sales force had been equipped with an information system – FISA – in 1989 that made it possible for them to analyze all relevant key figures among both the sales representatives and the customers.

The HHC were outdated after only a few years, so that the EDP-experts at Würth were forced to develop new software for the sales representatives in 1991 on the basis of the new laptop technology – the prices for far more efficient computers had in the meantime dropped considerably. Medium-term, the ADIS system – ADIS being an acronym for sales force information system – was supposed to be applied internationally, too, and so an international ADIS version was developed in 1994. As a first step, however, the prerequisites had to be created for "handling" 1,500 to 2,000 sales representatives who transmitted their orders to Adolf Würth GmbH & Co. KG all during the same period of time. [316]

A module for territory and route planning was added to ADIS in 1995 that helped the sales representatives to structure their work more efficiently. The company also started to research the possibility of transmitting data via mobile phone. Windows made its arrival in the sales force with the introduction of ADIS III in 1997. In 2000, the ADIS software was connected with the SAP system that had been introduced into the Group at the beginning of the 1990s. These changes ultimately saved a lot of work, yet always required comprehensive training for the staff.

Reinhold Würth was afraid that the creativity of the employees would be strangled by "overly rigid EDP processes firming up business operations:" "Customer service and service in general are limited by available EDP processes; initiative on the part of the staff is not only blocked, but even destroyed." [317] For this reason, the laptops of the sales representatives were replaced by desktops in 2003.

The company also developed EDP-service solutions for its customers. The so-called ORSYtel (order and system telephone) was developed following the ORSY-tradition, a complete PC-order system that was placed at the customers' disposal by Würth. The components: a shelf system for screws and accessories as well as a PC-order system with direct telephone link to Würth. 2,000 ORSYtel systems were installed in 1995.

"War for Ten Days" [318]

More and more qualified employees were needed by the company for expanding the field of logistics, for updating and developing programs, and for training the users. The training system in place at Würth did its part, with the new technology leading to new professions. In 1978, the first two apprentices were trained as data processing clerks. Young people were trained in business data processing (vocational academy) for the first time in 1989 and the DP clerk had now turned into the IT clerk. Later, computer scientists, information and telecommunication electronics engineers, and others could be found working at Würth. However, skilled staff and particularly programmers were often difficult to find, and were frequently hired away from other companies. Quite a few shied away from the location in Künzelsau. In the middle of the 1980s, Reinhold Würth said that EDP experts could sometimes only be convinced to join the company by adding a "desert allowance" to their salary. [319] Since the required staff was not only difficult to find, but also expensive, the company tried to find a way to obtain EDP services at a lower price at the end of the 1990s. In 1997, a group of people traveled to India to check if software developments could be purchased at more favorable conditions there.

There was, and still is, enormous potential for rationalization in the field of EDP. It contributes to higher productivity and therefore also to lower personnel costs. Technologies are developed at such breakneck speed, however, that the people responsible at Würth always have to carefully consider which trend to follow and where to identify long-term trends. EDP developments and their implementation are very expensive, and a company must carefully weigh its investments.

In 1975, the computing performance of the first EDP installation had already to be expanded, a process that would repeat itself constantly from that moment on. In 1979, the company already had 80 computer screens and had upgraded the IBM computer to 4 MB – a figure that fails to impress us today in view of the memory capacity of even the most inexpensive PCs, though at the time this represented a great leap forward.

For smaller subsidiaries, Würth started the introduction of EDP with PC with BASIC-programming in 1985, one example of this being order processing at Würth Construction.

A strategic DP study was commissioned for the overall Würth Group in 1986 that pointed the way for the next few years. It was decided to gear the Group to the Unix operating system medium-term. The advantage: this operating system worked very well on both small and large computers and facilitated the networking of computers by way of so-called client-server structures. "The organizational structure of the business determines the DP structures in the Group," was how Jürgen Häckel summarized this development for a professional journal.[320] Würth set up the first PC network in 1988 and three years later the PCs at Adolf Würth GmbH & Co. KG were networked throughout the company. As protocol, TCP/IP was established in all Würth networks that drastically reduced transmission time: instead of 8 hours, data from sales representatives could be transmitted in 15 minutes.

However, the management of the enormous data volume made possible by EDP sometimes also proved to be quite tricky. If its computers crash the whole company comes to a standstill – a situation that nobody can or wants to afford. The employees of the EDP department were and are requested to act quickly, identifying problems in advance and solving them. Data security has been a problem from the start, yet particularly since the 1990s such problems have become more frequent and more serious, owing to increased complexity and exposure to the Internet.

The year 1994 started with a data crash that kept several specialists busy around the clock for a number of days. In 1996, a database crash in the accounting department caused major problems. Everything there went down for ten long days, from August 13–23, 1996. Within the company this was described as a "war for ten days."[321] The crash occurred all of a sudden during the attempt to install a new backup system, and the magnetic tapes that held backup copies proved defective. Computer specialists in England were consulted who tried to restore the tapes – a very expensive project – yet they did not really succeed either. It was only ten days later that a parallel system could be established, which, however, was only able to restore the figures as of August 9. Within a period of few days the EDP staff therefore had to make a supreme effort to rework the missing entries. On September 7, the company was "up to date" again, with all systems operating smoothly. The reason for the overstretched magnetic tapes that had held the backup copies, however, remained a mystery.[322]

To avoid such problems in the future the hardware at Adolf Würth GmbH & Co. KG has been configured in such a way since 2001 that data are stored in two different DP centers. In an emergency, the second system can take over the function of the first one within 20 minutes.

The increasing use of the Internet also resulted in new risks. In 1997, a virus in the Internet that spread at terrific speed and knocked out almost the entire processes in both the offices and the warehouses caused major problems. This problem, however, was solved by having the staff work on the weekend. As a consequence, Würth attached increasing importance to antivirus programs, something that soon proved to be worthwhile. The notorious "I love you" virus could do no harm to Würth in 2000.

The year before, though, as Reinhold Würth complained[323], "at least 30 per cent of working time" had to be spent dealing with the infamous Y2K problem that kept EDP departments all over the world on their toes. The effort paid off, however, and Würth succeeded in overcoming this obstacle without serious difficulties. For years, the US term "Y2K" as synonym for the "year 2000" changeover problem was the talk of the town.

World Wide Würth

In the middle of the 1990s, Würth realized a future-oriented field of business in worldwide networking that would lead to a "completely new consumption pattern" in the long run. This is why Würth became active on the Internet for the first time in 1995. Together with industrial corporations, the Heilbronn University of Applied Sciences as well as Bausparkasse Schwäbisch Hall and Audi AG, a cooperative project was initiated aimed at "developing commercial application systems for the Internet." [324] For the first time the Annual Report 1994 was stored on a WWW-server and modified for the Internet. The competent employees also worked on a company presentation as well as product catalogs for the Internet, which offered the facility to place orders online and inquire about the status of the shipment. On April 20, 1996, the boss's birthday, Würth was represented on the Internet with a homepage of its own – a result of the cooperation between Würth and the so-called software lab at the Heilbronn University of Applied Sciences sponsored by 850,000 DM from the state of Baden-Württemberg. [325] In April 1998, a new Würth appearance in the Internet was started, which also marked the beginning of the Würth-Intranet that is intended to make daily work easier for the employees.

The Internet was and is becoming more and more important for companies. In contrast to the beginning, when businesses merely put a kind of self-projection on the Internet, Würth – like many other companies – is now concentrating on the possibilities of generating sales through the Internet and communicating with customers. In 1999, the company started to think about and discuss the issue of e-commerce: a Würth shop and the first online-shop for the Automotive Division.

Würth closely studies user behavior. The most important principle of all Web-activities was and is the question how customer wishes can be fulfilled long-term – not "what can we, the company, do?", but "what do our customers want?" [326] are the decisive issues.

It was particularly the collapse of the so-called new market in 2001 that resulted in the development of a completely new WüKO-online ordering system. Through competence and qualification in this field also, the company sought to achieve competitive advantage in a difficult situation in which customers increasingly requested electronically transmitted data and electronic communication. It was important to dovetail the online ordering system with that of internal order processing. In 2002, the design of the Würth website was taken a step further, even though it was decided to stick with tried and tested principles and only make small modifications. Now, the user can obtain information about the Group in general, at www.würth.com, and also about individual companies. There is a module that provides information about fire protection systems and relevant products the company carries in the range, as well as an electronic spare parts catalog. A new portal called "Commitment for Art and Culture" carries information on the activities of the Würth museums.

A problem is getting a standardized global design accepted; the foreign Würth Companies in part still present themselves individually.

Using the Company's Own Resources – Würth Software

Even though large software projects have in past months slid into crisis – they are not only extremely expensive, but, what is more, nobody is really surprised that they do not function properly anyway – Würth has in recent years successfully countered this development with a positive example.

In the early 1990s it was already foreseeable that "all businesses that did not thoroughly get to grips with the medium of electronic data processing (EDP) software would soon be left behind," [327] which is why Würth has time and again designed new plans for individual activities. According to Reinhold Würth, however, it was at the time not foreseeable if the future lay in the company's own solutions or in standard software. For this reason Würth opted for both approaches, one after the other. The company had already gathered experience with MSP/X, self-developed software based on Unix and relational databases that could be applied internationally – many large Würth Companies are still using it. For smaller companies, a solution based on a PC network of an existing package was modified. As a result, MSP/A was installed in 40 companies. [328]

COMPUTERS, NETWORKS AND PHOENIX
USING THE COMPANY'S OWN RESOURCES – WÜRTH SOFTWARE

A first project aimed at developing a software package for product management at Würth (AIDA), which was intended to replace the old systems in the middle of the 1990s, was halted again owing to insufficient fulfillment of the prerequisites, and the company decided to purchase non-Group products. It was only with the development of Würth Phoenix that the business accomplished the leap forward to become a supplier of complete IT packages.

Let us trace this development step by step. When it became clear at the end of the 1980s that the company urgently needed new software in the field of financial accounting, a project group was formed that was commissioned to develop an appropriate system – suitable not only for Adolf Würth GmbH & Co. KG, but also for smaller companies within the Group. This posed a rather difficult problem and the group failed in formulating the highly complex demands. The program R/3 by SAP based on Unix-hardware was expected for 1991 so that "the framework for a joint project" was defined together with the Walldorf-based software company. [329] Würth became SAP's VIP customer, with the changeover of the business to SAP R/3 starting after 1992. The staff working in the finance and EDP departments had to go to Walldorf for a few weeks for on-site training. In April 1993, Adolf Würth GmbH & Co. KG accounting was started with R/3 [330] – a huge success also for SAP. In July the program was started at Würth Denmark, too, and an R/3 congress in the Alma Würth Auditorium of Adolf Würth GmbH & Co. KG with 150 paying participants turned out to be a sweeping success. [331]

And yet, in the spring of 1994 Würth opted in favor of developing an individual organization and software concept geared toward the specific requirements of the company. It seemed to offer the best possibilities for "tailoring a system to the needs of Würth that will enable us to gain a competitive advantage through information technology in the years to come." [332]

The project, which went by the name of AIDA – Architecture of Information Systems for Development of Applications and Organization Structures – was supposed to start in 1995, but the group of experts involved met with unexpectedly serious difficulties. It was planned to have the entire project programmed in a net-based and object-oriented fashion – a programming technology that obliged the members of the project group to forget almost everything they had learned and applied so far. This completely new start was not only a very time-consuming process, but also the involvement of university graduates, who were a lot more familiar with these new technologies, resulted in conflict as had been expected. [333] To make things worse, there were too few tools on the market, and the available programming languages were still too unstable. Subsequently, the parameters of this project were tightened more and more – with incalculable consequences for its duration. Reinhold Würth did not expect it to be finished until 2002. [334]

So it was almost inevitable that by 1996 this ambitious plan had been put on ice . This decision was made easier by developments achieved by the external supplier SAP. "Intensive and fresh analysis of SAP's development environment has shown that it is nearly impossible for our Group to keep pace with SAP. After nights and nights of discussions and meetings, we have decided to develop the AIDA project with SAP technology in the future." [335] Many people were happy about this decision taken by FÜKO in 1997 because they had been afraid that AIDA would tie up too many resources that would be better invested in the "commercial and organizational aspects of our businesses." [336] Others had perceived the company to be moving in the direction of a Group-constrained software solution with AIDA and were relieved, too. However, some members of the AIDA-project group were deeply disappointed about the decision and left the company. Würth Italy, too, where Hubert Kofler was in charge of EDP, saw things in a different light. The company had always had good experience with customized software development, not least because this helped to save the sometimes astronomically high license fees and independent developments required less expensive hardware. [337]

The first pilot installation of SAP software at Würth Austria was a foretaste of the double-edged nature of the decision taken. The installation was quite difficult: "It needed too much expertise, time and capacity" [338] to modify the system. There was considerable demand for rework and adjustment to the specific requirements of Würth. It was particularly Würth's order-processing demands that could not be fulfilled by any standard software.

And yet, "external EDP software packages of the same type were installed at seven companies within the Würth Group between 1996 and 2000, which unexpectedly incurred high costs, more than 10 million DM on average per installation." [339] Independent businesses that would not have been able to rely on the support of group capital would either have gone bankrupt with such an action or would not have been able to finance it in the first place.

Würth Phoenix

In the summer of 1998, Reinhold Würth decided to appoint Hubert Kofler from Würth Italy, the committed advocate of independent software development, project manager of a program package to be developed independently. It was successfully completed in 2001 under the name of Würth Phoenix. Würth Phoenix GmbH had already been founded in Italy in the year 2000, with 50 employees on the payroll under the direction of Hubert Kofler. Reinhold Würth remarked: "We will develop our own software without becoming dependent on any software giant." [340]

With the modules "purchasing," "order processing," logistics, and "Speedy" – the successor of ADIS as international sales force system – purchasing, merchandise management, and order processing could now be handled. Experience gathered by many Group companies had shaped the development of the system.

Technically, the program package is based on Unix, Linux, and Windows operating systems and Java as programming language. Additionally, the object-oriented database, Versant, and the development system, Cobra, were used. [341] In 2002, when a book on the Phoenix success story was published by the Group's own publishing house, Swiridoff, Würth-Phoenix was already in use by Würth Italy and Würth Netherlands was in the process of implementing the system. During the FÜKO-conference 2003 in Kupferzell, Reinhold Würth said it was the objective to create planning security for new business first in the world of Würth. The prerequisite for this was a "clear commitment on the part of the companies as to the point in time of the planned installation of Phoenix." [342] Würth Phoenix is intended to become the standardized IT system in the Group, without the need for additional solutions. This is to speed up future centralization in the Würth Group's field of IT. The Phoenix Academy was established in Bad Mergentheim in November 2003 as a training facility for Würth employees.

Meanwhile, the range of Würth-Phoenix products is not only being installed at Würth Companies, but is also being offered to customers outside of Würth. The company wants to become a supplier in the market of business software, of which companies such as Microsoft, apart from the large-scale supplier SAP, have also recently sought to carve a piece for themselves. [343] This is why in recent years external sales have been increased by the acquisition of IT-companies and why a company called Portolan was purchased in 2004 that sells an accounting system reporting the highest sales figures worldwide after SAP. [344]

The customers – small, medium-sized, and large companies – are also offered consulting in process optimization as well as staff training, apart from the installation and maintenance of merchandise management and sales- force information systems.

On January 1, 2003, Würth Phoenix International B.V. and WIC-Consulting AG, having developed from Würth Finance and the IT department of Würth Holding in Chur, merged to become Würth Phoenix B.V. [345] Meanwhile, Würth Phoenix has 200 employees working in such different international locations as Germany, Hungary, Italy, The Netherlands, Switzerland, and China.

Würth Phoenix is intended to generate 50 per cent of sales externally in 2006. With the aim of working more cost-efficiently in the future, the development of software will gradually be transferred to Asia. [346] The company plans on having 50 developers working in Shanghai by the end of 2004. [347]

"As Much EDP as Necessary, but Not One Tiny Bit More!" [348]

As much as Reinhold Würth pushed ahead with the development of the Würth Group in the direction of becoming a software development company and as much as he – after the long-forgotten start-up difficulties of 1970 – realized and promoted the significant role that EDP is playing for his company, he also holds a critical view of the process. Not everything that is feasible actually makes sense in his opinion. This is why, on the occasion of the Congress of the Würth Group in Dubai in the summer of 2003, he spoke out in favor of a more humane and more people-oriented corporate culture: "We need to revive the old values that our Group is based on; we need to woo back our employees on the basis of honesty and being role models, with optimism and zest for life, with boundless willingness to perform and by showing them that we see the job as our hobby. In this time, which is characterized by far-reaching sociological changes, by more and more leisure time, by changes on an intellectual and even a religious level, our employees are in part caught in a vast and limitless vacuum of insecurity that very clearly has something to do with the excessive computerization of our businesses. It is this mechanization of our companies, the icy and pitiless disturbance of Würth's corporate culture by computer science, that finally results in our employees' incapability of identifying themselves with our company and the fact that they feel much more at home in their leisure-time activities and on their vacations than in our companies. Ladies and gentlemen, in your function as managers you are requested and challenged to restore the balance between things that are necessary and things that are feasible. Over the last 15 years, computer science has been insidiously seizing power in all our businesses, callously, unemotionally: creativity was killed mercilessly in favor of brainless processes and organizational forms that have turned our group of companies into a mechanical, Disneyland-like dinosaur which, at the touch of a button, flashes and grunts, roars and wags its tail, yet lacks human warmth, shared mirth, sensitivity, enthusiasm, and zeal." [349]

9 THE WÜRTH IDEA FOR THE 80s: SATISFIED EMPLOYEES! [350]

The 80s

In the decade between 1980 and 1990, it became obvious that the Würth Group could now reap the rewards of the reorganization measures that had been initiated since the middle of the 1970s. The "Happy Days" of 1985 when the company celebrated its 40th anniversary, which, as always, coincided with Reinhold Würth's "big 0" – he turned 50 – symbolize this development. The planning of a new administration building for Adolf Würth GmbH & Co. KG also illustrated the success of the company.

As in previous years, Reinhold Würth and his colleagues focused on issues of management development, marketing, and personnel development.

Reinhold Würth, who had started to deal with management issues in the mid-1970s when he had first come in contact with Professor Tietz from Saarbrücken, now summarized his thoughts and ideas, first for the staff working in the Würth Group, but also for the general public. Particularly since the award of the Marketing Prize to Adolf Würth GmbH & Co. KG in 1989, his popularity as speaker on issues of business strategy had greatly increased.

The second focus of his entrepreneurial thoughts was safeguarding and shaping the future of his company after his time. As early as 1987, business assets had been transferred to several family foundations, which created the prerequisite for further growth and prosperity of the Würth

> "Reinhold Würth's secrets of success? In my opinion, it is his concentration on the 'perfection of things trivial,' that is, doing what's self-evident and doing it perfectly, and his courage to simplify things in an actually inadmissible fashion, putting complex and contradictory matters in a non-academic nutshell."
>
> Dieter Krämer, former FÜKO-Member

Group unhindered by possible unforeseeable inheritance disputes within the family.

The Opening of the Wall and Continuity – Economy and Politics in the 80s" [351]

At the beginning of the 1980s, the relationship between the two ruling parties of the social-liberal coalition was no longer peaceful, owing in particular to differences in opinion regarding both economic and fiscal issues. This led to a breaking-off in the summer of 1982. The Schmidt government was brought down by a vote of non-confidence. The political constellation changed permanently when the Greens joined the Bundestag for the first time in 1983 and were able to put down roots there. However, triggered by controversies on issues such as NATO-rearmament and the deployment of Pershing intermediate-range ballistic missiles, the political parties saw themselves confronted with the so-called citizens' action groups that developed out of people's dissatisfaction with the ruling political party system. The efforts of people working in these new social movements, though, were mainly targeted at social injustices in people's immediate environment and were not really aimed at a fundamental change in society. Only the peace movement and the protest against the expansion of nuclear energy constituted general movements. The issue of environmental protection was increasingly integrated into official politics, not least because of the disaster at the nuclear power station in Chernobyl, Ukraine, in April 1986. Since that time, no nuclear power station has been built in Germany.

The fact that the Republicans gained strength and achieved more than seven per cent of the votes both in the elections for the European Parliament and for the Berlin Parliament in 1989 gave the parties hit by political affairs such as the "Flick scandal" a hard time.

In view of the dramatic and unexpected events of East-West German unification in 1989/90, however, these matters ranked second in the field of politics at the end of the decade. After Mikhail Gorbachev had created the prerequisites for the opening of the Eastern bloc and the Fall of the Berlin Wall in November 1989, the effects were felt in Baden-Württemberg primarily in the form of an influx of thousands of GDR citizens and so-called "late repatriates" from the Soviet Union.

Economically speaking, the 80s were initially characterized by a global crisis in the period 1980 to 1982. The economic concept of the

Christian Democrats and the Liberals in Bonn was based on a consolidation of the budget by cutting social spending and promoting a tax policy favoring businesses. The motto was "less state and more market." The economic upswing that soon followed was initially based on brisk domestic demand, but foreign trade had also been responsible for positive impulses since the middle of the 1980s. The regional focus of foreign trade was still on Europe as before: European countries accounted for more than 80 per cent of imports and exports. Favored by the Eastern Treaties, East-West trade in particular showed higher-than-average growth rates. The country, though, did not succeed in bringing down the unemployment rate, which was a structural problem related to Germany's change from an industrial to a service economy. The number of unemployed rose dramatically and remained at roughly nine per cent until the end of the 1980s, a circumstance that not even the "reunification boom" could address. Unskilled labor was hit particularly hard. Expenses for supplementary welfare benefits in Baden-Württemberg increased by 60 per cent between 1982 and 1988, causing the communities great problems.

The crisis-ridden development in the 1970s had coincided with speedy technological change characterized by the advance of the so-called "new technologies." The "third industrial revolution" as the triumphant advance of the new technologies was also called, fundamentally changed both people's private and professional lives.

The population of the Federal Republic of Germany increased from 61 to 62.7 million during the 1970s and 1980s. The decline in the birthrate, which gives cause for concern today, and the increase in life expectancy were already identified then, but compensated for by migration patterns. The Federal Republic of Germany had de facto become a country with an open immigration policy, mainly because of the work-related immigration of so-called foreign workers from southern Europe and southeast Europe, of which Turkish nationals constituted the biggest group. In the meantime, many families had followed so that they became a permanent part of the German population.

Despite unemployment and crises, prosperity increased – at least for many. Disposable income per person in the Federal Republic of Germany rose by more than 50 per cent between 1970 and 1991. One of the most striking characteristics is the increase in the number of cars, which very clearly symbolizes the demand for individual freedom. After the number of cars had tripled in the 1960s, it doubled in the Federal Republic of Germany between 1970 and 1990: from nearly 14 to 30.7 million.

The Company

Even though the economic development was not altogether positive, especially at the beginning of the decade – people complained about high oil prices, a tendency toward economic recession, inflationary trends, rising interest rates, and more than two million unemployed in the Federal Republic of Germany – Würth continued to achieve good overall results worldwide. In 1980, the Group generated sales of more than 550 million DM, of which Adolf Würth GmbH & Co. KG produced more than 200 million DM.[352] The pre-tax operating result, however, only made up 2.4 per cent of sales since the Automotive Division in Germany was particularly hard hit by the recession.

Despite a record number of company failures, Adolf Würth GmbH & Co. KG reported a further six per cent sales growth in 1982. By that time, Würth had for more than two years ranked among the top 500 German companies in terms of sales, and in 1983 the sales volume in Germany was higher than all the other countries where Würth was represented taken together. The management thought long and hard about how the productivity of the company could be stepped up, something that would have a positive effect on profit. Apart from the opening of many new branch offices in the 1980s, the divisionalization started at the end of the 1970s was continued. In 1983, the craft sector was once again subdivided into Wood and Metal. The business also tried to reduce costs in the field of staff. After a hiring freeze in the internal administration at the beginning of the decade, the Würth Group recovered its "dynamism of the founding years" only in 1984.[353] The Würth Group continued to grow despite dollar and stock market crises. In 1985 – the Würth anniversary year – the business exceeded its first billion in sales; in 1986, sales of Adolf Würth GmbH & Co. KG alone increased by 58.4 million DM; and 1987 turned into yet another "record year"[354]: Würth achieved global sales of 1.3 billion DM with roughly 6,000 employees.[355]

At the end of the 1980s, low interest rates encouraged domestic demand. The economic situation was positive, with Würth reporting further sales growth both at home and abroad. In the construction sector, business was particularly good, and the worldwide production of cars reached a record level for the fourth consecutive year. Finance costs and oil prices had dropped to a low level again, such that Reinhold Würth was very optimistic about his plans for capturing a further market share. In his opinion, the as yet untapped market potential was enormous, even though he identified certain risks in the increasing scarcity of energy and raw materials as well as in the unclear international political situation. [356] Since the middle of the decade his entrepreneurial vision had therefore been initially geared toward achieving two billion DM in sales in 1992. In 1987, however, he formulated his "Vision 2000" in view of the rapid development of the Würth Group and predicted ten billion DM in sales toward the turn of the millennium.

"The Fast Ones Eat Up the Slow"

The successes enjoyed by Würth were the result of hard work. In the 1980s, the company managed successfully to follow the principle formulated by Reinhold Würth that he had taken over from the Swiss businessman Nicolas Hayek, "the fast ones eat up the slow," and to maintain the momentum of the Würth Group. The business again distanced itself from the competition at the end of the 1980s, in the transition from the first to the second billion in sales. In this situation, additional external consultants were involved in the business. The management-consulting firm, McKinsey & Partners, analyzed the Würth Group and was highly impressed. Together with the management of Würth, McKinsey designed approaches to divisionalization – successfully carried out in the 1990s – that was aimed at further exploiting the market potential.

Meanwhile, the areas of purchasing, customer satisfaction, and personnel were important steps on the way to greater success. The purchasing department at Würth was optimized further. At the time, the staff sourced products in Asia, and also in the extant Eastern bloc, Poland and the GDR. However, 75 per cent of the products sold by Würth were manufactured in the Federal Republic of Germany in the middle of the 1980s, with only 15 per cent coming from Europe and 10 per cent from other parts of the world. [357]

Purchasing matters were becoming increasingly complex both in respect of the number of products, which had reached 30,000, and the number of suppliers, which now stood at 2,500. Since 1980, this area has been centralized throughout the Group, so that under the direction of Werner Rau and with EDP support more favorable conditions can be enjoyed all the time, following the motto that Reinhold Würth had already quoted in his 1975 corporate philosophy: "Profit lies in the purchasing of goods." [358]

The profit generated by the company has been the focus at Würth from the start, a circumstance that resulted in an equity ratio of almost 50 per cent that Würth has available today, which is quite unusual for German businesses. The solid growth of the Würth Group facilitated the issue of corporate bonds at the end of the 1980s, which helped to finance further growth. Time and again, expansion in the field of logistics required large investments. In 1990, the company was forced to start building a second distribution center, since the add-ons to the Würth distribution center completed in 1983 and 1897, a high-bay warehouse and a warehouse for chemicals as well as a new goods receiving department, had been outgrown after just a few years – despite the introduction of a driverless transport system in 1988.[359] Permanent lack of space, however, had not kept Adolf Würth GmbH & Co. KG from achieving a service degree of 96 per cent by 1986.

The foreign Würth Companies increased in size in the 1980s, too. In 1982, Würth Italy made a leap forward to become a really "big" company[360], while in the same year mobile data collection was introduced at Würth Italy, France, and Austria, and Würth Italy's branch office in Rome was officially opened. In 1983, Würth Canada, South Africa, Finland, and Holland moved into new premises, followed by the USA, Belgium, and Norway in 1984, Würth Austria in 1985, and Würth Great Britain, Switzerland, and Brazil in 1986. In 1987, the new corporate building of Würth Spain was completed, Würth Sweden moved from Stockholm to Avesta, and Würth Italy opened a new central warehouse in Neumarkt.

In Greece and in Australia new foreign subsidiaries were founded in 1981, followed by Würth Ireland in 1982.

Companies in the field of assembly and fastener technology were acquired in Great Britain and Canada in 1986. 1987 marked the year of the foundation of Würth Malaysia, the purchase of a company in Japan, and the foundation of Würth Iceland, Malta, New Zealand, and Uruguay; in 1988, the company Fime S.r.l. Verona, one of Würth Italy's competitors, was bought. At the end of the decade the companies in Argentina, Taiwan, and Turkey were set up. To be able to manage this impressive number of foreign subsidiaries – in 1989, 46 companies outside of the Federal Republic of Germany in 30 countries belonged to the Würth Group – Günter Theurer and Dieter Krämer presented a controlling system for the foreign subsidiaries to Reinhold Würth in 1986.

"Happy Days"

In 1985, the year of the company anniversary, Würth exceeded one billion DM in sales for the first time, though the costs involved meant that the Advisory Board was not altogether happy about the profit.[361]

A huge celebration was organized in Künzelsau-Gaisbach with the theme of "Happy Days:" the 40th anniversary of the business and Reinhold Würth's 50th birthday. For three days, from May 10–12, company premises were the scene of magnificent celebrations. Five thousand people were invited to join the party, among them representatives from the world of politics and finance, but also Würth employees and customers. As is still a tradition with Würth today, the celebrations were extensive, with multimedia and a circus, talk shows and classical concerts, fairgrounds and fireworks. It was an event that many people still remember very fondly. As a sign of appreciation of his achievements, Reinhold Würth was awarded the Order of Merit of the Federal Republic of Germany by Philipp Jenninger, President of the Bundestag.

Anticipation in the tent of Circus Krone (1985)

The construction of a new corporate headquarters building directly following the splendid celebration was intended as a symbolic expression of the new corporate culture. In the summer of 1985, an architectural competition for the new administrative headquarters of Adolf Würth GmbH & Co. KG was organized.

The subject of the competition was the "design of an administrative building connected with a communications and exhibition space appropriately representing the headquarters of a worldwide operating group of companies." The "contemporary architectural ideas" were supposed to be "poignantly expressed" [362] – similar to the building designed by Sep Ruf in the 1970s. The jury, which Reinhold Würth and members of the management also belonged to, opted in favor of the design by Siegfried Müller and Maja Heuser-Djordjevic.

Start of construction work and laying of the foundation stone would have to wait until June 1, 1989, however, because a replacement for a warehouse had to be built first, as the warehouse had to be vacated to make room for the new headquarters. The new administrative building was completed in 1991. In the planned, integrated exhibition space, the Würth Collection was to be put on display. Reinhold Würth, who had started collecting works of art back in the 1960s following an idea by his friend and photographer, Paul Swiridoff, sold his private collection to the company in 1987, thus marking the start of the era of public relations through the arts at Würth. Apart from Reinhold Würth, who in his function as collector is still behind all the Würth art campaigns and purchases of artworks, C. Sylvia Weber, who originally joined Würth as librarian in the middle of the 1980s, is responsible for the development of the art collection.

Reinhold Würth initiated yet another important development in 1985. To be equipped for company anniversaries and for company histories to be written in the future, company archives were set up at Adolf Würth GmbH & Co. KG, following his explicit wish. In the PAP ("Policy and Procedure,") the internal set of rules, he remarked on this topic: "A knowledge of the history is a precondition for an understanding of the present. History, myths, and symbols represent the tradition of the company's culture and code." This marked the beginning of the era of the "company histories:" all top Würth executives were requested to report regularly on the events in their daily work from now on. The reports would then be put in the archives. [363] "Just as every village has a 'museum of local history and culture' to stand in awe of itself and its history, every company should keep some 'historical items' with a company cultural value […]." [364] Würth central archives developed out of a crate with documents, recalls C. Sylvia Weber; it also serves as filing department and is today managed professionally by the historian Ludger Drüeke.

Products and Customers

As impressive as it was for the general public to see the celebrations and notice the company's opening up toward the outside, Würth customers were interested in other things, too. First of all, they concentrated on prices and the quality of the articles sold by Würth. The company was interested in achieving the highest possible prices and improving its profit situation, yet customers had to be convinced by high quality and perfect service. Würth therefore went to a lot of effort to permanently improve quality in many areas of the business. After all, the company had almost 250,000 customers worldwide by the middle of the 1980s, each of whom was supposed to be supplied better and faster all the time. In 1985, Würth recorded 40,000 customer contacts daily around the world. [365]

Quality control had been developed further since 1982, and Adolf Würth GmbH & Co. KG succeeded in considerably stepping up the service degree again owing to the use of so-called Hand-Held-Computers (HHC) in the sales force, starting in 1985. "As a consequence, merchandise reached the customers on average two days earlier," [366] and whoever wanted to pick up smaller quantities himself or decided not to wait for the visit of the Würth sales representative could drive over to one of the service depots that Würth continued to open up in the 1980s. Whereas there had only been 18 Würth branch offices in 1981, there were 30 just seven years later.

Würth attached importance to the continuous improvement of products. The R&D department run by Karl Weidner presented a number of new items. In 1981, almost 40 per cent of overall sales were generated with products that had not featured in the range 5 years previously.[367] This percentage increased, reaching 50 per cent by 1987.[368] The "Master" brand was created in 1981 for high-quality power and pneumatic tools. In 1984, Würth launched newly-developed bonding agents for bodywork technology and new types of screws – ECO-Fast and JAMO – that helped customers to save time. The latter were manufactured in Würth's own SWG company – Schraubenwerk Gaisbach, where the largest European range of chipboard screws was produced. Research in the field of ergonomic tools played an important role at Würth, too, one example of this being the range of nippers with new handles that was developed in cooperation with the Fraunhofer Institute.

Always a role model: Reinhold Würth stocking an ORSY rack (1995)

Würth closely monitored technical innovations in the field of assembly and fastening technology all over the world and aimed to offer customers a comprehensive product range for the solution of all types of fastener and assembly-related problems.

For quality inspection and quality assurance, the company further invested in corporate testing labs that were in part equipped with testing devices that had been developed by the company itself.[369] Environmental protection was an issue for Würth, too. In 1987, more than 200 chemical products had been changed over to environmentally-friendly propellants.[370] To be able to do customer-oriented research and development, a Customer Advisory Board as well as a Product Advisory Board[371] staffed by sales representatives had been established at Würth in 1980, whose aim was to provide fresh ideas for innovative product development and the set-up of product ranges. Another project aimed at customer commitment was investing in particularly loyal customers. From 1987,

Würth appointed good customers so-called "partner customers." These businesses received a special certificate and the wives of the owners were given a bouquet of flowers. The 2,600 partner businesses registered by the end of 1988 received the "Partner Magazine" every three months and were invited to special partner events with celebrations on company premises. To make sure that all Würth customers learned to appreciate the company not only in its role as supplier of goods, but also in its function as supplier of information, the sales representatives were trained as product consultants, starting in the middle of the 1980s. [372]

In 1982, Würth offered its customers a completely new sales model with the development of the ORSY rack. [373] This metal shelf system, invented by Würth's own product development department, was tailored to the specific needs of the individual customer and could be stacked with boxes specifically designed for this purpose. An important aspect in this connection: the customer rented this ORSY rack, and a Würth sales representative dropped by at regular intervals to reorder depleted items. This model of customer commitment, which proved to be very successful for Würth, also contributed to higher sales. Twenty-five thousand shelf systems had been put up by 1990. [374] For the customers it was a relief not to have to deal with ordering the products supplied by Würth any longer, sales being partly automated in that way. One prerequisite, though, was regular service visits by a sales representative.

Focus on Staff – Satisfied Employees

Successful customer commitment could not be achieved without qualified and motivated employees; this was one of the preconditions for achieving planned sales and profit growth, apart from increasing staff productivity with the help of EDP and new sales methods.

Human labor was valuable – and expensive. Reinhold Würth and his managers realized that this was one of the company's opportunities for success that had to be developed further. The basis of Reinhold Würth's thinking was that the human being must always be given priority over the matter, despite all rationalization measures and despite his exhortation addressed to the employees to think "in terms of seconds." [375]

And yet, it was not always easy to recruit qualified personnel, and for this reason further qualifications, motivation, and rewards for good performance were introduced to act as incentives for further efficiency increases.

The people in charge of personnel were preoccupied by the realization that staff fluctuation, predominantly in the sales force, cost the company a great deal of money. The hiring of a new sales representative equaled the value of investment capital amounting to approximately 500,000 DM [376], and so every unnecessary fluctuation had to be avoided in the interests of the business. The performance requirements of the Würth sales representatives were high, and the same applied to their income's dependence on success in sales. The basic salary merely constituted a small proportion of the sales representatives' overall income, and sales manager Karl Specht remembers that he always showed understanding for the problems of the sales representatives. The salary of the Würth sales representatives was generally high, but not everybody could cope with the psychological burden of an unsuccessful day in the field: "The job can be pretty tough sometimes." [377] If the situation was aggravated by problems with the superior, the performance often lagged behind the expectations of the company. At the beginning of the 1980s, per-capita sales achieved at Würth were at the lower end of the scale compared to wholesalers operating in other industries. It was Reinhold Würth's objective to change this situation and to improve the figures. [378] This was supposed to be supported by such measures as the presentation of the Würth Honor Pins and the establishment of the Würth Success Club in 1987, which rewarded particularly successful sales representatives with incentive trips.

Not least because of the use of EDP, the sales figures of every working day could now be compared with those of the corresponding day of the previous year and with planned targets. This opened up new possibilities for controlling the sales force.

    An external consultant who had dealt with the sales representatives of Adolf Würth GmbH & Co. KG within the framework of training sessions at the beginning of the 1980s came to the conclusion that only about half of the sales representatives were really excellent. This was also confirmed by Reinhold Würth, who closely monitored the work of the sales force. [379] Of course the conditions were not the same everywhere, but research had shown that some sales representatives were under psychological pressure and, as a consequence, experienced failure in the field and suffered damage to their health. It was mainly the behavior and attitude of many superiors that was criticized by the sales representatives. [380] Quite a few area managers merely concentrated on closing deals instead of leading and supporting their sales representatives. Instead of being motivated, many felt insulted and criticized all the time. Karl Specht, however, always considered it one of his responsibilities to show his sales representatives the way to more success, to higher sales, and to more new business, and to encourage them on an ongoing basis. [381]

"A successful field service crew can also never be controlled from a warm bunker back in the homeland and thus motivated to work;" [382] for this reason Reinhold Würth insisted on better supervision of mainly the area managers "to convey a more outlined, neater structure and a suitable amount of control to the field service organization of Würth KG." [383]

Improved further training and qualification of the sales representatives was the second component of the concept aimed at stepping up the performance of the sales force. New sales representatives who before had only received two weeks' training were now granted three months of product and field training. They were given the opportunity to get to know corporate headquarters and, together with their wives, were invited to Künzelsau for a weekend, all expenses paid. During the three-month training period the company paid guaranteed salaries with the result that the fluctuation in the sales force dropped considerably. In retrospect, Reinhold Würth evaluated this prolonged training period as one of the best investments made in his lifetime. [384]

The demands made on the sales representatives working for Würth had to be seen in the context of the services of the company: a market-conforming product range, top-quality products, and very high readiness to deliver. The sales representatives should not have to justify themselves vis-à-vis the customers for defects in Würth products or lack of services rendered by the company. The "allegedly puzzling" [385] sales price system often criticized by sales representatives was supposed to be simplified by a better method of customer classification that also guaranteed fair treatment of the customers. Those who ordered higher quantities and placed a higher number of orders would be granted preferential rates. The same principle applied to the sales representatives: good performance was supposed to be paid well, but better performance earned a higher reward. The lion's share of their income was still a performance-oriented portion based on sales commission and target attainment bonus. The successes of the new training model became obvious very quickly: monthly sales of the sales representatives increased considerably, and Reinhold Würth also recommended this training model, tested at Adolf Würth GmbH & Co. KG, to all the other established Group member companies. [386]

However, Reinhold Würth did not only focus on the sales force, but also on the in-house staff. The management in Künzelsau was particularly sensitive to issues regarding the working climate, since in the 1980s it was very difficult to find qualified employees in the region. Self-realization and quality of life were the catchwords supposed to guarantee a good working atmosphere. Flexitime without attendance recording introduced in Künzelsau at the end of the 1980s as well as the "corporate culture teams" expected to come up with suggestions for "a cheerful, trusting, and calculable working climate" [387] contributed to this aim. A questionnaire surfaced incentives that promoted staff willingness to perform.

In the in-house sector, too, the individual's productivity and performance increase was prioritized. The principle of performance having applied in the sales force from the start was to be utilized in the administration, too, and so the company started to appoint the "employee of the month" around 1986. From 1987, in-house employees received a bonus of 100 DM provided Adolf Würth KG achieved the monthly target. Würth also focused on further training and qualifications; last, but not least, the speedy development of EDP required keenness and eagerness to learn on the part of the staff.

Growth through Diversification

Apart from the principle of multiplication in the sales force, the more intensive penetration of the market with more and more sales representatives and more clearly separated divisions, as well as multiplication by way of establishing more foreign Würth Companies, Reinhold Würth from the very beginning considered the acquisition of companies to be an instrument of further growth, too. This was another way of opening up new business and new markets.

Initially, Würth had predominantly acquired screw-wholesaling companies. In May 1980, the 11th meeting of the Advisory Board decided to merge five of the acquired and competing subsidiaries into RECA NORM: Detmering KG, Hans Zander KG, and the companies Schrauben Listl, Schrauben Schmid, and Schrauben Müller. The objective was to "save costs through synergy effects," but very soon after the merger of the Reca-subsidiaries a "very emotional discussion about in-house competition" [388] started since the business segments of RECA NORM and Adolf Würth GmbH & Co. KG were largely identical. And yet, Reinhold Würth was of the opinion that the best competition was in-house competition: it not only stimulated business, but also "emotional waves" within the company. As long as the competing Reca Companies belonged to Adolf Würth GmbH & Co. KG from an administrative point of view, though, this circumstance occasionally caused negative friction. The organizational separation from Adolf Würth GmbH & Co. KG was only completed in 1986 when the business moved to a new Reca building in Kupferzell. [389] RECA NORM now had an independent administration, independent purchasing, and a logistics center of its own. Other companies that had in part been acquired by Würth during the 1970s were Baier & Michels GmbH & Co. KG that – being close to going bankrupt – had been taken over in 1973, IMS Verbindungstechnik GmbH & Co. KG, established in 1981 by Reinhold Würth's younger brother, Klaus-Frieder Würth and incorporated into the Würth Group in 1985, the tool and machine tool trading company Hommel Hercules that has been reorganized completely since being taken over in 1988, and the hardware and tool trading company Sartorius whose business was profitable when sold to Würth in 1989. [390] Companies were also acquired outside of Germany. Reinhold Würth bought Kellner & Kunz AG in Vienna in 1978 through Würth Holding, a wholesaling company selling screws and standard parts – a highly problematic acquisition in the beginning since the work of the Würth management was complicated by fraud and corruption on the part of the old management team [391] S. Kisling & Cie. AG in Zurich was acquired in 1980.

Companies working in other branches of industry, too, belonged to the Würth Group from very early on. On June 1, 1970, Würth Construction was founded, which, after losses of 10 million DM in 1983 and internal problems owing to unreliable employees, was closed down in 1984. According to Rolf Bauer, this was "a novelty in the Würth Group." [392]

The car dealership Autodienst Schubert GmbH & Co. KG was in charge of supplying and repairing the many Würth cars. In 1987, Adolf Würth GmbH & Co. KG took over Panorama Hotel in Waldenburg and had it renovated. Guests of Würth Group could now be accommodated in style at the hotel.

Schraubenwerk Gaisbach

All company acquisitions – whether profitable or in need of reorganization from the start – required very high commitment on the part of the Würth managers, as will be illustrated in the following two examples: SWG – Schraubenwerk Gaisbach – and Würth Elektronik.

Screw production within Würth had already begun at the end of November 1958, with three machines located in the basement of the company building at the Künzelsau railroad station that was enlarged the same year. In 1962, the company built a production hall in Gaisbach, and in 1966, SWG – Schraubenwerk Gaisbach – was spun off as independent enterprise.

However, business did not develop as expected in the long run, and so Reinhold Würth commissioned Rolf Bauer to support SWG in 1975. [393] In that year the business had incurred losses of almost one million DM, with 50 employees having to be dismissed and taken over by Adolf Würth GmbH & Co. KG.

Reinhold Würth expected Rolf Bauer to reorganize the company during two half days of the week, yet for the latter a project started that would take up more and more of his working time. On the other hand, he acquired all the necessary skills and qualifications – learning by doing – as the person in charge of the reorganization of a company, qualifications he would put to good use in similar cases in the future. In retrospect, Rolf Bauer considers this to be "an interesting field of activity" that he is still responsible for in the Würth Group. [394]

> "A manager employed by a company who has to answer to controlling bodies has the advantage that his decisions are shared, yet he also has the disadvantage that he cannot act on the spur of the moment."
>
> Rolf Bauer, deputy spokesman of the Board of Directors

Time and again Würth thought of closing down SWG, since the brass screws and nuts manufactured there could be purchased at much more favorable prices in the Far East. "Sometimes I no longer believed that this company would go on existing" [395] recalls Rolf Bauer, who took his job very seriously. In 1981, after lots of internal difficulties, he had to take over management of the business completely. In 1988/89, the company moved to new premises in Waldenburg. Initially, the investment in new production facilities and a fully automated warehouse in Waldenburg caused the company to go into the red again. And yet, Bauer succeeded again this time, too, with a reorganization concept based on two pillars. He drastically increased the prices and at the same time the service degree of the company, which latter he managed to step up to almost 99 per cent.

Würth Elektronik

Rolf Bauer's second major project during these years was Würth Elektronik, which started as a department of Adolf Würth KG in 1971. [396]

THE WÜRTH IDEA FOR THE 80s: SATISFIED EMPLOYEES!
WÜRTH ELEKTRONIK

Reinhold Würth realized that electronics was a modern technology that could become another profitable field of business for his company. Two engineers were appointed to develop electronic measuring devices, but one soon switched over to producing printed circuit boards instead. Customers got interested in the project, and so the company produced and sold these. Würth Elektronik became an independent company in 1975.

Rolf Bauer relates that Würth Elektronik is the outcome of a typical entrepreneurial decision.[397] Reinhold Würth had immediately put his idea regarding electronics into action by establishing the department and, despite all difficulties and also objections on the part of his corporate Advisory Board, he stuck to his decision. Meanwhile, the success of the company has proven him right.

For a number of years people were very skeptical concerning Würth Elektronik. After all, Reinhold Würth wanted to put down roots in a totally alien industry. Even though Würth Elektronik never was a business in need of reorganization in the opinion of Rolf Bauer, the company incurred losses around 1980. As was also the case with SWG, many of the problems were related to the management. Furthermore, there was not enough space, and investments had to be made if the business were to be successfully developed further. In 1987, it was decided to erect a new company building in Niedernhall, even though banks criticized the high investment volume of 20 million DM. Sales of the scale that had become a tradition with Würth could for the time being not be expected of such a manufacturing company. However, Rolf Bauer worked very hard for his project and for a certain time also took over management of the company himself. Looking back, he explains his success in terms of his communication skills, since he lacked in-depth knowledge of the industry. Occasionally, he spent 80 to 90 per cent of his working time at Würth Elektronik. With the help of many one-on-one talks and by making the business more transparent – the staff always knew for whom they had just finished this or that project – Rolf Bauer created an atmosphere that motivated everybody to join forces despite the start-up difficulties. Every morning at nine o'clock sharp he met with the most important people, one of his most successful measures in the reorganization business. He cultivated this type of communication in other companies, too, even if the focus was more on motivation than on factual issues there. Hardly ever did he spend time in his office; most of the time he could be found talking to staff members or customers. Since the products manufactured by Würth Elektronik did not fit in with Würth's core business, Bauer time and again had to vindicate himself vis-à-vis the corporate Advisory

Board. The members of this body urged Würth to sell the business all the more since there were people interested in buying it. However, Reinhold Würth opposed this suggestion; he also supported Rolf Bauer when the latter was heavily attacked by Georg Krupp, member of the Advisory Board, in 1990. The stubbornness shown by Reinhold Würth and Rolf Bauer paid off: today, Würth Elektronik is a profitable member of the Würth Group with more than 800 employees. [398]

Management with Visions

In the 1980s, Reinhold Würth increasingly focused on management techniques and on what he called "management culture." [399] "Management signifies modifying subject matter to the benefit of the company aim." [400] It was this company aim that needed to be redefined so that over the coming years employees' ways of thinking and acting could be positively guided in the direction of target attainment.

In 1983, during a conference in Nice, Reinhold Würth took stock: "We in the Federal Republic of Germany have intentionally launched a relatively wide attack on the market by means of diversification and the purchase of new companies. At the same time, we quite consciously put up with the disadvantage that even the management was not able to fully digest these "large bites", so to speak, in the short term. By means of hard work, I and the German managements have nevertheless succeeded in towing the German company group into the safe waters of success." [401] His company was now increasingly being noticed by the public, with his list of successes becoming quite respectable.

What Reinhold Würth aimed at now was setting a different priority in the image of the Würth Group. He wanted to move away from the reputation of being an unrelenting conqueror of the market in the direction of being perceived as a solid market leader. The seller's market of the 1950s and 1960s had meanwhile turned into a buyer's market. Quality and company profile became more important.

"I am not afraid to admit that, in the 60s and 70s, we sometimes elbowed ourselves into the market with quite rough and ready methods, whereby the limits of aggressive marketing always lay at the boundaries set up by the laws against unfair competition. Aggressive market assumption policies or "cannibalizing" as the Americans say, are the absolutely right method for a young sales organization. However, the switch to the soundness of the market leader, as propagated by me above, must be found at the right time during the course of an organization's growth," is how Reinhold Würth described the situation on the occasion of a sa-

THE WÜRTH IDEA FOR THE 80s: SATISFIED EMPLOYEES!
MANAGEMENT WITH VISIONS

les representatives' conference in Schwäbisch Hall in 1985. Joint efforts were made to improve the reputation of the company, to strengthen corporate identity. Successful PR work and the highlight of the "Happy Days" 1985 resulted in Würth achieving respect, acknowledgment, and esteem by business partners, the banks, and the public.[402]

Within only a few years Reinhold Würth and his team succeeded in convincing customers and corroborating the reputation of the solid, efficient, powerful, and reliable market leader in the Federal Republic of Germany. Würth's group of companies grew more quickly than the average of the economy and faster than comparable businesses in the industry. "All of this would have been impossible if we had employed the patriarchal and fusty management methods devoid of ideas characteristic of the traditional screw trade. […] Nowadays, I would compare the present phase of life of our company with that of a 25 year old who has sown his wild oats, gathered his experience, and has now made the decision to mold a sound career for the rest of his life."[403] And yet, the Würth Group had, according to Reinhold Würth, not turned into a "spongy giant," but rather looked like a "spindly young man." This lengthwise growth in terms of sales was now supposed to be followed by horizontal growth in terms of profit.[404]

This meant that Reinhold Würth and his managers needed to permanently check the procedures and measures applied so far for increasing company profit. Concrete measures aimed at stepping up profit were increasing liquidity by unrelenting improvement of credit control, the reduction of collection days, and – first and foremost – the increase in stock turns: the company tracked the life and sales cycle of every article since it could safely be assumed that the number of stock turns had significant influence on operating profit. The management tried to rationalize wherever possible. As for the rest, the maxim was that the "quality of growth can only be improved from the roots."[389] This is why all Würth managers were expected to be out in the field, accompanying sales representatives on five days out of every month.

The fact that this was not really anything new at Würth was specifically emphasized by Reinhold Würth: "In the 50s and 60s, neither I nor Mr. Lastdrager, Mr. Drexler or Mr. Clausen was able to call up the "big mother company" somewhere and ask for a 100,000 or 500,000 DM bank transfer to cover losses or even to just fill a liquidity gap. We were forced to earn every single mark, every guilder, every schilling and every crown ourselves to ensure a healthy capital investment in the companies." [406] Profit was always one of the guiding principles of entrepreneurial activity at Würth.

Now that the forward plans of the company's boss included further, substantial expansion of the business by the end of the decade, it had to be ensured that the additional capital resources necessary were provided for.

Whereas in 1985 Reinhold Würth assumed that the Würth Group would achieve sales of roughly 2 billion DM in 1992, he revised his plans in 1987 and developed his "Vision 2000." By the turn of the millennium, the aim was for Group generation of 10 billion in sales with around 30,000 employees.

Precise plans and targets were necessary for these objectives to be achieved. They were decided on during the managers' conferences and consequently put into practice on site in all the Würth Companies worldwide. By analyzing the sales figures every day and extrapolating the monthly result, the management was able to monitor performance; whether it was on target or if corrective measures had to be initiated. The sales representatives needed to be informed about the actual situation at all times and this was the responsibility of the sales management. During the 1981 Fall Conference in Bad Mergentheim, the first attempt was made at getting the managing directors both to forecast progress for the current year and make a statement on targets for the following year. Or, as Dieter Krämer described the process in retrospect: "You know, a farmer also has to know which yield he gets from which field, and this per hectare." [407]

For the first time a profitability list of the individual companies was compiled, and on top of this the contribution margins achieved by the individual Group member companies in addition to the balance sheet profit were credited, subsidies paid were charged to the respective businesses. Krämer 1982: "Out of this "internal list of liabilities in TDM," the TIS (Treasury Information System) emerged, initiated by Reinhold Würth: one of the most important controlling instruments of the Group." [408]

Degrees of Freedom

Concerning the management structures in the Group that also needed to be continuously reviewed in light of the planned growth, Reinhold Würth remarked about himself that he was a "convinced decentralist," [409] something he once again emphasized in retrospect: "Wherever things developed positively we let them ride. That's what using time to the max is all about. That's efficiency!" [410]

THE WÜRTH IDEA FOR THE 80s: SATISFIED EMPLOYEES!
DEGREES OF FREEDOM

Würth favored flat hierarchies and enabled talented and committed employees to progress to management level. Provided there was a vacant position they could also join the Group's Board of Management, which constituted central management and determined business policy. "Under the direction of Reinhold Würth, the managers of the Group's special functions and divisions are responsible for the long-term prosperous and safe development of the group of companies subsumed under the name of 'Würth Group'." [411]

The success of Würth had "many fathers," [412] yet Reinhold Würth said: "There's one thing that I want to claim for myself, namely that I have taken on all these competent men and women myself or indirectly." It was very important to him to nurture the solidarity and extraordinary stability in his top management and to promote his employees' loyalty towards the company. "The most important task of the manager is to place the right man (or the right woman) in the right position at the right time […].Thirty, twenty and even ten years ago, I was personally capable of keeping an eye on company matters down to the last details and of assessing them appropriately." However, in the meantime the company had grown to an order of magnitude that limited these opportunities. "I have been compelled to concentrate and specialize my own activities and, as the result of this, nowadays I can really only intensively keep an eye on the sectors of marketing and sales areas, in which I am also active to the greatest extent. The rest of my time is taken up with strategic fundamental decision-making activities in the specialized, but above all in the motivatory, sector within the entire company group." [413] The managers' conferences taking place annually served and still serve not only the exchange of experience, but also the implementation of a "team spirit, a working atmosphere, a corporate culture." [414]

Since the 1970s, conferences and congresses have become key pillars of Würth's corporate culture, and therefore ample time is also set aside for socializing and cultural events.

Reinhold Würth has always attached great importance to the development of a specific corporate culture, by which he understands the sum

> "Reinhold Würth has an uncanny ability: he knows who to assign responsibility to. He could have found more qualified people for certain tasks. But not believing someone to be capable of doing something, that's not for him."
>
> Peter Zürn, spokesman of the management of Adolf Würth GmbH & Co. KG

total of all activities, events, and memories that occur during the life cycle of a company and fuse to a sort of corporate code.

"Intuition, background information, and sensitivity in management" are some of the most important characteristics in his opinion – more important than "dogged and unquestioning faith in systems" or "plain management information figures." [415]

Marketing Prize Awarded to Würth

Reinhold Würth's efforts to create a new company image were crowned with success. In the 1980s, he was appointed member of several consulting bodies and supervisory boards: in 1980, for example, as member of the regional advisory board of Deutsche Bank Stuttgart and, in 1989, member of the supervisory board of Mercedes-Benz AG. The prestige connected with these positions also had a positive influence on his company that the press increasingly reported on. In 1986, an article about Reinhold Würth and the Würth Group appeared in "Manager Magazin" and the magazine "Capital" published an article on him in September 1989, one month before Adolf Würth GmbH & Co. KG was awarded the German Marketing Prize in Frankfurt. [416]

Congratulations: Dr. h.c. Walter Trux, chairman of the German Marketing Association, presenting the German Marketing Prize to Reinhold Würth in 1989

The German Marketing Prize is awarded by the German Marketing Association (DMV). On the occasion of the 17th German Marketing Day in the old Opera House in Frankfurt/Main on October 27, 1989, Reinhold Würth accepted the prize. In a brilliant presentation he introduced his company, which was honored for its professional marketing and Reinhold Würth's innovative projects as entrepreneur. [417]

Gerhard Fried, head of the marketing department at the time, recalls that the Marketing Prize greatly helped to boost the company's reputation. [418] However, measures in the field of PR were also needed to increase the company's degree of fame. After 1980, the new company slogan was: "Würth – the Complete Assembly Technology;" in 1983, the logo was revised; and after the "Happy Days," the Würth Group came up with yet another, very catchy slogan, namely "Würth – the Assembly Professionals," which is the catchphrase under which the Würth Group has been offering its products and services from 1987 until today.

Openness toward the outside has been emphasized since 1978 by way of the Annual Reports. They inform customers and investors alike about the previous business year at Würth in the form of figures and interesting reports.

In the 1980s, the company also intensified its philanthropic activities. Würth was active as a sports sponsor by the end of the 1970s. Initially, the company had focused on automobile sports and supported a team of its own, the BMW-junior team, Formula One and Formula Two as well as rally sports. Now, the business branched out into other areas: in 1987, Reinhold Würth inaugurated the International Reinhold Würth Women's Épée World Cup. Sports sponsorship in this field was obvious since an exclusive training center for fencing is located in nearby Tauberbischofsheim.

Apart from volleyball and gymnastics, Würth has been represented in soccer stadiums by way of touchline advertising since the beginning of the 1990s and also in the field of ice hockey since 1999. Since 2001, sponsorship of ONCE, the professional Spanish cycling team, is aimed at heightening awareness of the Würth Group in Europe and, since May 2004, Würth has been the principal sponsor of the German Skiing Association.

Sports sponsorship is very clearly aimed at raising the profile of the Würth brand. On top of this, it has a positive effect on customer loyalty by giving clients the opportunity of attending attractive sports events.

The company always ponders the extent to which it really benefits from such investment. Peter Zürn, member of the management of Adolf Würth GmbH & Co. KG, remarked as follows about the company's cooperation with the German Skiing Association: "Apart from our affinity with skiing, we see team sponsoring as a very useful instrument for enhancing the company's reputation and intensifying the emotions our customers associate with our brand. For Würth, the partnership with the German Skiing Association is therefore first-rate support for our sales activities." [419] Apart from large-scale sports events, the company also sponsors regional sports clubs.

Succession Settled in Time – the Family Foundations

Not for the first time in his life, but precisely then, at the zenith of his professional success, Reinhold Würth started thinking in earnest about the development of the company after his departure. Already by then it was part of his self-image as a successful entrepreneur to not only take care of business, but to also make provision for the future of the group of companies that one day would inevitably have to do without him.

He nominated both Dr. Walter Jaeger upon his joining the company in 1989 and Rolf Bauer, who had already been Reinhold Würth's official representative since 1985,[420] as his successors. Within the framework of the FÜKO he passed over more and more tasks to the two of them.

However, provisions also had to be made for the future of the company assets that would be inherited by his family in the case of his death. To solve this problem, Reinhold Würth put together a team of consultants consisting of the attorney Dr. Mark K. Binz, the tax adviser Dr. Martin H. Sorg, the notary public Werner Haag, Dr. Walter Jaeger, and the attorney Dr. Peter Beglinger.

After the Adolf Würth Foundation had been integrated into the limited liability company shares of Würth-Verwaltungs-GmbH in 1984, and when the Reinhold Würth Foundation had been set up in Chur in 1985, the Würth Succession Foundation Rules were stipulated in 1987.

That year, Reinhold Würth established four family foundations in Germany to which he and his wife Carmen transferred their assets.[421] Their two daughters, Marion and Bettina, contractually waive the legal portion of their parents' inheritance in exchange for financial indemnity, but are remembered as beneficiaries of the family foundations. It is their objective to guarantee the members of the Würth family a "fair and reasonable livelihood" and at the same time to further promote the companies of the Würth Group. Reinhold Würth comments: "Safeguarding the further existence of the Würth Group as a whole was […] much more important than the aspect of inheritance tax, income tax, and net assets tax. Experience of life shows that healthy and prosperous family-owned businesses must be sold in the second, third, or fourth generation only because a majority of the heirs consider the business a cash cow or want to cash in – to serve their own shortsighted interests. In doing so, the quarrelling family members completely forget that their own contribution to the building up or expansion of the business was either very modest or absolutely non-existent and that the founders and people who have grown the business would by no means approve of cashing in and using the company as cash cow. […] Let me put this very clearly: it is my idea to continue running and expanding the Würth Group, if possible, as a family-owned business."[422]

If they are interested, family members can play an active role in the company, but are in no way forced to do so. However, the Advisory

Board of the Würth Group is obliged to give preference to family members in cases where they are "on a par" with other applicants for the position of managing director. [423]

On the Foundation supervisory boards, decisions are taken by family members and external members. During Reinhold Würth's lifetime, however, he has the final say if he so desires. [424]

Administration Building of the Adolf Würth GmbH & Co. KG
with Museum Würth in Künzelsau-Gaisbach

THE HUMAN BEING – THE FOCUS OF ATTENTION

10

Working at Würth

According to the corporate philosophy, the focus of all entrepreneurial activities undertaken by Würth is the human being. During the Fall Conference of the Würth International Division in 1979, Reinhold Würth propagated the "Würth Idea for the 80s: Satisfied Employees!" [425] In his opinion, favorable "environmental conditions" in the business are a prerequisite for achieving the company's objectives. Würth defined five golden rules for dealing with staff. First: The company's goals must be stated clearly for everybody. Second: Responsible tasks and projects should be delegated to the highest possible extent. Würth knows: "This shows that the company has confidence in its employees, leading them to develop an astonishing degree of creativity and produce outstanding performances." Third: Above-average achievements must be recognized and rewarded. Fourth: Social communications within the company must be systematized, with both corporate philosophy and management culture contributing to this aim. Fifth: Staff should be treated as fellow human beings. People spend the best part of their lives at their place of work. Provided the staff experience the working atmosphere as positive and fulfilling, they will be all the more ready and willing to work harder for "their" company. [426]

Personnel Development from 1955 to 2005

Within a period of 50 years, the number of employees working at Würth has increased tremendously. When Reinhold Würth took over management of the company at the turn of 1954/55, he only had two employees, yet the 100-people mark had already been exceeded by the early 1960s. Not even ten years later the Würth Group had more than 1,000 people on the payroll. In 2003, the Würth Group had almost 42,000 employees worldwide, with about 13,000 of these in Germany and more than 29,000 working at the Group's foreign subsidiaries. [427] And this growth is continuing: in the past year, more than 3,000 new Würth employees have joined the Group worldwide.

Development of the Number of Employees of the Würth Group 1955–2003

	WÜRTH GROUP TOTAL	FOREIGN SUBSIDIARIES
1955	2	–
1960	51	–
1965	217	56
1970	821	213
1975	1.788	651
1980	3.363	1.732
1985	4.717	2.965
1990	10.318	7.259
1995	18.348	11.672
2000	36.161	23.500
2004	46.973	33.032

In the first two decades, the fast growth in staff numbers was mainly the result of Reinhold Würth's success strategy based on the multiplication of the sales force. As early as 1966, when the company had only 35 sales representatives, Reinhold Würth had announced his intention to quadruple this figure within a number of years.

In 2003, the Würth Group had a total of more than 23,000 sales representatives working in the field worldwide. Such a quickly-growing sales force generates an increase in order volume that needs to be handled by administrative as well as sales and marketing personnel. This is why the number of sales representatives is in almost all cases matched with an equally large number of

Reinhold Würth accompanied by his daughter Marion, as guests on the outing organized for retired employees (1995)

THE HUMAN BEING – THE FOCUS OF ATTENTION
PERSONNEL DEVELOPMENT FROM 1955 TO 2005

in-house staff: in 2000, the latter accounted for roughly 49 per cent of the overall staff of the Group. However, it needs to be taken into consideration that a large number of employees no longer work in the core business, i.e., in companies belonging to the Würth Line, but in the so-called "Allied Companies." Since 1999, the number of staff working in German subsidiaries has exceeded that of Würth Line employees in Germany; in 2004, almost 62,6 per cent of the staff in Germany belonged to the Allied Companies.

Employees of Würth Line and Allied Companies in Germany [428]

	WÜRTH LINE	ALLIED COMPANIES
1980	1.067	564
1985	1.234	517
1990	1.921	1.138
1995	4.022	2.654
1999	4.610	5.220
2000	4.884	7.777
2004	5.067	8.874

Since 1980, the number of staff working in foreign subsidiaries has gradually exceeded the number of staff working in Germany. Whereas in 1980 roughly 52 per cent of all Würth employees belonged to foreign subsidiaries, this had increased to more than 67 per cent in 1988 and 70 per cent in 2003.

Until the turn of the millennium, the overall number of staff at Würth has in most cases increased by double-digit percentages every year, with redundancies as were necessary at Adolf Würth KG in 1975 so far constituting an absolute exception in the company's history. However, during a meeting of the managing directors of the foreign subsidiaries at the beginning of the 1980s, Reinhold Würth explained that the per-capita sales achieved at Würth ranked very low compared with wholesaling companies operating in other branches of industry, and requested rationalization measures. "The human working capacity, one which is becoming more and more valuable, must be put to more efficient use by means of rationalization measures. When asking ourselves if a new employee is to be taken on, or whether the work can be done just as well by machines, the decision in all cases must be made in favor of machines." Würth also warned, though, that this recommendation must under no circumstances lead to a situation in which the workers and employees were slave-driven "to work with tongues hanging out and using their very last resources." [429]

The parent company of the business, Adolf Würth GmbH & Co. KG, that had roughly 4.651 employees on the payroll in 2004 and therefore accounts for 9,9 per cent of the total staff of the Würth Group, [430] is the focus of the statements made below about working at Würth. The basic principles of the corporate philosophy apply to all companies belonging to the Würth Group; regarding the detailed application of these principles, however, the individual companies have certain leeway. In the following section, the areas of activity in Würth's core business are explained, taking the example of Adolf Würth GmbH & Co. KG.

The Sales Force – the Foundation of the Business

"Sales and finally also profit are generated by selling. Sales are the pillar of every business, be it a manufacturing or a selling company. If a company cannot sell its products or services, it does not need to deal with other things, its days are numbered," according to Reinhold Würth. [431] Today, additional market shares can only be captured with the help of qualified sales representatives. At Würth, the sales force constitutes the basis of the success or failure of the company. This realization leads to an important conclusion: the sales representative is "the first among equals."

At the beginning of the 1970s, the future profession of sales representative was seen in a rather depressing light, in view of the new possibilities of electronic data processing. At

THE HUMAN BEING – THE FOCUS OF ATTENTION
THE SALES FORCE – THE FOUNDATION OF THE BUSINESS

that time, received opinion held that the main task of the sales representative was to find out when and where products were needed, the quantity and the price. People thought that this task could in the future be handled more quickly and more cost-efficiently by computers. However, Reinhold Würth realized that this assumption was wrong: "Today, […] sales representatives are just as important as in the past; I believe that the importance of sales and marketing has even increased in times of the virtual enterprise and the post-capitalist society." [432] At Würth, direct contact with customers still enjoys priority over e-commerce. In the business year 2002, the company further invested in expanding the worldwide sales force. Never before had so many new sales representatives been hired in one year: 2,800 in total, which corresponded to an increase of 14.2 per cent. [433]

The typical tasks of a sales representative are conducting sales negotiations with the customers and giving them information about the products and the company, thereby supporting sales and promoting the company's image. The sales representative must plan his customer visits, deal with logistical issues such as the distribution of goods and inventory management, check the orders received, and prepare reports on his work.

Starting with the divisionalization at the end of the 1970s, the field of sales at Würth has been subdivided into Cargo, Automotive, Wood, Construction, Electrical, Sanitary, Metal, and Industry as well as into geographical areas. Depending on the branch of industry, the customers are visited by sales representatives belonging to the corresponding division. The system was fine-tuned further with the introduction of an additional regional structure in 1999. It is now primarily the Würth branch offices in every region that serve as points of contact for the Group's customers. In another step, the sales representatives were also assigned customers according to size of business. A small craft customer can receive products from all divisions via his Würth sales representative, whereas large customers can be served by several Würth representatives working for different divisions.

Würth has had the experience that well-trained sales representatives generate higher sales than their poorly-trained colleagues. It therefore pays off to invest in further education and on-site training. Before starting their practical work in the field, Würth sales representatives are trained in the company's own Würth Academy for three months. The company pays a guaranteed salary during this time, yet this was not always the case. In the beginning, new sales representatives were sent out into the field without much ado. In the 1960s, they accompanied an experienced colleague for about two weeks, but in the 1970s a twelve-week induction plan was developed for new sales representatives. [434] Finally, in the middle of the 1980s, the three-month training model for sales representatives was developed at Adolf Würth GmbH & Co. KG, concentrating on product training and sales training. [435]

Good Sales Representatives Require Good Leadership

The interplay of sales representatives and market will only work well if the management of the business creates a climate for the traveling sales representatives and the customers in which they both feel at home and have sufficient room for personal development. Reinhold Würth believes that in most cases it is the management and not so much the sales representatives themselves that are responsible for lasting failure on the part of the sales force. A business solely focused on its sales figures will run the risk of putting so much pressure on the sales representatives that they feel forced to sell whatever the price. This price, however, will always be too high since it leads to annoyed customers and frustrated sales representatives. Frustrated sales representatives give notice and need to be replaced at shorter intervals all the time. Annoyed customers will in most cases be lost to the company forever. Reinhold Würth: "To avoid this spiral of failure, the management must fuse the requirements of the sales representatives and those of the customers into an indivisible, interactive connection." [436]

Selling is hard work every day in the field of tension between the company and the customers. The sales representative needs to be supported by his company to be able to tolerate the physical and mental strains connected with the job. The management is requested to help the sales representatives come to grips with the negative experiences and inevitable frustrations, something that Reinhold Würth is very well aware of, too. Würth has also created the prerequisites for supporting the sales force that can be subdivided into three categories – depending on whether they refer to the Würth Group as a whole, the individual sales representative, or the individual customer. Included in the first category are a market-conforming product range, top-quality products and services, a high service degree and a well-defined company image. The second category includes appropriate fixed salaries, an attractive commission system, company cars and bonuses, sales promotion campaigns, frequent special offers, and attractive advertising. Within the third category are probability models used to assess buying potential with related prices and discounts, fair handling of complaints, prompt reimbursement for supported complaints, and involvement in a partner system. The objective of all these measures is to turn sales representatives and customers into satisfied sales representatives and customers.

The characteristics that Reinhold Würth requires of a sales representative include average intelligence, delight in work, eagerness to learn, determination to make optimal use of working hours, healthy ambition, interest in motivation programs, and "a number of personality traits such as optimism, reliability and persistence, loyalty and enthusiasm, and seeing the job as a hobby." [437] Above and beyond the mere act of selling, the work of a sales representative must be targeted at establishing and cultivating long-term cooperation with the customer. Even if not mentioned explicitly, it is for the most part men working in the sales force of Würth. This might be explained by the products sold by the company and the customers requiring these products: even today, there are not too many women working in the crafts sector, on construction sites, or in automotive repair shops. Working in the field also entails long absences from home, a circumstance that makes the compatibility of job and family seem almost impossible for women. Great authorities on the field of sales such as the former Würth manager Karl Specht can hardly imagine women working in this profession. However, he also knows that a sales representative who wants to perform well needs the support of his partner. Karl Specht's wife supported him in every way she could; for a long time, she handled all the back office administration. [438] Since 2001, a woman, Bettina Würth, has been a member of the top governing body, the Board of Directors of the Würth Group.

Good Pay in Exchange for Good Work

One of the prerequisites for recruiting and keeping good sales representatives is an attractive salary. The management must determine an income level that is in line with the sales representative's market value. This is not an easy task and can only be performed well if the labor market for sales representatives is relatively transparent. In the middle of the 1970s, the company had introduced fixed salaries for the sales representatives, but the experience proved negative; as a result, a strongly performance-oriented salary system was introduced instead. The income of a sales representative now consisted of a fixed base salary and performance-related components. Every sales representative received a fixed salary depending on his years of affiliation with the company. He was able to increase this fixed portion by commission payments based on the orders he obtained. Outstanding achievements were rewarded by additional performance bonuses.

Würth employees are categorized according to their respective performance. Every performance category contains certain incentives depending on the respective sales representative's status as C, B, A, Success Club, or Top Club sales representative. This standing becomes apparent by the different types of company car, each of which signifies the performance category a sales representative belongs. If a sales representative fulfils the criteria for admission to the Success Club or the Top Club, he will receive additional bonuses and invitations to incentive trips. [439]

For many sales representatives, the trips to which their partners are also invited are the highlights of their working life. Because they are organized together with the other members of the clubs from the entire Würth Group – very often Reinhold Würth will attend, too – they strengthen the solidarity and the sense of togetherness of the top-performing sales representatives in the Group. The "company histories" written by top executives about their respective areas of responsibility eloquently testify to this. As a member of the Success and the Top Club, the former sales manager Hans Hügel together with his wife traveled to Turkey, Sicily, Portugal, Greece, Hong Kong and Bali, South Africa, Australia, and Brazil and went on a cruise in the Caribbean. For him, these trips were the "highlight of all incentives." [440]

The use of incentives is not undisputed: critics find fault both with the loss of quality in the work of the sales representative in favor of quantity and with a certain "effect of saturation." [441] However, in the meantime the Würth Company can look back on many years of experience with incentives. At the start, in the 1970s, the company had to realize that sometimes sales figures were dressed up so that the sales representatives were able to receive the incentives or that sales representatives wrote down orders that no customer had placed, something that caused a lot of trouble with the customers who received merchandise they had not ordered. Today, incentives are integrated into a comprehensive concept of staff leadership and motivation and used accordingly. [442] At Würth, the management is well aware that incentives by no means guarantee successes in sales and cannot act as replacement of leadership on the part of the managers.

Successful sales representatives do not only receive bonuses, they are also rewarded by being admitted to the Success or Top Club or are awarded the Golden Honor Pin, with or without diamonds. Additionally, they can attend further training seminars within the framework of the Würth Career Model, take over tasks and projects in the training of new sales representatives, or be promoted to management level within the sales force. [443] On top of all this, Reinhold Würth has always attached great importance to expressly thanking the sales representatives for outstanding achievements – not as an irksome task, but always as honest and heartfelt appreciation.

Structures in the Sales Force

Some of the model prerequisites described in this book are, of course, not always identical with the day-to-day reality faced by the sales representatives, and in the quickly expanding business it took quite some time for the corresponding structures to be built up. Employment contracts in the sales force were only introduced at the end of 1962 and in the 1970s the department "sales management – sales force" was established, which deals with the administrative tasks of the sales force and both manages and supervises the sales representatives. [444] One issue that has always played an important role in the history of the Würth Group and given rise to controversial discussions between the sales representatives and management is pricing. The introduction of a new pricing and commission system at the end of the 1970s constituted an important first step in the direction of more transparency.

Even if the salary, the working atmosphere, and the conditions of operation are fine, staff turnover rate in the sales force is always higher than in other departments of the company. By 1979 it had risen to 28 per cent at Würth, but was able to be reduced in the following years, a circumstance explained by Reinhold Würth through the introduction of a new training model. [445]

Every new sales representative means an investment for the business, and therefore fluctuation must be avoided as much as possible. Having to part with a sales representative costs the company a great deal of money every time, and for this reason the so-called "Roth's early warning system" was introduced at Würth in October 2002. It is based on the doctoral thesis of the economist Ulrich Roth [446] and focuses on the issue of staff turnover in the sales force. As soon as a sales representative has been identified as being likely to leave the company, the competent manager will take action. Upon the sales representative's leaving the company, an "exit interview" is carried out with him to better understand his motives and to derive strategies from the interview aimed at intensifying the sales representatives' ties with the company. [447]

"For me, staff turnover has always been the epitome of a success parameter, particularly for the management. In my opinion, staff turnover in the sales force is the early indicator of a company's strategic stability. Or, phrased differently: every sales representative leaving the company constitutes a defeat for the management. If the management loses many such battles it must be feared that the company will lose the war entirely," Reinhold Würth remarked in one of his lectures to the students at the University of Karlsruhe. [448]

Sales, Administration, Distribution – Order Processing at Würth

Even though the sales force – being the foundation, as it were – enjoys a special position within the Würth Group, Reinhold Würth also points out the importance of the other functions in the company: "Without the in-house staff, the financial experts, or the warehouse workers, the sales representatives would be completely helpless." [449] In a lecture to his students in Karlsruhe, Reinhold Würth described the way orders are processed at Würth, which is sketched briefly below.

The sales representative contacts the customers and obtains orders. [450] As a rule, the customer requests a quote for different items that either the sales representative draws up in writing himself or has his dedicated office worker deal with. Once the customer has agreed the price and selected the desired products he orders these, with the sales representative taking the order. The customer receives a copy of the order, and the Würth sales representative enters the order in his PC at home. The order is transmitted to the EDP system at corporate headquarters in Künzelsau via modem in the evening, when all the orders obtained that day are completed. Once the orders are received there, they are checked so that any anomalies can be identified and corrected. At the time the orders are checked for correctness, the financial standing of the customers is also verified and, in case of problems with a customer's credit profile, the order is transferred to accounts. Specialist workers in that department check if, in the case of only a minimal increase in the credit line agreed, the order can still be released. An order is held back, however, if a customer is already on dunning level 3 or 4 or if the credit line has already been considerably exceeded. Orders having successfully completed this process are then passed on to serial creation within EDP.

The employees in warehousing and shipping work in a two-shift system from 6 a.m. to 10 p.m. Reinhold Würth knows that the warehouse manager bears an "immense strategic responsibility" because the survival of the company also depends on how quickly and cost-efficiently a customer order can be processed. [451]

The orders received by the distribution center are first subdivided into so-called "pick positions" within individual series consisting of roughly 250 orders each. A picking slip is made out for every pick position that accompanies the merchandise taken off the shelves throughout the warehouse, which contains all pertinent information about the origin (shelf) and the order. An order can receive merchandise from different picking areas of the warehouse.

The products are put into plastic containers together with the corresponding picking slips and passed on automatically via a system of conveyor belts which, with the help of the bar code on the picking slip, ensure that the products ultimately arrive at the correct sorting station. There, the person in charge accepts the picking containers, once again checking the items and comparing them with the delivery note. If everything is correct, he or she stamps and signs the delivery note so that, in case of later inspections or customer complaint, it is possible to trace who packed and completed the order.

The merchandise is then put in a suitable box and passed on to the shipping department on a conveyor belt. There, packing material is used to fill any remaining gaps in the shipping carton, which is then closed. Next, the address label included with the shipping documents is put on the carton. Robots place the boxes ready for shipping on pallets, divided according to the type of delivery: parcel service, forwarding agency, or express service. Everyone who has the opportunity to take a look at Würth's logistics system in Künzelsau is highly impressed by the efficiency of the process.

Standard orders are delivered by the parcel service DPD. Shipments that exceed a certain weight or are extremely bulky are delivered by a forwarding agency. Shipping by TNT is fastest, but also most expensive. This is why more than 90 per cent of deliveries are made by parcel service. The pallets are handed over to trucks that pass them on to the parcel distribution center in Heilbronn in the course of the day. There, the boxes are assigned to the principal courses and DPD depots. Shipping to far-away depots is scheduled earlier, so that the trucks with the merchandise ordered arrive in the respective depot at the latest by early morning the following day.

Delivery drivers in the area of the receiving depot take over the parcels that they have to deliver to the respective customers on the same day. This completes the process of ordering and delivery. Parallel to the issue of pick positions in serial creation, the invoice for the merchandise delivered is printed out and sent to the customer under separate cover. If the customer does not pay the invoice in full within a certain period, a dunning procedure is started. The sales representative is informed about dunning letters so that he can talk about outstanding invoices with the customer during his next visit. A well-functioning dunning system is important for the company, since it contributes to a reduction in bad debt and therefore to higher liquidity.[452]

The above is the description of the individual steps of the process that are necessary for the customer to receive the merchandise he has ordered. However, without the work of the purchasing department the warehouse would be empty. "The purchasing department wanders along a very narrow ridge. It should not keep stocks too low and must never have too many goods in the warehouse," says Reinhold Würth. [453] The rate of stock turnover impacts directly on the company's operating figures. Würth realized very early that a stock turnover coefficient of 4, which means that the entire stock is shifted four times a year, is optimal concerning the relation between capital used and the service degree. Today (2004), the Würth Group achieves a coefficient of 6. This goal, however, can only be attained if both the warehouse and the purchasing department cooperate closely.

To make sure that the individual departments at Würth work hand-in-hand, it has become a tradition that employees not only familiarize themselves with their own positions, but also with the areas of responsibility of their fellow employees. Upcoming top managers are supposed in particular to visit the grass-roots level: they spend a couple of weeks in the warehouse or in sales to gather some experience in these fields. Members of management all the way down to the group leaders are requested to spend at least one full day per quarter in the field, visiting customers. This very close contact with the market through accompanying sales representatives means the in-house staff no longer see the 14,000–16,000 orders received daily in the distribution center in Künzelsau as an amorphous mass of work and orders. The sales representatives fought for every one of these orders. Every order, on the other hand, is proof of the confidence that customers have in Würth. Reinhold Würth is convinced that all the employees in purchasing, financial accounting, and distribution who understand this will work much more reliably than before. They comprehend that they are actually not paid by the Würth Company, but by the customers, and will act accordingly.

Corporate Culture and Employee Participation

Irrespective of the position the employees work in, be it in the sales force, the in-house sales department, the purchasing department, the accounting department, or the warehouse, or be it as office worker or manager, Reinhold Würth wants to create the prerequisites for continuous and successful work "not only by appropriate pay, attractive working conditions, and social benefits, but also by creating an emotional and intellectual bond between the staff and 'their' company. In my experience, this second element is more important than the first." [454]

> "The way I was received both during the job interview and when I took up my job here – friendly and respectful, irrespective of the position one was to fill – this impressed me greatly from the start."
>
> Michael Kübler, former chairman of the Council of Trustees; Würth Academy

Corporate culture plays an important role in this connection. Reinhold Würth defines corporate culture as the sum of all the activities, events, and memories – including deficiencies and mistakes – that occur in the course of a company's life-cycle; which can be experienced by the staff, which are mentally and emotionally comprehensible, and which have solidified into a specific company code, an unmistakable hallmark, a corporate identity. [455] At Würth, specifically developed forms of employee participation also constitute important elements of corporate culture.

In 1983, a Council of Trustees was set up at Adolf Würth GmbH & Co. KG, whose founding chairman was Manfred Binder. It constitutes the "conciliation committee and connecting link between the employees and the management of Adolf Würth GmbH & Co. KG and is responsible for promoting cooperation based on mutual trust,' the statutes record. This Würth-specific body aims at reaching a consensus and does not dispose of the comprehensive rights of a works council as specified by the Industrial Constitution Law. In the opinion of its former chairman, Michael Kübler, "the Council of Trustees is the model of employee participation best suited for Würth," because it is more flexible and more consensus-oriented. Flexibility is absolutely indispensable for a direct sales company that does not work with long-term orders on the book. If, for example, the order volume is higher than average on a Thursday evening, an additional shift on Saturday is necessary so that the merchandise is with the customers by Monday. In such a case, the

Council of Trustees will decide which employees can be deployed or which employees could voluntarily take over the shift.[456] The current chairman of the Council of Trustees, Thomas Wagner, also considers the Würth-specific model of employee participation orientated toward flexibility and consensus to be absolutely in keeping with the times.[457]

The Council of Trustees is elected for a term of office of four years by all employees working in the sales force and in-house administration with a contract of employment unlimited in time; the sales managers, regional sales managers, and members of the management are not entitled to vote. Work on the Council of Trustees is carried out in an honorary capacity.[458] All over Germany, the Council of Trustees of Adolf Würth GmbH & Co. KG has 25 members, 10 of whom are at the Künzelsau location (6 from administration and 4 from logistics) as well as 15 from the sales force. Meanwhile, other Councils of Trustees have also emerged in other companies belonging to the Würth Group, with a joint meeting taking place once a year. Some of the Allied Companies such as Hahn & Kolb have works councils in place with which the Council of Trustees also keeps in touch.[459]

Working for the Colleagues – the Members of the Council of Trustees

During the term of office of the chairmen of the Council of Trustees – Hermann Leiser, who held this office until 1994, and Michael Kübler (1994 to 1998) – several improvements could be achieved for the staff: for example, regarding workplace conditions or the establishment of a company restaurant in the new administrative block; the introduction of capital-forming payments, the award of a Christmas and vacation bonus; and orientation toward the pay of the German engineering workers' union, which is above the standard rates of the trade.[460] Working hours and compensation are agreed upon between the management and Council of Trustees and laid down in company agreements. A corporate overall wage agreement regulates the employment contracts of the in-house staff. Regular working hours at Adolf Würth GmbH & Co. KG average 37 hours per week on an annual basis.[461] Flexitime was introduced in commercial administration at the end of the 1980s, yet there are no clocking-in machines. Management trusts people to fulfil their duties and complete the work they have before them and for which they are paid. Reinhold Würth: "Checking up on them is not necessary, because staff appreciate the liberal trust that is put in them." [462] In 1998, however, agreement was reached regarding working hours, which guarantee customers can talk to staff from 7 a.m. to 6 p.m. during the week, and time sheets were introduced.

The Council of Trustees must be informed in case of dismissals and has the right to file an objection. In such cases, the objective is to reach an amicable settlement with the management. When the company decided to reduce staff in view of the economic situation in 2003, the Council of Trustees negotiated the exercise of socially acceptable measures such as early retirement schemes or transfer to subsidiaries for a period of one-and-a half to two years with the management. [463]

At Würth, one-on-one talks take place twice a year. In addition to these, anonymous staff surveys both in the sales force and the in-house administration are carried out at regular intervals. The objective is to offer a "secure space" for feedback, to receive information about both management quality and management culture, and to identify starting points for improvements as well as long-term trends. [464] The staff survey in the sales force, carried out by personnel development/sales management, aims at concrete measures for improvement, and particularly to minimize the staff turnover that all sales organizations experience. After the questionnaires have been evaluated, commitments – that is, discussions between superiors and employees resulting in the definition of concrete measures – are carried out. The implementation of these measures is monitored. The relatively high feedback rate of 70 per cent in 2003 can certainly be explained by the fact that the survey is followed by concrete changes.

The Council of Trustees started carrying out the survey among in-house staff in 1995, regarding this survey as the basis of its work. The turnover rate is relatively low among in-house employees, and so the survey focuses more on equipment and workplace design, working conditions, and the general "mood" in the company. Meanwhile, the questionnaire has also been taken over by individual subsidiaries, e.g., by Würth Netherlands. Evaluation of the questionnaire takes some time, and occasionally employees may doubt its worth and whether the findings will really bear fruit. However, the feedback rate increased continuously. At the start, it was 35 per cent, in 1999 it went up to 44 per cent, and in 2000, more than half of the staff, 51 per cent to be exact, returned a completed questionnaire. The survey is evaluated separately for every division. The division managers receive the complete evaluation and discuss it with their department managers, the department managers discuss it with their group leaders, and the group leaders in turn discuss it with their employees. This is, at least, the ideal scenario; there are no binding rules, as the company trusts in the understanding of the people responsible and the ones concerned. The evaluation of the survey of the entire company is then fed into the Würth intranet. [465]

In 2003, more than 77 per cent of the in-house staff participating in the survey said that they liked their job or even liked it very much, the majority of the staff particularly appreciating the versatility of their tasks. Staff were dissatisfied with the environmental conditions at their place of work, with ventilation, and air conditioning. Roughly 38 per cent were satisfied or very satisfied with their income in relation to their performance; more than 40 per cent remarked "so-so"; and about 21 per cent were dissatisfied or very dissatisfied with their income. Concerning the social benefits of the company, more than 85 per cent of the staff considered the vacation bonus, the Christmas allowance, and the target attainment bonus to be very important. People were highly satisfied with the working hours and shift schedules.

Management culture at Würth was rated very highly. Three-quarters of the staff were either satisfied or very satisfied with the management culture, and 81 per cent stated that they "wholeheartedly" or "fully" identified with Würth. Even in times of economic instability, most of the in-house staff considered their place of work secure. [466]

Life-Long-Learning – Further Education and Training at Würth

Würth sees the qualification of its employees and efficient personnel development as strategic success components. This is why the company takes great pains over selecting trainees. Further education and training of employees plays an important role at Würth, too.

"For Reinhold Würth, human skills are just as important as professional qualifications. From the start, he gives his employees the opportunity to show what they are made of. That's good, because I think most of the careers missed out on are the result of people not being challenged enough and not the result of excessive challenges."

Peter Zürn, spokesman of
the management of Adolf Würth GmbH & Co. KG

Commercial training has been offered by Würth since 1974, and careers "from trainee to top manager" are to be found at Würth, too, as is proven by Hans Hügel, who started his apprenticeship at Würth in 1955, or Rolf Bauer, who joined the company as an apprentice in 1963. Another example is the career of the spokesman of the management of Adolf Würth GmbH & Co. KG, Peter Zürn. He acted as spokesman of the apprentices during his commercial apprenticeship at Würth. Owing to his foreign language skills, Zürn was sent to Spain for a while, and afterward worked in the export department before being appointed managing director of Würth Australia in 1986. Back in Künzelsau, Rolf Bauer took him under his wing, and it was from him that Zürn took over the Automotive Division. Since 2003, Peter Zürn has been the spokesman of the management of Adolf Würth GmbH & Co. KG.

Today, at the start of the 21st century, traineeships in companies are hard to come by, yet in the 1960s businesses actually advertised for apprentices. A letter by Adolf Würth KG to the Schwäbisch Hall Employment Office in 1969 read: "Now that we have moved into our new administrative offices in Gaisbach close to Künzelsau, we would like to draw your attention to our favorable training opportunities and job prospects for young businessmen." Now that the company had sufficient space in Gaisbach, the apprentices received two hours of in-company classes to deepen the knowledge gained in the vocational school. Particularly gifted apprentices were given the opportunity to spend some time in a foreign subsidiary. The ladies and gentlemen from careers guidance were invited to get a first-hand impression of the modern places of work at Würth and to have lunch together with the employees in the newly- established company restaurant "offering a panoramic view of the Hohenlohe region." [467]

Times have changed, though, and today the quality of training at Würth is no longer a secret. Every year, many hundreds of young people apply for a training place at Würth. In 1997, the business created an additional eight openings for apprentices shortly before the official start of the training period, within the framework of an initiative aimed at fighting unemployment among young people. [468] In 1999, Adolf Würth GmbH & Co. KG received 800 applications for training places and in 2004 this number had increased to 2,000, according to Thomas Wagner, head of the training department. Contrary to business policy, the company trained more young people than were actually needed at Würth in the years 2001 and 2002, but now the number of openings for apprentices has been reduced. In 2004, ca. 80 new training places will be available, though this is still double the number originally planned. [469]

Apprentices at Adolf Würth GmbH & Co. KG [470]

	NUMBER OF APPRENTICES
1978	77
1988	183
1992	289
2002	384

In view of the high number of applicants, a selection procedure has become necessary to decide which young people are suitable for training at Würth. The evaluation is not solely based on their academic grades. First, the general knowledge of potential candidates is tested, with the help of a multiple-choice questionnaire. They are furthermore invited to interviews, during which their personality and character are assessed. The "optimum Würth apprentice" is supposed to be "smart, flexible, nimble-minded, optimistic, and positive". [471]

Synergy Effects between Schools and the Business

In an integrated training system of Adolf Würth GmbH & Co. KG with Würth Industrie and Würth Phoenix Academy, young people are trained in 18 different professions today, among others wholesale, import and export merchant, specialist in inventory management, industrial clerk, informatics clerk, specialist information scientist, and IT systems electronics engineer. Roughly one-third of the apprentices are made up of students of the Mosbach vocational academy, branch office Bad Mergentheim. Apart from the fields of trade, electronic commerce, service marketing, information technology, and merchandise management and logistics, they can also earn the degree of BA/International Business Administration and BA/Facility Management (BA standing for vocational academy).[472]

Within the training framework, the school-related part of the schedule is complemented by in-house seminars. Furthermore, the trainees can attend external promotion courses that are offered in cooperation with the Heilbronn Chamber of Commerce and Industry. The trainees of the Würth Company for the most part achieve results that are higher than the German average.

Würth places a lot of trust and confidence in its trainees. Following an initiative by Reinhold Würth, the junior company Auto-Hifi & Design GmbH (AHD) was founded in 1986. This is a retail business run independently by trainees that specializes in the sale and installation of car radios and special accessories. In the very first year of its existence, AHD succeeded in exceeding its sales target.[473]

In 1998, the pilot project "International Economic Management" was developed in cooperation with the commercial vocational school in Baden-Württemberg, for young people with a high school diploma. Group-wide, Würth offers 23 young men and women of one training year of the field of "wholesale and export and import merchant" the opportunity of acquiring an additional qualification within the framework of their training. This additional qualification covers in-depth studies in international business management as well as classes in English and French or Spanish. A four-week stay in a

European company belonging to the Würth Group is also part of this additional qualification. Würth Companies in 17 different countries participate in the program for the international exchange of trainees. [474]

A special training program for young talent in sales was introduced in 1999 in cooperation with the Heilbronn Chamber of Commerce and Industry (IHK). As the first company in Germany, Würth offers young people the opportunity to learn the profession of sales representative. The two-year training course leads to the degree of "specialist consultant in sales," with the final examination being carried out by the IHK. Apart from product knowledge, marketing, and business administration, the young students also learn corporate accounting and how to negotiate. [475] The current composition of the participants, 36 male and 2 female junior sales representatives, shows that selling in Germany remains a male-dominated area of activity even in the 21st century.

At least once a year, the management gets together with the trainees in a round of discussions lasting several hours. Reinhold Würth makes one or two presentations to the trainees every year. For his efforts in improving the field of training, he received a certificate of honor from the German President in 1984.

Qualification and Career

The business, though, does not only take good care of its trainees; Würth attaches great importance to the further development of all staff members. In cooperation with the IHK Heilbronn, further qualification opportunities were offered for the first time in 1981 to employees in the field of logistics, in the form of in-house seminars on the new profession "specialized commercial packer," thus paving the way for further professional advancement. [476]

It has been one of Reinhold Würth's maxims that management positions be filled by people from the company's own ranks, if possible; a measure that so far has proven to be worthwhile as is illustrated by the careers of top managers at Würth.

In the meantime there are two different career paths at Würth – the management career and the specialist career. A career in management is aimed at assuming responsibility for personnel and covers the steps clerk – senior clerk – group leader – department manager – general manager. The specialist's career is connected with the enlargement of the technical qualification of the employee concerned and covers the steps clerk – senior clerk – specialist – specialist advisor. [477] The Annual Report 2002 reads: "[…] at Würth, every employee has the prospect of taking on increasing responsibility." A survey in 1994 revealed that 73 per cent of the employees believed career development prospects in the business to be very good, with 68 per cent considering a career in the Würth Company desirable. [478]

"Reinhold Würth is a fascinating person. His own career is unconventional, and this is exactly what he lets others experience, too."

Siegfried Müller, architect, designed and built the Würth corporate headquarters in Künzelsau together with Maja Djordjevic-Müller

At the beginning of the 21st century, the group of companies is continuing to grow worldwide, with management being taken over by a new generation. It is in this process that personnel development is becoming very important. For this reason, a Group-wide human resources development program was started in September 2001. The Würth Academy had already been commissioned to build up a personnel development system in 1995. [479]

One part of the overall concept aimed at the Group-wide advancement of young employees is a promotion program for international upcoming managers, called "MC Würth." Well-targeted seminars and the assignment of special projects further qualify the upcoming managers for their specialist and management functions. In 2002, 26 upcoming managers from 7 nations and completely different areas of responsibility participated in this 3-year promotion program. [448]

With the personnel development team in charge, a so-called High Potential Program was developed in 2003 for upcoming top managers. Its objective is to prepare top, upcoming employees from the Würth Group's own ranks for taking over top management responsibility in the future. The potential candidates are selected in the respective companies and assigned concrete working projects that help them further to develop their skills and capabilities. In the long run, the program is meant to ensure that a sufficient number of qualified young managers are ready to take over management responsibility during the transition.

Furthermore, a course of studies running parallel with the job and leading to the Master of Business Administration (MBA) was developed. This is an internationally recognized postgraduate degree offered in cooperation with the University of Louisville, Kentucky (USA), Grand Valley State University of Allendale, Michigan (USA), and the Heilbronn University of Applied Sciences. The course of studies in "International Management and Entrepreneurship" for Würth employees takes 13 months. Half of it is carried out in the USA and the other half in Germany. Classes are taught by part-time lecturers from the Heilbronn University of Applied Sciences, top managers of the company, and by Reinhold Würth himself. The training finishes with the MBA degree taken in the USA. In November 2003, the first 14 graduates from 2 countries and 5 Würth Companies successfully passed their final exams. [481]

Würth Phoenix Academy was officially opened in Bad Mergentheim in November 2003 and constitutes yet another training institute of the Würth Group, offering workshops and seminars to the staff, the latter covering processes of change in Würth Companies including change management, optimization of business processes, and the implementation of IT projects. With specific training measures, Würth Phoenix Academy conveys comprehensive knowledge about the use of the Group's own ERP system, Würth Phoenix.

An In-House Campus – the Würth Academy

In 1986, Reinhold Würth came up with the idea of a "Würth Campus" during a presentation at an international managing directors' conference of the Würth Group. Following the example of US American universities, he wanted his business to be turned into a mini-campus in whose free and liberal atmosphere all employees – not only top executives – were to be perpetually stimulated to develop their personalities and knowledge further, and in which "the business and its employees would be knit together in an elitist team." [482]

As a consequence of these ideas, the Würth Academy was founded in 1991. Today, it constitutes the umbrella of all measures aimed at further education and training at Würth. Here, courses on technical and professional further qualification are offered to the staff. The courses and seminars range from informatics know-how, foreign languages, business and technical know-how, physical fitness, and introduction to Excel through to courses on self-organization at the individual's place of work and step aerobics, and are increasing all the time – just like the number of participants. In 1995, the Würth Academy offered more than 200 courses and had roughly 2,500 participants from Würth Companies in Germany and abroad; just 2 years later, the number of participants exceeded 7,000. At that time, the business had invested more than 5 million DM in further qualification measures. [483] However, it is not only practical knowledge that is taught at the Würth Academy; concerts, the arts, literature, lectures, and sports are also covered. Lisa Fitz was the first artist to perform at the Würth Academy, in February 1991. She came back nearly a decade later – on the occasion of the tenth anniversary of the Würth Academy. It has already organized a large number of events, and many well-known artists and celebrities have performed there: Hanns-Dieter Hüsch, Hannes Wader, Ilja Richter, Senta Berger, Gerhard Polt, Harald Schmidt, Dieter Hildebrandt, Klaus Doldinger, Götz Alsmann, Wolfgang Ambros, Justus Frantz, Max Greger, and Franz Beckenbauer, to name but a few. Not only the Würth employees, but also people living in the surrounding area are invited to the cultural events. Therefore, the Würth Academy adds to the region's cultural attractions. It also opens itself up to users outside of the company in other fields: customers of the Würth Company have the opportunity to attend seminars on product knowledge, assembly technology, and business-related topics.

The Academy also supports the field of music via Edition Würth, with the aim of promoting mainly unknown artists and pieces. Since 1997, a three-day open-air festival has taken place annually, organized by the Würth Academy and attracting more than 12,000 visitors each time.

THE HUMAN BEING – THE FOCUS OF ATTENTION
AN IN-HOUSE CAMPUS – THE WÜRTH ACADEMY

Michael Kübler is one of the founding members of the Würth Academy; today, he is events manager. Among other things, he introduced the health program in 1994 that is used either during the lunch break or after work. Kübler also initiated the open-air festival. He says: "This is what's so special about Würth: people are very open to ideas here, with staff being given the opportunity to put ideas into practice." [484]

The first in-house sports group had developed by 1972, many years before the establishment of the Würth Academy. Today, about 300 employees are members of Würth's sports teams – in eleven sections ranging from soccer, volleyball or bowling to archery and scuba-diving. "In-house sports teams are very important for corporate culture. Sports, joint activities, and socializing strengthen the staff's sense of togetherness," Reinhold Würth said in an interview with Frankfurter Rundschau. [485]

Würth employees can also use the company's library. It was opened in 1986 at a time when other businesses such as Daimler-Benz were closing down these facilities, according to C. Sylvia Weber, who was then the librarian at Würth and is today head of Würth's art collection. [486]

The varied offer of further education and cultural events by the company and the Würth Academy contributes to the attractiveness of Würth as an employer of the future. Reinhold Würth says: "The idealistic, mental and emotional ties which exist between our employees and our Company must be strengthened and improved in as friendly and as pleasant a way as possible." [487] And he is convinced that corporate culture will become even more important in the future, not only in relation to staff turnover: "When producers, consumers, and employees are faced with a choice between this or that company, they will opt for the one that has the most highly developed corporate culture." [488] Therefore, comprehensive corporate culture constitutes a strategic advantage over the competitors: "In the future, a company can only garner competitive advantages if it provides fun." [489]

11 HE'S STILL THE BOSS, YOU KNOW [490]

The 1990s

At the end of the 1980s, the well-known management consulting company McKinsey had been commissioned to analyze the Würth Group and identify additional potential for development together with the Würth managers with whose help Reinhold Würth's "Vision 2000" was to be realized. The catchwords that come to mind in this connection are "divisionalization" and "regionalization" of the company's structures. In the opinion of everybody involved, they accounted for the Würth Group's major leap forward in the 1990s. However, political turmoil also had a positive influence on the growth of the Würth Group's sales volume. The opening of the Eastern bloc and the tapping of new markets in its wake, particularly in the former GDR, contributed to the realization of Reinhold Würth's entrepreneurial targets.

Certainly the most important event of the decade within the company was Reinhold Würth's announcement that he intended to retire from business on January 1, 1994. His transfer from operative management to the Advisory Board and the structural and personal changes at management level connected with this move are also dealt with in this chapter.

Reunification Boom and Social Change – Germany in the 1990s [491]

For Würth, a worldwide business for the past 30 years, the global economic situation became increasingly important, a circumstance that is also reflected in the company's Annual Report and its commentary on the previous trading year.

As had been the case in the 1970s, the 1990s saw oil prices spiralling upward, this time as a direct consequence of conflict in the Gulf, with this increase impacting directly on the international economy.
    Although in 1990 a recession loomed in the USA, demand from the five new Länder resulted in an economic upswing in Germany. The unemployment rate rose dramatically, however, especially in eastern

Germany, although in the West it dropped slightly. By February 1991, 800,000 people were unemployed in the new Länder, with 1.9 million working shorter hours. After the fall of the Berlin Wall on November 9, 1989, events moved swiftly. In May 1990, an international treaty on a monetary, economic and social union between the Federal Republic of Germany and the GDR was signed. After July 1, the German Mark became the sole means of payment in the GDR, and a social security system modeled after that of the Federal Republic of Germany was set up with the help of funds from the West. On October 3, 1990, the unification treaty came into effect, and the GDR ceased to exist.

However, the promise of flowering countrysides and a unification of the two German states at no additional cost soon turned out to be unrealizable. Tax increases and a mountain of debt left behind by the Treuhandanstalt privatization agency of more than 200 billion DM verify this. The German automotive industry, however, reported record results in 1991, even though economic development in Europe was rather slow and was to stay that way during the next few years. Almost all western industrialized nations suffered from flat growth.

In the Federal Republic of Germany, too, a 10-year phase of growth came to an end in 1992, something that became particularly obvious in the field of mechanical engineering. At the beginning of the 1990s and after the end of the so-called reunification boom, Baden-Württemberg experienced the most severe recession in the history of the state. The decline of gross domestic product by 1.1 per cent was by far exceeded by Baden-Württemberg's 4.3 per cent, and the unemployment rate went up to almost 9 per cent in 1997. Large and medium-sized businesses were affected.

In the crafts sector and in the construction industry, business was still quite good, however, with the structural crisis becoming apparent in these fields of industry only after 1995, in the form of a high number of business failures. In 1997, the German economy gradually started to improve again, yet the upswing was mainly based on the export business; domestic demand was weak and investments in construction declined further until the end of the decade, since the communities were awarding fewer and fewer contracts. The end of international economic crises was announced in 1999. The USA was back on the path of growth and the crisis in Asia was tapering off. In Europe, too, business started to look up.

In Germany, though, the number of unemployed continued to increase despite the economic upswing. In 1998, 82 million people lived in the Federal Republic of Germany, roughly 17 million or 27 per cent more than in 1946. Apart from the baby boom of the 1950s and 1960s, the reason for this was the immigration of refugees and displaced persons from the former East German territories, East German migrants as well as migrant workers recruited from southern Europe, and later millions of so-called ethnic German (late) repatriates from eastern and southeast Europe. Slightly more than one million refugees and political refugees, particularly since the middle of the 1980s and predominantly from European war and crisis regions, but also from countries outside of Europe, caused a controversial debate in Germany about the issue of whether, and how, immigration should be regulated.

In contrast, the decline of the indigenous population through the fall in birthrate has been viewed as increasingly problematic since the 1990s. A second significant trend is the aging population: progress in the field of medicine, health care, hygiene, and a generally higher level of affluence has resulted in a dramatic increase in life expectancy since the 1950s.

By the end of the decade, it had become obvious that this modern, industrial, service-oriented society, which could offer employment in the production sector or agriculture to just a third of the workforce, was facing major problems of social adjustment.

In 1998, the Kohl administration – increasingly associated with the catchword "reform jam" – lost the parliamentary elections. Gerhard Schröder was elected seventh German Chancellor and formed a coalition government of the Social Democratic Party and the Greens. Eliminating mass unemployment was the declared aim of the new government, and consequently an "alliance for work" that had already existed under Helmut Kohl was revived again in 1998, with funds for further training and the creation of new jobs being made available.

On April 1, 1999, the new, so-called "ecotax" came into force, increasing the price of energy in favor of pension benefits and also encouraging people to be more careful in their use of energy. By March, Oskar Lafontaine, the Minister of Finance and leader of the Social Democratic Party, had unexpectedly resigned, thus paving the way for a retrenchment policy to consolidate public finances. This step, as well as internationally disputed decisions such as the involvement of German troops in Kosovo, put the new government under pressure; this was, however, softened considerably, not least because of the CDU donation scandal that was revealed at the end of 1999. In 2000, Angela Merkel became the new leader of the Christian Democratic Union.

A Slow Start and a Record Finish – the 1990s at Würth

At Würth, spiralling operating costs within the Group and disappointing returns in the period 1990–1992 led to cost-cutting measures and hiring freezes. [492] It was particularly the unsatisfactory development of sales that induced Reinhold Würth and the Board of Management to cancel the Würth Congress in Athens planned for 1991. "We wanted to set a warning example and make people do everything in their power to get the sales development under control," [493] is how Karl Specht, sales manager, recalls the incident in his company history. However, while the international economic situation deteriorated all around, at least Adolf Würth GmbH & Co. KG continued to live in a "safe haven," [494] with the company benefiting from the reunification of Germany.

The "summer price high 1992" initiated by Rolf Bauer, which was based on Bauer's positive experience with higher prices going hand in hand with improved service during the reorganization of SWG [495], resulted in considerably higher profits in 1993. And yet, in his autobiography Management Culture: the Secret of Success, Reinhold Würth describes this period of time as the third crisis in the company's history. [496] He was very worried about the international economic situation because at home, in Baden-Württemberg, mechanical engineering and the automotive industry were also experiencing crisis.

Despite record results in profit – measured against the balance sheet total the company had 39 per cent equity capital in 1993 – Würth had to say goodbye to double-digit growth rates in sales for the time being. [497] Therefore, measures aimed at improving the situation were initiated in the Würth Group in 1994 as a reaction to worldwide recession. Training courses were organized and analyses commissioned to identify areas in which the business had potential for improvement.

A market research institute had analyzed the degree of fame of the Würth brand with very positive results. According to the study, touchline advertising in soccer stadiums and the PR work of the chairman of the Advisory Board, Reinhold Würth, in the form of public lectures as well as his cultural activities in connection with the Würth Museum, added to the Würth brand's profile. [498]

Another measure used to fight stagnating sales was not to replace employees who had handed in their notice, saving personnel costs without having to dismiss staff, through this process of "natural wastage." The performance-related portion of the managing directors' income was increased to motivate them to work even harder. In 1995, the Würth Group succeeded in generating record sales again worldwide to the tune of 4.3 billion DM [499]; in 1996, the Group reported sales growth of more than 1 billion DM for the first time in one year. However, at Adolf Würth GmbH & Co. KG the development of sales and profit was still unsatisfactory at the beginning of the year, with sales representatives who did not achieve their set targets now being dismissed. [500]

All in all, though, the late 1990s yielded positive results: in 1998, the annual sales volume of the Würth Group amounted to 7.1 billion DM – not least owing to the many companies that had been acquired. Worldwide, the business had 190 sales companies in 72 countries around the globe, and 1999, a year marked by record profits, was only marred by deepening recession in the construction business and a dramatic decline in construction-related trade. [501]

The New Länder – Würth Goes East

The opening of the borders toward the East enabled the Würth Group to open up new markets and mitigate the economic crisis that had befallen Europe at the beginning of the 1990s.

Whereas people moved westwards, the flow of goods went in the opposite direction. It was in 1990, a very successful year for Adolf Würth GmbH & Co. KG, that the expansion of the business toward eastern Europe and the then still GDR started.

One year before, in 1989, the first customer in the GDR, the Deutrans Company in Potsdam, had been supplied with goods. Even before the monetary union, in January 1990, the company began to talk to craftsmen in Dresden, the planned location for the first sales company. In May, when Dresdner Würth Montagetechnik GmbH was founded, a partner from the GDR still had to hold a 5 per cent share in the company. It appeared at a trade show in the same month, and the first sales representatives were already trained by June. Reconstruction work on the branch office in Dresden, the 35th as it was later noted, was completed in the summer of 1990. The office building and warehouse covering around 10,800 ft² (1,000 m²), whose reconstruction and enlargement had cost 600,000 DM, was officially opened on August 31. Two months after the sales representatives started selling, the sales volume had already exceeded 1,000,000 DM. In 1991, Adolf Würth GmbH & Co. KG made an appearance at the Autovision Fair in Leipzig.

Karl Specht was responsible for building up the sales force in eastern Germany. During a Coordinating Conference in Portugal in spring of that year, it had been decided to hire 2 or 3 sales representatives for the

GDR, yet Karl Specht already had 21 new employees. In retrospect, he admits that this was a risk, but it paid off in the end. In view of the successes achieved, Reinhold Würth accepted Specht's decision. [502]

Large job advertisements for the Würth Company were placed in newspapers such as the "Sächsische Neueste Nachrichten:" "This is the beginning of your future with entirely new professional opportunities in the GDR. Würth is your future." [503] The company looked for craftsmen and practical people who wanted to train as sales representatives. Fifteen hundred applications were received, with the best-suited candidates being identified. The next objective was to make customers in eastern Germany happy. According to Specht, many representatives of other companies went to the East and "pulled a fast one" on their customers, yet as a logical consequence of this they disappeared from the market just as quickly. [504] Würth, however, treated its customers in eastern Germany fairly and did not sell them products they did not need. Specht had a lot of fun with his activities in eastern Germany, since he felt transported back in time to his beginnings at Würth, reminding him of the "pioneering spirit" of the 1960s when everybody was full of motivation.

A step into a new era: inauguration of the Würth Dresden branch office in August 1990, ahead of the first all-German elections

After a period of adjustment and some start-up difficulties – many new sales representatives considered working for Würth stressful – the staff turned out to be competent and committed. Karl Specht always attached great importance to being a role model, and after only a short period of time the entire management team hailed from the East. Reinhold Würth advised Specht to be careful, since new managers from outside always had their own ideas about running a company. In his opinion, it was more advisable to recruit people from the company's own ranks for management positions: "We have gone very far with the Würth culture and the Würth philosophy, and this is something we must by no means neglect." [505]

Successes in eastern Germany could already be reported in the first few months of 1991, with the sales representatives achieving monthly per-capita sales of 200,000–250,000 DM [506], and therefore more and more sales representatives were hired. The first years of commitment in the new Länder resulted in considerable growth for Adolf Würth GmbH & Co. KG.

However, there was also conflict and friction, the main issue being the sales representatives' income. Even though some of the new sales representatives quickly achieved astonishingly high salaries – they had used the chances offered for professional advancement – nobody was willing to accept a pay differential between western and eastern Germany. It was only after a man "of the first hour" who had figured particularly prominently in this matter was invited by Karl Specht to come to Künzelsau for a discussion that things quieted down. Shortly afterward a plan was introduced, stipulating the incremental adjustment of salaries with the objective of equalizing income levels in the east and west by 1993, something that in Specht's opinion "singled us out again in the national economy as the trailblazer." [507]

After 1992, Würth considerably expanded its business in the new Länder, opening its 50th German branch office in Jena in 1995.

Expansion and Customer Commitment

Würth did not only expand in the East: many new Allied Companies were also acquired in Germany and abroad in the 1990s. It was not always easy to integrate these companies into the Würth Group, yet Würth was on the right track very early on with the realization that processes and strategies that had proven to be correct in other places also needed to be introduced in the new companies. Dieter Krämer recalls that it was very important to coin some sort of corporate lingo. "Macros" such as Reinhold Würth's statement "10 + 1 = 10" or "growth without profit is fatal" were transferred to the subsidiaries, and the same principle applied to processes such as the pricing techniques or forms of communication that were customary at Würth. Even the consulting experts at McKinsey had to admit that they had never seen anything like this before. Much could be learned from Würth: "Matters are OK here, and this can be transferred to companies joining the Würth Group." [508]

In 1993, Reinhold Würth bought the company Arnold in Ernsbach, in Dr. Walter Jaeger's opinion "one of the most successful acquisitions in the history of Würth." [509] The reason: the business came at a very favorable price. With Arnold, from which the Reisser Company had spun off in 1921, the company in which Reinhold Würth's father had once worked as authorized signatory, Würth somehow "rediscovered its roots." [510] Hahn & Kolb Werkzeuge GmbH in Stuttgart was acquired in 1995. In 1996, Würth purchased companies that manufactured operating equipment (Dringenberg) and fittings (Mepla Group) and with the FEGA Group acquired shares in the electrical wholesale business. 1997 marked the year of the biggest acquisition so far in the history of the Würth Group: Conmetall GmbH & Co. KG in Celle. [511] With this acquisition, Würth banked on the growing do-it-yourself market in Germany; after all, Conmetall ranked among the leading suppliers of sanitary articles, hardware, fittings, and tools, as well as articles for leisure-time activities and gardening products for DIY stores and chains, with subsidiaries in Belgium and Austria.

Acquisitions in Germany were supplemented by international acquisitions. Apart from many new sales companies in the countries of the former Eastern bloc, Würth established new companies across the globe – in Mexico, Thailand, Poland, and Canada in 1990; in South Korea in 1991; and in Hong Kong and the People's Republic of China, Indonesia, and India in 1994. In 1996, Würth founded companies in Israel, Kenya, and the Philippines, and further Allied Companies were established abroad. After 1997, the Würth Group intensified its market presence in the USA by acquiring the Baer Supply Company, Adams Nut & Bolt Company, and the Eastern Fastener Corporation, with the aim of opening up new business for the Würth Group in addition to the existing five Würth Companies in New Jersey, Florida, California, Illinois, and Texas. However, the returns of the Würth Companies in the USA were still proving unsatisfactory in the middle of the 1990s.

In 1998, sales companies for Würth Elektronik were set up in France and Italy, and in 1999 Würth approached the Gulf region for the first time with Würth Iran and Würth Dubai after having already founded Würth Jordan in 1998.

To be able to guarantee the well-known high Würth quality in the many new foreign companies, Otto Steck, responsible for quality control at Würth, introduced quality management at the foreign subsidiaries in 1995. [512] Furthermore, additional regional procurement centers were set up worldwide in Bratislava, Shanghai, New Jersey, and Milan in 1996, apart from Würth Holding in Chur and Germany.

Competent and Professional – the Würth Service

Even though most of the customers rated Würth as competent, reliable, and professional [513], Würth was constantly striving for further improvement in the field of customer service in the 1990s. One problem the company had, though, were those customers whose sales declined or who changed over to Würth's competitors. In 1991, Prof. Tietz, the long-term advisor of the Würth Group who was killed in a plane crash in 1995, was requested to research the reasons for customer fluctuation in a representative customer survey. Staff from the University of Saarbrücken traveled throughout Germany and interviewed 1,600 customers. According to this survey, the pivotal points of customer satisfaction were the reliability of the sales force and the quality of the products, the prices being of secondary importance. The result of the study confirmed Würth's corporate policy of delivering quality and service and not getting involved in price fights with the competition.

Therefore, quality assurance enjoyed top priority in the Würth Group and was a direct responsibility of the management. A quality assurance handbook was written and, in February 1993, Würth was certified according to DIN/ISO 9001. In 1996, all large Würth Companies appointed a quality assurance officer.

Würth further intensified its commitment to the environment – "Würth pro environment" – and organized a Würth waste disposal service. Since 1986, the company had refrained from using CFCs in aerosol cans, and after 1990 there were only products free from chlorinated hydrocarbons available in the chemical range. Biologically degradable products were developed for the Würth Eco Line, and the Würth Refillo system for cans was even awarded the Innovation Prize for Packaging by the German Dual System. [514] Adolf Würth GmbH & Co. KG underwent an ecological audit in 1995.

Prof. Bruno Tietz,
chairman of the Advisory Board of the Würth Group (1993)

It had become a tradition at Würth not only to focus on quality, but also on new developments. In 1996, the new ORSY 200-case system developed by the company for optimum storage of small parts, machines, and tools was put at the customers' disposal, and nominated "product of the year" by the Plastics Consumption trade association. [515] Tried and tested Würth brands such as ZEBRA or Würth Master were developed further and complemented by PRINETO for heating and sanitary installation systems, as well as TRESYS for mechanical and electronic security systems and COMkit mobile radiotelephone service accessories. The latter two have since declined in importance due to the changing market for accessories. Bosch became the new manufacturer of Würth private label battery-powered screwdrivers in 1994.

A total of 120 employees worked in the R&D department in 1996.[516] In 1998, an innovation offensive was started to intensify the efforts aimed at developing new products. Following an initiative by Rolf Bauer, Würth Modyf was founded in 1997, a mail-order business offering working clothes and boots to customers.

Ordering was made easier for customers, too: since 1997, Würth has been working with the ordering system "Würth Catalog on-line" (WÜKO) that was presented at CeBIT together with the Würth CD-Rom-Catalog.[517] Individual service teams[518] have developed from the sales departments and act as contacts for customers, sales representatives, and branch offices. The motto is "Service 24:" orders received by headquarters by 12 noon are delivered to customers in Germany the next day. Thanks to the establishment of the Customer Competence Center (CCC), the customer only requires one contact among the in-house staff.[519]

In 1990, the starting pistol had been fired in Künzelsau for construction of the new distribution center; this was put into operation two years later, but had to be enlarged again in 1996. The fully automated pallet warehouse and two high-bay warehouses required capital expenditure of 60 million DM.

Encouraged by the book The Virtual Corporation, Reinhold Würth came up with the idea of founding a Würth leasing company, which offered this financing option to customers.[520] At the end of 1993 it had initially been founded as a Group internal financing instrument. The Würth credit card, too, initiated by Reinhold Würth in 1994 and issued in 1996 first to employees and partner businesses, was intended as another means of customer commitment.

Reinhold Würth decided to establish the Würth Academy in 1991, not least to fulfil the requirements for well-trained employees desired by the customers. Everything having to do with learning in the company was supposed to take place under the roof of the Academy: management seminars, PC courses, courses aimed at attaining the driver's license for forklift trucks. On the other hand, the entrepreneur also wanted to make courses on personal development available to all his staff, and for this reason the people responsible for the Würth Academy put together a very varied cultural program at favorable prices, to encourage the exploration of new horizons.[521] At management level, Harald Unkelbach is responsible for the Würth Academy.

Since 1997, the Würth Academy has organized the annual Würth Open Air Festival, which has become a supra-regional draw for 12,000 visitors. Customers of Würth can also attend seminars on business management and staff motivation, but also specialist seminars on state-of-the-art dowel technology or window fitting in the Würth Academy. This is also a response to the problems of the company's craft customers who were increasingly threatened by business failures and the loss of jobs. [522]

The Transparent Company – the Würth Information System

Ever since the 1990s, the Würth Information System and the department for financial control, strategic planning, and reconciliation under the direction of Dr. Walter Jaeger have facilitated increased transparency and therefore tighter strategic control, particularly in times of crises. Dr. Walter Jaeger joined the company in 1989 and today is the spokesman of the Board of Directors.

Before joining the Würth Group, Dr. Jaeger had spent many years as tax consultant and auditor to the business. He knew the Würth Group from his time as an employee of the Heilbronn Treuhand Wirtschaftsprüfungs- und Steuerberatungsgesellschaft mbH as well as partner of the professional firm Kleinknecht, Rappold, Jaeger. Especially after the premature death of Dr. Kleinknecht, Dr. Jaeger had almost exclusively dealt with Würth for a number of years before a different solution needed to be found at the end of the 1980s as a result of the Group's growing size, with the mandate being handed over to the consulting firm Arthur Andersen.

Dr. Jaeger did not come to Würth primarily because of the money; he was, as he writes in his company history, financially independent at the time. Looking back, he says he was "fascinated by the entrepreneur and person Reinhold Würth." [523] He was impressed by the "striving for excellence, the challenging goals, the desire to permanently keep the company on the path of growth, by the optimism, but also by the naturalness, ease, and modesty radiated by the management and the people with whom I dealt as external auditor and tax adviser." [524]

Dr. Jaeger's new area of responsibility, the strategic control department of the Würth Group, was being reorganized at the time. He started his job by building up the Würth Information System (WIS) initiated by Dieter Krämer in cooperation with the University of Constance, which developed the first software for the system. The Würth Group thus received an information base that enabled the managers to identify both strengths and weaknesses better and faster every month. The system, having been modified and improved several times, is still being used today. In 1998, the WIS was put onto a new software basis.

HE'S STILL THE BOSS, YOU KNOW
A FAMILY-OWNED BUSINESS APPROACHES THE CAPITAL MARKET

For the decentralized approach cultivated by Reinhold Würth, which has also proven worthwhile because of the long distances within the Group, and its availability worldwide, the information system was "a real breakthrough." [525] Now, a ranking of all Würth Companies was possible. Dr. Jaeger sees one of the major success factors of Würth in the fact that the company knew quite early what was going on in the individual companies. This enabled Würth to maintain the decentralized management style – even though the size of the Würth Group continued to permanently increase. [526] Developing criteria for business acquisitions – strategic management – as well as the introduction of process-based accounting were some of Dr. Walter Jaeger's new responsibilities.

Group headquarters was and is the "data pool and information hub." [527] It is there that the Board of Directors keeps a close eye on the figures and can, if necessary, request a comment from the companies according to Reinhold Würth's motto: "The greater the successes, the greater the liberty and freedom granted, and, of course, vice versa." [528] During the Würth Commitment Conferences in the fall, the binding targets for the coming year are passed. Time and again the question is asked: to what extent have the companies put their current plans into action? Have they learned from past experience, and where are they headed? [529]

> "Here at Würth you won't find any stuck-up managers who want a separate elevator or a separate restaurant for the board of management. This made a big impression on me; these were practically-minded people, and working together with such a group of people appealed to me."
>
> Dr. Walter Jaeger, spokesman of the Board of Directors of the Würth Group

A Family-Owned Business Approaches the Capital Market

Together with the increasing degree of fame of the entrepreneur Reinhold Würth and his Würth Group, it was the confidence-building information policy, the plausible strategies and objectives of the company, its extraordinary stability, and the continuity in its top management as well as good operating results, even in times of a weak economy, that created the prerequisites for the successful launch of bonds. They supplied part of the capital needed for the further growth of the Würth Group, a field in which Würth proved to be highly prepared for innovation, too.

In Zurich in 1987, the Würth Group had presented itself for the first time to interested financiers on the occasion of the raising of an SFr loan. [530] For a family-owned business it is not so usual to raise capital on the capital market, as is emphasized by Dieter Gräter from Würth's financial department in his company history. [531]

In the opinion of Dr. Walter Jaeger, who had, at the time, prepared and carried out the presentation as external auditor, Reinhold Würth together with José Viana put an extraordinary idea into practice and made the company a lot less dependent on banks. In 1990, the second bond was placed and also offered for subscription to the staff. Since that time, the successful principle of launching bonds has been continued. Up to 2004, several bonds have been placed by Würth Finance, founded in Zurich in 1978 as the Würth Group's own house bank, on the capital market. On top of this, the Würth Group has successfully worked with other financial instruments to fund its gigantic investment budget, such as currency option transactions and the commercial paper programs newly introduced in Germany at the beginning of the 1990s.

Even though the company is not quoted on the stock exchange and is still a family-owned business, Reinhold Würth got in touch with the rating agencies Standard & Poor's and Fitch at the beginning of the 1990s "to discuss the question of how the Würth Group could be rated in view of its sales performance and earning power, the market risks and future prospects, as well as its management and legal structure." [532] Being a company not quoted on the stock exchange, the Würth Group had not met with major interest on the part of investors during the first bond placements, and this was why Reinhold Würth sought a rating.

"Negotiations showed us very quickly that the first and foremost prerequisite for a rating is absolute openness. All balance sheets, strategic plans, several management interviews, and analyses carried out by the analysts of both Standard & Poor's and Fitch over a period of several months were necessary until the first A-minus rating for long-term liabilities was granted by Standard & Poor's in 1995. This is a downright spectacular result for a German family-owned business; to my knowledge there is no other German family-owned business that has been granted a rating by Standard & Poor's. Meanwhile, the rating by Standard & Poor's has improved to "A outlook stable" which has something to do with the fact that we have succeeded in continually stepping up our equity ratio." [533]

Consulting by McKinsey – Structures in a State of Flux

The successes of the measures taken by Würth in the 1980s, which had resulted in a high degree of commercial success and a new level of standing in the eyes of the public, already had Reinhold Würth and his managers thinking about future growth. As early as 1985, the consulting company McKinsey had come up with a project plan entitled "Safeguarding the Future Growth of the Business." In the accompanying letter, McKinsey described the Würth Group as an "excellently managed business" and testified to its "high efficiency level." [534] It had been the objective of the planned project at that time to develop strategies for a doubling of the sales volume from one to two billion DM within a period of five years (1985–1990). The new sales target was supposed to be achieved with the help of "well-targeted expansion in profitable markets" and "generation of sufficient profit in the key markets." McKinsey attached particularly great importance to personnel development. "Extremely fast expansion harbors the risk of having the managers do too many things at the same time." [535] The business expanded very quickly indeed, with the Würth Group reaching its target one year earlier than originally planned.

When Würth entered into active consultancy with McKinsey in 1989, the Group had already set itself new targets. The objective now was to develop the "System 2000" that was based on Reinhold Würth's vision of the Würth Group achieving a sales growth of more than 10 billion DM by 2000.

In a meeting of FÜKO members in April 1989, the most important points of cooperation with McKinsey were laid down. [536] The management of Würth felt absolutely capable of developing strategies and structures for this major project, yet intended to use help from outside for "getting to know new instruments and techniques for structuring groups of companies," in order to moderate the process, and to recruit the "outside control necessary in view of the magnitude ("jumbo size") of all decisions." The project was intended to be based on the hypotheses formulated by Reinhold Würth about the "necessity of constant growth to maintain the company's youthfulness" as well as his maxim "growth without profit is fatal." It was assumed that – aside from social or political turmoil – the growth potential of the Würth Group was almost unlimited. Possible dangers from within the business such as "intellectual limitations" had to be avoided from the start. FÜKO and the management of Adolf Würth GmbH & Co. KG constituted the dedicated project team. An important aspect realized in this connection was the issue of the management personnel needed to shape and further such a business development. There was acute awareness of the fact that the existing management team would only be active "for another 10 or 20 years or so" and that new "entrepreneurial personalities" had to be trained and qualified in good time.

The final report by McKinsey & Company submitted in October 1989 [537] summarizes the results of the cooperation. The statement that, in 2000, each of the four marketing segments (Automotive, Craft Metal, Craft Wood, and "Rest") would be larger than the entire Würth Group of 1989, once again illustrates the magnitude of the project. The country with the highest sales volume was still reckoned to be the Federal Republic of Germany.

An analysis of the current situation yielded positive results: the managers were satisfied with the controlling instruments in place at Würth at the time, and the atmosphere was good: "hard, yet humane." The specialist skills in the field of sales and the sales representatives' self-image were rated equally positively as the "strategy of the core marketing segments." Problems were mainly detected in the need to enlarge the current management team with new managers "from the company's own ranks" and "academics and managers from outside."

The strategy of "feeling one's way into the market" so far adopted by Würth was also earmarked for change. To pre-empt potential competitors, the study by McKinsey favored international market penetration, further specialization of the marketing segments, the development of new distribution channels, and measures aimed at structuring the product range, as well as potential-oriented sales force controls that facilitated a more precise use of the sales representatives. The final report by McKinsey also stated that central functions of the business had to be developed carefully. The purchasing department required adaptation to the new targets, with a change of focus to "international procurement management." The objective was to achieve supply security, price advantages, and quality, while at the same time drastically reducing dependence on individual suppliers. According to McKinsey, the logistics sector posed one of the most important challenges to growth: it needed to be decentralized while at the same time maintaining its high efficiency levels. Würth Companies abroad required a great deal of consulting in this regard. Meanwhile, departments such as product development, EDP, human resources development, and financial accounting had to be prepared for the planned growth.

1 Feeling close to South Tyrol: Reinhold Würth after a hike in 1979 in conversation with Luis Trenker (†1990), a real South Tyrolean character and pioneer of mountaineering
2 Internationally successful, yet loyal to their Hohenlohe roots: the entrepreneurs Albert Berner, Gerhard Sturm and Reinhold Würth (2004)

PLATE 2

1

2

1 Reinhold Würth is a great admirer of former South African President, Nelson Mandela, opponent of apartheid and Nobel laureate. The two met in June 2000 **2** A gift for the host in Dubai: Reinhold Würth and Sheikh Ahmed bin Saeed Al Maktoum (second from left) in April 2000 **3** Reinhold Würth in audience with Pope John Paul II at the Vatican (2002) **4** Quite an event: Reinhold Würth and the Dalai Lama during his visit to corporate headquarters in Künzelsau (1999)

PLATE 4

1 Tycoons: Reinhold Würth and Lothar Späth, chief executive of JENOPTIK AG and former Prime Minister of Baden-Württemberg (2000) **2** Reinhold Würth in conversation with Erwin Teufel, Prime Minister of Baden-Württemberg (2000) **3** Reinhold Würth with German Chancellor Gerhard Schröder in the chancellery in Berlin in June 2002 **4** Reinhold Würth in conversation with former German President Roman Herzog (2001)

Divisionalization of the Würth Group

The principal issue of the study was a clear subdivision into marketing segments, in order to keep pace with the growing complexity of the business. This was the only way to keep the expanding product range under control and guarantee the industry-specific orientation of the range. Having dedicated managers assume responsibility for the success of a marketing segment promoted entrepreneurial thinking. "In the final stage, the members of the management team will look after one marketing segment worldwide as well as assume responsibility for one or more central functions." Furthermore: "In large countries/markets the marketing segments could, as a final step, become independent companies." [538]

Reinhold Würth is of the opinion that divisionalization shot the Würth Group "into a completely different orbit." [539] The whole project got off to such a successful start that Würth dispensed with the originally planned "check-up" by McKinsey. [540]

Initially, the Automotive, Metal, and Wood Divisions emerged of which, by the beginning of the 1990s, Automotive had progressed furthest. At that time Rolf Bauer planned to take over a fourth division developed in 1993: Industry. Even though industry customers worldwide made up the largest market segment for Würth, this section of the market was still relatively small. The company was only just beginning to develop a strategy for this target group: a total supply concept including logistics and ordering services. Therefore, Rolf Bauer took over the International Automotive Division, Karl Specht the Metal Division, and Gerhard Fried, head of the marketing department, the Wood Division. As early as 1994, on the occasion of a conference in Prague, the separation of the Automotive Division into the fields of trucks and passenger cars was decided. Since 1995, every salesman has represented a certain division. Product departments, too, have all been assigned to individual divisions.

The process continued with the Allied Companies (AC), which were united and then divisionalized. [541] Individual companies had a more product-oriented approach, and the Würth Group hoped for synergy effects in the fields of marketing, purchasing, and training. A "Specialist" Division was established for standard parts and screws as well as for tools, with the RECA and "Trade and Production" Divisions also being set up. The "Diversification" Division was in charge of businesses such as the car dealerships Schubert and AHS, Würth Elektronik, the junior company AHD established in 1986, and Panoramahotel Waldenburg.

Reinhold Würth Becomes Chairman of the Advisory Board

Concern about the continued existence of his business induced Reinhold Würth to transfer company assets to foundations in good time, as has already been reported in this book. Now, in the 1990s, he wanted this measure to be taken a step further by withdrawing from operative management and safeguarding continuity in the management team.

Having already announced this step a few years before, Reinhold Würth decided to leave operative management of the Würth Group behind and instead take over the chair of the Advisory Board on January 1, 1994. As his successors, he nominated Dr. Walter Jaeger as spokesman of the Board of Management and Rolf Bauer as his representative.

Preliminary talks on this subject had been taking place since 1992 to precisely define respective roles and responsibilities in the future.[542] It was discussed how Reinhold Würth expected the Würth Group to be run in the future, which meetings he would attend in his function as chairman of the Advisory Board, how he wanted to be informed about events in the Würth Group, and which communication channels should exist between him, FÜKO, the FÜKO spokesmen and the staff: e.g., should he in future address the employees solely through the new Group management or would the direct way still be an option for him? Who would be responsible for PR work and – the most delicate question – which role would Reinhold Würth play in Adolf Würth GmbH & Co. KG, still the biggest company of the Würth Group?

The successors designate were aware of the challenge and the marked differences in both personalities and potentialities. Dr. Walter Jaeger writes in his company history[543] that he and Rolf Bauer got along very well, but that what set them apart from their predecessor in their new position was "Reinhold Würth's innate charisma, his eloquence, the enthusiasm he can arouse in people. […] These characteristics can only be learned to a certain extent. […] We could by no means slip into Reinhold Würth's role, copy his behavioral patterns, use the idioms he used."

A few days before his official withdrawal as managing director and almost as a "farewell performance," Reinhold Würth walked the distance from the spot where once the Schlossmühle in Künzelsau and therefore also the first seat of his father's company had been to Künzelsau station, with a hand-drawn barrow he had loaded himself. This was something he had had to do quite often as a boy. In his autobiography he called this action "a lesson in humility and modesty."[544] Almost 300 employees shared this lesson with him.

HE'S STILL THE BOSS, YOU KNOW
REINHOLD WÜRTH BECOMES CHAIRMAN OF THE ADVISORY BOARD

On December 17, 1993, Reinhold Würth hosted his farewell dinner in the company's own Panoramahotel in Waldenburg, and his successor Dr. Walter Jaeger gave a farewell speech for him as befitted the occasion. He spoke about the responsibility that the new management team would take over and about the challenge of "continuing to run the business with the same dynamic force, the same success" as Reinhold Würth. "When we speak about saying good-bye tonight this has a final, irrevocable touch to it. Dear Mr. Würth, this only applies to your official activity in operative management, but not to your professional life, you will certainly not be out of work, but stepping into the breach." In the course of the evening Dr. Walter Jaeger explained: "Dear Mr. Würth, you have really made an extraordinary decision, but after all, you are an extraordinary man. You have written one of the German success stories of the post-war era, you have built up a company that is highly appreciated and admired by the public. Dear Mr. Würth, your reasons for getting away from the pressure of everyday routine in your prime as manager are logical and intellectually comprehensible: your wish to enjoy some freedom from the daily pressures of business, set other priorities in your daily routine, spend more time with your family and your hobbies, is certainly doubted by many, but respected by all, and everybody is really glad for you, you deserve it." [545]

Back to his roots: when Reinhold Würth withdrew from operative management in 1993, he once again pulled a handcart through the streets of Künzelsau, just as he had done as a young boy almost 50 years before

However, nobody, not even his successors, believed that Reinhold Würth would from now on devote his time first of all to his hobbies. Slowly, everybody involved came to realize that such a transition was not easy and could not be accomplished in a day. When, after a number of years, Dr. Walter Jaeger looked at the minutes again in which the new rules and regulations had been laid down, he discovered "how enormously wishes and reality differ even after a period of ten years." He wrote: "An entrepreneur like Reinhold Würth cannot do without the entrepreneurial field, without the many facets of his power and experience to push the business. An entrepreneur of his type will never find a successor who can fulfil his requirements. Therefore, he will always feel the urge to actively intervene in the business, merely checked by reason, by his intention not to offend too much against his own word, his own wishes." [546]

In Dr. Walter Jaeger's opinion, though, "the constellation is a critical one from the point of view of the separation of powers. Owing to Reinhold Würth's being the chairman of the Advisory Board, this body is clearly dominated by him. On the other hand, its strong involvement in operative business leads to the situation that neither one nor the other body can make decisions freely, the entire power and competence rests with him." This is an analysis that Reinhold Würth felt compelled to agree with in a letter written in 2003. According to Dr. Jaeger this is "perhaps a constellation [...] to be expected if one has a certain understanding of the human psyche of a full-blooded businessman and entrepreneur."

By 1997, this first official announcement had been made: since the development of business in the previous year had not proved satisfactory in Reinhold Würth's opinion, he had written in February to the employees and the managers, informing them that from that time on he saw himself as being forced to deal with the operative business of Adolf Würth GmbH & Co. KG more intensively than before:[547] "The greater the successes, the greater the liberty and freedom granted. [...] It is entirely up to you to keep the chairman of the Advisory Board out of your daily business!"

New Projects for Reinhold Würth

Despite the continued commitment to his company – in his position as chairman of the Advisory Board Reinhold Würth's diary remained full[548] – he also took some time out for new activities. It is particularly his public presence that has significantly increased since 1994. Apart from his function as chairman of the Advisory Board, Reinhold Würth has been kept busy by his many lecture tours, his commitment to the arts at Würth, to the citizens' action group "pro Region Heilbronn-Franken" that he helped to establish in 1997, and last but not least his activity as professor of entrepreneurship at the University of Karlsruhe, the chair being endowed in 1999.

Official opening of the new administrative building: Reinhold Würth together with the architects, Maja Djordjevic-Müller and Siegfried Müller (1992)

Until today (June 2004), Reinhold Würth has given more than 700 public speeches and has many times addressed the staff of the Würth Group – often also by videotape. He comments on this as follows: "This was nothing I designed or planned, it just happened that way. [...] One of my first lectures was at the Marketing Club in Cologne. […] When I give a speech today we receive at least one or two requests afterward for additional lectures. I have to turn down many such inquiries, but it goes without saying that I gladly accept requests that are close to the business, such as today the foremen's training institute of the German window construction trade, since these are our future customers. This is a great help and support for the business." [549]

Since that time, Reinhold Würth has also been making the headlines as patron of the arts, philanthropist, and university professor. When the staff moved into the new administrative building of Adolf Würth GmbH & Co. KG in Künzelsau at the end of 1991, into which a small museum of screws and threads as well as a concert and lecture hall with more than 200 seats had also been integrated, the Würth Museum with 10,000 ft² (900 m²) exhibition space was officially opened there in December of the same year. The square in front of the building had been designed by the Danish sculptor Robert Jacobsen – this was a very successful collaboration as the architect Siegfried Müller recalls. [550]

"A company opens up towards the outside – with a corporate collection of works of art of the 20th century on whose basis changing exhibitions are mounted in several museums and exhibition locations owned by the business, we receive a great response from the employees and the general public: this is how one of Reinhold Würth's visions becomes a reality."

C. Sylvia Weber, responsible for the arts at Würth

The first exhibition in the Würth Museum showed the most important paintings of the collection. The fact that 2,500 visitors came to the official opening was a good sign for the coming years, during which the museum succeeded in developing a unique profile. Successful exhibitions impressed Baden-Württemberg's art scene, and the Würth Museum – initially scrutinized rather suspiciously – has meanwhile become a respected and highly appreciated partner in the museum landscape of Baden-Württemberg. In particular, the interior installation "Wrapped Floors and Stairways and Covered Windows" staged by Christo and Jeanne-Claude in 1995 for the museum and parts of the office wing was a sweeping success shortly before the covering of the Berlin Reichstag, and even members of the Würth management who were less than enthusiastic about the project in the beginning are, with hindsight, convinced of its success because of its dramatic contribution to the Würth public image.

In 1997, the Danish architect Prof. Henning Larsen won the competition organized by Würth for the construction of an art gallery for the Würth Collection in Schwäbisch Hall. There, Reinhold Würth had been offered a plot that had originally been intended for the construction of the city's library. Reinhold Würth made a quick decision in favor of the construction of the art gallery, which on the part of the Würth Group was supervised by C. Sylvia Weber, who is responsible for the arts at Würth, until its official opening in 2001.

Reinhold Würth in conversation with composer Philip Glass in February 1995

By 1987, Reinhold Würth together with his wife Carmen had set up the "Würth Foundation" whose objective is the sponsorship of research and sciences as well as the arts and culture and the promotion of regional activities. One sponsorship priority of the Würth Foundation is research into the state's history and archaeology. As a consequence, Reinhold Würth, who since the 1990s has received several prizes for his cultural commitment, was awarded the Württemberg Archaeology Prize of People's Banks and Rural Credit Cooperatives in 1997. The Würth Foundation also sponsors historical exhibitions and publications, as well as festival performances; it also commissioned a composition by the composer Philip Glass (Symphony #3) on the occasion of the 50th anniversary of Adolf Würth GmbH & Co. KG, which was premiered within the framework of the Christo-installation.

After receiving the Order of Merit of the Federal Republic of Germany on the occasion of the 40th company anniversary in 1985, Reinhold Würth received many more decorations and awards in the course of the 1990s. In 1994 he was presented the Medal awarded by the state of Baden-Württemberg and in 1996 the First-Class Order of Merit of the Federal Republic of Germany in recognition of his varied cultural commitments. The visits by German Chancellor Gerhard Schröder and the Dalai Lama to Künzelsau in 1999 illustrate the increasing public respect and admiration being gained by both Reinhold Würth and his business.

In 1995, Reinhold Würth had his staff organize a ceremony in Stuttgart's Hanns-Martin-Schleyer-Auditorium on the occasion of the

Würth Group's 50th anniversary on April 20 – his 60th birthday. Many celebrities from the world of politics and industry, among others the former German President, Richard von Weizsäcker, paid tribute to his life's work. Georg Krupp from the board of management of Deutsche Bank, member of the Advisory Board of the Würth Group since 1983, gave the eulogy. He emphasized customer orientation and the business' "youthful mentality" as the most important success factors that were also expressed by the motto of the anniversary year: "Be Young." First of all, though, it was "Reinhold Würth's powerful and charismatic entrepreneurial personality" that had paved the way for the "extraordinary development of the Würth Group." [551] Baden-Württemberg's Prime Minister, Erwin Teufel, compared Reinhold Würth's achievements with the work of men such as Gottlieb Daimler, Karl Benz, and Robert Bosch. [552]

1 Former German President, Richard von Weizsäcker, was among the guests at the celebration in Stuttgart (1995) **2** Erwin Teufel, Prime Minister of Baden-Württemberg, bestows the service medal of the state of Baden-Württemberg upon Reinhold Würth in Ludwigsburg Castle (1994) **3** Former German President, Roman Herzog, awarding Reinhold Würth the First Class Order of Merit of the Federal Republic of Germany (1996)

HE'S STILL THE BOSS, YOU KNOW
NEW PROJECTS FOR REINHOLD WÜRTH

1 Reinhold Würth in conversation with Rolf Bauer and Dr. Walter Jaeger (1995) **2** A Harley for his 60th birthday: the staff's gift to Reinhold Würth (1995)
3 All smiles: Bettina Würth shares her father's joy over the Harley-Davidson, the staff's gift to Reinhold Würth on his 60th birthday.

Official opening of Kunsthalle Würth in Schwäbisch Hall in May 2001: Hermann-Josef Pelgrim, mayor of the city of Schwäbisch Hall, C. Sylvia Weber, curator of the Würth Collection, German Chancellor Gerhard Schröder and Reinhold Würth

REINHOLD WÜRTH 12

The Entrepreneur and His Contributions to Society

As an entrepreneur, Reinhold Würth constitutes an extraordinary success story. The development of his company from a small, two-man operation into an international group of companies and world market leader in the field of fasteners and assembly technology has been widely acknowledged by the public. Würth has in consequence been appointed a member of many bodies in the industry; e.g., he was a member of the supervisory board of Mercedes-Benz AG from 1989 to 1997, since 1980 he has served on the regional advisory board of Deutsche Bank AG, Stuttgart, and since 1999 on the advisory board of Landesbank Baden-Württemberg. Furthermore, Reinhold Würth is a partner and member of the board of trustees of Robert Bosch Stiftung GmbH, Stuttgart and has sat on the chairman's committee of the Federation of German Industries since 2000. On top of this, he has held the chair of the advisory board of entrepreneurs of GWZ Gesellschaft für internationale wirtschaftliche Zusammenarbeit Baden-Württemberg mbH, Stuttgart since 1993.

The entrepreneur from Baden-Württemberg now also features on the political scene of the federal capital, Berlin, with his representative office on the Isle of Schwanenwerder in the Wannsee.

In the years since 1994, Reinhold Würth has become well known primarily through his contributions to society. "Like hardly any other entrepreneur, Würth, the visionary, combines entrepreneurial determination with social and cultural commitment," remarks Manfred Kurz, his employee on the staff of the Advisory Board.[553]

Since the 1970s, Reinhold Würth has been intensifying the company's PR work and cultivating his contacts with representatives of the public. Through cultural events, he has created highlights in the business' daily routine. When the new distribution center in Künzelsau-Gaisbach was officially opened in May 1979, a ceremony was organized in Künzelsau's municipal hall with a highly acclaimed orchestra, which was attended by a number of regional political representatives.

One of the highlights in the company's history that staff still rave about today, and which promoted Würth's degree of fame both in the region and beyond, were the "Happy Days" organized on the occasion of the company's 40th anniversary in 1985. The ceremony lasted three days in a marquee of the Circus Krone, erected on the company's premises, and featured circus acts, fireworks, and a matinee concert by Philharmonica Hungarica and the pianist Justus Frantz. Five thousand guests, employees, and customers as well as numerous representatives from the worlds of politics and industry attended the festivities, including among others the Minister for Economic Affairs at that time, Martin Bangemann, and the speaker of the Bundestag, Philipp Jenninger. It was Jenninger who awarded the Order of Merit of the Federal Republic of Germany to Reinhold Würth, an honor that was intended both for the entrepreneur and the citizen "who contributes to society in many different ways – as patron of the arts and cultural sponsor […] and last but not least as a generous benefactor on many occasions." [554]

The "Happy Days" triggered a development at Würth that culminated in the official opening of Kunsthalle Würth in Schwäbisch Hall in May 2001, which not only Baden-Württemberg's Prime Minister, Erwin Teufel, attended, but also the German Chancellor, Gerhard Schröder.

The decorations, awards, and prizes that Reinhold Würth has received for his entrepreneurial and social commitment are too numerous to quote in full here, yet they are listed in the appendix. It will suffice here simply to describe the most recent accolades: the largest nationwide initiative for the promotion of entrepreneurship in Germany, StartUp, acknowledged his life's work with the German Founder's Prize in June 2004. This award paid tribute to Reinhold Würth's entrepreneurial achievements, the building up and exemplary management of a globally operating trading corporation, and at the same time Würth's contributions to society and his sponsorship in many areas of cultural life. Manager Magazin admitted Reinhold Würth to its "Hall of Fame," together with the head of Siemens, Heinrich von Pierer, in 2004 and in April that year Reinhold Würth was awarded the Ludwig-Erhard Medal in recognition of his outstanding services to the social economy. In his presentation speech, Dr. Christoph Palmer, secretary of Baden-Württemberg, said: "Economy, technology, arts, and culture are no isolated phenomena, but are closely correlated with each other. The history of businesses, but also of entire national economies, must primarily be understood in its cultural dimension – and desi-

REINHOLD WÜRTH
THE BUSINESSMAN AS ART COLLECTOR

> "You know, there are people who keep all the money they make to themselves, but Reinhold Würth has always generously shared with others. And he has had the experience that you get something back when you give to others."
>
> Prof. Dr. Hans Küng, Professor of Theology at the University of Tübingen

gned and adjusted accordingly."[555] This is exactly how Prof. Reinhold Würth lived and worked. In the eulogy given on the occasion of the presentation of the Knight's Order of the Legion of Honor to Reinhold Würth in March 2004, the French consul general paid tribute to Reinhold Würth as "a humanist who succeeded in bringing economy and culture, the human being and his work in line, a visionary who turned his Utopia into reality, a "wanderer" in the spirit of Goethe who has found his way from things useful, through things true, to things beautiful."[556]

The extent of Reinhold Würth's contribution to society and his official presence also become obvious from a glance at the shelves of the central archives of the Würth Company in Künzelsau. The files that hold the press reports of his activities occupy several feet. Whereas the press reports about Reinhold Würth from the period between 1985 until the spring of 1993 only fill a thin folder, a huge file is necessary to hold the reports from the three following years, and the collection of press reports covering the years from 1996 until the spring of 2004 takes up six weighty files, reports about the business not included. Going through this collection of press clippings one realizes how much the degree of fame and reputation of the entrepreneur have increased – not least because of Reinhold Würth's many lecture tours on the issues of staff leadership, staff motivation, and corporate culture, his commitment to the field of arts and cultural sponsorship, and his chair in entrepreneurship at the University of Karlsruhe.

The Businessman as Art Collector

In 1971, Reinhold Würth bought the watercolor "Marsh Landscape" by Emil Nolde. It was the first painting he acquired for the collection that today comprises roughly 7,000 exhibits.[557]

He was encouraged by his friend, the photographer Paul Swiridoff, whom he first met in 1969. At that time, the staff had just moved into the new administrative head-

"I have always felt that my art activities act as an emotional antithesis to the rationality of my business profession."

Reinhold Würth

quarters of the Würth Company in Gaisbach, and Carmen Würth wanted to surprise her husband with a number of photos taken of the building. She commissioned Paul Swiridoff, who was impressed by the architectural design of the new company building. This marked the beginning of a long friendship. Reinhold Würth developed an interest in art, not least inspired by the paintings he saw hanging on the walls at Paul Swiridoff's and by the latter's many stories of his time as a gallery owner after the end of the war, during which he had been very active exhibiting contemporary works of art. "This changed my friend's life who, in his position as successful businessman, had long since been one of the most highly esteemed among the successful," recalls Swiridoff. [558]

During his first 15 years' collecting art, Reinhold Würth followed a rather unsystematic approach and based his purchases merely on his personal predilections. Business trips that he soon began to combine with visits to art galleries played an important role in the acquisition of works of art.[559] Until about 1985, he was buying paintings, drawings, graphic art, and sculpture, as well as icons, tapestries, and ceramic and porcelain artefacts.[560]

Since then, the entrepreneur has had art historians, art dealers, and artists advise him. Würth and the well-known Paris gallery owner, Denise René, have been cooperating intensively for a long time. This grand old lady of the postwar modern art scene, who started her activities as a gallery owner and art dealer in 1947 with works by Vasarély, became acquainted with Würth through their mutual friend, Robert Jacobsen.[561]

Meanwhile, the Würth Collection is being developed around a number of key genres. One of these focal points is classical modern art, represented by artists such as Beckmann, Buffet, Dix, Ernst, Grieshaber, Jawlensky, Léger, Münter, Nolde, Poliakoff, Chagall, Miro, and Picasso. The second group of artists comprises contemporary expressionists from Germany and Austria such as Anzinger, Baselitz, Bohatsch, Damisch, Dorfer, Hacker, Hebenstreit, Immendorff, Lüpertz, Penck, Rainer, Scheibl, Schmalix, Sedlak, and Wölzl. Works by Rudolf Hausner and Wolfgang Hutter represent the third focus of the Würth Collection, the fantastic realists.

Immediate contact with painters and sculptors has shaped Würth's knowledge of art, and is also the reason why many works of artist friends of his can be found in the Collection, primarily the Danish sculptor Robert Jacobsen. The Würth Collection also contains works by Sonia Delaunay, Günter Fruhtrunk, Richard Mortensen, Lun Tuchnowski, and Victor Vasarély, who gathered around Jacobsen during his period in Paris and Munich. Other works of art, primarily in the field of sculpture, were purchased as a result of Reinhold Würth's close friendship with artists such as Alfred Hrdlicka, Horst Antes, Wolfgang and Gerda Bier, and Thomas Lenk. [562]

Würth's activities as an art collector became more widespread internationally in parallel with the international development of the Würth Group. The Würth Collection also features work by the following European artists: Piero Manzoni and Lucio Fontano (Italy); Juliao Sarmento and José de Guimarães (Portugal); and Eduardo Arroyo and Antoni Tapiès (Spain). The US American pop-artist Andy Warhol and the environmental artists Christo and Jeanne-Claude should not be ignored – Reinhold Würth owns the largest private collection of exhibits by Christo and Jeanne-Claude in the German-speaking area. For Christo and Jeanne-Claude, the Würth Collection is very important, since Reinhold Würth bought entire groups of their works, including some quite early ones. The two, who met Reinhold Würth almost 15 years ago during an event in Hamburg in the run-up to the wrapping of the Berlin Reichstag, say: "If a collector buys so many exhibits, a friendly relationship will develop in time." [563]

Despite the professional advice that Reinhold Würth seeks before purchasing artefacts, his motivation to

Danish sculptor Robert Jacobsen in conversation with Reinhold Würth and his wife Carmen (1992)

buy something is still a "mix of well-targeted and intuitive purchasing." Würth emphasizes that the works of art he acquires have to be to his liking, too. "I only add those objects to the Collection that appeal to me personally. I do not buy names or the image of an artist, but the work of art itself." [564]

At the end of the 1970s, Reinhold Würth conceived the idea of combining his art collection with his business. [565] The design of the new corporate headquarters in Künzelsau from the very start included the connection between working space and the world of art. Since Christmas 1991, large parts of the Würth Collection have been open to the public in the Würth Museum, which is an integral element of the new administrative building. The Würth Museum is immediately adjacent to the foyer. In 2001, Kunsthalle Würth was officially opened in Schwäbisch Hall as an annex to the museum in Künzelsau. Initially started as a private collection, the Würth Collection has thus been brought before the public and meets with great approval.

Reinhold Würth has received several awards and prizes for his outstanding cultural commitment. In 1995, he was presented with the Adam-Elsheimer Prize by Art Frankfurt. The Fondation d'Entreprise Montblanc de la Culture awarded Reinhold Würth the high-profile award "Montblanc de la Culture" for his cultural activities in 1998. In 2000, the entrepreneur was honored for his outstanding services to French culture by the decoration "Chevalier dans l'Ordre des Arts et des Lettres" and in March 2004 by the decoration Knight of the Legion of Honor, the Chevalier de l'Ordre de la Légion d'Honneur.

About his passion for collecting art, the entrepreneur himself remarks: "I have always felt that my art activities act as an emotional antithesis to the rationality of my business profession." [566] At the same time, there are sound commercial reasons favoring the establishment of an art collection.

> "Reinhold Würth is a collector with a lot of courage, daring, and interest. And many aspects of the spirit pervading our gallery can also be found in the Würth Collection."
>
> Denise René, art dealer in Paris

1 The aerial view from 2004 shows the impressive expanse of the premises in Künzelsau-Gaisbach

PLATE 6

1

2

1 View of the project "Wrapped Floors And Stairways And Covered Windows" by Christo and Jeanne-Claude, January through July 1995 in the Würth Museum, Künzelsau **2** View of the opening exhibition of Kunsthalle Würth, Schwäbisch Hall, "Einblick – Ausblick – Überblick. Rendezvous mit der Sammlung Würth", May through October 2001 **3** Reinhold Würth in conversation with British sculptor Anthony Caro (2004) **4** View of the installation of sculptures "The Last Judgement" by Anthony Caro in the Johanniterhalle close to Kunsthalle Würth in Schwäbisch Hall, May through September 2001 **5** View of the exhibition "Gauguin und die Schule von Pont-Aven", March through June 1997, Würth Museum, Künzelsau

PLATE 8

1

2

3

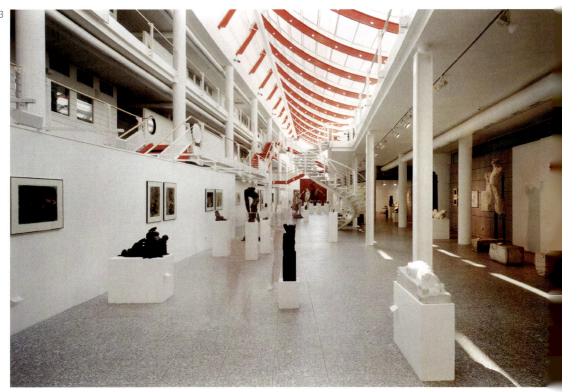

1 View of the exhibition "José de Guimarães. Bilder, Objekte und Figuren. Sammlung Würth und Privatbesitz", February through June 2001 in the Würth Museum, Künzelsau **2** View of the exhibition "Alfred Haberpointner – Konkrete Verwandlungen", January through September 2004 in the Würth Museum, Künzelsau **3** View of the exhibition "Alfred Hrdlicka. Arbeiten 1954–1993", July through October 1993 in the Würth Museum, Künzelsau **4** View of the exhibition "Hans Arp – eine Übersicht", September 1994 to January 1995 in the Würth Museum, Künzelsau **5** Reinhold Würth with Colombian artist, Fernando Botero **6** Reinhold Würth talking shop with artist Ben Willikens, born in Leipzig (2004)

PLATE 10

1

2

1 View of the exhibition "Pablo Picasso – Sein Dialog mit der Keramik"; works from the collection of Marina Picasso and paintings, drawings, ceramic objects from the Würth Collection, June through September 1999, Würth Museum, Künzelsau **2** View of the exhibition "Land auf, Land ab. Karlsruhe und Stuttgart im Kaleidoskop der Sammlung Würth", Kunsthalle Würth, Schwäbisch Hall, March through October 2004 **3** View of the cabinet exhibition "Aus der Kunstkammer Würth. Meisterwerke von 1500–1800", January 2003 to February 2004 in Kunsthalle Würth, Schwäbisch Hall **4** View of the Screw and Thread Museum at corporate headquarters in Künzelsau

1 Kunsthalle Würth (left) and Adolf Würth-Auditorium (right) provide an excellent view of Schwäbisch Hall's picturesque old town
2 A prominent sign: Exterior view of the Kunsthalle Würth

REINHOLD WÜRTH
THE COLLECTOR IN HIS ROLE AS BUSINESSMAN

The Collector in His Role as Businessman

"As a businessman, I must, of course, pay attention to whether the work of art that I intend to buy has a certain potential for increase in value," says Reinhold Würth. "So, if I see two equally beautiful and equally impressive works of art that have the same depth and I can or want to buy only one, I will, of course, choose the one that promises the higher increase in value." [567]

The increase in the value of artwork has to be considered over a long period of time; works of art are long-term investments, and their appreciation in value is not guaranteed. Art collections do, however, provide the opportunity to make substantial contribution to a company's asset growth. These considerations do play a role at Würth. [568] The watercolor by Nolde, the first one that Reinhold Würth bought at 60,000 DM at the start of his activities as a collector, is worth about five times this amount today. [569] Since 1987, the initially private collection has been held by Adolf Würth GmbH & Co. KG. [570]

Other commercial aspects have also turned the collection into a profitable asset for its owner. Würth is convinced that the symbiosis of art and the world of employment results in a positive attitude among the staff that contributes to the company's efficiency. The Würth Museum offers the employees changing exhibitions that generate debate and enliven the daily routine. Members of staff are invited to guided tours of the respective exhibitions, which take place during their lunch break. These tours are even a mandatory part of the apprentices' period of training. The company also organizes an attractive program of lectures and events around every exhibition.

The employees can bring their friends to the exhibitions, often impressing them with their unusual place of work. This promotes the sense of togetherness: the employees' willingness to perform and the pleasure they derive from their work both increase and they identify more closely with the business they work for.

Employees can borrow works of art from the museum depot for their offices, and from the company's picture lending gallery they can, upon payment of security, take home prints for a certain time, with explanatory specialized literature being available in the corporate library. It is true that the profitability of such measures cannot be calculated precisely, but Reinhold Würth is absolutely convinced that the works of art enhance the staff's identification with the company and that highly motivated employees constitute a competitive advantage.

Reinhold Würth has also reckoned the effect of his art collection on the general public: the exhibitions draw to the business premises many people who are not familiar with the Würth Group. The reports about art openings in the newspapers and other media certainly contribute to the company's reputation. "This increase in our degree of fame ultimately has a positive effect on our sales volume." [571]

This becomes obvious all the more whenever the Würth Museum brings large projects to Künzelsau that are of particular interest to the media. The most spectacular event took place in the beginning of 1995. Just a few days before the wrapping of the Berlin Reichstag, Christo and Jeanne-Claude realized their so far largest interior installation in the Würth Museum. The title of this temporary artwork was "Wrapped Floors and Stairways and Covered Windows" and it attracted almost 82,000 visitors to Künzelsau in the period from January 29 to June 4, 1995. The project realized by the New York-based artists together with a team of 25 people earned the Würth Group advertising contacts and advertising effects of between ten and fifteen million DM, according to estimates.

The art collector expects Kunsthalle Würth in Schwäbisch Hall to have a substantial effect on the public, too. When the Kunsthalle was officially opened in May 2001, Würth welcomed such distinguished guests as German Chancellor Gerhard Schröder, the Prime Minister of Baden-Württemberg, Erwin Teufel, Christo & Jeanne-Claude, Alfred Hrdlicka, the author Hans Magnus Enzensberger, and the British sculptor Anthony Caro. The Goethe Institute is located in Schwäbisch Hall, which guarantees that many future managers from different coun-

"We are very happy to see that employees of the Würth Company who would perhaps otherwise not visit art exhibitions now have access to art and to our work. This corresponds to our philosophy."

Christo und Jeanne-Claude, artists;
press conference in Arlesheim on May 4, 2004

Collector and artist:
Reinhold Würth in conversation with Christo (1993)

tries will learn the German language here. The name of "Würth" will certainly mean something to them even after their departure from the small Franconian town – Reinhold Würth expects this to have a "long-term PR effect." 572

In an interview with the magazine Kunsthandel Reinhold Würth remarked: "People often ask me if it is worthwhile investing money in an art collection. I always answer them: 'You know, I have been collecting art for 30 years now, and if you compare the development of the German economy with the development that our business has taken, you will realize that we have made considerably more progress. I therefore conclude that our occupation with art has at least not done us any harm.'" 573

Open to the Public – the Würth Collection

Christo believes that Reinhold Würth is so special because he grants the public access to his art collection – in contrast to many other collectors. 574 Meanwhile, Würth presents works of art from the Würth Collection in a growing number of museums in Germany and Europe. Company employees, like the general public, have the opportunity to get in touch with modern art completely free of charge. It all started with the Würth Museum in Künzelsau in 1991, followed by Kunsthalle in Schwäbisch Hall and other galleries in foreign subsidiaries; now, in 2004, people are talking of plans to establish an art gallery at Würth France in Erstein, Alsace. 575 In 1997, Paul Swiridoff wrote: "The art collector Reinhold Würth has long since become one of the great collectors and founders of private museums in Europe." 576

The Würth Museum in Künzelsau

When an architectural competition for a new Würth administrative building in Künzelsau was organized in 1985, it had already been decided to have a museum as an integral element of the new building. The Stuttgart-based architects Maja Djordjevic-Müller and Siegfried Müller won the competition, and their design was also appreciated by the public: in 1993, the Baden-Württemberg Chamber of Architects awarded the pair the Hugo-Häring Prize for the building. 577

In the atelier of Austrian painter and sculptor Alfred Hrdlicka (1995)

The central court in front of the administrative building gets visitors and staff into the right mood for the arts: it is dominated by three steel sculptures and two fountains by Robert Jacobsen. The Würth Museum was opened at Christmas 1991, even before the official opening of corporate headquarters, and the 50,000th visitor had been welcomed just eleven months later, on December 3, 1992. Meanwhile, more than one million people have visited the Würth Museum. The area of the Museum covers 9,900 ft^2 (920 m^2), with 800 ft (240 m) of hanging space offering ample room, not only for exhibits from the Würth Collection, but also for numerous objects on loan.

From an organizational point of view, the Würth Museum is an independent department within the business. C. Sylvia Weber is the director of the museum and can, like many other managers in the company, look back on a typical Würth career. She joined Adolf Würth GmbH & Co. KG as librarian in the middle of the 1980s with remit of building up the company's library. In 1987, she started working with the art collection, which she had already gotten to know as she made an inventory of the library. She studied art history in her spare time and today, from time to time, lectures at seminars in different universities and colleges. C. Sylvia Weber is responsible for the systematic development as well as for the setup and management of the Würth museums. 578

She is supported by her representative, Dr. Beate Elsen-Schwedler. The Würth Museum is open to the public seven days a week. As a rule, admission is free, with the exception of a few temporary exhibitions. The symbiosis of the corporate headquarters of a group of companies and a public museum under a single roof is an absolute novelty. "I claim to have been the first person worldwide to have had the idea to integrate an art museum open to the public into an office building," says Reinhold Würth about the unique character of his museum in Künzelsau. "It is true that there are many corporate collections, yet they are only open to visitors and business associates of a company or a corporation; in other words, the works of art are lost to the public." [579]

There are certainly corporate collections, that is, collections owned by companies that are open to the public in art galleries – for example, the Hypo gallery in Munich or the IBM gallery in New York – but these collections are presented in a separate location, at a distance from the respective businesses. In Künzelsau, visitors meet Würth employees in the museum and the cafeteria and have the opportunity to talk to each other – a circumstance that induced the French consul general to speak about a "place of cultural dialogue with the world around it." [580]

Every year, the Würth Museum offers its visitors four temporary exhibitions focusing on different subjects. These exhibitions give the visitor an insight into the work of individual artists who are represented in the Würth Collection. Since the official opening of the museum, there have been monographic exhibitions of work by Robert Jacobsen, Alfred Hrdlicka, Hans Arp, Rudolf Hausner, Paul Swiridoff, Serge Poliakoff, Max Ernst, Pablo Picasso, Günter Grass, Alberto Magnelli, José de Guimarães, Arnulf Rainer, Jean Michel Basquiat, Markus Lüpertz, Wolfgang Bier, and Klaus Zylla. Other exhibitions concentrate on abstract or figurative art, portraits and self-portraits, intense painting or representations of nature or landscapes. Some exhibitions by the Museum Würth present several artists of a certain geographical area. In past years there have been exhibitions on Austrian, Mexican, Polish, and Spanish art in Künzelsau.

Some projects and exhibitions not only succeed in attracting a huge number of visitors, but also in awakening interest in the arts at the Würth Museum among the media and the public.

So far, the absolute highlight has been Christo and Jeanne-Claude's interior installation in 1995, shortly before their wrapping of the Berlin Reichstag. From January 11 - 27, 1995, the New York environmental artist and his wife together with a team of 25 people created

"Wrapped Floors and Stairways and Covered Windows." The entire interior of the Würth Museum including the cafeteria and a part of the administrative building were included in the project. The artists covered a total of 10,000 ft² (900 m²) of floor space with a type of cloth used by painters in the US to protect furniture and floors from paint splatters. The insides of the windowpanes were covered with brown wrapping paper, creating a honey-colored light in the interior and at the same time blocking the outside view. The walls of the museum remained empty.

Christo's walk-in sculpture attracted almost 82,000 visitors to Künzelsau. The response in the press was overwhelming: more than 230 reports and commentaries from the period of time from the end of January to early June 1995 now fill two large volumes in Würth's central archives. Apart from many national newspapers, international publications such as the Wall Street Journal Europe, The Moscow Times, Art News, New York, and The Straits Times of Singapore also reported on the art event – for an instant, as it were, the whole world looked at Künzelsau.

Almost 78,000 visitors attended "Gauguin und die Schule von Pont-Aven" on display at the Würth Museum from March through June 1997; this exhibition therefore attracted almost as much attention as Christo's installation two years previously. It contained one hundred paintings by Paul Gauguin, Emile Bernard, Paul Sérusier, and seventeen other artists belonging to the important international group that went down in art history as the "school of Pont-Aven." The exhibits of a European private collection had before only been on display in the USA, Australia, and Israel. The Würth Museum was the only venue for this exhibition in Europe.

Kunsthalle Würth in Schwäbisch Hall

With the growth of the Würth Collection over the years and the Würth Museum in Künzelsau being limited in the number of art treasures it can present, the idea of a second "Würth art location" soon came up. In 2001, the vision became a reality with the official opening of the Kunsthalle Würth in Schwäbisch Hall.

REINHOLD WÜRTH
KUNSTHALLE WÜRTH IN SCHWÄBISCH HALL

"The dedication of the 'Kunsthalle' gallery is one of the greatest moments of my professional life," said Reinhold Würth at the press conference that marked the inaugural weekend. The event was celebrated for a whole weekend from May 18 – 20, 2001 with many prominent guests and more than 15,000 people interested in art.

In his opening speech, German Chancellor Gerhard Schröder emphasized the importance of art and culture: while not necessary to the survival of the state, they do make a vital, critical contribution to public discourse. Reinhold Würth shares this view in relation to his business: "I firmly believe that active and critical interaction with art leads to something that can truly be called corporate culture." [581]

Henning Larsen, the well-known architect from Copenhagen, designed the Kunsthalle with its 19,500 ft^2 (1,800 m^2) exhibition space spread over three floors. In the initial competition, Larsen was selected over colleagues such as Sir Norman Foster or Mario Botta. "In Schwäbisch Hall, the challenge was to create a building that dared to be modern and yet fit into both the architecture and the scale of this medieval city. And it had to be part of the ensemble with the striking brewery building and St. Katharine's Church, while, at the same time, being able to stand out and make a statement," [582] remarked the architect, who has realized such projects as the Physics Institute of the Free University of Berlin and the Royal Danish Embassy in Riyadh, Saudi Arabia.

The building that blends harmoniously with Schwäbisch Hall's historic old town was erected in two-and-a-half years. The architect placed the three-story building on an existing underground parking structure in the Katharinenvorstadt on the banks of the Kocher River. The exterior consists of local Crailsheim shell limestone, which had already been used for the medieval town wall and the base floor of the timber-frame houses. The steel and glass dome that houses the staircase is a striking element of the modern elevation that faces toward the town. The top floor opens up in the center to form a spacious assembly room, which affords a unique panorama over the rooftops of the town with the medieval church of St. Michael and the Baroque town hall. This is the ideal exhibition venue for sculptures from the collection.

The largest coherent exhibition room is on the first floor, which is reached by the staircase in the glass dome. A series of smaller rooms on the ground floor also provides a setting for the presentation of graphic works. Construction costs of more than 20 million DM were financed by Adolf Würth GmbH & Co. KG, which also maintains the Kunsthalle – the town of Schwäbisch Hall contributed the site. Admission is free like in the other Würth museums.

At the opening, the Kunsthalle presented about 300 selected works from the Würth Collection. In conjunction with Museum Würth in Künzelsau, special exhibitions in the Kunsthalle take a look at the different aspects of the Würth Collection: masterpieces from 1500 to 1800, expressionist artists like Edvard Munch, impressionist and post-impressionist works, and monographic exhibitions on Eduardo Chillida, Robert Jacobsen, and Max Liebermann.

The Hirschwirtscheuer in Künzelsau

In 1984, "Förderverein Künstlerfamilie Sommer" was founded in Künzelsau. Its stated mission was to explore the history and the works of the Sommer family of artists who lived and worked in Künzelsau for five generations from the middle of the 17th to the beginning of the 19th century. Representatives of the Sommer family of artists worked in many different fields, as sculptors, wood carvers, bridge-builders, stock-makers for rifles, cabinet-makers, and barrel painters. Among many others, the most important works are the stone bridge across the Kocher River in Künzelsau (1694–95), the 16 stone figures of the cabinet of dwarves on the Weikersheim Castle grounds (1713–14), figures and the balustrade of the castle garden in Rügland (1713–1715), the Stephanus Altar in the Schöntal monastery church (1729), the organ pipes in the church of St. John in Künzelsau (1768) and the Bonhoeffer epitaph in the church of St. Michael in Schwäbisch Hall (1770–1773).[583]

Until the beginning of the 19th century, the Sommer family, who had a lasting influence on the Baroque period in Hohenlohe, lived and worked in the Hirschwirtscheuer in Künzelsau. The Förderverein rebuilt it into a museum intended to preserve the memory of the Sommer family.

Fritz Kellermann, who passed away in 1988, took the initiative to rebuild the Hirschwirtscheuer, since he thought it suitable as a museum for the presentation of works by the Sommer family.

The Hirschwirtscheuer had been built in 1760 by the Hohenlohe court mason Johann Georg Scharpf (1726–1785). Originally, it was constructed as a residential building with barn; later on, it was only used a barn. This is why the Hirschwirtscheuer was not in a state of conservation before 1986. It was torn down to the foundation walls so that in 1988–89 a new building in accordance with the old ground plans could be erected on the historical cellar.

The symbol of the Hirschwirtscheuer is the so-called "atlas," a male caryatid by Johann Andreas Sommer (1716–1776). Before, the atlas was positioned on the façade, but in 1989 it was moved inside for reasons of conservation and put on display there. The original position is now occupied by a replica by Peter Nedwal from Rothenburg.

The reconstruction of the Hirschwirtscheuer resulted in roughly 2,800 ft^2 (260 m^2) usable area on three floors. On the first and second floors, visitors can take a look at a permanent exhibition on the Sommer family as well as works of art by the family members; photographs document the life and work of the Sommer family. Temporary exhibitions of modern and contemporary art from the Würth Collection are presented on the top floor.

The cellar preserved in its original state serves as a multi-functional venue for lectures, concerts, and readings. The Förderverein, following an initiative by its chairman, Reinhold Würth, and the Würth Foundation, act as sponsors of the museum, with the reconstruction of the building with its historical cellar being financed by Adolf Würth GmbH & Co. KG.

The Museum of Screws and Threads

Apart from the Würth Museum, a Museum of Screws and Threads is also integrated into the Würth headquarters in Künzelsau. A permanent exhibition displays technical exhibits that are related to fastening and assembly technology, the principal focus of the business. Nine different areas of the application of screws and threads in industry, technology, and everyday life are presented in a space of approximately 2,700 ft^2 (250m^2).

After an introduction on screws and threads, screw shapes in nature and their uses in art are examined. Additional aspects are the Archimedean screw, the airscrew, screws used for lifting, pressing, and clamping as well as fastening, and adjusting screws. In closing, the exhibition explains which role the screw plays in everyday use. With the help of original works on display and models explained by drawings and texts, visitors can understand the historical development of the screw and its importance in the present time.

This section of the museum is mainly intended for customers, trade schools, and the staff of Würth. The special exhibition shown in 1995 entitled "The Screw between Power and Splendor. The Thread in Antiquity," however, attracted many more visitors: 17,000 people saw this exhibition, which was presented in cooperation with the Archaeological Museum Constance and the Stuttgart Monument Authority. The Museum of Screws and Threads of the Würth Company is the only one of its kind in Germany.

The Würth Collection in International Würth Subsidiaries

Being the international entrepreneur that he is, Reinhold Würth does not limit his cultural activities to Germany. For a number of years, the Künzelsau model has been applied to numerous Würth Companies abroad: art and culture are connected with the world of employment by establishing an art gallery or museum either inside the company building itself or right next to it.

The art gallery "Gallerie Würth" was opened in September 2003 right next to Würth Norge in Oslo. The museum covers 6,500 ft^2 (600 m^2) and dedicated its opening exhibition to Pablo Picasso. His works from the Würth Collection constituted the start of a series of temporary exhibitions presenting both modern and contemporary art.

Würth Netherlands in s'Hertogenbosch opened "Kunstlocatie Würth" in 2002 and only one year later had already mounted its third exhibition. "Marc Chagall. Illustraties voor de bijbel" contained 25 original color lithographs from Chagall's bible series that had rarely been shown in such completeness.

The art exhibitions of Würth Austria in Böheimkirchen, Würth Switzerland in Arlesheim, Würth Holding in Chur, and Würth Denmark have for quite some time been

REINHOLD WÜRTH
THE WÜRTH COLLECTION ON THE ROAD

enjoying a positive response, and only recently plans have been made to set up an art gallery at Würth France in Erstein, Alsace.

The Würth Collection on the Road

In the meantime, Reinhold Würth's collection has also been taken note of outside the traditional Würth art locations. Works on loan from the Würth Collection have been shown not only in Hamburg, Frankfurt, Bonn, Constance, and Düsseldorf, but also in Strasbourg, Budapest, Venice, Barcelona, Mexico City, and Hong Kong. In the summer of 1997, a representative cross-section of the corporate collection was shown in Asia for the first time. The 120 pictures, sculptures, and graphics from the Würth Collection were displayed in the National Museum of Contemporary Art in Seoul, the Taipei Museum of Fine Arts, the Kaohsiung Museum of Fine Arts, and the Hong Kong Arts Center. More than 350,000 visitors saw the exhibition of the Würth Collection. The project received a very positive response in all the media.

About 50 works by Christo and Jeanne-Claude were shown in Hong Kong and Guangzhou in China in 1999. In 2000, drawings and watercolors by Günter Grass traveled to exhibitions in the USA and to Singapore. Every year, museums all over the world show exhibits from the Würth Collection. Vice versa, lenders from all over the world are willing to cooperate with the Würth museums. When the Museum on Screws and Threads showed the exhibition "The Screw between Power and Splendor – The Thread in Antiquity" on the occasion of the 50th company anniversary, leading museums of the world made exhibits available. Among them were the Eremitage in St. Petersburg, the Vatican Collections in Rome, the J. Paul Getty Museum in Malibu, and the Stiftung Preußischer Kulturbesitz.[584]

Opening of the exhibition "The Dialogue between Art and Corporate Culture – Modern Art in the Würth Collection" in the Taipei Fine Arts Museum (1997)

Patronage of the Arts within the Framework of the Würth Foundation

In 1987, the entire company assets were transferred to four newly-established family foundations. Concomitant with proprietary regulations governing his succession, Reinhold Würth together with his wife Carmen established the charitable Würth Foundation. Its objective is sponsoring projects from the areas of art, culture, research, and science with income from the Foundation's capital. The Würth Foundation primarily focuses on the Hohenlohe region, to which Reinhold Würth feels closely connected by origin and birth. The Würth Foundation awards research grants, promotes universities, and presents prizes to all kinds of different artists. The Foundation, consisting of a supervisory board and board of management, is endowed with appropriate assets so that its long-term existence is safeguarded.

Würth Prize of the Jeunesses Musicales Deutschland e.V.

Since 1991, this prize has been awarded annually to excellent young ensembles or outstanding personalities from the world of music who feel a special rapport with the objectives of the Jeunesses Musicales Deutschland (JMD). Prize-winners are chosen by the managing board of the JMD, with the award including prize money of EUR 10,000 being sponsored by the Würth Foundation.

REINHOLD WÜRTH
WÜRTH PRIZE OF THE JEUNESSES MUSICALES DEUTSCHLAND E.V.

Prize Winners of the Jeunesses Musicales Deutschland

1991	Dennis Russell Davis
1992	Arcis-Quintett, München
1993	Philip Glass
1994	Dietmar Schönherr for the Nicaragua project Casa de los Tres Mundos in Granada
1995	The three children's choirs Tölz Boys' Choir, the Philharmonic Choir Prague, and the Polish Nightingales, Poznan, for the realization of the children's opera project Brundibár
1996	Yakov Kreizberg
1997	Young German Philharmonic Orchestra, Frankfurt
1998	Prof. Henry W. Meyer, Cincinnati (USA)
1999	Tabea Zimmermann, viola
2000	National Children's Orchestra of Venezuela
2001	Claudio Abbado
2002	Ensemble Resonanz
2003	Theo Geißler (publisher and editor-in-chief of "neue musikzeitung")
2004	The Berlin Philharmonic Orchestra for their educational program Zukunft@BPhil

The Robert-Jacobsen Prize

Since 1993, this prize has been awarded by the Würth Foundation every other year to an artist from the field of fine arts. Following an initiative by Reinhold Würth, the award was inaugurated the year the Danish sculptor Robert Jacobsen passed away. It comes with prize money of EUR 15,000.

Winners of the Robert-Jacobsen Prize

1993	Lun Tuchnowski
1995	Richard Deacon
1997	Magdalena Jetelovà
1999	Gereon Lepper
2001	Stephan Kern
2003	Rui Chafes

The Tübingen Visiting Professorship in Poetry

The Visiting Professorship in Poetry awarded since 1996 enables the University of Tübingen to invite prominent writers to give lectures and workshop seminars. The members of the Visiting Professorship in Poetry change every semester.

Tübingen Visiting Professorship in Poetry

1996	Marlene Streeruwitz, João Ubaldo Ribeiro
1997	Tankred Dorst, Aleksander Tisma
1998	Yoko Tawada, Andrzej Szczypiorski
1999	Gerhard Köpf, Günter Grass
2000	Aras Ören and eight other authors, among them Herta Müller, Yoko Tawada, and Alissa Walser
2001	Herta Müller, Peter Rühmkorf
2002	Amos Oz, Juan Goytisolo
2003	Peter Turrini

Würth Literature Prize

In close cooperation with the Tübingen Visiting Professorship in Poetry, the Würth Literature Prize has been awarded since 1996. The author who occupies the Professorship chooses the topic and has a considerable influence on the awarding of the prize. The prize money of the award can be subdivided among several winners. The prize money of the Würth Literature Prize is EUR 7,500.

1ST WÜRTH LITERATURE PRIZE 1996
Subject: "Breakfast and Violence"; Prize winners: Odile Kennel, Chris Ohnemus, Doris Reckewell, Ingeborg Schulte, Daniel Zahno

2ND WÜRTH LITERATURE PRIZE 1996
Subject: "The Teachings of Foreign Parts – the Inner Void of the Foreigner"; Prize winners: Josiane Alfonsi, Friedrich K. Rumpf, Anette Puttmann

3RD WÜRTH LITERATURE PRIZE 1997
Subject: "Money or Your Life"; Prize winners: Terèzia Kriedemann and Horst von Buttlar

4TH WÜRTH LITERATURE PRIZE 1997
Subject: "Power and Women"; 1st prize: Bruno Preisendörfer, 2nd prize: Karla Reimert, Beate Schlachter, Antje Telgenbüscher

5TH WÜRTH LITERATURE PRIZE 1998
Subject: "Metamorphoses"; Prize winners: Elke Domhardt, Anne Hauschild, Stefan Thomas

6TH WÜRTH LITERATURE PRIZE 1998
Subject: "Gun and Dignity"; Prize winners: Marcus Hammerschmitt, Irmgard Hierdeis, Heinrich Steinfest

7TH WÜRTH LITERATURE PRIZE 1999
Subject: "Noble-Mindedness – Style – Elegance";
Prize winners: Gerhard Engbarth, Volker Just, Kirsten Kühlke,
Sylvie Schenk-Gonsolin, Jochen Schmidt

8TH WÜRTH LITERATURE PRIZE 1999
Subject: "Mixed Class"; Prize winners: Martina Kieninger,
Eckhard Schmidt-Dubro, Patrick Wilden

9TH WÜRTH LITERATURE PRIZE 2000
Subject: "The Shark in My Head"; Prize winners: Fabienne Pakleppa,
Friedrun Schütze-Schröder, Hellmut Seiler

10TH WÜRTH LITERATURE PRIZE 2000
Subject: "If the Cat Were a Horse One Could Ride Through the Trees";
Prize winners: Zoran Drvenkar, Mike Markart

11TH WÜRTH LITERATURE PRIZE 2001
Subject: "The Handbag"; Prize winners: Birgit Müller-Wieland
and Jutta Reichelt

12TH WÜRTH LITERATURE PRIZE 2001
Subject: "The Story of the Crane that Wanted to be a Ship's Siren";
Prize winners: Stefanie Golisch, Mathias Jeschke, Harald Winter

13TH WÜRTH LITERATURE PRIZE 2002
Subject: "A Love Affair"; Prize winners: Alexandra Lavizzari,
Sandra Niermeyer, Guido Rademacher, Beate Rygiert

14TH WÜRTH LITERATURE PRIZE 2002
Subject: "Naivety – Variety"; Prize winners: Marcus Jensen
and Rebekka Malter

15TH WÜRTH LITERATURE PRIZE 2003
Subject: "Goodbye Tübingen?"; Prize winners: Annette de Jong
and Daniela Arbeiter

REINHOLD WÜRTH
WÜRTH PRIZE FOR EUROPEAN LITERATURE

Würth Prize for European Literature

Since 1997, the Würth Prize for European Literature with EUR 25,000 prize money has been awarded every other year. After 2004, the Würth Literature Prize and the Würth Prize for European Literature will be awarded alternately every other year.

Prizewinner: author Hermann Lenz (†1998) receives the newly established "Würth Prize for European Literature" from Reinhold Würth (1997)

Winners of the Würth Prize for European Literature

1997	Hermann Lenz
1999	Claudio Magris
2001	Claude Vigée
2003	Harald Hartung

Support for Universities

The Würth Foundation also supports regional universities and colleges. The Foundation has a long-standing association with the Heilbronn University of Applied Sciences, making it possible for students to spend time abroad to gain practical experience and new insights. In 2000, a chair in sports management was endowed for a period of 10 years at the Künzelsau branch of the Heilbronn University of Applied Sciences. The Universities of Tübingen and Karlsruhe also receive assistance from the Würth Foundation on a regular basis for a wide variety of projects.

Positions held by Reinhold Würth in the Sponsorship of Art and Culture

- Member of the board of trustees of the Philharmonic Orchestra of Nations
- Member of the board of trustees of the Birgit Keil Dance Foundation
- Member of the board of trustees of the European Cultural Forum Mainau
- Deputy chairman of the board of trustees of the Cultural Foundation of the Länder
- Partner and patron of the Baden-Württemberg Art Foundation
- Chairman of the Friends of the Wiener Männergesang-Verein e.V. (founder chairman)
- Chairman of the Association of the Friends of the Burgfestspiele Jagsthausen e.V. (successor of Prof. Roman Herzog)
- Patron of the Burgfestspiele Jagsthausen
- Deputy chairman of the managing board of the Carmel Foundation
- Chairman of the Society for the Promotion of the Württembergische Landesmuseum e.V., Stuttgart
- Member of the managing board of the Stuttgart Gallery Association
- Member of the board of trustees of the Hohenlohe Cultural Foundation

Reinhold Würth together with Kurt Schuh,
former chairman of the Vienna Men's Choir (1997)

Swiridoff Publishing Company

A large number of publications result from Reinhold Würth's widespread cultural commitments, be they the catalogs of the Würth Museum and the Kunsthalle Würth, the Hirschwirtscheuer, or the publications by the winners of the literature prizes. In 1999, Würth took over the Swiridoff Publishing Company founded by Paul Swiridoff, in order to concentrate this wide variety of publications in one place, and integrated it into the Würth Group. The company is run by C. Sylvia Weber, director of the field of art at Würth, and the managing director of the publishing house is Norbert Brey.

Reinhold Würth in conversation with Paul Swiridoff during his exhibition "Gesichter einer Epoche" in the Würth Museum in Künzelsau (1997)

The publishing company bears the name of the photographer Paul Swiridoff (1914–2002) who lived in Schwäbisch Hall for many decades and became known through many illustrated books on cities, though mostly by portraits of personalities who have shaped Germany since 1945. Swiridoff, who became friends with Reinhold Würth at the end of the 1960s, also acted as editor and publisher of the successful company magazine Würth-report from 1970–1992. In a retrospective, the publishing company honors the lifetime achievements of the late Paul Swiridoff, the man who gave the publishing house his name.

The Swiridoff Publishing Company carries many catalogs on exhibitions and literary publications in its range, and also up-market volumes on photography and architecture. These are complemented by an increasing number of publications on the cultural history of southwest Germany; recently, a new guide to Hohenlohe was published that shows the home of Würth in its true light. In cooperation with the chair of entrepreneurship at the University of Karlsruhe, which was held by Reinhold Würth from 1999 to 2003, a number of specialist books on management and economic issues have also been published.

"The Most Public Form of Art" – Architecture at Würth

"Corporate art is […] nothing new," says Reinhold Würth, giving as examples the office design of the commercial companies and banking houses of the 18th century or the industrial architecture of the early 20th century, such as the AEG turbine shed in Berlin (1909) or the Fiat plant by Matté Truco in Turin (1919–1926). In addition to large-scale sculptures and the plastic arts, he considers architecture to be "the most public form of art" since it can be experienced by each and every one of us, day and night. Industrial architecture can thus claim to have an especially intense effect on corporate identity and corporate culture. With the company buildings of the Würth Group, Reinhold Würth wants his staff to experience "open-mindedness, cosmopolitanism, and joie de vivre […] in the working environment." [585]

At Würth it has become a tradition to erect company buildings going beyond everyday commercial architecture. "There can be few companies in Germany in which the economic recovery after the second world war is reflected as directly and as impressively in its architecture", states the book Building for the World. Architecture at Würth. It was published in 2000 and illustrates the wide variety and quality of the company buildings worldwide. [586]

The first and comparatively modest administrative building designed by the architect Hans-Peter Sperling in Gaisbach in 1969 already differed greatly from the then-popular industrial buildings, owing to its shape. Sep Ruf, one of the most distinguished architects of post-war modernism, set the standards with the extension to this building in 1974. When, eleven years later, the company ran out of space and thought about the construction of a new administrative headquarters for the entire Würth Group, it was clear from the outset that the building should also provide a forum for its burgeoning cultural and social interests. The wishes and ideas of the building owner were specified in the announcement for the architectural competition in 1985: in addition to operations-related space that could meet the evolving demands of a flexible business organization, Rein-

REINHOLD WÜRTH
"THE MOST PUBLIC FORM OF ART" – ARCHITECTURE AT WÜRTH

> "What's so nice about Reinhold Würth is that he makes decisions quickly. And it is this speed that's one of the success factors of his family-owned business – always a step ahead of the competition."
>
> Siegfried Müller, architect, designed and built the Würth corporate headquarters in Künzelsau together with Maja Djordjevic-Müller

hold Würth wanted to have a distinctive communications and exhibition area to "take into account the special interest of the promisor and owner as promoter of the arts and music, but also the obligations resulting from worldwide activities and business relations." The planned museum for screws and technical connectors, a gallery for art exhibitions and a hall for presentations and concerts were all supposed to be accessible through a prestigious entrance. The announcement continued: "The promisor expects proposals and suggestions which concisely express contemporary architectural conceptions in their quality and design," with anticipation of "a qualified statement about the architecture of the eighties."

Finally, the young architects from Stuttgart, Maja Djordjevic and Siegfried Müller, were awarded the contract. In the competition they had beaten everybody, including the stars of the architectural scene, and convinced both Reinhold Würth and the eleven jury members, among them professors of architecture, banking experts, and representatives of the company.

With its wide hall, its large glass roof, and open railings and gangways, the headquarters building officially opened in 1991 "quite intentionally creates the impression of a ship, an ocean steamer" and thus expresses open-mindedness and cosmopolitanism.[587] The museum on the first floor of the building aims to demonstrate to the company's employees that Würth is "not merely a commercial enterprise with a provincial focus, with its eye solely on turnover and profits, but that it is in fact the fine arts that make working life worth living." On the other hand, it also gives the people who live in this neighborhood the opportunity to find out more about commercial activities and developments at the Würth Group as an incidental part of their visit to the museum.[588]

At Würth, there is no formal guideline that specifies creative instructions or demands Group-specific designs. Reinhold Würth explains that an architectural or building department to handle the planning of administrative and warehouse buildings worldwide would contradict the principles of decentralization and liberalization. "Instead, Würth allows every company in the Group to have its own culture under an umbrella of integrity, calculability, and reliability." This is why the company buildings at Würth are widely heterogeneous in style and architecture and designed very differently. The newly erected offices and warehouse buildings of the foreign subsidiaries represent examples of the industrial architecture of the respective countries in the respective periods of time. It is Würth's desire to "make a modest contribution to the cultural history of industrial architecture." [589]

Entrepreneurship in Theory and Practice – the Entrepreneur on His Way to Professorship

Dr. h.c. Reinhold Würth's life work, the outstanding development of the Würth Group, has also impressed academic institutions. He has been appointed honorary senator and honorary doctor of the University of Tübingen as well as professor at the University of Karlsruhe, where he held Germany's first chair of entrepreneurship from 1999 to 2003. Today, Reinhold Würth, the practician of the trade, can count on the respect of academic dignitaries: "I would be lying if I didn't admit that the right to hold these titles flatters my self-esteem." [590]

Honorary Senator of the University of Tübingen

On February 22, 1991, Reinhold Würth was appointed honorary senator of the University of Tübingen. In his eulogy, Prof. Joachim Starbatty of the economics faculty emphasized that a "strong determination to shape things" was discernible both in Reinhold Würth's business activities and in his commitment to art and culture. The secret of Würth's commercial success could certainly also be explained by the "symbiosis of art and commerce." Prof. Starbatty continued that Würth did not focus on management technique alone in describing the task of running a business, but rather stressed the importance of management culture: "Anybody who knows management technique inside out is merely a "business manager;" it is management culture that will turn him or her into a real 'entrepreneur.'" [591]

The Eberhard-Karls-University Tübingen paying tribute to Reinhold Würth: he is appointed honorary senator. Next to him Prof. Dr. Adolf Theis, president of the University at the time (1991)

Würth elaborated on this subject in his speech on the occasion of his appointment: from the sociological perspective of the business, both subjective and emotional matters influenced the success of the company to an extent that the overall economy had not yet sufficiently recognized. For many people, time spent at their place of work offered the most important opportunity for communicating with others, "a marketplace used for the exchange of ideas, opinions and views." [592] The business was therefore challenged to offer a corporate culture to its employees that "radiates harmony, human warmth, and security."

Honorary Doctor of the University of Tübingen

"This is one of the most important days in my life," Reinhold Würth said upon being awarded an honorary doctorate by the University of Tübingen on April 30, 1999. In the 20 years before that, the economics faculty of the Eberhard-Karls-University only awarded four such honorary titles.

In his eulogy, the economist Franz X. Bea stated that Würth's success was based on the realization of a management concept characterized by corporate culture. For this reason, it was neither the successful entrepreneur nor the long-time sponsor of the University of Tübingen appointed honorary doctor. First and foremost, the cosmopolitan visionary was honoured who not only had innovative ideas, but also put these ideas into practice. At Würth, not only management know-how or sales strategies were important, but also simple human virtues emphasizing a "moral dimension believed to have disappeared in the sphere of the market." [593]

In his acceptance speech, Reinhold Würth remarked that he did not explain his success solely with his 50 years of experience in his business, but also owed these achievements to his staff and his wife. Afterward, he summarized the principal aspects of his corporate philosophy that were mainly responsible for the international successes of the Würth Group. In his speech, Reinhold Würth said: "Management in my business is characterized by its decentralized organization and liberal ethos. According to this principle, management positions in individual countries are almost exclusively filled by locals: a Thai, a New Zealander, or a Brazilian will naturally evaluate and assess the mentality and historical roots of his fellow countrymen much better than somebody from Group headquarters."

Dr. Werner Neus presenting Reinhold Würth with an honorary doctorate from the Eberhard-Karls-University Tübingen (1999)

In his function as member of the newly established university council of the Eberhard-Karls-University, Reinhold Würth has continued to watch over the further development of this academic institution since the fall of 2000.

Professor of Entrepreneurship at the University of Karlsruhe

In the winter semester 1999/2000, Dr. h.c. Reinhold Würth was offered the chair in entrepreneurship, the first of its kind in Germany. Following a comment by the Federal Ministry of Economics and Research in the summer of 1999, the universities felt obliged to make a contribution to increasing the number of business formations. In the period following, 35 chairs of entrepreneurship were established, the one at the University of Karlsruhe being the first. Reinhold Würth ran the Entrepreneurship Institute until September 2003.

PLATE 13

1 Würth Spain is situated in Palau-Solità i Plegamans close to Barcelona
2 The administrative building of Würth Austria in Böheimkirchen, about 44 miles (70 km) from Vienna

PLATE 14

1 The impressive facade of Würth Greece can be seen in Krioneri close to Athens
2 What a beauty: Würth Finland is located in Riihimäki, about 40 miles (65 km) from Helsinki
3 Steadfast: the administrative building of Würth Norway in Hagan, about 15 miles (25 km) from Oslo
4 A sea of lights: Würth Netherlands s situated in s'Hertogenbosch in the vicinity of Eindhoven
5 The administrative building of Würth Belux in Turnhout/Belgium, about 28 miles (45 km) from Antwerp
6 A true oasis: the administrative building of Würth Portugal in Sintra, about 15 miles (25 km) from Lisbon

PLATE 15

1 The administrative building of Würth France in Erstein close to Strasbourg **2** The Würth House Berlin on Schwanenwerder peninsula at the Wannsee was officially opened in June 2003

REINHOLD WÜRTH
PROFESSOR OF ENTREPRENEURSHIP AT THE UNIVERSITY OF KARLSRUHE

The Karlsruhe chair in entrepreneurship had been endowed by the Walldorf-based software manufacturer, SAP. At first there had been a lot of conflict within the university over the question of where the chair should be established. It was finally decided that it would be best set up in the engineering department, to stimulate students and convey to them basic knowledge for a possible later job as entrepreneur. Prof. Dr.-Ing. Volker Krebs, head of the Institute of Servo- and Control Mechanisms (IRS) and at that time dean of the electrical engineering faculty, succeeded in attracting the chair to his faculty. A so-called "search committee" comprising members of the participating faculties, the presidency, and the students looked for suitable personalities for the professorial position and made the unanimous decision to approach the entrepreneur Reinhold Würth.

Prof. Krebs is convinced: "In Reinhold Würth the faculty had won a personality who represents and conveys interdisciplinary qualifications." [594] The appointment met with widespread response in the press since it was a novelty in the German university scene, which was very much characterized by academic titles and formal qualifications, that somebody merely on the basis of his practical experience without a university education should receive an honorary professorship.

In an interview, Reinhold Würth remarked: "I believe that the idea of the former president, Sigmar Wittig, to give the chair of entrepreneurship to a man of practice, was certainly a very courageous one for Germany." [595] However, he is of the opinion that such courage is definitely called for, since young entrepreneurs are absolutely indispensable for a country's economic growth. "Over the next ten years it is […] important to dramatically increase the number of business start-ups. In 1999, Reynolds and others asked a representative group of adults in the G-7 nations as well as in Israel, Denmark, and Finland if they were currently thinking about starting their own business. The study shows that at the time 8.4 % of the persons asked in the USA pondered self-employment, 3.3 % in Great Britain, but only 2.2 % in Germany." [596]

> "Veni vidi vici – that's how one could describe Reinhold Würth's activities as professor at the University of Karlsruhe."
>
> Prof. Dr. Hans Joachim Klein,
> Institute of Sociology at the University of Karlsruhe

An Entrepreneur's Curriculum

Together with three academic assistants and a secretary, Reinhold Würth developed a two-semester curriculum that consisted of 16 lectures in the winter semester and twelve in the summer semester. It was the Institute's objective to give all the students at the University of Karlsruhe the opportunity to familiarize themselves with the concepts of career and self-employment. Reinhold Würth's lectures, in which he talked about the art of starting your own business, were attended by up to 200 students.

Würth does not only see the businessman or businesswoman as an entrepreneur, but also as "someone who is prepared to assume responsibility, to render exemplary performances in his or her career, and to handle facts with readiness to achieve, inventiveness and entrepreneurial courage so as to dissolve obsolete structures through creative destruction, as proposed by Schumpeter, to the benefit of one's company, one's own career or the community, and someone who brings forth modern, up-to-date, future-oriented innovations." [597] Among the entrepreneurs invited by him to give lectures were business founders, the president of the University of Karlsruhe, and the mayor of Schwäbisch Hall.

Reinhold Würth published the results of his work at the Entrepreneurship Institute in a series of writings (IEP) of the Swiridoff Publishing Company. In the first volume "Entrepreneurship in Germany – Ways toward responsibility" he shares his own wealth of entrepreneurial experience, whereas in two other volumes young entrepreneurs whom Prof. Würth invited to guest lectures describe their experience as founders of businesses. Another volume of the series, which comprises 12 volumes in total, is dedicated to the results of a study of the economic knowledge of young people in Baden-Württemberg carried out in cooperation with Prof. Dr. Hans Joachim Klein from the Institute of Sociology of the University of Karlsruhe. [598]

"At the university, Mr. Würth taught entrepreneurial thinking on all levels. This means that employees also learn how to think like entrepreneurs."

Prof. Dr. Ing. Volker Krebs,
vice-president of the University of Karlsruhe

REINHOLD WÜRTH
AN ENTREPRENEUR'S CURRICULUM

Relaxed: Prof. Dr. Reinhold Würth during his inaugural lecture to students of the University of Karlsruhe (1999)

After only a few months of Prof. Würth's activities, it became obvious that the Interdisciplinary Entrepreneurship Institute established at the electrical engineering faculty had also developed close ties with the economics faculty. The latter therefore offered double membership to the Entrepreneurship Institute so that Reinhold Würth was now also in a position to supervise economic dissertations and doctoral theses. In his teaching post, Reinhold Würth focused on imparting the so-called "soft skills" that are of paramount importance for success in business: "In lectures and seminars I try to make the students aware of the importance of soft skills, to make them understand what it means to build up a positive attitude in one's colleagues and superiors by being predictable, willing to perform, showing keenness, and by pursuing goal-directed career marketing." [599]

Taking the example of his own business' expansion, together with other positive examples, Reinhold Würth explained to the students what is important in the process of starting up one's own business. At the beginning of every company formation, there is a vision: "The successful businessman differs from his average colleague by his ability to visualize, to conceive the inconceivable. In my long career as an entrepreneur, I have often been smiled and even laughed at by my staff. Every person in a leading position must understand that normally nothing will develop positively in an evolutionary fashion in a club, in a family, in a business, or in a country that has not already been anticipated in the hearts and minds of those people leading such institutions," observed Würth in one of his introductory lectures. [600]

To show how visions can be realized successfully, he described the development of the Würth Group and also used examples such as Sam Walton (WalMart), Richard and Maurice McDonalds, and Henry Ford. The historical development of entrepreneurship since early industrialization was the subject of one of his lectures, as was the current socio-political environment as a factor influencing business start-ups. In his lectures at the university, Würth also shed light on aspects such as globalization or corporate PR work, using many examples from his own business.

"In theory, everybody can learn the tools of the trade and read up on the pre-requisites for self-employment. What is much more important, though, is the ability to lead people and to be enthusiastic, reliable, persevering and unwavering enough to get one's own convictions accepted. I have always said: 'The world is full of giants in knowledge, but also full of dwarves in implementation.'" [601]

Stimulus for Self-Employment

Reinhold Würth saw his lectures as a "medium to long-term investment." The majority of students initially became salaried employees, but, encouraged by his example, would possibly develop a business idea and "[become] self-employed perhaps two to three years earlier than they would have without my lectures." [602]

Würth indeed encouraged some of his students to start up their own business, among them Mirko Holzer, "an enthusiastic informatics student" who one day heard from a friend "some multibillionaire" [603] gave lectures on business formation. He attended Prof. Würth's inaugural lecture, thought it "inspiring and motivating," and was won over. Holzer finally got his idea accepted that entrepreneurship was also recognized as supplementary subject for informatics students. When he won a business plan competition organized by Würth, he was given the opportunity to accompany Reinhold Würth to a conference of Würth Spain. In Holzer's opinion, Würth's "entrepreneurial fervor" was extremely infectious, and upon Reinhold Würth's advice he started his own business, founding pi-consult GmbH even before finishing his university studies. He takes Reinhold Würth as an example and intellectual mentor, still maintains contact with him, and at regular intervals updates Würth on the progress of his young company. [604]

Prof. Würth's interest in, and commitment to, the University of Karlsruhe went beyond his lectureship at the Entrepreneurship Institute. Time permitting, he also dealt with the concerns of the faculty and attended faculty meetings "to learn more about

REINHOLD WÜRTH
STIMULUS FOR SELF-EMPLOYMENT

the processes of a faculty and find out how they differ from the processes in a company," noted Prof. Krebs. [605] He recapitulates that Würth's activities at the Fridericiana and his many contacts with public figures and personalities from the world of finance made an

> "The business of our company is completely different from classical trade, but we nevertheless put some of Würth's principles into practice, first of all the rule to finance growth from corporate profit without taking out loans, raising money through the stock exchange, or using venture capital."
>
> Mirko Holzer,
> general manager of pi-consult; former student of Reinhold Würth

"enormous impact" that turned out to be highly advantageous for the university as a whole. Following an invitation by Reinhold Würth, a number of highly acclaimed speakers visited the University of Karlsruhe. The by far most prominent example was the visit by German Chancellor Gerhard Schröder, who came to the Fridericiana on May 5, 2003 to discuss with the students reforms aimed at supporting Germany's economic efficiency. After four years, in September 2003, Reinhold Würth concluded his activities at the Entrepreneurship Institute. However, this step has not put an end to his lecturing activities in general. Within the framework of studies accompanying the job and finishing with the Master of Business Administration (MBA) for employees of the Würth Group developed in cooperation with the Heilbronn University of Applied Sciences, the University of Louisville, Kentucky (USA), and the Grand Valley State University of Allendale, Michigan (USA), he continues to teach students and in September 2002 was appointed professor at the College of Business and Public Administration at the University of Louisville, Kentucky.

13 CONQUERING NEW TERRITORY

Würth in the New Millennium

After Reinhold Würth had taken the chair of the Advisory Board of the Würth Group in January 1994, the business under his direction and under the direction of his official successors, Group spokesman Dr. Walter Jaeger and Rolf Bauer, successfully moved in the direction of fulfilling the "Vision 2000" whose forecasts were realized right on time in the year 2000.

Neither Reinhold Würth nor his managers rested on their laurels, however. New fields of business and many new acquisitions also accounted for the Würth Group's growth in the first few years of the new millennium.

Turbulent Times – the First Few Years of the New Century

All over the world the new millennium was noisily celebrated on the night of New Year's Eve 1999.[606] Fortunately, apprehensions about the predicted computer chaos were unfounded.

However, the second and unforeseeable IT problem of the year, the computer virus "I l love you" that circulated in May 2000, caused worldwide damage of 20 billion DM. In theory, it also affected those 20 per cent of the inhabitants of Baden-Württemberg who had access to the Internet. Fifty per cent of all households in the state had a PC in 2000 and 30 per cent owned a mobile phone – the age of communication had set in. In the course of year, the bursting of the so-called "dotcom bubble" loomed owing to the collapse of technology equities on the US stock exchange. Stock prices hit a low. In Germany, the most important event of the summer was the EXPO in Hanover that, however, only turned out to be a modest commercial success because of the unexpectedly low number of visitors (who nevertheless had to stand in line to get in).

In retrospect, the year 2001 was dominated solely by the events of 9/11 in the USA. Almost simultaneously, four hijacked passenger planes flew into the twin towers of the World Trade Center, the Pentagon, and in the direction of Camp David. Several thousand people died. Since then, the USA has declared war on international terrorism. After the attacks, NATO invoked Article 5 of the North Atlantic Treaty. German Chancellor Schröder assured US President Bush of Germany's complete support, yet the question of German soldiers being deployed in Afghanistan initially caused a crisis in the Red-Green ruling coalition.

War and terrorism would preoccupy Germany and the world in 2002 as well. Terrorist attacks alarmed the population worldwide, with atrocities such as those on the Tunisian vacation island of Jerba, where 21 people were killed when a tank truck exploded in front of a synagogue, and on the island of Bali, where a terrorist attack killed almost 200 people. Sixteen tourists were killed by a suicide attack in Kenya and, in Moscow, 700 theater-goers were taken hostage, with tragic outcome. The hostage-takers, who were demanding an end to the war in Chechnya, were killed alongside 130 hostages when a special Russian task force stormed the theater. Apolitical acts of violence and accidents also made headlines, however. In the US, two serial killers terrorized the surroundings of Washington. Before they could be arrested, the two men had killed 14 people, and in Germany a 19-year old student ran amok, killing 17 people and finally himself in his high school in Erfurt. When air traffic control failed at Lake Constance, a Russian passenger plane and a cargo plane collided, killing 71 people.

The imminent war in Iraq became a campaign issue in 2002 and, after German Chancellor Gerhard Schröder had categorically refused the participation of German troops, tension increased between Berlin and Washington. Even though UN inspectors searching for weapons of mass destruction did not find any such weapons, US troops and their allies marched into Iraq in March 2003. In May 2003, US President George W. Bush declared the main military action to be over.

The most negative event of 2002 in Germany was the flooding of the Elbe River in Eastern Germany. This caused 21 deaths, billion-euro damage, and left tens of thousands of people homeless. On the other hand, this disaster led people to donate the huge amount of 250 million euro to the relief fund, which possibly contributed to the success of the ruling coalition of SPD and the Greens in the parliamentary elections in September, even if only by a slim majority.

The year 2002 had started with the introduction of euro currency in Germany and eleven other European countries. The transition was very smooth, but the question of whether the introduction of the euro led to price increases is still being debated today – the term "Teuro" was named word of the year. But it was not just in Germany that the financial year was characterized by business failures and industrial scandal.

In the US, the energy trader Enron Corp had to answer charges of corruption and mismanagement. In Germany, Ron Sommer, chief executive of Deutsche Telekom, finally resigned under pressure. Billion-euro debts caused the T-share to plummet to less than a tenth of its highest value, with almost three million private investors losing a lot of money in the process. The company MobilCom, too, was close to insolvency. Almost half of the 4,200 employees were laid off, experiencing the same fate as the other four million unemployed. The Federal Government placed its hopes on the suggestions submitted by a body of experts, the so-called Hartz Committee. Catchwords such as "Ich-AG" and personnel service agencies were expected to find ways out of the crisis; the Federal Labor Office was supposed to be reformed.

In eastern Germany, the unemployment rate of 17.6 per cent was still twice as high as in the west at 7.8 per cent. The global economic situation was not much better. In the USA and South America, too, people experienced a climate of tension, particularly so in Argentina where mass protests turned into street riots.

In 2002, Baden-Württemberg turned 50. People were quite satisfied with the economic situation here; at the time of the state's anniversary, four times as many goods and services were being produced per capita than at the time of the state's founding in 1952. Since its high in 1997, the unemployment rate had declined slightly again, even though Baden-Württemberg has been experiencing a structural change for ten years now that primarily affects the industrial sector, a traditional stronghold in Baden-Württemberg.

It is generally believed that – as a consequence of the development of the population, which has been an issue of discussion since the 1990s, and in view of the long-term high unemployment rate – German society is facing major challenges at the beginning of the new millennium. People in Germany, however, are increasingly disenchanted with politics, a circumstance that became particularly obvious at the start of the new millennium. Only about 62 per cent of the electorate actually voted in the Baden-Württemberg state elections in 2001.

The Vision Becomes a Reality – the New Millennium at Würth

For Adolf Würth GmbH & Co. KG, the millennium got off to a positive start. In Germany, a boom in the export industry resulted in the strongest economic growth since the reunification of the country, even though both the construction industry and the auto repair trade had ample reason to complain. The Würth Group achieved the goal of generating sales of more than ten billion DM worldwide with more than 30,000 employees in 2000, a target that Reinhold Würth had already envisioned in 1987: his "Vision 2000" made a precision landing. Two hundred and thirty-six companies in seventy-six countries worldwide – many of these purchased in the 1990s – had helped to achieve this goal. The 500,000 German customers of Würth could rely on the company's 98 per cent service level, and in 2001, roughly 22,000 shipments left the distribution center in Künzelsau-Gaisbach with its 560,000 ft² (52,000m²) warehouse space every day. [607]

Recessionary trends in the global economy had started to emerge in 2001, however, and were intensified by insecurity on the part of consumers and investors as well as by massive turbulence on international financial markets as a consequence of 9/11. The German economy, too, did not develop as expected, with the anticipated economic upturn failing to materialize. Growth almost came to a standstill because of people's unwillingness to invest and their anti-consumption attitude. For the first time since the reunification of Germany, private consumption, so far the strongest support of the economy, was weaker than in the previous year: "German consumers were more inclined to save than to spend." [608] Sales dropped by almost 5 per cent in the construction sector. Since the peak of the construction boom in the middle of the 1990s, 40 per cent of jobs in this industry had been lost. The situation was particularly serious in the new Länder.

And yet, the Würth Group succeeded in increasing its sales volume in the year 2001 to the record high of 5.28 billion euro worldwide. 2002 also turned out to be a record year, with sales amounting to 5.35 billion euro and an operating result that had grown by 10 per cent over the previous year and reached almost 300 million euro. [609]

2003 was still a critical year, particularly for Adolf Würth GmbH & Co. KG. Sales figures were not satisfactory, and the measures initiated caused a lot of unrest among the staff. In cooperation with the Council of Trustees, 200 jobs were cut, as far as possible through natural wastage. Employees were asked to go into early retirement or transferred to subsidiaries. The number of trainees in the 18 different professions was reduced considerably.

The other side of the coin was not satisfactory for Adolf Würth GmbH & Co. KG either: despite a crisis on the labor market, many sales representatives left the company voluntarily. In the summer of 2003, the spokesman of the management of Adolf Würth GmbH & Co. KG, Peter Zürn, submitted a study on fluctuation in the sales force to the Board of Management.[610] The result was not positive at all: fluctuation had reached a record high in April and May. Never before had so many sales representatives left the company in one month, a fact that had been looming on the horizon during the preceding months and which proved very expensive for Adolf Würth GmbH & Co. KG.

As is typical of the company, though, action was taken immediately. Peter Zürn, appointed member of the Board of Management in 1996 – he had at that time taken over the International Automotive Division from Rolf Bauer – declared the fight against fluctuation in the sales force to be the most important task. The management anticipated that an improved hiring procedure[611], the installation of an early warning system, and the evaluation of leaving interviews would all have a positive effect. The early warning system, which was developed specifically for Würth, identifies sales representatives likely to leave so that management can initiate appropriate countermeasures in good time.[612]

The Chairman of the Advisory Board at Grass Roots Level

There were different opinions about the reason for the crisis: after all, competitors and even the Reca Group, a member of the Würth Group, were not as hard hit by the crisis as Adolf Würth GmbH & Co. KG. General opinion was that the overall economic crisis was only a marginal factor, even though the small and medium-scale sector of the German economy was suffering from real problems for the first time since the end of the war: the domestic market had developed poorly whereas other European countries such as Spain had invested a great deal of money.

Reinhold Würth, too, was worried about his first business, Adolf Würth GmbH & Co. KG, but on the other hand he was also optimistic. During a meeting of the Board of Management in Kupferzell in the summer of 2003, he stated that economic theory, too, said that a company in its "phase of maturity" would, after having overcome the crisis, quite often experience much more dynamic growth than before.[613] In his opinion, it was very important for the further growth of the Würth Group to develop so-called "high potentials," upcoming top managers in the Würth Companies to preserve the identity of the Würth Group. Having an outsider take over a top management position, as happened recently at Würth Netherlands, had to remain an exception.

During the Würth Congress in Dubai, which had been postponed to the summer because of the Iraq war, he analyzed the figures of the first seven months of 2003. His summary was by no means totally negative. "External sales have gone up by 1.2 per cent, the operating result increased by 3.4 per cent to 211.0 million euro, the number of sales representatives was stepped up by 7.7 per cent to 22,695, and the number of in-house staff remained almost constant at 18,275. We succeeded in further improving stock turns to 5.7 [...] disappointments and successes are close together. [...] It is true that we can only report very modest growth for the last three years. A few months ago Rolf Bauer said something very important: he remarked that Würth probably no longer had a concept of its opponents in the market! Indeed, we have left all of our competitors way behind, and now we suddenly find ourselves in a (relative) vacuum of success; it seems as if some of our managers no longer know what to do next." [614]

In his speech, the chairman of the Advisory Board of the Würth Group indicated the one direction that his managers could head for. "Because of their age, the oldest companies of our Group, AW KG and Würth Netherlands, are currently experiencing a phase of insecurity, a lack of orientation, yet both businesses are heading in the right direction toward optimism and upswing – it would indeed be ridiculous if this group of companies were not able to mobilize enough self-healing power so that in the future we can continue to experience almost limitless growth, first and foremost by not letting this go to our heads and losing respect and appreciation for our employees! Time and again I notice how the atmosphere in a Group member company is influenced by the attitude and the behavior of the management team. If the managing director is friendly, obliging, and hard but fair in his dealings with the staff, this will be respected by the entire team, and the atmosphere in the company will be as the motto: "birds of a feather flock together." However, the opposite is true, too. If the managing director is supercilious or even arrogant, this will have a deleterious effect on the working climate, with arrogance and lack of motivation following automatically. This, of course, will in turn lead to high fluctuation in staffing levels, especially in the sales force, and, as a logical consequence, stagnating or even declining sales." [615]

To set a good example, Reinhold Würth decided to spend a couple of months in sales himself after January 2004 and, with the help of the success achieved in his area, demonstrate that the problems either did not exist at all or could at least be solved.

> "My father and I get along extremely well. We know what to think of each other."
>
> Bettina Würth, member of the Board of Directors

Bettina Würth, for the Board of Directors, and the spokesman of the management of Adolf Würth GmbH & Co. KG, Peter Zürn, also said in an interview with Hohenloher Zeitung that they were optimistic that the Würth Group had the right solutions at hand even for very critical situations. [616]

New Structures in the Group

Following an initiative by the consulting company Simon, Kucher, & Partner, the Group's organizational structures were once again adjusted to the growth of Würth in the new millennium. In the opinion of the consultants, the existing Board of Management was not up to the demands in the long run, a situation that McKinsey & Partner had already remarked on in their final report in 1989. [617] Moreover, the original FÜKO members had started to retire from 1997: Gerhard Fried, Otto Beilharz, Dieter Krämer, José Viana, and Karl Specht. Dr. Walter Jaeger and Rolf Bauer, too, would soon end their career with Würth, so this seemed to be the right time for reorganization. The successor of the old FÜKO was supposed to be assigned "precisely defined business areas by geographical regions, functions, and divisions." [618] Strategic management of the Group would rest with a different body.

When founded in 1979, the Board of Management (FÜKO) was almost identical with the managing directors of Adolf Würth GmbH & Co. KG, even though not all managers of Adolf Würth GmbH & Co. KG were also FÜKO members. During the reorganization process in 2001, however, the FÜKO was enlarged considerably to 25 members, as the Coordinating Conference that had existed since 1976, but had now been dissolved, was for the most part assimilated by the new FÜKO. [619] The FÜKO members constitute the operative management of the Würth Group and are each responsible for running a strategic business unit.

On top of the new Board of Management, a Board of Directors was established whose key management tasks include strategic corporate planning, the selection of executive staff, and controlling the strategic business units and functional areas. [620] It is the supreme decision-making body of the Würth Group. Its members are Dr. Walter Jaeger, spokesman of the Board of Directors, Rolf Bauer, his representative, Bettina Würth [621], Harald Unkelbach and – as successor of Dr. Walter Jaeger who will retire in May 2005 – Robert Friedmann. Friedmann, who started his career at Würth in 1992 as assistant to Rolf Bauer, last filled the position of spokesman of the management of Hahn & Kolb in Stuttgart.

In addition, there is still the Advisory Board that – chaired by Reinhold Würth since 1994 – constitutes the supreme monitoring and controlling body of the Würth Group. The Advisory Board discusses strategic questions with the Board of Directors and approves the corporate budget and use of funds. It furthermore appoints the members of the Board of Directors, the members of the Board of Management, and the managing directors of the large Würth Companies. The Advisory Board is a body that is certainly much more powerful under Reinhold Würth's chairmanship than it was prior to 1994.

Robert Friedmann, member and after May 2005, spokesman of the Board of Directors

These new structures give the Würth Group a framework that is also flexible, in the opinion of the deputy spokesman of the Board of Directors, Rolf Bauer. In reality, many things are settled much more informally than is stipulated in writing – at least while Reinhold Würth remains at the helm. Bauer says that this is not a disadvantage at all. Reinhold Würth still has things firmly under control; his role as entrepreneur has not undergone major change since 1994. On the other hand, the Würth Group is managed in a highly decentralized fashion, something that gives talented managing directors a lot of freedom and scope. Bauer says that, the larger the Group becomes, the more this freedom and scope must be balanced by controlling mechanisms such as the Würth Information System. The most important thing – and so far the Würth Group has been very successful at doing this – is to achieve a balance between security and supervision on the one hand and freedom and motivation on the other. [622]

Risk Management

After numerous corporate crises both in Germany and worldwide at the start of the 1990s, the law on control and transparency in company operations (KonTraG) took effect in Germany in May 1998. The law was, and is, aimed at improving corporate supervision by means of identifying in good time any risks that could jeopardize the continued existence of the business. Even though this law is not binding for family-owned businesses, Reinhold Würth used the new legislation as an opportunity to establish a risk management office in his company in 2000. The Würth Group therefore voluntarily subjects itself to the rigid demands made on German stock corporations.

Dr. Ute Roth, an economist from the University of Würzburg who supported Reinhold Würth in her role as assistant during his time at the University of Karlsruhe, is responsible for the office. Risk Controlling reports directly to the chairman of the Advisory Board and serves to evaluate both opportunities and risks. [623] The introduction of voluntary risk management illustrates that the Würth Group still adheres to its transparent and solid corporate policy. The measures initiated were also aimed at promoting public confidence in the company.

New Ways of Selling – Regionalization and Customer Segmentation

Divisionalization of the Würth Group, having been successfully introduced at the beginning of the 1990s, had been superseded by a second, regional structure in 1999 at Adolf Würth GmbH & Co. KG.

This was a change that some of the sales representatives viewed with distrust, since they are always concerned if the system is modified. Regionalization of the sales sector of Adolf Würth GmbH & Co. KG implied a change in the entire sales force and branch office organization, with the conversion of the sales force and the branch offices to a shared organizational structure. The new, matrix organization that consists of divisions and regions is highly complex, and many a sales representative at the outset was afraid of having to "serve two masters." [624] In some places, competition between different divisions had to be abandoned in favor of the new regional structure. [625]

The introduction of regionalization was triggered by the often very different competitive situation that seemed to require flexible adjustment of the organizational design. The regional units were intended as quasi-autonomous companies that could operate more flexibly in the local market. Würth anticipated a more intense regional opening up of the market to complement the growth generated by divisionalization. One manager each was appointed for the new regional business units, with responsibility for all the divisions in his area. [626] The sales representatives were hooked up with the now more than 90 branch offices in

Germany and the customers – this was the stated aim – were meant to have only one contact for their region. According to Dr. Walter Jaeger, the company expected this change to bring it closer to its customers. [627] Regionalization was completed in 2001. Since that time, the regions have, as expected, become increasingly independent.

In the past two years, the concept of regionalization has been developed further. The company has also made progress by developing a model of customer segmentation. [628] According to Peter Zürn, this will lead to a new model of multiplication at Adolf Würth GmbH & Co. KG. The so-called "potential sales representatives' customer service groups" are subdivided by customer size. Zürn explains that the company increasingly needs to distinguish between those customers that have reached a size where the sales representative must be capable of carrying out negotiations at board level and the more traditional, craft customers. [629]

Würth still has the objective of supplying its customers quickly and efficiently with the required "low interest products" as Prof. Bruno Tietz calls them in his preface to the Würth company history published in 1991. [630] The core business of the Würth Group is still concentrated on "C" parts: items that the customer needs, but does not really focus on. Therefore, the dedicated Würth employees devote a lot of time and energy to optimizing the purchasing process and making purchasing easier for the customer.

ORSY, the success product of the 1980s, has meanwhile been developed into a regular warehouse management system. The ORSY products are part of a process management concept for the procurement of "C" items and the services that Würth offers its customers. This concept is aimed at optimizing the flow of materials and ordering processes so as to "achieve significant and quantifiable savings," as is aptly described in Würth's advertising. [631]

Apart from the well-known ORSY racks there are ORSY case systems for the storage of small parts and tools, a scan system making it easier for the customer to order Würth products, ORSY storage and retrieval systems, and the ORSYmat whose modular system can be tailored to the customer's needs, allowing for the retrieval of products by entering a PIN and tracking the customer's buying pattern with the help of a retrieval record. ORSYmobil stands for the design of individual vehicle outfitting for Würth customers. For industry customers, Würth has developed a demand-controlled supply system on a container basis.

Selling products through the Internet with the help of the Würth Online Catalog has been improved, too, and placed on a new system platform. As a result, Würth generated sales amounting to eight million euro through the Internet in 2002. [632]

Conquering New Territory: Würth Diversifies

The fact that more sophisticated concepts are required by customers is illustrated by the example of the industry. Large, industrial customers need to be serviced by the Würth sales representatives in a different way to the traditional, craft customers. This was the reason behind the spin-off of the Industry Division, which had "become a burden" [633] on Adolf Würth GmbH & Co. KG owing to its completely different organizational processes, as an independent subsidiary in January 1999. The new company, WIS Würth Industrie Service GmbH & Co. KG, which deals with the specific requirements of industrial customers, is located in the new Würth industry park in Bad Mergentheim in the former Drillberg barracks area.

It was during the 1970s when Würth took over Baier & Michels, which Dieter Krämer upon Reinhold Würth's request had looked after for many years, that Würth learned the lesson that "the use of the Würth strategy […] is unsuitable and too expensive" [634] for industry customers.

Now Würth Industrie Service GmbH & Co. KG concludes service agreements with industrial heavyweights, a concept that is supposed to be transferred to large craft businesses, too, since the latter also require different services to smaller enterprises. Therefore, Würth Industrie Service GmbH & Co. KG presents itself to its customers as a supplier of "C" parts, offering more than 50,000 articles specifically for industrial purposes in the fields of production, plant construction, and maintenance. Furthermore, the company offers supply concepts enabling the Würth industry customer to minimize his expenses in the procurement of small parts. Since the costs of ordering, storing, and handling "C" parts by far exceed the actual material value, industry customers are particularly interested in reducing process-related costs. To this aim, Würth Industrie Service GmbH & Co. KG has developed scanner-supported rack systems and just-in-time supply with the help of Kanban container systems. These systems enable the Würth industry customer to track merchandise received to its place of assembly.

Würth Industrie Service GmbH & Co. KG is a very dynamic company. In February 2000, it officially opened a Kanban logistics center in the Würth industry park Bad Mergentheim, with work starting only two months later on an extension wing. In June 2001, Würth Industrie Service GmbH & Co. KG, together with its customer Liebherr, won the WIN/WIN Cup of the VDI (Association of German Engineers) for a jointly realized, large-scale logistics project.

Construction of a new high-bay warehouse that will extend the existing logistics facilities in the industry park by a building for goods received and shipping, covering roughly 43,000 ft2 (4,000m2) and creating more than 13,500 pallet spaces, was started in February 2004.

Würth Solar GmbH & Co. KG founded in 1999 belongs to the Electronics Division of the Würth Group. Apart from Adolf Würth GmbH & Co. KG, which holds 99.5 per cent of the business, a member of the partnership is the Institute for Solar Energy and Hydrogen Research Baden-Württemberg, which developed the company's production technology.

In 2000, the most modern pilot plant worldwide for thin-layer CIS solar modules was put into operation in a decommissioned power plant in Marbach am Neckar; in 2003, the company invested in a second CIS plant. The modules are subjected to a number of tests, among others at Würth Elektronik in Waldenburg and Würth Holding in Chur. A decision about investing in mass production of the CIS modules will in all probability be made in 2004 according to Rolf Bauer, the company has the technical aspects of the "small membranes"[635] under control. If matters continue to show such a positive development, Reinhold Würth will be satisfied with this future-oriented technology, too.

Good or Bad? Diversification at Würth

The initiatives that opened up areas outside the core Würth business and the many acquisitions never went undisputed. As early as the 1980s, the Advisory Board had criticized the situation at Würth Elektronik, and the consultants from McKinsey, too, had always been quite skeptical regarding the "other" companies whose results often differed from projected profit percentages.[636] It was assumed they would tie up too much management capacity, with critical questions being asked about possible "synergies with the core business," and whether such companies as RECA Norm, which had an almost identical product and customer structure, could lead to in-house competition, dissension, and dissatisfaction – an issue that was still being hotly debated a number of years later. As late as 1992, one of the McKinsey people in his letter to Reinhold Würth quoted terms such as "millstones" or "expensive hobbies" that he claimed to have heard from Würth employees.[637]

However, Reinhold Würth insisted – success would prove him right – and also gave his reasons: "Recent management literature, too, illustrates how immensely important it is for a company's ability to cope with economic or corporate crises to have the management steeled and toughened by giving them the possibility to experience reorganization and crisis management. [...] I therefore believe that it is good training for the immune system of a company to permanently have a handful of problem cases to deal with, problems the management can learn from and use as training ground for really big crises. The easier way of selling, that is, unloading 'millstones,' is the option taken by a real softie who will later be incapable of getting truly critical situations under control." [638] He referred to the experience gained first of all by Rolf Bauer with SWG and Würth Elektronik, Otto Beilharz with Hommel Hercules, Dr. Walter Jaeger with Monks & Crane, and Dieter Krämer with Baier & Michels and Würth Canada – businesses that have in the meantime operated very profitably.

A master's thesis on the acquisition policy of the Würth Group written during the time that Reinhold Würth held the chair of the Interdisciplinary Institute for Entrepreneurship at the University of Karlsruhe also focused on these issues. The author, Martin Schulteis, analyzed research literature that assumes the most successful companies will be those that "diversify around their special business." [639] He specifically describes Rolf Bauer's outstanding achievements in reorganizing companies and identifies the communication skills of the Würth management as a success factor. Rolf Bauer's conclusion after more than twenty years of restructuring businesses at Würth is positive, too. [640] However, the master's thesis does not ignore the challenges posed by Würth's new acquisitions in the tool and electrical wholesale trades, which required different strategies to the traditional, direct selling business of Würth owing to differences in customer needs, market structures, and corporate culture.

In the meantime, the Würth Group has also gone into the insurance business, beginning in 2000 with Waldenburger Versicherung AG. It also has the successful company Würth Leasing GmbH & Co. KG, the Würth Logistics Center in Adelsheim, and the software and IT-consulting business Würth Phoenix, and offers its customers business protection packages. The purchase of the Reutlingen-based insurance broker Kirsch in the spring of 2004 marked the beginning of the Würth Group's future as a financial services provider. For the time being, Würth employees and customers located in the region are the targets of the insurance policies on offer. [641]

Reinhold Würth considers this development to be something perfectly normal, a process whose result will ultimately depend on both the commitment of the employees and the managers involved: "It is always a philosophical question, you know, if diversification is good or bad. I believe that it is neither one nor the other, since you can find a whole range of examples for both hypotheses." [642]

Würth – Where to Now?

With a sales volume of 6,2 billion euro in the business year 2004, more than 2.5 million customers, and over 46,000 employees, the Würth Group is the largest direct selling company worldwide in the field of fasteners and assembly material. The Würth Group is represented in 80 countries of the world, with 314 companies.

The core business of Adolf Würth GmbH & Co. KG is still the sale of screws, screw accessories, chemical-technical products, hardware and furniture fittings, dowel technology and fire protection systems, insulating material, hand tools, power tools and pneumatic tools, service and maintenance products, connectors and fastening material, storage and retrieval systems, and special solutions for the automotive, woodworking, construction, and metalworking industries.

Würth customers can expect quality products, service, and qualified technical advice from more than 90 branch offices in Germany and almost 25,000 sales representatives worldwide, whether they are an industry customer or work in the automotive, metalworking, woodworking, or construction industry.

At international level, the operational business units are: the Automotive Division, with the sub-divisions Auto and Cargo; the Metal Division, with the sub-divisions Metal, Household Technology, and Maintenance Workshops; the Wood Division; the Construction Division; and the Industry Division. The Allied Companies, too, which belong to Würth yet trade under their own name, are subdivided according to their business activities: apart from the traditional, direct selling companies united in the reca Group, there is Electrical Wholesale, Trade, the Electronics group, and companies offering industry supply concepts united in a group named "Screws and Standard Parts." [643] The companies that have joined the Würth Group by way of diversification are listed separately, with the company's own hotels and car dealerships among them.

The Würth Group continues to grow, even though the targets laid down in "Vision 2000" have been achieved, thanks in no small measure to the newly established companies and acquisitions. On January 1, 2000, the Würth Group made its biggest acquisition in the company's history to date, by purchasing EGG Elektrogroßhandel AG, the holding company of the Uni Elektro Group located in Eschborn. In addition to this, Würth acquired businesses in the field of fittings and stainless steel. In the next two years, two IT companies among others were integrated into the Würth Group by way of acquisition, and with Würth Phoenix the Würth Group has meanwhile become an IT-developing business itself.

The wave of new foundations of Würth Companies abroad continued in uninterrupted fashion after the turn of the millennium. In 2000, Würth Egypt and Würth Kosovo, in 2001, Würth Central America, Panama, Lebanon, and Cambodia, and, in 2002, Würth Dominican Republic were all established. Furthermore, several Würth Modyf companies were established in Europe, and Würth bought a few businesses in the field of the Allied Companies. In April 2004, almost 1,400 new employees joined the Würth Group through the acquisition of LICHT Zentrale Thurner GmbH, the Austrian fittings manufacturer Grass, and DIY World GmbH Wuppertal that supplies do-it-yourself markets across Europe with tools, electrical machines, hardware, furniture fittings, and gardening tools. [644]

> "I have learned so much from Reinhold Würth in many discussions, meetings, conversations, and during many hours of celebrating together. What I admire him most for is the joy he feels when making others happy."
>
> Prof. Hans Joachim Dr. Klein, Institute for Sociology at the University of Karlsruhe

According to information from Dr. Walter Jaeger, spokesman of the Board of Directors, the Würth Group is still "being driven by Reinhold Würth. And it is his entrepreneurial curiosity that piques him to try out new things, to develop financial services, the insurance business, solar technology, Würth Phoenix." [645]

Dr. Jaeger expects the Würth Group to achieve a market share worldwide of at least 15 to 20 per cent – the current market share lies slightly below 5 per cent. Markets such as China and the former Eastern bloc have so far only been scratched on the surface.

Reinhold Würth agrees: "I am absolutely convinced that we can easily generate 10 per cent of the growth reported by WalMart with the product range we have and in view of the many marketplaces in which we are active today – fastening technology, electronics, and electrical equipment all the way to chemicals and bonding technology – and this, in turn, would equal US$21.78 billion or 19.5 billion euro with 140,000 employees worldwide. […] All our calculations show very clearly the unbelievable reserves in the market that still exist out there." [646]

Reinhold Würth im Gespräch

"I always wanted to be in front, get ahead, move up …"

INTERVIEW WITH REINHOLD WÜRTH

Das letzte Wort hat Reinhold Würth. In einem Interview fasst er rückblickend wichtige Stationen in der Entwicklung seines Unternehmens zusammen und erläutert den heutigen Standort der Würth-Gruppe.

GG Prof. Würth, the Würth Group can look back on 60 years of history; for 50 years now you have been in charge of running the business. When you took over the company, did you ever imagine it could develop into such an extraordinary enterprise?

REINHOLD WÜRTH When all of a sudden you find yourself in charge of running a company, you don't have that much time to think about it. You can't expect this from a nineteen-year-old anyway. I just got cracking, did not really think about the job a whole lot, least of all that the company could one day have 45,000 employees which is the case right now. Surviving was the number one priority then. After about three or four months, I realized that we would make it. What also helped us was the German economic miracle, during which it was more difficult to purchase goods than to sell them.

GG Can you remember an exact point in time when you realized that this could turn into something really big?

REINHOLD WÜRTH I really can't, it was more of an evolutionary process. And this applies irrespective of the yardstick you use. You know, first we moved to Hermersberg, and at the beginning it was a major change for us, from a bungalow in Gaisbach to Hermersberg Castle, but after one or two years you just take things for granted, you don't really see anymore what's so special about it. When you have guests, though, and they remark: "Wow, this is really beautiful," that's when you see your environment from a different angle again. It's the same thing with my wife. When a friend tells me that she is such a warm, charming, and witty lady, then I feel embarrassed and have to admit to myself that my friend is right and that my wife is indeed a wonderful person.

GG When did you start developing entrepreneurial visions?

REINHOLD WÜRTH At the latest in 1978, when I publicly announced that I intended to triple the company's sales volume within seven years. In principle I got into the habit of planning 10 years ahead; I always considered a 12-month plan to be much too short-term. I always wanted to be in front, get ahead, move up. My venturing into terra incognita was always connected with a purpose; and I always wanted to find out if this or that could be done, too. And every time it was a thrill to find out, yes, it is indeed possible.

GG So, would it be correct to say that the larger the company, the more daring your moves?

REINHOLD WÜRTH The standards grew, too. In the past, sales increases of 100 million euro were simply inconceivable, yet today we take something like this almost for granted. Everything is relative in this world.

GG You said your business developed in an evolutionary fashion in the beginning. A growing company needs certain structures, though. Looking back today, can you explain the most important steps on the way to a more structured organization?

REINHOLD WÜRTH It was certainly very important that I structured the entire business in a very decentralized manner from the start. I always delegated a lot of responsibility and actually only stepped in in case of deviations. Whenever negative developments became apparent I either went to the respective company myself or had somebody go in my place. Corporate headquarters never meddled with companies where everything went as expected. This also had something to do with efficiency and making optimum use of the time available.

About 20 years ago, we started working with the first Würth Information System, which was certainly one of the success factors since it gave us the opportunity to learn

"I ALWAYS WANTED TO BE IN FRONT, GET AHEAD, MOVE UP ..."
INTERVIEW WITH REINHOLD WÜRTH

what was going on in every company belonging to the Würth Group at an early stage. When we organize the Commitment Conferences or the FÜKO Checks (FÜKO = Board of Management) today, we have all the necessary information available at the click of a button: the number of stock turns, or staff fluctuation, or the calculation factor. We are certainly also tops both nationally and internationally owing to the scope and networking of information offered by the Würth Information System: our swift reaction to potential problems is exemplary.

> **GG** Does this mean that the Würth Company plays a leading role not only in your branch of industry, but also in other industries?

REINHOLD WÜRTH If we weren't better than the competition we would never have developed into the world market leader for fasteners. All in all we must have done some things better than our competitors, and this particularly applies to our balance sheet: after all, the Würth Group reports 6 stock turns of the entire inventory annually; in 2003, the ratio of equity to total assets was 48.5 %. This can only be achieved by having stock turns under control, tightening credit control, and optimizing processes in general.

So, our success is certainly a combination of the figures on the one hand – mechanistic processes, computer science, rational thinking – and the emotion of the corporate spirit on the other; one simply should not ignore the human factor. This is exactly what I said recently on the occasion of the 50th anniversary of the Baden-Baden Meeting of Entrepreneurs on June 11, 2004: we are currently experiencing the biggest revolution of all times, with the exception of the founding of religion. Owing to informatics, computerization, and robotics, people's lives have undergone more far-reaching changes in the last 30 years than in the 500 years before that! Human contact, relationships, and networks suffer because of excessive communication via computer screens; today's economy is driven by mechanistic processes and terms such as confidence, personal contact with others, and business acquaintance lose some of their meaning because face to face conversations are replaced by bland, soulless, e-mail messages that all look the same, no matter if they are sent from Hong Kong or Untermaßholderbach.

The service of a company will suffer, too, because the businesses are computer-driven and because every service that does not fit into the concept of the computer will lead to errors and seven consequential errors.

It is my firm belief that, especially in trading companies, the quality of management in terms of staff leadership and the cultivation of relationship networks is much more important than sleek and stylish computer programs.

> **GG** In other words, the success of the Würth Group is to a large part due to entrepreneurial inspiration, intuition, and a good team?

REINHOLD WÜRTH I always said that it is the most important task of an entrepreneur to place the right man, the right woman, in the right position at the right time. If this can be accomplished, there should be no problems.

> **GG** In part, you take a critical stance towards the use of EDP in your business and also emphasize this critical attitude. At the same time you have intensified your efforts in this field with the Würth Phoenix project and also want to launch this product on the market.

REINHOLD WÜRTH I am very well aware that we would not be able to survive today without EDP and informatics. We need informatics to come to grips with certain problems, there is no alternative. On the other hand, the computer experts talked us into developing this and that, telling us what's feasible and possible, yet we completely ignored what is really and truly necessary. Let me give you a practical example to show you what I mean: designers are nuts about miniature components and completely forget that people still have pudgy fingers. Miniaturization fails when it encounters the normal dimensions of people. Take a video camera, for example. It offers a thousand different functions – time-lapse motion, slow motion, fade-over, underexposure, single frame, night for day and day for night shots, the works. For an amateur, 90% of these functions are useless since he only wants to press a button and shoot a few video scenes. There is certainly a big difference between the things that designers work out in their offices, far removed from the real world, and the things that are really necessary in everyday business. This principle does not only apply to many products, but to informatics, too.

This is exactly what brought me to the Würth Phoenix project. I had to learn that it sometimes cost us between 10 and 15 million DM to change over a medium-sized Würth Company to standard software – amounts of money that a business of that size would not have been able to pay and would therefore have gone bankrupt had it not been for the Group carrying the financial burden. If you look around in the industry you will see many business failures that are causally connected with the fact that these businesses did not master the exaggerated EDP-changeovers. To cut costs, I decided to have our staff develop special software for trading companies, primarily with modules for purchasing, order processing, and inventory management plus financial accounting, without any fancy bits and frills – elegant, fast, and cost-efficient.

I wanted to use the experience I have had in the past: in a figurative sense, many software companies unload a huge truck full of Lego® building blocks on the customer's yard and let him make the decision himself as to which blocks could fit his purposes and which components could come in handy – a very time-consuming and expensive process. Our specific Würth software was developed by experts – cybernetics experts, system analysts, people who know how to optimize processes on Java-basis – and it is therefore more than a match to many completely outdated software packages of even the largest software companies.

Just recently, one of my businesses changed over their purchasing to Würth Phoenix: in with the plug, and you can start playing with it. This is great, and it is cost-efficient, too, so that I don't see any problems whatsoever in selling the Würth Phoenix package to other companies outside of the Würth Group.

GG Let's go back to the past again, to the history of the business. Your father started up the business in Hohenlohe; you decided to stay there. What were your reasons except for the feeling of personal closeness with the region? Has the location played a role in the success of your company?

REINHOLD WÜRTH I never really thought much about the question of staying or leaving. I was there, and I stayed there without giving this issue much thought. There wasn't anything that spoke against staying in the Hohenlohe region. However, it was certainly one of the success factors that the Hohenlohe region experienced a major process of transformation after World War II. When a large number of agricultural machines were introduced in this primarily agricultural region, a huge number of industrious, hard-working, and upright people were released who then were available for the building up of our trading company in Hohenlohe. Many of our employees still have a small farm and do part-time farming after work and on the weekends. This attachment to the region and to the company is downright exemplary: even though the company will only turn 60, there are families whose third-generation members already work for Würth.

Another locational advantage was the fact that the wages and salaries compared to the population centers of Stuttgart or Munich are still about 10% lower even today.

GG You are very committed to the region. What is it you want to achieve with the citizens' action group pro Region Heilbronn-Franken?

REINHOLD WÜRTH It is the principal objective of the citizens' action group to bring the citizens from Franconia and Hohenlohe closer together, including the intellectual sense of the word. The area of Heilbronn-Franconia never had a state territory of its own. Traditionally, the knights in this area were particularly loyal to the emperor. Until the beginning of the 19th century, the territory from Gaildorf to Wertheim and from Crailsheim to Eppingen was ruled by knights: the imperial cities of Heilbronn, Schwäbisch Hall and Wimpfen, the clergy, the very small counties and principalities. In short, particularism prevailed.

It was only in 1803 that Napoleon made a clean sweep, and this can still be felt today. The frontier between Württemberg and Baden drawn in 1806 is still visible today. Both my representative, Frank Stroh, and I want to give all the citizens of the region the opportunity to experience at first hand the Heilbronn-Franconia region and to develop a certain pride in our joint activities in time – after all, Heilbronn-Franconia is absolute tops among the 12 regions of the country in terms of percentage economic growth.

"I ALWAYS WANTED TO BE IN FRONT, GET AHEAD, MOVE UP …"
INTERVIEW WITH REINHOLD WÜRTH

GG You ventured out into the world from this region at a very early point in time and established subsidiaries abroad at the beginning of the 1960s. This was rather unusual for a company of this size. What were your reasons?

REINHOLD WÜRTH This is actually due to my father's influence. When he still worked for his first employer, the Reisser Company, he traveled first to Austria and then to Switzerland to sell screws.

After he had started up his own business, my father continued along these lines. Between 1949 and 1954, I often accompanied him to Switzerland to open up new business there so that the idea of internationalization was something very natural for me, albeit on a small scale. From an intellectual point of view, Switzerland was further away from Germany after the end of World War II than California is today. I am still very grateful to my father today for planting the seed of internationalization in my head: without him I would certainly not have had the idea of founding companies abroad at such an early point in time.

Looking back today, I would say that 50% of our success is due to this early internationalization of the business. We feel at home in the world not only on the sales side, but also concerning purchasing: shortly after the Cultural Revolution in China, we started to make contact with local vendors and imported huge amounts of nuts to Europe. As a second step we established and cultivated purchasing contacts with Japan, Taiwan, Hong Kong, and Thailand.

GG Could you name a few especially successful foreign Würth Companies?

REINHOLD WÜRTH There are two categories here: quantity and quality. Concerning quantity, Würth Italy absolutely stands out, followed by Würth France and Würth Spain. These three companies generate the highest sales among the foreign Würth Companies and all three of them are highly profitable, too. Concerning quality, both Würth Finland and Würth Portugal play an important role: these two companies generate the highest profit percentages. The success stories of these companies are very clearly associated with the personalities of the respective managing directors: the managing directors of Würth Finland and Würth Portugal are very unique, entrepreneurial personalities – they are visionaries, they are modest, obliging, true role models, persevering, absolute professionals, in short, true AAA-men who are not only good sports, but with whom you could conquer the whole world.

> **GG** Where would you draw the line between the two categories of quantity and quality?

REINHOLD WÜRTH The main difference is the pro rata results: that is, the per-capita performance. If I compare the sales volume of Würth Italy with the sales volume of Würth Finland, I see that the latter achieves a per-capita performance that is 3.2 times higher than that achieved by our Italian friends. It's more or less the same with the operating result: in Finland, the profit is 7.5 times higher than in Italy, in Portugal 1.5 times higher. These are enormous differences indeed that do not have anything to do with products, competition or processes, but simply with the quality of the management and the mangers' motivational skills.

> **GG** Much has been said about the success of your business. Can you remember times of crises, too?

REINHOLD WÜRTH Of course we experienced crises; one of them was particularly remarkable. In 1970, I founded the company Würth Bau (Construction), which during its peak times had up to 300 employees on the payroll. During the construction industry's crisis in 1985, I had to shut down the business with a 10 million DM loss. This was certainly not a crisis that jeopardized the existence of our business, but a burden that even affected my private life. To cover the loss and spare corporate assets I had at the time taken out a private loan! Please let me emphasize very clearly that Würth Bau did not go bankrupt, but was liquidated. Neither a customer nor a vendor of Würth Bau lost so much as a single cent in the process. All construction projects and complaints were handled professionally. We also took care of the employees who lost their jobs. About half of them found employment within the Würth Group in Hohenlohe and we approached other companies in the region to find jobs there for the remaining people.

Other than that, I have had a number of sleepless nights during my professional career, but we have actually never experienced a crisis that put the existence of the Würth Group at a risk.

Würth has remained a company without major risks. There are different risk factors such as dependence on a handful of large customers, yet this isn't the case with Würth. We have more than two million customers worldwide. We are not dependent on a few manufacturers either, with a few exceptions: for example, concerning fittings. The global market for fittings is very clearly an oligopoly that is dominated by four or five manufacturers. We realized the danger of having Würth suffer from lack of supplies. I solved this problem by acquiring the fittings manufacturers Mepla, Alfit, and in 2004 the Grass Company as well. This reduced our dependency on suppliers.

I mentioned before that the Würth Group stands on a very solid financial footing, with equity capital accounting for 48.5 % of total assets in 2003. We are very well prepared for further growth.

> **GG** In 1984, during a conference, you said that Würth could afford to completely disregard the market, the economic situation. Is that still true today? Were the declining sales figures of Adolf Würth GmbH & Co. KG during the last two years due to the economic slowdown?

REINHOLD WÜRTH In past years, too, the Würth Group has continued to grow, albeit not that rapidly. The small drop in sales of Adolf Würth GmbH & Co. KG in Germany certainly has something to do with the overall economy, but first and foremost it was a mental block: AW KG was excessively computerized, mechanized, and rationalized, with the advocates of this mentality pushing emotions, enthusiasm, and personal contact far into the background. The new management of AW KG that has been in place now for roughly two years succeeded in reversing this trend; Würth KG, too, is back on track towards growth in 2004.

Worldwide, we presently have a market share of below 5%, so the economy doesn't play that much of a role. In practice, it doesn't make any difference if you can still capture 95% of the market in a normal economic situation or 2% less, that is, only 93% in an economic trough. No businessman will be able to conceptualize a 2% difference in demand. I therefore believe that a company in our industry that doesn't grow in an economic low has an attitude problem and not an economic one. If we pay heed to the negative reports in the media, if we give in to people complaining, lamenting, wailing, moaning, and groaning, activities we Germans have really perfected, the performance of a business will almost automatically stagnate or even decline.

It is still my objective to develop the Würth Group into an oligopolist with 15–18% market share. This means that, even after 60 years in the market, Würth is still at the very beginning of its development; doubling or even tripling our sales volume worldwide is certainly conceivable without major problems.

GG At the beginning of 2004, you took over a sales region and went back to grass roots level, as it were. What were your reasons for doing so, and how did the company react?

REINHOLD WÜRTH The main reason for my decision was certainly the fact that, during the previous three or four years, Adolf Würth KG had more or less trudged along and either had zero per cent sales growth or even a deficit of one or two per cent. In October 2003, I decided that this was it and said: "Let's see if I can't get the business going again." Last year, we took away the laptops from our sales representatives and restructured the sales force a bit. The sales representatives were not too happy about the changes, and this, in turn, led to lack of enthusiasm and stagnating sales.

I therefore went into the field during January 2004 and spent 12 or 13 full days there until June. I personally took over management of one of the 10 regions in Germany. Throughout 2003, this region ranked 3rd in the statistics, but from January through September 2004 it came in first. I do feel responsible for part of this success.

One of my closer colleagues told me I should have taken the decision to go into the

"I ALWAYS WANTED TO BE IN FRONT, GET AHEAD, MOVE UP ..."
INTERVIEW WITH REINHOLD WÜRTH

field a lot earlier, since the sales representatives now work hard again instead of thinking about what else they can criticize and complain about.

The lack of notebook computers didn't seem all that important any longer either because I was able to say: "I just spent a full 7 days in the field, and not one single item was missed from the order form, because there was no laptop (as a replacement we had made desktops available to the sales representatives, which are better and much easier to handle than the notebooks).

Being a role model is of paramount importance. The sales representatives were impressed about my work in the field; all of a sudden, there was a mood change in the sales force.

I had unlimited access to the grass roots, to the market. I got first-hand information about what was going on in our industry. It is interesting to see that the pessimistic mood in Germany is actually homemade and that the attitude of some people is actually a lot worse than the situation itself.

Let me give you an example: last week I was on the road, during which time I visited two larger companies and spoke to the bosses. When I asked them: "How's it going?" they answered: "Very bad, the situation is rotten, you know, the taxes, the government." I replied: "But listen, it doesn't look that bad here, people in your workshops seem to have enough to do, I really have the impression your business is running very smoothly." Their answer: "Well, yes, in a way you are right, our business seems to be doing okay." This happened to me I don't know how many times. In Germany, people obviously feel compelled to complain as if this were part of their business – I'm so fed up with all this moaning and groaning.

When I held the chair in entrepreneurship at the University of Karlsruhe, I always told my students: "Actually, you should jump up and down on your mattresses every morning, loudly shouting "hooray," because you live in peace and freedom!!!" Unfortunately, young people don't understand what this means! I was ten years old during World War II and almost got killed by a US fighter-bomber in 1944. In view of this, it seems really trivial when there is almost a national uprising in Germany about the EUR 10 fee you have to pay at the doctor's office every quarter! If you see the whole picture, people's complaining and lamenting becomes a real banality. We still live in the land of milk and honey, even those who are close to the poverty line: if I remember my childhood, my God, there were so many refugees crossing the country, wearing hand-me-down shoes, freezing in the winter time. Nobody needs to freeze in Germany, nobody needs to be hungry, everybody has a place to live, even though in some cases the situation of the individual has taken a negative turn compared to the situation 10 years ago.

> **GG** Let's get back to the issue of "selling;" you have been in the business for 50 years. Do you see any fundamental changes?

REINHOLD WÜRTH Actually, nothing has changed in this regard. People are still as complex as before. If you work as a sales representative you will get to know every single type of person. This is extremely interesting, and this is exactly my reason for saying that the job of a sales representative is the most interesting profession there is. You are in constant contact with people; you get an insight into human nature relatively quickly and can assess people. For me, selling is still fascinating and I must admit that accompanying sales representatives in the field is real fun. Well, you know, things are very pleasant nowadays: when the customers know that Mr. Würth is coming to pay them a visit, they have coffee ready, and some of our partner customers even hoist the Würth flag, but selling still reminds me of my early days in the job – standing in front of the shelves, taking down the items needed. I thoroughly enjoy this.

> **GG** The extent of your fame has increased enormously since the middle of the 1980s. You are in the public eye not only as a businessman, but also as an art collector, lecturer, and professor at the university. How did all this happen?

REINHOLD WÜRTH This was by no means planned or designed in some way, it just happened. Sales were constantly increasing and the press reported this. As a consequence, I was frequently invited to give lectures. One of my first lectures was at the Marketing Club in Cologne. If I also include my in-house speeches, the number comes close to 2,000. In

"I ALWAYS WANTED TO BE IN FRONT, GET AHEAD, MOVE UP ..."
INTERVIEW WITH REINHOLD WÜRTH

1989, Würth was awarded the German Marketing Prize. Traditionally, the prize-winner goes on the road afterwards, and Würth made presentations to 10 marketing clubs from Lindau to Hamburg.

When I give a speech somewhere today, we receive at least one or two requests for lectures at other institutes afterwards. For reasons of time I have to turn down many such invitations, but I readily make exceptions for those audiences that are close to the Würth Group. Today I will still give a lecture at the master craftsman's institute of the German window construction trade in Karlsruhe, since it is there that our future customers are being trained. I can combine business with pleasure: for my business, these lectures of mine are long-term PR activities.

> **GG** Your company's degree of fame has certainly increased with these activities. However, you have also become known as an entrepreneur committed to the world of fine arts. What prompted you to collect art, not for yourself as a private person or as an investment, but to open your art collection to the public?

REINHOLD WÜRTH I started out collecting art in private. Whenever we organized an "Open House" weekend in Künzelsau, we always had between 20,000 and 30,000 visitors. I then had the idea of setting some space aside for my collection in a museum in Künzelsau/Gaisbach, in the new administrative building that was to be constructed, and presenting the art to the public. This idea, which became a reality with the official opening of the new corporate headquarters building in 1991, was more successful than I could ever have imagined. Since 1991, more than a million people have visited the Würth Museum! On the one hand, this art museum in our corporate headquarters adds another spot of color to the cultural landscape in Hohenlohe; on the other, it was a sober business decision to communicate the name of the company to the public through art. It is obvious that this leads to a positive attitude towards the business: a few days ago, I went to Kunsthalle Würth in Schwäbisch Hall. A woman I did not know came up to me and said: "You know, all the things you organize here, they are really wonderful and I just wanted to say, 'Thank you!'" These brief meetings make me happy. Making other people happy is a wonderful experience that adds color to one's life. I would be telling lies if I didn't admit that I like to see the exhibits hanging on the wall when I visit the Kunsthalle. Recently, I was visited by one of the leading art experts in Germany. We took a stroll through the current exhibition "Land auf, Land ab" that presents the work of painters and sculptors of the academies of art in Stuttgart and Karlsruhe, when he told me: "To be honest with you, I am almost envious. It is great to see that you can put together such an exhibition on the basis of your own collection." This is indeed a comment that fills me with pride.

> **GG** Your chair in entrepreneurship at the University of Karlsruhe lifted you in people's estimation, too. What did you want to teach the students, what did you want them to learn from you? And is there something you learned from your activities there also?

REINHOLD WÜRTH I wanted to encourage these young people to become self-employed, and I wanted to share my experience with them. This was a plan that met with great approval on the part of the students. They were very keen and wanted to know how to start up their own businesses. I, too, learned a lot since I had never before seen a university from the inside. It took me about two or three months to find my bearings and find out what makes a university tick. I went through the same process as all the freshmen at the start of their studies. They, too, have to find their way around first. I was lucky, though, in being able to recruit the economist Dr. Ute Roth from the University of Würzburg as my assistant. She quickly and efficiently showed me the ropes. We have a saying: "Teach, and you will learn," and I must say I learned a great deal from my teaching activities, particularly in the field of economic history. This would never have happened had I not been forced to do research for my lectures.

> **GG** You are also active politically. You are a member of the Liberal Democratic Party, you are in touch with many politicians. What do you want to achieve with your political commitment, and what is it you don't like about politics?

"I ALWAYS WANTED TO BE IN FRONT, GET AHEAD, MOVE UP ..."
INTERVIEW WITH REINHOLD WÜRTH

REINHOLD WÜRTH For 40 years we have been talking about tax reform, about reducing taxes, about the security of our pensions system, but we don't really see any changes. It is only the power of facts, the globalization that will make all the decision-makers understand that Germany cannot evade changes either. Another 15 to 20 years will certainly go by before we reach the situation that Great Britain initiated owing to Thatcher's reforms in the 1980s and has achieved today.

What I consider to be a big problem all the way down to the level of district and community politics is the different dates for the elections. When I was chairman of the Aviation Association Schwäbisch Hall, I was in frequent contact with the Schwäbisch Hall municipal authorities. Crucial changes were postponed by the authorities time and again because dates were either fixed for the elections for the municipal council, the state elections, the district council elections, the parliamentary elections, or the elections for the mayor of Schwäbisch Hall. If one date was over and we thought that now changes could be initiated, there was always the next election just around the corner.

I would recommend coordinating any kind of election, at least per Federal Land, and fixing the same dates for these. The current mayor of the city of Schwäbisch Hall, Hermann-Josef Pelgrim (Social Democratic Party), shows that not all politicians are alike. Pelgrim is a man of action, he makes headway with his city, takes a stand, and is not afraid of conflict with his parliamentary party and prevailing through different majorities. I am deeply impressed by people of his kind, and I am sure the citizens feel the same.

GG Did you want to become politically active yourself, time permitting?

REINHOLD WÜRTH I tried it once, but experience showed me that political parties don't readily accept lateral entries. It is constantly suggested that people from industry should enter politics. I have learned that this isn't all that easy. Let me give you an example: I was once invited as guest speaker to an election meeting of the FDP. I dared to say: "The FDP is the party of people who are willing to perform, the party of the elite, and therefore the FDP is the party of the higher-paid." After my lecture the party leaders were very upset. They said it was an absolute no-no to call the FDP the party of the higher-paid. This illustrates the problem that the FDP has: if it is the party of the elite and the people who are willing to perform (and no party leader would ever deny that), the logical consequence is that the FDP is the party of the higher-paid.

The illogical attitude of the FDP leadership does not end here, though: the FDP tries to copy the people's parties and cover the entire political spectrum from foreign policy to educational and social policy all the way to economic policy. However, they lack the manpower required for such a broad range; the FDP leadership does not understand that it would be best for them to go in for niche politics. The party should actually canvass on the basis of "The FDP is the party of the higher-paid," and then they would garner 18% of the votes in no time. It is precisely the higher-paid who feel misunderstood by the FDP at the moment. These are some of the ideas that got me involved in politics. However, being close to 70, I am simply too old today to become politically active.

GG Let's turn from Reinhold Würth, the "public person," back to the entrepreneur and his business. At quite an early point in time, you thought about your succession and opted for setting up foundations. At the end of 1993, you retired from operative management and took the chair of the Advisory Board. What were your reasons for doing so?

REINHOLD WÜRTH I had already started dealing with the issue of my succession at the age of 40, in 1975. The reason behind it was actually my intention to leave active business behind as early as possible, so as to see how the company would fare after my retirement. This was the principal reason behind the early transfer of assets to the foundations and delegation of management responsibility, to create the opportunity to adjust the power and administrative structures in the right direction, to watch from the sidelines, and to shape the entire conglomerate according to my ideas. Something like this cannot, of course, be done from the grave.

GG And did it work out as expected? Are you really that detached that you simply watch the business from the sidelines? In actual fact, you are still very active; isn't the company still being run by Reinhold Würth?

REINHOLD WÜRTH This might be a bit misleading. All in all, the company works very well without me. And anybody who knows what the spokesman of the Board of Directors, Dr. Jaeger, does will realize that the business is developing away from me. Dr. Jaeger works largely independently as regards the Würth Group. It happens quite often that we don't see each other for three weeks, even though we have our offices on the same floor. The only exception is AW KG (Adolf Würth GmbH & Co. KG) because it is right under my nose, geographically speaking, and because the results achieved by AW KG for quite some time were not at all what I expected them to be. If I see the company suffering and trudging along, I simply cannot stand back and say, too bad, this is not my responsibility. This company is the "apple of my eye," as it were. It was the first business I started up and I want to protect it from drifting off course. Würth KG has been back on track since January 2004, and this certainly has something to do with my assistance. For all the staff and the managers this was a great learning process. If you know where the company comes from, you also know which screws to adjust to bring it back on track. On the other hand, I also have to win the acceptance of the young people, who might feel slighted and offended if I intervene all of a sudden. Last week I talked to the chairman of the Council of Trustees, Mr. Wagner, and he told me: "It is great to see the boss making sure that everything is alright." We have a very good and positive atmosphere in the company again and, now that this has been achieved, I am happy, too.

GG The business has seen a new generation taking over in past years. Your daughter, Bettina, was appointed member of the Board of Directors in 2000. What do you think about the new generation, and about your daughter's role in the company? How do you want the business to develop from here?

REINHOLD WÜRTH My decision and the decision of the Advisory Board to announce Robert Friedmann as the successor of Dr. Jaeger was made very early, and deliberately so. It is definitely quite unusual for a company with more than 45,000 employees to appoint a young man of 38 spokesman of the Board of Directors. However, there is a certain philosophy behind it: with the appointment of Robert Friedmann, the business shows that is still young, that we don't adhere to antiquated customs, but are capable of pushing through with innovations and trying out new things. I am convinced that Robert Friedmann will gain a lot of respect; we are therefore on the right track! We also have a large number of "young tigers" in the Würth Group who want to advance their careers and make progress with the company.

We are in a fortunate situation to be able to recruit 95% of our upcoming top managers from our own ranks, and this is certainly another one of our success factors.

Everyone knows companies that simply cannot find any upcoming managers, either from within or outside, because their management style is so authoritarian that the company in its role as employer scares off potential candidates. To intensify our efforts, we have been cooperating very closely with the University of Louisville, Kentucky for two years now and jointly organize Würth-specific MBA study courses. The young graduates from Würth already now rank among those with the highest grades of the entire university – if selected properly, one can also find excellent upcoming managers in Germany, ranking so low in the PISA-study.

As for my daughter Bettina, she does an excellent job; I am really proud of that girl. The two of us agreed that she will not become the No. 1; I simply do not want to burden her, a mother of four, with such a task. Bettina is a member of the Board of Directors consisting of five members; she is responsible for all national and international businesses trading under the name of Würth. Very deliberately, though, she leaves the role of spokesman of the Board of Directors to Mr. Robert Friedmann.

By the way, Bettina had to fight really hard for her position. It is not that I gave her this or that job because of the position of power I have in the business. Bettina has rather gained her colleagues' and staff's respect because of her commitment, achievements, and her professionalism.

"I ALWAYS WANTED TO BE IN FRONT, GET AHEAD, MOVE UP ..."
INTERVIEW WITH REINHOLD WÜRTH

GG One question in closing, a brief look into the future: where will the company go from here in your opinion? Which markets still need to be captured? What is your vision regarding the future of the Würth Group?

REINHOLD WÜRTH Well, apart from our core business in the market for fasteners and assembly materials, I have already been diversifying for a number of decades; let me just mention Würth Elektronik and the tool wholesalers, Hommel Hercules and Hahn & Kolb, and the electrical wholesalers Fega, Uni Elektro, and Schmitt.

We want to intensify our efforts in peripheral market places, such as perhaps the electrical wholesale business, the tool wholesale business, and the more recent financial services sector and IT-software sales.

All these issues also have a philosophical aspect, concerning the question of whether diversification is good or bad. I believe that it is neither one nor the other, since you can find a large number of positive and negative examples for both. The hypothesis "diversification is bad" ultimately means "cobbler, stick to your last." Take the example of Daimler-Benz: under the direction of Edzard Reuter, the company came up with the idea of building up a worldwide technology group. The project failed abysmally, not because Edzard Reuter's idea was wrong, but because of the fact that Daimler-Benz was so focused on building cars that the automobile managers couldn't think of anything else – the current board of managers of DaimlerChrysler is focused on building cars – and yet the business still suffers from the decision. This is a classic example of diversification being neither good nor bad: it actually boils down to the people in charge, the people taking action, and their powers of persuasion. However, there is also the case of General Electric: originally active in the electrical engineering industry, General Electric has turned into a highly successful, global conglomerate today. The company does not only build electrical and electronic appliances and components, but also engines; they can fall back on a tight network of banks and insurances; and all of these businesses are highly successful and highly profitable.

On an international level, we are still way below 5 per cent market share in our core business. In Germany we have about 5 per cent, in Finland perhaps 15 or 20 per cent, but in the US, Spain, and Italy we are still way below; in other words, even after 60 years we are still at the very beginning of our development.

I envision the Würth Group to be an oligopolist with 14, 16, or even 18 per cent market share. Provided we reckon with 4 per cent market share today, 16 per cent would equal a quadrupling of our sales; we would therefore have to generate sales of 20 billion euro. And even this is not the limit in our market.

The interview with Prof. Dr. h.c. Reinhold Würth
was carried out by Ute Grau and Dr. Barbara Guttmann on June 17, 2004

FOOTNOTES

1. Paul Erker: Aufbruch zu neuen Paradigmen. Unternehmensgeschichte zwischen sozialgeschichtlicher und betriebswirtschaftlicher Erweiterung. In: Archiv für Sozialgeschichte 37, 1997, pp. 321–365, p. 365
2. Manfred Pohl: Zwischen Weihrauch und Wissenschaft? Zum Standort der modernen Unternehmensgeschichte. Eine Replik auf Toni Pierenkemper. In: ZUG 2/1999, pp. 150–163
3. Toni Pierenkemper: Unternehmensgeschichte. Eine Einführung in ihre Methoden und Ergebnisse. Stuttgart 2000 (Grundzüge der modernen Wirtschaftsgeschichte, Vol.1), p. 13, pp. 40
4. At the end of the eighties the Working Group for Critical Business and Industry History was established at the University of Bochum, which publishes the magazine "Akkumulation"
5. Toni Pierenkemper: Was kann eine moderne Unternehmensgeschichtsschreibung leisten? Und was sollte sie tunlichst vermeiden. In: ZUG 1/1999, pp. 15–31
6. Manfred Pohl: Zwischen Weihrauch und Wissenschaft? Zum Standort der modernen Unternehmensgeschichte. Eine Replik auf Toni Pierenkemper. In: ZUG 2/1999, pp. 150–163, p. 154
7. Florian Triebel, Jürgen Seidl: Ein Analyserahmen für das Fach Unternehmensgeschichte. In: ZUG 1/2000, pp. 11–26, p. 25
8. Hans-Ulrich Wehler: What is the "History of Society"? In: Geschichte der Geschichtsschreibung 18/1990, pp. 5–19, p. 15
9. See Paul Erker: Aufbruch zu neuen Paradigmen. Unternehmensgeschichte zwischen sozialgeschichtlicher und betriebswirtschaftlicher Erweiterung. In: Archiv für Sozialgeschichte 37, 1997, pp. 321–365, pp. 334
10. Karl Helfferich: Georg von Siemens. Ein Lebensbild aus Deutschlands großer Zeit. 3 vols. Berlin 1921–1923
11. Theodor Heuss: Robert Bosch. Leben und Leistung. Stuttgart 1946. Neuauflage Stuttgart 2002
12. The entrepreneurial pioneer as conceived by the Austrian economist Joseph Schumpeter is a symbol of innovation and revolution. Today, he is a dynamic of the free market system. Joseph Alois Schumpeter: Das Wesen und der Hauptinhalt der theoretischen Nationalökonomie; Theorie der wirtschaftlichen Entwicklung. Eine Untersuchung über Unternehmergewinn, Kapital, Kredit, Zins und den Konjunkturzyklus; Kapitalismus, Sozialismus und Demokratie
13. Albert Pfiffner: Henry Nestlé (1814–1890). Zürich: 1993; Sidney Pollard, Roland Möller: Dr. August Oetker (1862–1918).In: J. Kocka, R. Vogelsang (publishers): Rheinisch-Westfälische Wirtschaftsbiographien. vol. 14, Münster 1991, pp. 354–377; Ingunn Possehl: Unternehmer und technischer Fortschritt zu Beginn der Feinchemikalienindustrie. In: F. Schinzinger (publisher): Unternehmer und technischer Fortschritt. Munich 1996, pp. 265–282
14. Gerald D. Feldman: Hugo Stinnes. Biographie eines Industriellen 1870–1924. Translated into German by Karl Heinz Siber. Munich 1998. Gerald D. Feldman is the director of the Institute of European Studies, University of California, Berkeley
15. Theodor Heuss: Robert Bosch. Leben und Leistung. Stuttgart 2002, p. 13
16. Reinhold Würth: Management Culture: the Secret of Success. An Entrepreneur Takes Stock. 2nd edition. Künzelsau 1999, pp. 89
17. Manfred Pohl: Zwischen Weihrauch und Wissenschaft? Zum Standort der modernen Unternehmensgeschichte. Eine Replik auf Toni Pierenkemper. In: ZUG 2/1999, pp. 150–163, p. 154
18. Reinhold Würth: The Würth idea for the 80s. In: Thoughts on Company Management. Schwäbisch Hall 1985, pp. 81–90

CHAPTER 1

1. A detailed description of the foundation history of the company can be found in: Karlheinz Schönherr: Nach oben geschraubt. Reinhold Würth. Die Karriere eines Unternehmers. 3rdunchanged edition. Künzelsau 2001, pp. 19–41
2. Reinhold Würth: Thoughts on Company Management. Schwäbisch Hall 1985, p.10
3. Quote in Karlheinz Schönherr: Nach oben geschraubt. Reinhold Würth. Die Karriere eines Unternehmers. 3rd unchanged edition. Künzelsau 2001, p. 29
4. Willi A. Boelcke: Wirtschaftsgeschichte Baden-Württembergs. Von den Römern bis heute. Stuttgart 1987, p. 459
5. Willi A. Boelcke: Wirtschaftsgeschichte Baden-Württembergs. Von den Römern bis heute. Stuttgart 1987, pp. 579
6. Willi A. Boelcke: Wirtschaftsgeschichte Baden-Württembergs. Von den Römern bis heute. Stuttgart 1987, p. 480
7. Künzelsau city archives, trade tax 1945 – 1974
8. Reinhold Würth: Thoughts on Company Management. Schwäbisch Hall 1985, p.10
9. Quote in Karlheinz Schönherr: Nach oben geschraubt. Reinhold Würth. Die Karriere eines Unternehmers. 3rd unchanged edition. Künzelsau 2001, p. 39
10. Reinhold Würth: Thoughts on Company Management. Schwäbisch Hall 1985, p. 10

CHAPTER 2

11. Reinhold Würth: the Secret of Success. An Entrepreneur Takes Stock. 2nd edition. Künzelsau 1999, p. 17
12. Reinhold Würth: the Secret of Success. An Entrepreneur Takes Stock. 2nd edition. Künzelsau 1999, p. 20
13. Excerpt from the entry on the Commercial Register District Court, Register Court Schwäbisch Hall
14. Company History Dieter Krämer, Würth Central Archives
15. Excerpt from the entries on the Commercial Register District Court, Register Court Schwäbisch Hall
16. Paul Swiridoff: Gesichter einer Epoche. Begegnungen aus fünf Jahrzehnten. Stuttgart, Zurich 1997, p. 37

17 All quotes if not expressly marked otherwise: Interview with Carmen Würth on July 22, 2004
18 Schloss Hermersberg – Gedanken von Reinhold Würth. In: Gerhard Taddey: Hermersberg. Die Geschichte von Schloss und Wildfuhr. Sigmaringen 1992, p. 188
19 Company History Karl Weidner, Würth Central Archives.
20 Carmen Würth: Zur Eröffnung des Hauses "Anne-Sophie" March 14, 2003. Printed manuscript 2004
21 Hohenlohe Trends 5/2003
22 Reinhold Würth: the Secret of Success. An Entrepreneur Takes Stock. 2nd edition. Künzelsau 1999, p. 17

CHAPTER 3

23 Willi A. Boelcke: Wirtschaftsgeschichte Baden-Württembergs. Von den Römern bis heute. Stuttgart 1987, p. 461
24 50 Jahre Baden-Württemberg. Hg. V. Statistischen Landesamt Baden-Württemberg. Stuttgart 2002
25 Reinhold Würth: the Secret of Success. An Entrepreneur Takes Stock. 2nd edition. Künzelsau 1999, p. 32
26 Company History Hans Hügel, Würth Central Archives
27 Würth Handbook 2002. Facts and Figures worldwide. Künzelsau 2002, p. 73
28 Interview with Albert Berner on November 27, 2003
29 Company History Hans Hügel, Würth Central Archives
30 Company History Hans Hügel, Würth Central Archives
31 Company History Hermann Leiser, Würth Central Archives
32 Company History Hermann Leiser, Würth Central Archives
33 Company History Hans Hügel, Würth Central Archives
34 Quote in Karlheinz Schönherr: Nach oben geschraubt. Reinhold Würth. Die Karriere eines Unternehmers. 3rd unchanged edition. Künzelsau 2001, pp. 55
35 Company History Karl Specht, Würth Central Archives
36 Reinhold Würth: the Secret of Success. An Entrepreneur Takes Stock. 2nd edition. Künzelsau 1999, p. 16
37 Interview with Hans Hügel on February 16, 2004
38 Company History Hans Hügel, Würth Central Archives
39 Company History Christoph Walter, Würth Central Archives
40 Company History Christoph Walter, Würth Central Archives
41 Company History Hermann Leiser, Würth Central Archives
42 Quote in Karlheinz Schönherr: Nach oben geschraubt. Reinhold Würth. Die Karriere eines Unternehmers. 3rd unchanged edition. Künzelsau 2001, pp. 64
43 Company History Herrmann Leiser, Würth Central Archives
44 Company History Hermann Leiser, Würth Central Archives
45 Interview with Hermine Künast on January 12, 2004
46 Company History Christoph Walter, Würth Central Archives

CHAPTER 4

47 Reinhold Würth: Management Culture: the Secret of Success. An Entrepreneur Takes Stock. 2nd issue. Künzelsau 1999, p. 19

48 For the history of Hohenlohe see Hohenlohe. Published by Otto Bauschert, Stuttgart 1993 (Schriften zur politischen Landeskunde Baden-Württembergs; vol. 21); Karin Wohlschlegel: Hohenlohe: Burgenland Württembergs. In: Baden-Württemberg. Vielfalt und Stärke der Regionen. Published by Hans-Georg Wehling, Angelika Hauser-Hauswirth, Fred Ludwig Sepaintner commissioned by Landeszentrale f. pol. Bildung Baden-Württemberg. Leinfelden-Echterdingen 2002, pp. 240–277
49 Walter Hampele: Die politische Kultur Hohenlohes. In: Hohenlohe. Published by Otto Bauschert. Stuttgart 1993 (Schriften zur politischen Landeskunde Baden-Württembergs; vol 21), p. 142
50 See Walter Hampele: Die politische Kultur Hohenlohes. In: Hohenlohe. Published by Otto Bauschert. Stuttgart 1993 (Schriften zur politischen Landeskunde Baden-Württembergs; vol. 21), pp. 141–165
51 See population statistics Künzelsau with suburbs according to the situation of the region from Jan. 1, 1977, Künzelsau municipal archives; Peter Giehrl: Entwicklung von Bevölkerung und Wirtschaft. In: Hohenlohe. Published by Otto Bauschert. Stuttgart 1993 (Schriften zur politischen Landeskunde Baden-Württembergs; vol 21), pp. 109
52 Report by the Baden-Württemberg Statistical Office, www.heilbronn.ihk.de/Information/Statistics_KB.htm. November 11, 2003
53 Willi A. Boelcke: Wirtschaftsgeschichte Baden-Württembergs von den Römern bis heute. Stuttgart 1987, pp– 449.
54 Dieter Schweikhardt: Die Industriegeographischen Veränderungen in Künzelsau seit 1945. Päd. Inst. Esslingen 1957, p.11
55 Der Kreis Künzelsau. Published by Konrad Theiss et al. Aalen 1965 (Heimat und Arbeit), pp. 18
56 Minister of Finance Dr. Herrmann Müller: Die finanziellen Beziehungen des Landes zum Landkreis Künzelsau und dessen Gemeinden. In: Der Kreis Künzelsau. Published by Konrad Theiss et al. Aalen 1965 (Heimat und Arbeit), pp. 21
57 Peter Giehrl: Entwicklung von Bevölkerung und Wirtschaft. In : Hohenlohe. Published by Otto Bauschert. Stuttgart 1993 (Schriften zur politischen Landeskunde Baden-Württembergs; vol. 21), pp. 117
58 www.stadt-kuenzelsau.de/cms. April 29, 2004
59 Speech by Walter Döring on the occasion of the 2nd Regional Day of the citizens' action group pro Region Heilbronn-Franken e.V. on June 20, 1999
60 Die Region Franken mit Stadtkreis und Landkreisen. Statistisches Landesamt Baden-Württemberg. Materialien und Berichte. H. 11. Stuttgart 1998
61 Peter Giehrl: Entwicklung von Bevölkerung und Wirtschaft. In : Hohenlohe. Published by Otto Bauschert. Stuttgart 1993 (Schriften zur politischen Landeskunde Baden-Württembergs; vol. 21), pp. 122

FOOTNOTES

62 Die Region Franken mit Stadtkreis und Landkreisen. Statistisches Landesamt Baden-Württemberg. Materialien und Berichte, H. 11. Stuttgart 1998

63 Reinhold Würth: Chancen und Probleme der wirtschaftlichen Entwicklung in ländlichen Räumen. Vortrag am Institut für Raumordnung und Entwicklungsplanung an der Universität Stuttgart, December 16, 1986

64 Die Region Heilbronn-Franken in Zahlen. Statistik 2002. Published by the Heilbronn-Franken Chamber of Commerce and Industry, 4th edition November 2002, p. 22

65 District administrator Helmut M. Jahn: Hohenlohekreis – Der Standort mit Zukunft. www.pro-region.de/3wissenswerteshohenlohekreis.pdf. April 2004

66 Haller Tagblatt from April 29, 2003 and www.heilbronn-franken.com/DATA/REGION/region-perspektive-deutschland.php. November 2003

67 Compilation of Adolf Würth GmbH & Co. KG, May 2004

68 Reinhold Würth: Chancen und Probleme der wirtschaftlichen Entwicklung in ländlichen Räumen. Vortrag am Institut für Raumordnung und Entwicklungsplanung an der Universität Stuttgart, December 16, 1986

69 HAT-Gespräch mit Prof. Reinhold Würth and the mayor of Hall, Herrmann-Josef Pelgrim, about the future of Schwäbisch Hall in the Heilbronn-Franconia region. Haller Tagblatt from November 25, 1999

70 Stuttgarter Zeitung from August 25, 2004

71 See results of an inquiry carried out by the citizens' action group pro Region Heilbronn-Franken in the summer of 2000, Würth Central Archives

72 Die Wirtschaft von Baden-Württemberg im Umbruch. Published by Hilde Cost, Margot Körber-Weik. Stuttgart 2002 (Schriften zur politischen Landeskunde Baden-Württembergs, vol. 29), p. 19

73 Reinhold Würth: Chancen und Probleme der wirtschaftlichen Entwicklung in ländlichen Räumen. Vortrag am Institut für Raumordnung und Entwicklungsplanung an der Universität Stuttgart, December 16, 1986

74 Annual Report of the Würth Group 2002

75 Annual Report of the Würth Group 2003

76 Reinhold Würth: Chancen und Probleme der wirtschaftlichen Entwicklung in ländlichen Räumen. Vortrag am Institut für Raumordnung und Entwicklungsplanung an der Universität Stuttgart, December 16, 1986

77 Reinhold Würth: Chancen und Probleme der wirtschaftlichen Entwicklung in ländlichen Räumen. Vortrag am Institut für Raumordnung und Entwicklungsplanung an der Universität Stuttgart, December 16, 1986

78 Reinhold Würth: Chancen und Probleme der wirtschaftlichen Entwicklung in ländlichen Räumen. Vortrag am Institut für Raumordnung und Entwicklungsplanung an der Universität Stuttgart, December 16, 1986

79 Rolf Bauer, Company History, Würth Central Archives

80 Correspondence between Reinhold Würth and mayor Wilhelm Balbach, Würth Central Archives

81 Conversation with Wilhelm Balbach, mayor of Niedernhall from 1951–1993, on January 20, 2004

82 www.Niedernhall.de. May 2004

83 Würth Handbook 2002. Facts and Figures worldwide. Künzelsau 2002, pp. 96

84 Würth Handbook 2002. Facts and Figures worldwide. Künzelsau 2002, pp. 88

85 See Eberhard Kugler: Vom Bauern- zum Industriedorf: dargestellt an der Entwicklung Ernsbachs am Kocher. Festschrift anlässlich des 100jährigen Bestehens der Schraubenfertigung in Ernsbach. Sigmaringen 1998 (Forschungen aus Württemberg-Franken / Historischer Verein für Württembergisch-Franken 46)

86 Würth Handbook 2002. Facts and Figures worldwide. Künzelsau 2002, p. 109, p.140

87 Opening words by Prof. Reinhold Würth. In: Neues Leben im alten Sudhaus. Supplement to Haller Tagblatt, Hohenloher Tagblatt and Rundschau, Friday, May 21, 2004

88 Neues Leben im alten Sudhaus. Supplement to Haller Tagblatt, Hohenloher Tagblatt and Rundschau, Friday, May 21, 2004

89 Reinhold Würth: Meine Ehrenbürgerschaft. Manuscript.

90 Reinhold Würth: Chancen und Probleme der wirtschaftlichen Entwicklung in ländlichen Räumen. Vortrag am Institut für Raumordnung und Entwicklungsplanung an der Universität Stuttgart, December 16, 1986

91 Reinhold Würth: Schloß Hermersberg – Gedanken. In: Gerhard Taddey: Hermersberg. Die Geschichte von Schloß und Wildfuhr. Sigmaringen 1992 (Forschungen aus Württembergisch Franken, vol. 41), p. 184

92 Reinhold Würth: Schloß Hermersberg – Gedanken. In: Gerhard Taddey: Hermersberg. Die Geschichte von Schloß und Wildfuhr. Sigmaringen 1992 (Forschungen aus Württembergisch Franken, vol. 41), p. 189

93 Quote according to Carl Heinz Gräter: Im grünen Licht Hohenlohes. Stuttgart 1989, p. 78

94 Reinhold Würth: Der deutsche Südwesten – Das Land der Tüftler und Schaffer. Ceremonial address on the occasion of the presentation of the Wirtschaftsmedaille des Landes Baden-Württemberg (medal awarded by the state of Baden-Württemberg) in Stuttgart on April 6, 1990

95 www.wir-koennen-alles.de August 2004

96 Reinhold Würth: Der deutsche Südwesten – Das Land der Tüftler und Schaffer. Ceremonial address on the occasion of the presentation of the Wirtschaftsmedaille des Landes Baden-Württemberg (medal awarded by the state of Baden-Württemberg) in Stuttgart on April 6, 1990

97 Wertheimer Zeitung from July 14, 2001

98 Heilbronner Stimme, no date (www.pro-region.de/pages/presse.html. February 2004)

99 Correspondence with Dr. Franz Susset, Würth Central Archives

100 www.uni-karlsruhe.de/~iep. March 27, 2003

101 Heilbronner Stimme, no date (www.pro-region.de/pages/presse.html February 2004)
102 Stuttgarter Nachrichten, no date (www.pro-region.de/pages/presse.html February 2004)
103 Werbung mit Nebenwirkung? Einsatz für "Pro Region" stößt aus verschiedenen Gründen auf Kritik. Hohenloher Tagblatt from October 10, 2000
104 Company History Karl Specht, Würth Central Archives

CHAPTER 5
105 Quote according to Willi A. Boelcke: Wirtschaftsgeschichte Baden-Württembergs. Von den Römern bis heute. Stuttgart 1987, p. 462
106 Willi A. Boelcke: Wirtschaftsgeschichte Baden-Württembergs. Von den Römern bis heute. Stuttgart 1987, pp. 550.
107 Karlheinz Schönherr: Nach oben geschraubt. Reinhold Würth. Die Karriere eines Unternehmers. 3rd unchanged edition. Künzelsau 2001, p.77
108 50 Jahre Baden-Württemberg. Published by the Baden-Württemberg Statistical Office. Stuttgart 2002
109 Quote in Karlheinz Schönherr: Nach oben geschraubt. Reinhold Würth. Die Karriere eines Unternehmers. 3rd unchanged edition. Künzelsau 2001, p.72
110 Quote in Karlheinz Schönherr: Nach oben geschraubt. Reinhold Würth. Die Karriere eines Unternehmers. 3rd unchanged edition. Künzelsau 2001, p.73
111 Interview with Reinhold Würth on June 17, 2004
112 Company History Rolf Bauer, Würth Central Archives
113 Company History Hans Hügel, Würth Central Archives
114 Reinhold Würth: Profit – the wages of clever economic management? Managers' Conference of the Würth Group in the spring of 1981. Rottach-Egern/Tegernsee, April 24 – May 1, 1981. In: Thoughts on Company Management. Schwäbisch Hall 1985, p. 128–140
115 See Reinhold Würth: Profit – the wages of clever economic management? Managers' Conference of the Würth Group in the spring of 1981. Rottach-Egern/Tegernsee, April 24 – May 1, 1981. In: Beiträge zur Unternehmensführung. Schwäbisch Hall 1985, p. 128–140
116 Quote in Karlheinz Schönherr: Nach oben geschraubt. Reinhold Würth. Die Karriere eines Unternehmers. 3rd unchanged edition. Künzelsau 2001, p. 70
117 Interview with Reinhold Würth on June 17, 2004
118 Company History Hans Hügel, Würth Central Archives
119 Letter by Adolf Würth OHG from October 13, 1961. Company History Hans Hügel, Würth Central Archives
120 Company History Karl Specht, Würth Central Archives
121 Company History Rolf Bauer, Würth Central Archives
122 Company History Karl Specht, Würth Central Archives
123 Company History Rolf Bauer, Würth Central Archives
124 Company History Rolf Bauer, Würth Central Archives
125 Company History Rolf Bauer, Würth Central Archives
126 Interview with Rolf Bauer on February 16, 2004
127 Company History Otto Beilharz, Würth Central Archives
128 Company History Otto Beilharz, Würth Central Archives
129 Company History Karl Specht, Würth Central Archives
130 Company History Hermann Leiser, Würth Central Archives
131 Letter from Adolf Würth OHG from October 13, 1961. Company History Hans Hügel, Würth Central Archives
132 Company History Hans Hügel, Würth Central Archives
133 Company History Hermann Leiser, Würth Central Archives
134 Company History Christoph Walter, Würth Central Archives
135 Company History Hans Hügel, Würth Central Archives
136 Also in the following quotef from the Company History of Christoph Walther, Würth Central Archives
137 Company History Karl Specht, Würth Central Archives
138 Reinhold Würth: Würth field service – the foundation for progress. Würth Congress ‚76 in Willingen from December 17 – 19, 1976. In: Thoughts on Company Management. Schwäbisch Hall 1985, pp. 13–23, pp. 16
139 Company History Rolf Bauer, Würth Central Archives.
140 Company History Christoph Walther, Würth Central Archives
141 Quote in Karlheinz Schönherr: Nach oben geschraubt. Reinhold Würth. Die Karriere eines Unternehmers. 3rd unchanged edition. Künzelsau 2001, p. 74
142 Company History Christoph Walther, Würth Central Archives
143 Company History Christoph Walther, Würth Central Archives
144 Company History Karl Specht, Würth Central Archives
145 Company History Hans Hügel, Würth Central Archives
146 Company History Karl Specht, Würth Central Archives
147 Company History Rolf Bauer, Würth Central Archives
148 Company History Rolf Bauer, Würth Central Archives
149 Karlheinz Schönherr: Nach oben geschraubt. Reinhold Würth. Die Karriere eines Unternehmers. 3rd unchanged edition. Künzelsau 2001, p. 103
150 Company History Otto Beilharz, Würth Central Archives
151 See Gottfried Knapp, Andreas Schmid: Building for the World. Architecture at Würth. Bauen für die Welt. Architektur bei Würth. Künzelsau 2001, p. 18
152 Letter from Adolf Würth KG to the Schwäbisch Hall employment office, May 20, 1969, Würth Central Archives
153 Company History Otto Beilharz, Würth Central Archives.
154 Letter from Adolf Würth KG to the Schwäbisch Hall employment office, May 20, 1969, Würth Central Archives

CHAPTER 6
155 Interview with Reinhold Würth on June 17, 2004
156 Reinhold Würth: Globalisierung der Geschäftsidee. Lecture manuscript. Entrepreneurship Institute. University of Karlsruhe (TH), summer semester 2002
157 Interview with Reinhold Würth on June 17, 2004
158 Reinhold Würth: Management Culture: the Secret of Success. An Entrepreneur Takes Stock. 2nd issue. Künzelsau 1999, pp. 269
159 Karlheinz Schönherr: Nach oben geschraubt. Reinhold Würth. Die Karriere eines Unternehmers. 3rd unchanged edition. Künzelsau 2001, pp. 79

FOOTNOTES

160 Figures taken from Karlheinz Schönherr: Nach oben geschraubt. Reinhold Würth. Die Karriere eines Unternehmers. 3rd unchanged edition. Künzelsau 2001, pp. 79
161 Company History Hendrik Lastdrager. In: Company History Würth Netherlands, Würth Central Archives.
162 Karlheinz Schönherr: Nach oben geschraubt. Reinhold Würth. Die Karriere eines Unternehmers. 3rd unchanged edition. Künzelsau 2001, pp. 87
163 Würth Handbook 2002. Facts and Figures worldwide. Künzelsau 2002, p. 230
164 Karlheinz Schönherr: Nach oben geschraubt. Reinhold Würth. Die Karriere eines Unternehmers. 3rd unchanged edition. Künzelsau 2001, pp. 92
165 Handbook 2002. Facts and Figures worldwide. Künzelsau 2002, p. 21
166 Company History Würth Italy, Würth Central Archives
167 Helmut Gschnell: Abenteuer Umsatz. Chronik der Erfolgsstory von Würth Italien. Unpublished manuscript. February 2004, p. 15
168 Helmut Gschnell: Abenteuer Umsatz. Chronik der Erfolgsstory von Würth Italien. Unpublished manuscript. February 2004, p. 27
169 Helmut Gschnell: Abenteuer Umsatz. Chronik der Erfolgsstory von Würth Italien. Unpublished manuscript. February 2004, p. 28
170 Helmut Gschnell: Abenteuer Umsatz. Chronik der Erfolgsstory von Würth Italien. Unpublished manuscript. February 2004, p. 31
171 Helmut Gschnell: Abenteuer Umsatz. Chronik der Erfolgsstory von Würth Italien. Unpublished manuscript. February 2004, p. 45
172 Helmut Gschnell: Abenteuer Umsatz. Chronik der Erfolgsstory von Würth Italien. Unpublished manuscript. February 2004, p. 56
173 Helmut Gschnell: Abenteuer Umsatz. Chronik der Erfolgsstory von Würth Italien. Unpublished manuscript. February 2004, p. 72
174 Company History Dieter Krämer, Würth Central Archives.
175 Helmut Gschnell: Abenteuer Umsatz. Chronik der Erfolgsstory von Würth Italien. Unpublished manuscript. February 2004, p. 73
176 Helmut Gschnell: Abenteuer Umsatz. Chronik der Erfolgsstory von Würth Italien. Unpublished manuscript. February 2004, p. 5
177 www.wuerth.it, August 2004
178 Company History Richard Burgstahler. In: Company History Würth France, Würth Central Archives
179 Figures taken from the Company History of Richard Burgstahler. In: Company History Würth France, Würth Central Archives
180 Company History Richard Burgstahler. In: Company History Würth France, Würth Central Archives
181 Company HIstory Mutschler. In: Company History Würth France, Würth Central Archives
182 Company History Karl Specht, Würth Central Archives
183 www.wuerth.fr, August 2004
184 Interview with Ernst Clausen on November 8, 2003
185 Reinhold Würth: Management Culture: the Secret of Success. An Entrepreneur Takes Stock. 2nd edition. Künzelsau 1999, pp. 273
186 Interview with Ernst Clausen on November 8, 2003
187 Company History José Viana, Würth Central Archives
188 www.wuerth.es, August 2004
189 Reinhold Würth: Globalisierung der Geschäftsidee. Lecture manuscript. Entrepreneurship Institute. University of Karlsruhe (TH), summer semester 2002
190 Interview with Peter Zürn on January 26, 2004
191 Company History Günter Theurer, Würth Central Archives
192 Reinhold Würth: Management Culture: the Secret of Success. An Entrepreneur Takes Stock. 2nd edition. Künzelsau 1999, p. 270
193 Reinhold Würth: The Würth Idea for the 80s. In: Thoughts on Company Management. Schwäbisch Hall 1985, p. 81–90
194 Interview with Dieter Krämer on November 6, 2003
195 Company History José Viana, Würth Central Archives
196 Interview with Ernst Clausen on November 8, 2003
197 Minutes of the FÜKO on June 10/11, 2002 in Künzelsau-Gaisbach. Würth Central Archives
198 Company History Günter Theurer, Würth Central Archives
199 Würth-Report. 1st issue 1971
200 Haller Tagblatt from May 23, 1987, "Deutsche Wirtschaftspolitik stabilisiert Apartheidsystem"
201 Interview with Peter Zürn on January 26, 2004
202 Interview with Peter Zürn on January 26, 2004
203 Würth Handbook 2002. Facts and Figures worldwide. KÜnzelsau 2002, pp. 270
204 Company History Dieter Krämer, Würth Central Archives
205 Annual Report of the Würth Group 1987
206 Annual Report of the Würth Group 1997, do. 1998, 1999
207 Company History Peter Zürn, Würth Central Archives
208 Annual Report of the Würth Group 2001
209 Würth Handbook 2002. Facts and Figures worldwide. Künzelsau 2002, p. 231
210 Company History José Viana, Würth Central Archives
211 Reinhold Würth: Management Culture: the Secret of Success. An Entrepreneur Takes Stock. 2nd edition. Künzelsau 1999, p. 321
212 Würth Handbook 2002. Facts and Figures worldwide. Künzelsau 2002, p. 192
213 Reinhold Würth: Management Culture: the Secret of Success. An Entrepreneur Takes Stock. 2nd edition. Künzelsau 1999, p. 276
214 Reinhold Würth: Globalisierung der Geschäftsidee. Lecture manuscript. Entrepreneurship Institute. University of Karlsruhe (TH), summer semester 2002
215 Würth Handbook 2002. Facts and Figures worldwide. Künzelsau 2002, p. 11
216 Company History José Viana, Würth Central Archives

217 Company History José Viana, Würth Central Archives
218 Company History Dieter Krämer, Würth Central Archives
219 Reinhold Würth: Globalisierung der Geschäftsidee. Lecture manuscript. Entrepreneurship Institute. University of Karlsruhe (TH), summer semester 2002
220 Interview with Ernst Clausen on November 8, 2003
221 Interview with Rolf Bauer on February 16, 2004
222 Interview with Dieter Krämer on November 6, 2003
223 Reinhold Würth: Globalisierung der Geschäftsidee. Lecture manuscript. Entrepreneurship Institute. University of Karlsruhe (TH), summer semester 2002

CHAPTER 7

224 For figures on personnel development and sales development see Karlheinz Schönherr: Nach oben geschraubt. Reinhold Würth. Die Karriere eines Unternehmers. 3rd unchanged edition. Künzelsau 2001, p. 252, p. 254
225 50 Jahre Baden-Württemberg. Published by the Baden-Württemberg Statistical Office. Stuttgart 2002
226 50 Jahre Baden-Württemberg. Published by the Baden-Württemberg Statistical Office. Stuttgart 2002
227 Karlheinz Schönherr: Nach oben geschraubt. Reinhold Würth. Die Karriere eines Unternehmers. 3rd unchanged edition. Künzelsau 2001, p. 112. Also see Reinhold Würth: Management Culture: the Secret of Success. An Entrepreneur Takes Stock. 2nd edition. Künzelsau 1999, p. 323
228 Quote in Karlheinz Schönherr: Nach oben geschraubt. Reinhold Würth. Die Karriere eines Unternehmers. 3rd unchanged edition. Künzelsau 2001, p. 111
229 Company History Gerhard Knoblauch, Würth Central Archives
230 Company History Günter Theurer, Würth Central Archives.
231 Karlheinz Schönherr: Nach oben geschraubt. Reinhold Würth. Die Karriere eines Unternehmers. 3rd unchanged edition. Künzelsau 2001, p. 108
232 Company History Günter Theurer, Würth Central Archives
233 Company History Walter Jaeger, Würth Central Archives
234 Karlheinz Schönherr: Nach oben geschraubt. Reinhold Würth. Die Karriere eines Unternehmers. 3rd unchanged edition. Künzelsau 2001, p. 254
235 See Reinhold Würth: Profit – the wages of clever economic management? Managers' Conference of the Würth Group in the spring of 1981. Rottach-Egern/Tegernsee from April 24 – May 1, 1981. In: Thoughts on Company Management. Schwäbisch Hall 1985, pp. 128–140
236 Reinhold Würth: Corporate Philosophy of the Würth Group. 1975 version. Unchanged reprint 1979
237 Also in the following Company History Dieter Krämer, Würth Central Archives
238 Reinhold Würth: Management Culture: the Secret of Success. An Entrepreneur Takes Stock. 2nd edition. Künzelsau1999, p. 94
239 Minutes of the constituent meeting of the Advisory Board of Adolf Würth KG, April 16, 1975, Würth Central Archives
240 All quotes in this section from Reinhold Würth: Corporate Philosophy of the Würth Group. 1975 version. Unchanged reprint 1979
241 Company History Dieter Krämer, Würth Central Archives.
242 Reinhold Würth: Management Culture: the Secret of Success. An Entrepreneur Takes Stock. 2nd edition. Künzelsau1999, p. 96
243 This development is also confirmed by Dieter Krämer in his Company History of the year 1977, Würth Central Archives
244 Reinhold Würth: Management Culture: the Secret of Success. An Entrepreneur Takes Stock. 2nd edition. Künzelsau1999, p. 86
245 Karlheinz Schönherr: Nach oben geschraubt. Reinhold Würth. Die Karriere eines Unternehmers. 3rd unchanged edition. Künzelsau 2001, p. 133
246 All quotes in this section taken from the Company History of Dieter Krämer, Würth Central Archives
247 All quotes in this section taken from the Company History of Werner Rau, Würth Central Archives
248 Reinhold Würth: Thoughts on Company Management, Schwäbisch Hall 1985, p. 21
249 Company History Dieter Krämer, Würth Central Archives
250 Reinhold Würth: Würth field service – the foundation for progress. Würth Congress ,76 in Willingen from December 17 – 19, 1976. In: Thoughts on Company Management. Schwäbisch Hall 1985, pp. 13
251 Company History Karl Specht, Würth Central Archives
252 Karlheinz Schönherr: Nach oben geschraubt. Reinhold Würth. Die Karriere eines Unternehmers. 3rd unchanged edition. Künzelsau 2001, pp. 118. Also see Company History Karl Specht, Würth Central Archives
253 Company History Hans Hügel, Würth Central Archives
254 Also in the following Reinhold Würth: Success = motivation + information. Fall Conference of the foreign Würth Companies in Bolzano from October 22 – 26, 1979. In: Thoughts on Company Management. Schwäbisch Hall 1985, p. 61–102
255 Reinhold Würth: Management Culture: The Secret of Success. An Entrepreneur Takes Stock. 2nd edition. Künzelsau 1999, p. 71
256 Company History Karl Specht, Würth Central Archives
257 Company History Karl Specht, Würth Central Archives
258 Company History Karl Specht, Würth Central Archives
259 Reinhold Würth: Würth field service – the foundation for progress. Würth Congress ,76 in Willingen from December 17 – 19, 1976. In: Thoughts on Company Management. Schwäbisch Hall 1985, p. 20
260 Company History Karl Specht, Würth Central Archives
261 Company History Hans Hügel, Würth Central Archives
262 Gottfried Knapp, Andreas Schmid: Building for the World. Architecture at Würth. Bauen für die Welt. Architektur bei Würth. Künzelsau 2001, pp. 17

263 Reinhold Würth: Würth field service – the foundation for progress. Würth Congress '76 in Willingen from December 17 – 19, 1976. In: Thoughts on Company Management. Schwäbisch Hall 1985, pp. 21
264 Reinhold Würth: Würth field service – the foundation for progress. Würth Congress '76 in Willingen from December 17 – 19, 1976. In: Thoughts on Company Management. Schwäbisch Hall 1985, pp. 21
265 Company History Paul Jakob, Würth Central Archives
266 Quote in Karlheinz Schönherr: Nach oben geschraubt. Reinhold Würth. Die Karriere eines Unternehmers. 3rd unchanged edition. Künzelsau 2001, p. 128
267 Company History Karl Specht, Würth Central Archives
268 Quote in Karlheinz Schönherr: Nach oben geschraubt. Reinhold Würth. Die Karriere eines Unternehmers. 3rd unchanged edition. Künzelsau 2001, p. 128
269 Company History Otto Beilharz and Company History Günter Theurer, Würth Central Archives
270 On this in detail the Company History Gerhard Fried, Würth Central Archives
271 Company History Karl Weidner., Würth Central Archives
272 Company History Karl Weidner., Würth Central Archives
273 Annual Report of the Würth Group 1978
274 Paul Swiridoff: Gesichter einer Epoche. Begegnungen aus fünf Jahrzehnten. Stuttgart, Zurich 1997, p. 38
275 Interview with Hermine Künast on January 12, 2004
276 Reinhold Würth: Corporate Philosophy of the Würth Group. 1975 version. Unchanged reprint 1979
277 Company History Rolf Bauer and Company History Karl Weidner, Würth Central Archives
278 Annual Report of the Würth Group 1978
279 See Karlheinz Schönherr: Nach oben geschraubt. Reinhold Würth. Die Karriere eines Unternehmers. 3rd unchanged edition. Künzelsau 2001, p. 113
280 Company History Rolf Bauer, Würth Central Archives
281 Minutes of the 7th Meeting of the Advisory Board of Adolf Würth KG, April 22, 1978, Würth Central Archives
282 Annual Report of the Würth Group 1978
283 All figures from Karlheinz Schönherr: Nach oben geschraubt. Reinhold Würth. Die Karriere eines Unterneh-mers. 3rd unchanged edition. Künzelsau 2001, p. 254, p. 252. Percentage figures based on calculations by the authors
284 Quote in Karlheinz Schönherr: Nach oben geschraubt. Reinhold Würth. Die Karriere eines Unternehmers. 3rd unchanged edition. Künzelsau 2001, p. 134

CHAPTER 8

285 Reinhold Würth: Gedanken zur Entwicklung des Hauses Würth bis zur Jahrtausendwende. Conference of the managing directors of the International Division, Künzelsau in the fall of 1986
286 Reinhold Würth: Gedanken zur Entwicklung des Hauses Würth bis zur Jahrtausendwende. Conference of the managing directors of the International Division, Künzelsau in the fall of 1986
287 Reinhold Würth: Gedanken zur Entwicklung des Hauses Würth bis zur Jahrtausendwende. Conference of the managing directors of the International Division, Künzelsau in the fall of 1986
288 Letter by Reinhold Würth to Jürgen Häckel from December 21, 1993, Würth Central Archives
289 Reinhold Würth: Gedanken zur Entwicklung des Hauses Würth bis zur Jahrtausendwende. Conference of the managing directors of the International Division, Künzelsau in the fall of 1986
290 Willi A. Boelcke: Wirtschaftsgeschichte Baden-Württembergs von den Römern bis heute. Stuttgart 1987, pp. 475
291 For the following see: Company History Otto Beilharz, Company History Rolf Bauer
292 Karlheinz Schönherr: Nach oben geschraubt. Reinhold Würth. Die Karriere eines Unternehmers. 3rd unchanged edition. Künzelsau, 2001, pp. 104
293 Company History Erika Jungfer. In: Company History Jürgen Häckel, Würth Central Archives
294 Company History Rolf Bauer, Würth Central Archives
295 Company History Bernd Wanke. In: Company History Jürgen Häckel, Würth Central Archives
296 Company History Erika Jungfer. In: Company History Jürgen Häckel, Würth Central Archives
297 Company History Hans-Dieter Fuhr. In: Company History Jürgen Häckel, Würth Central Archives
298 Company History Bernd Wanke. In: Company History Jürgen Häckel, Würth Central Archives
299 Company History Bernd Wanke. In: Company History Jürgen Häckel, Würth Central Archives
300 Karlheinz Schönherr: Nach oben geschraubt. Reinhold Würth. Die Karriere eines Unternehmers. 3rd unchanged edition. Künzelsau, 2001, p. 128
301 Karlheinz Schönherr: Nach oben geschraubt. Reinhold Würth. Die Karriere eines Unternehmers. 3rd unchanged edition. Künzelsau, 2001, pp. 126
302 Company History Dieter Krämer, Würth Central Archives.
303 Harald Unkelbach: Software development at Würth. In: "würth-phoenix_the book". Development and implementation of a merchandise management system. Künzelsau 2002, pp. 11–18
304 Company History Jürgen Häckel, Würth Central Archives.
305 For the EDP-history of the company also see: Harald Unkelbach: Software development at Würth. In: "würth-phoenix_the book". Development and implementation of a merchandise management system. Künzelsau 2002, pp. 11–18
306 Company History Dieter Krämer, Würth Central Archives
307 Interview with Dieter Krämer on November 6, 2003
308 Company History Jürgen Häckel, Würth Central Archives

309 Company History Dieter Krämer, Würth Central Archives
310 Company History Jürgen Häckel, Würth Central Archives
311 Key figures mentioned in tours of the company. Adolf Würth GmbH & Co. KG. July 2003
312 Company History Jürgen Häckel, Würth Central Archives. Also see Karlheinz Schönherr: Nach oben geschraubt. Reinhold Würth. Die Karriere eines Unternehmers. 3rd unchanged edition. Künzelsau, 2001, pp. 141
313 Harald Unkelbach: Software development at Würth. In: "würth-phoenix_the book". Development and implementation of a merchandise management system. Künzelsau 2002, pp. 11–18
314 Company History Walter Jaeger, Würth Central Archives
315 Company History Jürgen Häckel, Würth Central Archives
316 Company History Jürgen Häckel, Würth Central Archives
317 Annual Report of the Würth Group 2001
318 Company History Jürgen Häckel, Würth Central Archives
319 Reinhold Würth: Chancen und Probleme der wirtschaftlichen Entwicklung in ländlichen Räumen. Vortrag am Institut für Raumordnung und Entwicklungsplanung an der Universität Stuttgart, December 16, 1986
320 Jürgen Häckel: Schrittweise zum Ziel. In: Personalwirtschaft/SAP-Supplement
321 Company History Jürgen Häckel, Würth Central Archives
322 Company History Jürgen Häckel, Würth Central Archives
323 Company History Jürgen Häckel, Würth Central Archives
324 Company History Jürgen Häckel, Würth Central Archives
325 Company History Jürgen Häckel, Würth Central Archives
326 Company History Jürgen Häckel, Würth Central Archives
327 Reinhold Würth: Introduction to "würth-phoenix_the book". Development and implementation of a merchandise management system. Künzelsau 2002, pp. 7–9
328 Harald Unkelbach: Software development at Würth. In: "würth-phoenix_the book". Development and implementation of a merchandise management system. Künzelsau 2002, pp. 11–18
329 Company History Jürgen Häckel, Würth Central Archives
330 Annual Report of the Würth Group 1993
331 Company History Jürgen Häckel, Würth Central Archives
332 Company History Jürgen Häckel, Würth Central Archives
333 Company History Jürgen Häckel, Würth Central Archives
334 Letter by Reinhold Würth to Jürgen Häckel from May 8, 1996, Würth Central Archives
335 Company History Jürgen Häckel, Würth Central Archives
336 Company History Jürgen Häckel, Würth Central Archives
337 Hubert Kofler: würth_phoenix_the project. In: "würth-phoenix_the book". Development and implementation of a merchandise management system. Künzelsau 2002, pp. 19–54
338 Harald Unkelbach: Software development at Würth. In: "würth-phoenix_the book". Development and implementation of a merchandise management system. Künzelsau 2002, pp. 11–18
339 Reinhold Würth: Introduction to "würth-phoenix_the book". Development and implementation of a merchandise management system. Künzelsau 2002, pp. 7–9
340 Minutes of the FÜKO 06 in Künzelsau-Gaisbach on June 10 – 11, 2002, Würth Central Archives
341 Harald Unkelbach: Software development at Würth. In: "würth-phoenix_the book". Development and implementation of a merchandise management system. Künzelsau 2002, pp. 11–18
342 Minutes of the FÜKO 10 in Kupferzell, June 30 – July 1, 2003, Würth Central Archives
343 "Auch Microsoft tummelt sich inzwischen auf dem Markt der Unternehmenssoftware". In: Frankfurter Allgemeine Zeitung from June 9, 2004
344 Minutes of the FÜKO 12 in Künzelsau-Gaisbach from January 19 – 20, 2004, Würth Central Archives
345 www.wuerth-phoenix.com, August 2004
346 Minutes of the FÜKO 11 in Künzelsau-Gaisbach from December 8 – 9, 2003, Würth Central Archives
347 Minutes of the FÜKO 12 in Künzelsau-Gaisbach from January 19 – 20, 2004, Würth Central Archives.
348 Minutes of the FÜKO 10 in Kupferzell, June 30 – July 1, 2003, Würth Central Archives
349 "Address by the Chairman of the Advisory Board of the Würth Group. Presence and Future of the Würth Group." Speech by Reinhold Würth on the occasion of the Würth Congress in Dubai in September of 2003

CHAPTER 9
350 Reinhold Würth: The Würth Idea for the 80s. In: Thoughts on Company Management. Schwäbisch Hall, 1985, p. 81–90
351 Bundeszentrale für politische Bildung: Informationen zur politischen Bildung
352 Annual Report of the Würth Group 1980
353 Company History Dieter Krämer, Würth Central Archives.
354 Karlheinz Schönherr: Nach oben geschraubt. Reinhold Würth. Die Karriere eines Unternehmers. 3rd unchanged edition. Künzelsau 2001, p. 157
355 Annual Report of the Würth Group 1987
356 Reinhold Würth: The Würth Idea for the 80s. In: Thoughts on Company Management. Schwäbisch Hall, 1985, p. 81–90
357 Karlheinz Schönherr: Nach oben geschraubt. Reinhold Würth. Die Karriere eines Unternehmers. 3rd unchanged edition. Künzelsau 2001, p. 155
358 Reinhold Würth: Corporate Philosophy of the Würth Group. Fourth revised edition. October 2000
359 Karlheinz Schönherr: Nach oben geschraubt. Reinhold Würth. Die Karriere eines Unternehmers. 3rd unchanged edition. Künzelsau 2001, p. 156
360 Company History Dieter Krämer, Würth Central Archives
361 Annual Report of the Würth Group 1985; Company History Dr. Walter Jaeger, Würth Central Archives
362 Würth Handbook 2002. Facts and Figures worldwide, Künzelsau 2002

FOOTNOTES

363 PAP – Policy and Procedure 08.86-06-030, p.1, Würth Central Archives
364 PAP – Policy and Procedure 08.86-06-030, p.1, Würth Central Archives
365 Annual Reports of the Würth Group 1980 and 1985
366 Annual Report of the Würth Group 1987
367 Annual Report of the Würth Group 1981
368 Annual Report of the Würth Group 1987
369 Since 1976, see Company History Karl Weidner, Würth Central Archives
370 Annual Report of the Würth Group 1987
371 Company History Karl Specht, Würth Central Archives
372 Annual Report of the Würth Group 1984
373 Company History Gerhard Fried, Würth Central Archives
374 Karlheinz Schönherr: Nach oben geschraubt. Reinhold Würth. Die Karriere eines Unternehmers. 3rd unchanged edition. Künzelsau 2001, p. 140
375 Reinhold Würth: Corporate Philosophy of the Würth Group. Fourth revised edition. October 2000
376 Reinhold Würth: Management style in the field service. Regional managers' conference in South Tyrol. May 29 – 30, 1981. In: Thoughts on Company Management. Schwäbisch Hall 1985, p. 149
377 Interview with Karl Specht on January 20, 2004
378 Reinhold Würth: Companies need targets. International division conference from 26th to 30th October 1981 in Bad Mergentheim. In: Thoughts on Company Management. Schwäbisch Hall 1985, p. 179
379 Reinhold Würth: Management style in the field service. Regional managers' conference in South Tyrol. May 29 – 30, 1981. In: Thoughts on Company Management. Schwäbisch Hall 1985, pp. 141–151. And: Reinhold Würth: Management by example and consistency in the field service. Regional sales managers' conference on 19.3.1982 in Schwäbisch Hall. In: Thoughts on Company Management. Schwäbisch Hall 1985, pp. 171–181
380 Reinhold Würth: Management style in the field service. Regional managers' conference in South Tyrol. May 29 – 30, 1981. In: Thoughts on Company Management. Schwäbisch Hall 1985, pp. 141–151
381 Interview with Karl Specht on January 20, 2004
382 Reinhold Würth: Do it! Special sales conference of field service V from 13th to 16th September 1982 in Heilbronn. In: Thoughts on Company Management. Schwäbisch Hall 1985, pp. 199–208
383 Reinhold Würth: Management by example and consistency in the field service. In: Thoughts on Company Management. Schwäbisch Hall 1985, pp. 171–181
384 Reinhold Würth: The new training model of Adolf Würth GmbH & Co. KG. International Division conference on 7th November 1983 in Bad Mergentheim. In: Thoughts on Company Management. Schwäbisch Hall 1985, pp. 277–284
385 Reinhold Würth: Management style in the field service. Regional managers' conference in South Tyrol. May 29 – 30, 1981. In: Thoughts on Company Management. Schwäbisch Hall 1985, pp. 141–151
386 Reinhold Würth: Field service employee training model. Würth managers' conference, International Division. Spring 1984/Istanbul. In: Thoughts on Company Management. Schwäbisch Hall 1985, pp. 377–385
387 Karlheinz Schönherr: Nach oben geschraubt. Reinhold Würth. Die Karriere eines Unternehmers. 3rd unchanged edition. Künzelsau 2001, p. 170
388 Company History Dieter Krämer, Würth Central Archives
389 Company History Rolf Bauer, Würth Central Archives
390 Würth Handbook 2002. Facts and Figures worldwide. Künzelsau 2002, pp. 90
391 Martin Schulteis: Voraussetzungen für den Erfolg von Unternehmensakquisitionen unter besonderer Berücksichtigung der Würth-Gruppe. Dissertation submitted for a diploma at the University of Karlsruhe 2000, pp. 94
392 Company History Rolf Bauer, Würth Central Archives
393 Company History Rolf Bauer, Würth Central Archives
394 Interview with Rolf Bauer on January 12, 2004
395 Company History Rolf Bauer, Würth Central Archives
396 Würth Handbook 2002. Facts and Figures worldwide. Künzelsau 2002, pp. 96
397 Interview with Rolf Bauer on January 12, 2004
398 Würth Handbook 2002. Facts and Figures worldwide. Künzelsau 2002, pp. 96
399 See Thoughts on Company Management. Schwäbisch Hall 1985
400 Reinhold Würth: The manager and his task. Young Management staff conference from 21st to 24th September 1981 in Bad Mergentheim. In: Thoughts on Company Management. Schwäbisch Hall 1985, pp. 153–162
401 Reinhold Würth: Catch the chance. International division conference from 25th to 30th April 1983 in Nice. In: Thoughts on Company Management. Schwäbisch Hall 1985, p. 238
402 Reinhold Würth: Do it ,83. International managers' conference from 25th to 28th October 1982 in Alsace. In: Thoughts on Company Management. Schwäbisch Hall 1985, pp. 209–219
403 Reinhold Würth: Do it ,83. International managers' conference from 25th to 28th October 1982 in Alsace. In: Thoughts on Company Management. Schwäbisch Hall 1985, p. 215, p. 216
404 Reinhold Würth: Improving the quality of growth. International Division conference in Portugal from 3rd to 7th May 1982. In: Thoughts on Company Management. Schwäbisch Hall 1985, pp. 183–198
405 Reinhold Würth: Improving the quality of growth. International Division conference in Portugal from 3rd to 7th May 1982. In: Thoughts on Company Management. Schwäbisch Hall 1985, pp. 183–198

406 Reinhold Würth: Profit – the wages of clever economic management? Managers' conference of the Würth group in spring 1981 27.4. to 1.5.1981 in Rottach-Egern/Tegernsee. In: Thoughts on Company Management. Schwäbisch Hall 1985, pp. 127–140
407 Company History Dieter Krämer, Würth Central Archives
408 Company History Dieter Krämer, Würth Central Archives
409 Reinhold Würth: Do it '83. International managers' conference from 25th to 28th October 1982 in Alsace. In: Thoughts on Company Management. Schwäbisch Hall 1985, pp. 209–219
410 Interview with Reinhold Würth on June 17, 2004
411 See Annual Report of the Würth Group 1988
412 Reinhold Würth: Management by ... Young management staff B/I conference from 27th to 30th June 1983 in Waldenburg. In: Thoughts on Company Management. Schwäbisch Hall 1985, pp. 253–261
413 Reinhold Würth: Management by ... Young management staff B/I conference from 27th to 30th June 1983 in Waldenburg. In: Thoughts on Company Management. Schwäbisch Hall 1985, pp. 253–261
414 Reinhold Würth: Management Culture: the Secret of Success. An Entrepreneur Takes Stock. 2nd edition. Künzelsau1999, p. 308
415 Memo by Reinhold Würth to the Füko and the members of the management team of KG from May 13, 1983, Würth Central Archives
416 Capital, September 1989
417 Regarding the reasons given fort he awarding of the prize see Karlheinz Schönherr: Nach oben geschraubt. Reinhold Würth. Die Karriere eines Unternehmers. 3rd unchanged edition. Künzelsau 2001, p. 160
418 Company History Gerhard Fried, Würth Central Archives
419 www.wuerth.de. Press release from May 12, 2004
420 Company History Rolf Bauer, Würth Central Archives
421 Reinhold Würth: Management Culture: the Secret of Success. An Entrepreneur Takes Stock. 2nd edition. Künzelsau1999, pp. 331. Also see Company History Dr. Walter Jaeger, Würth Central Archives
422 Kompendium der rechtlichen Struktur der Würth-Gruppe, Stand März 2001. Preface of the first edition 1990, pp. 9
423 Also see Reinhold Würth: Application submitted to the Foundation supervisory board and Advisory Board: Application for nomination of Bettina Würth as member of the new Board of Directors from February 24, 2000, Würth Central Archives
424 Reinhold Würth stipulated the precise rules regarding members of the Foundation supervisory boards in a compendium on the "legal structure of the Würth Group"

CHAPTER 10

425 Reinhold Würth: The Würth Idea for the 80s. In: Thoughts on Company Management. Schwäbisch Hall 1985, pp. 81–90
426 Reinhold Würth: Management Culture: the Secret of Success. An Entrepreneur Takes Stock. 2nd edition. Künzelsau 1999, p. 284
427 Annual Report of the Würth Group 2003, percentages calculated by the authors.
428 All figures taken from the Annual Reports of the Würth Group
429 Reinhold Würth: Companies need targets. International division conference from 26th to 30th _October 1981in Bad Mergentheim. In: Thoughts on Company Management. Schwäbisch Hall 1985, p. 168
430 All figures taken from the Annual Reports of the Würth Group, percentages calculated by the authors
431 Also in the following Reinhold Würth: Sales technique and marketing. Lecture manuscript. Entrepreneurship Institute. University of Karlsruhe (TH), summer semester 2002
432 Reinhold Würth: Sales technique and marketing. Lecture manuscript. Entrepreneurship Institute. University of Karlsruhe (TH), summer semester 2002
433 Annual Report of the Würth Group 2002
434 Company History Karl Specht, Würth Central Archives
435 Reinhold Würth: Field service employee training model. Würth managers' conference, International Division Spring 1984/Istanbul. In: Thoughts on Company Management. Schwäbisch Hall 1985, pp. 377–388
436 Also in the following Reinhold Würth: Sales technique and marketing. Lecture manuscript. Entrepreneurship Institute. University of Karlsruhe (TH), summer semester 2002
437 Reinhold Würth: Sales technique and marketing. Lecture manuscript. Entrepreneurship Institute. University of Karlsruhe (TH), summer semester 2002
438 Interview with Karl Specht on January 20, 2004
439 Yvonne Thein: Incentives – Pro und Contra. Kritische Analyse der motivationalen Wirkung von Incentives. Master's thesis FH Rhineland-Palatinate, Worms 1993, pp. 76
440 Company History Hans Hügel, Würth Central Archives
441 Yvonne Thein: Incentives – Pro und Contra. Kritische Analyse der motivationalen Wirkung von Incentives. Master's thesis FH Rhineland-Palatinate, Worms 1993, p. 67–72
442 Company History Karl Specht, Würth Central Archives
443 Yvonne Thein: Incentives – Pro und Contra. Kritische Analyse der motivationalen Wirkung von Incentives. Master's thesis FH Rhineland-Palatinate, Worms 1993, pp. 76
444 Company History Karl Specht, Würth Central Archives
445 Reinhold Würth: Field service employee training model. Würth managers' conference, International Division Spring 1984 / Istanbul. In: Thoughts on Company Management. Schwäbisch Hall 1985, pp. 377–388
446 Ulrich Roth: Theoretische und empirische Untersuchungen von Fluktuation und Leistungsanreizen im Außendienst eines Handelsunternehmens. Künzelsau 2003 (Schriften des Interfakultativen Instituts für Entrepreneurship an der Universität Karlsruhe (TH), vol. 6)

FOOTNOTES

447 Minutes of the FÜKO 10, June 30 – July 1, 2003 in Kupferzell, Würth Central Archives
448 Reinhold Würth: Sales technique and marketing. Lecture manuscript. Entrepreneurship Institute. University of Karlsruhe (TH), summer semester 2002
449 Reinhold Würth: Sales technique and marketing. Lecture manuscript. Entrepreneurship Institute. University of Karlsruhe (TH), summer semester 2002.
450 All pieces of information of the following description taken from Reinhold Würth: Management technique and management culture. Lecture manuscript. Entrepreneurship Institute. University of Karlsruhe (TH), summer semester 2003, pp. 5–9
451 Reinhold Würth: Presentation on the occasion of the conference on warehousing and distribution of the Würth Group, Hotel Stadt Waldenburg, June 2 – 5, 1985
452 See Reinhold Würth: Improving the quality of growth. International Division conference in Portugal from 3rd to 7th May 1982. In: Thoughts on Company Management. Schwäbisch Hall 1985, p. 196
453 Reinhold Würth: Improving the quality of growth. International Division conference in Portugal from 3rd to 7th May 1982. In: Thoughts on Company Management. Schwäbisch Hall 1985, p. 195
454 Reinhold Würth: Management Culture: the Secret of Success. An Entrepreneur Takes Stock. 2nd edition Künzelsau 1999, p. 283
455 Reinhold Würth: Management Culture: the Secret of Success. An Entrepreneur Takes Stock. 2nd edition Künzelsau 1999, p. 283 and p. 306
456 Interview with Michael Kübler on December 4, 2003
457 Interview with Thomas Wagner on July 22, 2004
458 Statutes of the Council of Trustees of Adolf Würth GmbH & Co. KG, version 2000
459 Interview with Thomas Wagner, chairman of the Council of Trustees of Adolf Würth GmbH & Co. KG on July 22, 2004
460 Interview with Hermann Leiser on October 29, 2003
461 Corporate overall wage agreement for in-house employees of Adolf Würth GmbH & Co. KG, Künzelsau 2001
462 Reinhold Würth: Management Culture: the Secret of Success. An Entrepreneur Takes Stock. 2nd edition Künzelsau 1999, p. 298
463 Interview with Thomas Wagner on July 22, 2004
464 Bernhard Nebl: Der Prozess der Mitarbeiterbefragung in der AW KG. February 11, 2004. (Sales force)
465 Interview with Thomas Wagner on July 22, 2004
466 Evaluation of the Würth in-house employee survey 2003
467 Adolf Würth KG to the Schwäbisch Hall Employment Office, May 20, 1969, Würth Central Archives
468 Annual Report of the Würth Group 1997
469 Interview with Thomas Wagner on July 22, 2004.
470 All figures taken from the Annual Reports of the Würth Group
471 Annual Report of the Würth Group 1984
472 Interview with Thomas Wagner on July 22, 2004
473 Annual Report of the Würth Group 1987
474 Annual Reports of the Würth Group 1997 and 1998
475 Annual Report of the Würth Group 1999
476 Annual Report of the Würth Group 1981
477 Annual Report of the Würth Group 1994
478 Annual Report of the Würth Group 1994
479 Annual Reports of the Würth Group 2001 and 1995
480 Annual Reports of the Würth Group 2001 and 2002
481 Annual Report of the Würth Group 2003
482 Reinhold Würth: Gedanken zur Entwicklung des Hauses Würth bis zur Jahrtausendwende. Managing directors' conference Division International, fall 1986 Künzelsau
483 Annual Reports of the Würth Group 1995, 1996 and 1997
484 Interview with Michael Kübler on December 4, 2003
485 Interview Frankfurter Rundschau from March 8, 2004
486 Interview with C. Sylvia Weber on October 23, 2003
487 Würth and the Arts. A company's commitment to culture. Künzelsau 1999, p. 44
488 Reinhold Würth: Management Culture: the Secret of Success. An Entrepreneur Takes Stock. 2nd edition Künzelsau 1999, p. 304
489 Annual Report of the Würth Group 1991

CHAPTER 11
490 Answer of a Würth employee to the question what had changed after Reinhold Würth's transfer to the office of chairman of the Advisory Board
491 See for this paragraph: Bundeszentrale für politische Bildung. Informationen zur politischen Bildung; Annual Reports of the Würth Group; 50 Jahre Baden-Württemberg. Published by the Baden-Württemberg Statistical Office. Stuttgart 2002
492 Company History Günter Theurer, Würth Central Archives
493 Company History Karl Specht, Würth Central Archives
494 Company History Gerhard Fried, Würth Central Archives
495 Company History Rolf Bauer, Würth Central Archives
496 Reinhold Würth: Management Culture: the Secret of Success. An Entrepreneur Takes Stock. 2nd edition Künzelsau 1999, pp. 322
497 Company History José Viana, Würth Central Archives
498 Company History Gerhard Fried, Würth Central Archives
499 Annual Report of the Würth Group 1999
500 Company History Rolf Bauer, Würth Central Archives
501 Annual Report of the Würth Group 1999
502 Company History Karl Specht, Würth Central Archives
503 Sächsische Neueste Nachrichten from April 5, 1990
504 Company History Karl Specht, Würth Central Archives
505 Company History Karl Specht, Würth Central Archives
506 Company History Karl Specht, Würth Central Archives
507 Company History Karl Specht, Würth Central Archives
508 Interview with Dieter Krämer on November 6, 2003
509 Company History Dr. Walter Jaeger, Würth Central Archives
510 Company History Dr. Walter Jaeger, Würth Central Archives

511 Annual Report of the Würth Group 1997
512 Company History Otto Steck, Würth Central Archives
513 Annual Report of the Würth Group 1990. Study by the Consumer Research Association Nuremberg
514 Annual Report of the Würth Group 1993
515 Annual Report of the Würth Group 1996
516 Annual Report of the Würth Group 1996
517 Annual Report of the Würth Group 1997
518 Annual Report of the Würth Group 1998
519 Annual Report of the Würth Group 1994
520 William H. Davidow, Michael S. Malone: The Virtual Corporation. New York 1992 (published in German by Campus in 1994)
521 Interview with Michael Kübler on December 4, 2003
522 Economic journal "handwerk magazin", Adolf Würth GmbH & Co. KG, Signal Iduna Gruppe
523 Company History Dr. Walter Jaeger, Würth Central Archives
524 Company History Dr. Walter Jaeger, Würth Central Archives
525 Company History Dr. Walter Jaeger, Würth Central Archives
526 Company History Dr. Walter Jaeger, Würth Central Archives
527 Company History Dr. Walter Jaeger, Würth Central Archives
528 Company History Dr. Walter Jaeger, Würth Central Archives
529 Company History Günter Theurer, Würth Central Archives.
530 Annual Report of the Würth Group 1987
531 Company History Dieter Gräter, Würth Central Archives
532 Address by the Chairman of the Advisory Board of the Würth Group. On the occasion of the Würth Congress in Dubai. September 2003
533 Address by the Chairman of the Advisory Board of the Würth Group. On the occasion of the Würth Congress in Dubai. September 2003
534 Letter by McKinsey & Company (Dr. Hagemann) addressed to Reinhold Würth from March 22, 1985, Würth Central Archives
535 McKinsey & Company: Safeguarding the Future Growth of the Business. Würth Group. May 1985, Würth Central Archives
536 McKinsey-Memo from April 19, 1989, Würth Central Archives. The following quotes are taken from said memo
537 McKinsey & Company: Mastering the Planned Growth. Würth Group. Final report October 1989, Würth Central Archives
538 McKinsey & Company: Mastering the Planned Growth. Würth Group. Final report October 1989, Würth Central Archives
539 Reinhold Würth: Management Culture: the Secret of Success. An Entrepreneur Takes Stock. 2nd issue Künzelsau 1999, p. 296
540 Letter by A. Timmermann (McKinsey) addressed to Reinhold Würth from January 10, 1992, Würth Central Archives
541 Annual Report of the Würth Group 1991
542 Company History Dr. Walter Jaeger and Company History Rolf Bauer, Würth Central Archives
543 Company History Dr. Walter Jaeger, Würth Central Archives
544 Reinhold Würth: Management Culture: the Secret of Success. An Entrepreneur Takes Stock. 2nd edition Künzelsau 1999, p. 14
545 Company History Dr. Walter Jaeger, Würth Central Archives
546 Company History Dr. Walter Jaeger, Würth Central Archives
547 Letter from February 17, 1997 "To all members of the sales force" on the issue of the "development of AW KG", Würth Central Archives
548 Reinhold Würth: Management Culture: the Secret of Success. An Entrepreneur Takes Stock. 2nd edition, Künzelsau 1999, p. 342
549 Interview with Reinhold Würth on June 17, 2003
550 Interview with Siegfried Müller on November 5, 2003
551 Speech on the occasion of the 50th anniversary of the Würth Group, Künzelsau and Reinhold Würth's 60th birthday in the Hanns-Martin-Schleyer-Auditorium, Stuttgart, on April 20, 1995
552 Annual Report of the Würth Group 1995

CHAPTER 12
553 Manfred Kurz: Unternehmer und Philosoph. In: Values. Zeitschrift der Doertenbach GmbH & Co.KG. Frankfurt. Winter 2001/2002
554 Quote according to Karlheinz Schönherr: Nach oben geschraubt. Reinhold Würth. Die Karriere eines Unternehmers. 3rd unchanged edition Künzelsau 2001, p. 150
555 Speech by secretary of state Dr. Christoph-E. Palmer on the occasion of the ceremony on the presentation of the Ludwig-Erhard-Medal to Prof. Reinhold Würth in Stuttgart on April 27, 2004
556 Eulogy of the French consul general in Stuttgart on the occasion of the presentation of the Order Cgevalier de l'Ordre de la Légion d'Honneur to Prof. Reinhold Würth in Künzelsau-Gaisbach on March 9, 2004
557 Conversation with C. Sylvia Weber on October 28, 2003.
558 Paul Swiridoff: Gesichter einer Epoche. Begegnungen aus fünf Jahrzehnten. Stuttgart, Zurich 1997, p. 38
559 Interview with Reinhold Würth in Kunsthandel 4/2002, p. 40
560 Reinhold Würth: Management Culture: the Secret of Success. An Entrepreneur Takes Stock. 2nd edition Künzelsau 1999, p. 24
561 Interview with Denise René on November 20, 2003
562 For this section see Reinhold Würth: Management Culture: the Secret of Success. An Entrepreneur Takes Stock. 2nd edition Künzelsau 1999, p. 25
563 Press interview with Christo, Jeanne-Claude and Reinhold Würth on May 4, 2004, Würth Arlesheim, Switzerland
564 Interview with Reinhold Würth in Kunstzeitung 04/90
565 Manuel Wally: Zehn Sammler zeitgenössischer Kunst und ihre Museumsinitiativen. Doctoral thesis. University of Salzburg 1993, p. 142

566 Reinhold Würth: Management Culture: the Secret of Success. An Entrepreneur Takes Stock. 2nd edition Künzelsau 1999, p. 24
567 Interview with Reinhold Würth in Kunsthandel 4/2002, p. 41
568 See Manuel Wally: Zehn Sammler zeitgenössischer Kunst und ihre Museumsinitiativen. Doctoral thesis. University of Salzburg 1993, p. 145
569 Frankfurter Allgemeine Zeitung from September 9, 2001
570 Conversation with C. Sylvia Weber on October 28, 2003
571 Interview with Reinhold Würth in Kunsthandel 4/2002, p. 41
572 Nürtinger Zeitung from October 20, 2001
573 Interview with Reinhold Würth in Kunsthandel 4/2002, p. 41
574 Press interview with Christo, Jaenne-Claude and Reinhold Würth on May 4, 2004, Würth Arlesheim, Switzerland
575 See eulogy of the French consul general in Stuttgart on the occasion of the presentation of the decoration Chevalier de l'Ordre de la Légion d'Honneur to Prof. Reinhold Würth Künzelsau-Gaisbach on March 9, 2004
576 Paul Swiridoff: Gesichter einer Epoche. Begegnungen aus fünf Jahrzehnten. Stuttgart, Zurich 1997, p. 38
577 See Reinhold Würth: Kunst als Investition – Reflektionen eines privaten Kunstsammlers. Lecture at the 11th Churburger Wirtschaftsgespräche on October 12, 1996, p. 4
578 Conversation with C. Sylvia Weber on October 28, 2003
579 Reinhold Würth: Kunst als Investition – Reflektionen eines privaten Kunstsammlers. Lecture at the 11th Churburger Wirtschaftsgespräche on October 12, 1996, p. 7
580 Eulogy of the French consul general in Stuttgart on the occasion of the presentation of the decoration Chevalier de l'Ordre de la Légion d'Honneur to Prof. Reinhold Würth Künzelsau-Gaisbach on March 9, 2004
581 All quotes in this section taken from: Kunst und Kultur 2001. Lebendige Unternehmenskultur bei Würth. Published by Adolf Würth GmbH & Co. KG. Künzelsau 2002
582 Annual Report of the Würth Group 2002
583 Rolf Stadel: Kunst- und Kulturförderung als wichtiger Bestandteil der Unternehmensimagepolitik aufgezeigt am Beispiel der Firma Würth. Master's thesis. Stuttgart 1990, p. 55
584 This section follows Reinhold Würth: Kunst als Investition – Reflektionen eines privaten Kunstsammlers. Lecture at the 11th Churburger Wirtschaftsgespräche on October 12, 1996, p. 9
585 Reinhold Würth: Architecture at Würth. In: Gottfried Knapp, Andreas Schmid: Building for the World. Architecture at Würth. Bauen für die Welt. Architektur bei Würth. Künzelsau 2001
586 Also in the following Gottfried Knapp, Andreas Schmid: Building for the World. Architecture at Würth. Bauen für die Welt. Architektur bei Würth. Künzelsau 2001
587 Reinhold Würth: Architecture at Würth. In: Würth and the Arts. A company's commitment to culture. Künzelsau 1999, p. 106
588 Reinhold Würth: Architecture at Würth. In: Gottfried Knapp, Andreas Schmid: Building for the World. Architecture at Würth. Bauen für die Welt. Architektur bei Würth. Künzelsau 2001, 8
589 Reinhold Würth: Architecture at Würth. In: Würth and the Arts. A company's commitment to culture. Künzelsau 1999, p. 105
590 Stuttgarter Zeitung from October 20, 1999
591 Eulogy. In: Tübinger Universitätsreden volume 42: Bestowing the title of honorary senator. Reinhold Würth. February 22, 1991, p. 9, pp. 12
592 Reinhold Würth: Unternehmensführung – Quo vadis? In: Tübinger Universitätsreden volume 42: Bestowing the title of honorary senator. Reinhold Würth. February 22, 1991, p. 19
593 Quotes taken from the newspaper article "Wissenschaft ehrt Praktiker", Hohenloher Zeitung, May 3, 1999
594 Interview with Prof. Dr. Volker Krebs on November 17, 2003
595 Interview with Reinhold Würth in UNIKATH 4/2003, p. 74
596 Karlsruher Transfer, number 24, WS 2000/2001, p. 32
597 Reinhold Würth: Entrepreneurship in Germany. Ways Towards Responsibility. Künzelsau 2001 (Schriften des Interfakultativen Instituts für Entrepreneurship an der Universität Karlsruhe (TH). IEP volume 1), p. 5
598 Schriften des Interfakultativen Instituts für Entrepreneurship an der Universität Karlsruhe (TH). Künzelsau.
Vol. 1: Reinhold Würth: Entrepreneurship in Germany – Ways Towards Responsibility. 2001
Vol. 2: Reinhold Würth (publisher): Wer wagt? Unternehmensgründungen in Deutschland. 2001
Vol. 3: Reinhold Würth: The Tides of Change. Economics and Society on the Verge of the 21st Century. 2001
Vol. 4: Reinhold Würth/Hans Joachim Klein: Wirtschaftswissen Jugendlicher in Baden-Württemberg. Eine empirische Analyse. 2001
Vol. 5: Herbert Grüner: Personalmanagement in der Zeit nach der New Economy. 2002
Vol. 6: Ulrich Roth: Theoretische und empirische Untersuchungen von Fluktuation und Leistungsanreizen im Außendienst eines Handelsunternehmens. 2003
Vol. 7: Reinhold Würth (publisher): Wirtschaftsunterricht an Schulen im Aufwind? 2003
Vol. 7a: Reinhold Würth/Hans Joachim Klein: Ökonomie als erweitertes schulisches Lehr-Lern-Fach: Einstellungen von Lehrern an allgemeinbildenden Schulen in Baden-Württemberg. 2003
Vol. 8: Reinhold Würth (publisher): Wer wagt, gewinnt. 2003
Vol. 9: Tobias Walter: Segmentspezifische Vertriebsstrategien im Großhandel. 2003
Vol. 10: Roland Janner: Erfolgsfaktoren technologieorientierter Unternehmensgründungen in Baden-Württemberg. 2004
599 Karlsruher Transfer, number 24, WS 2000/2001, p. 32

600 Reinhold Würth: Das Beispiel Würth. Lecture manuscript. Entrepreneurship Institute. University of Karlsruhe (TH)
601 Handelsblatt. Junge Karriere. June 2001
602 Interview with Reinhold Würth in UNIKATH 4/2003, p. 74
603 Interview with Mirko Holzer on November 4, 2003
604 Interview with Mirko Holzer on November 4, 2003
605 Interview with Prof. Dr. Volker Krebs on November 17, 2003

CHAPTER 13

606 This chapter is mainly based on www.tagesschau.de as well as on the Annual Reports of the Würth Group and 50 Jahre Baden-Württemberg. Published by the Baden-Württemberg Statistical Office. Stuttgart 2002
607 Figures taken from the Würth Handbook 2002. Facts and Figures worldwide. Künzelsau 2002, pp. 73 (2001 version)
608 Annual Report of the Würth Group 2002
609 Annual Report of the Würth Group 2002
610 Minutes of the FÜKO 10 from June 30 – July 1 in Kupferzell, Würth Central Archives
611 Minutes of the FÜKO 10 from June 30 – July 1 in Kupferzell, Würth Central Archives
612 Ulrich Roth: Theoretische und empirische Untersuchungen von Fluktuation und Leistungsanreizen im Außendienst eines Handelsunternehmens. Schriften des Interfakultativen Instituts für Entrepreneurship an der Universität Karlsruhe (TH), vol. 6, Künzelsau 2003
613 Minutes of the FÜKO 10 from June 30 – July 1 in Kupferzell, Würth Central Archives
614 "Address by the Chairman of the Advisory Board of the Würth Group. Present Situation and Future of the Würth Group." Lecture by Reinhold Würth at the Würth Congress in Dubai in September 2003
615 "Address by the Chairman of the Advisory Board of the Würth Group. Present Situation and Future of the Würth Group." Lecture by Reinhold Würth at the Würth Congress in Dubai in September 2003
616 "Erfolg ist auch in rückläufigen Märkten möglich". In: Hohenloher Zeitung from July 25, 2003
617 McKinsey & Company: Mastering the Planned Growth. Würth Group. Final Report October 1989, Würth Central Archives
618 Letter by Reinhold Würth "Application to the Foundation Supervisory Board and the Advisory Board. Application for the appointment of Bettina Würth to the new Group Management Team." February 24, 2000. Würth Central Archives
619 Interview with Rolf Bauer on February 16, 2004.
620 Wüth Handbook 2002. Facts and Figures worldwide. Künzelsau 2002, p. 9
621 Letter by Reinhold Würth "Application to the Foundation Supervisory Board and the Advisory Board. Application for the appointment of Bettina Würth to the new Group Management Team." February 24, 2000. Würth Central Archives
622 Interview with Rolf Bauer on February 16, 2004
623 Annual Report of the Würth Group 2000
624 Interview with Dr. Walter Jaeger on December 10, 2003
625 Interview with Bettina Würth on October 29, 2003
626 Würth Handbook 2002. Facts and Figures worldwide. Künzelsau 2002, p. 71
627 Interview with Dr. Walter Jaeger on December 10, 2004
628 Annual Report of the Würth Group 2002
629 Interview with Peter Zürn on January 26, 2004
630 Karlheinz Schönherr: Nach oben geschraubt. Reinhold Würth. Die Karriere eines Unternehmers. 3rd unchanged edition Künzelsau 2001, p. 7
631 www.wuerth.de. August 2004
632 Annual Report of the Würth Group 2002
633 Company History Günter Theurer, Würth Central Archives
634 Company History Dieter Krämer, Würth Central Archives
635 Interview with Rolf Bauer on February 16, 2004
636 McKinsey & Company: Mastering the Planned Growth.Würth Group. Final Report October 1989, Würth Central Archives
637 Letter by A. Timmermann (McKinsey) to Reinhold Würth from January 10, 1992, Würth Central Archives
638 Letter by Reinhold Würth to A. Timmermann (McKinsey) from February 12, 1992. Würth Central Archives
639 Martin Schulteis: Voraussetzungen für den Erfolg von Unternehmensakquisitionen unter besonderer Berücksichtigung der Würth-Gruppe. Eine theoretische und empirische Analyse. Master's thesis University of Karlsruhe 2000. P. 148
640 Interview with Rolf Bauer on February 16, 2004
641 "Würth, der Finanzdienstleister". In: Hohenloher Zeitung from May 11, 2004
642 Interview with Reinhold Würth on June 17, 2004
643 Recent information taken from www.wuerth.com
644 Künzelsau press report from April 15, 2004 www.wuerth.com/konzern/presse/pm/040416-grassgruppe.html
645 Interview with Dr. Walter Jaeger on December 10, 2003
646 "Address by the Chairman of the Advisory Board of the Würth Group. Present Situation and Future of the Würth Group." Lecture by Reinhold Würth at the Würth Congress in Dubai in September 2003

INDEX OF PERSONS

Abbado, Claudio 253
Adenauer, Konrad 22, 70
Alfonsi, Josiane 255
Al Maktoum, Ahmed bin Saeed Plate 2/2
Alsmann, Götz 208
Ambros, Wolfgang 208
Antes, Horst 239
Anzinger, Siegfried 239
Arbeiter, Daniela 256
Armstrong, Neil 72
Arp, Hans 245
Arroyo, Eduardo 239

Bak, Pieter 92
Balbach, Wilhelm 63
Bamberger, Norbert 14
Bangemann, Martin 236
Baselitz, Georg 239
Basquiat, Jean Michel 245
Bauer, Rolf 30, 78et seq, 82, 84et seq, 87, 101, 111, 121et sqq., 135et seq., 141et seq, 173et sqq, 182, 202, 213, 219, 225et seq, 232, 270, 275et sqq, 281et seq
Bea, Franz X. 263
Beckenbauer, Franz 208
Beckmann, Max 238
Beglinger, Peter 182
Beilharz, Otto 30, 80, 86, 115, 117, 121et seq, 132, 141, 276, 282
Benz, Karl 231
Berger, Senta 208
Bernard, Emile 246
Berner, Albert 36et sqq, 81, Plate 1/2
Bier, Gerda 239
Bier, Wolfgang 239, 245
Binder, Manfred 198
Binz, Mark K. 182
Bohatsch, Erwin 239
Bombala, Anna 101
Bosch, Robert 10, 231
Botero, Fernando Plate 9/5
Botta, Mario 247
Brandt, Willy 72, 114, 135
Braun, Wolfgang 118
Brey, Norbert 259
Buffet, Bernard 238
Bugelnig, Gerhard 147
Burgstahler, Richard 96
Bush, George 271
Buttlar, Horst von 255

Caro, Anthony 242, Plate 6/3
Chafes, Rui 254
Chagall, Marc 238, 250

Chillida, Eduardo 248
Christo und Jeanne Claude 229et seq, 239, 242et seq, 245et seq, 251
Clausen, Ernst 90, 96et sqq, 103et seq, 109, 177
Clausen, Otto 97

Daimler, Gottlieb 231
Dalai Lama 230, Plate 3/4
Damisch, Gunter 239
Davis, Dennis Russel 253
Deacon, Richard 254
Dehnelt, Hubert 38, 42, 84
Delaunay, Sonia 239
Dias, Nuno 99
Dix, Otto 238
Djordjevic-Müller, Maja 166, 206, 228, 244, 261
Djotirto Sjifong 92
Doldinger, Klaus 208
Domhardt, Elke 255
Dorfer, Oliver 239
Döring, Walter 51
Dorst, Tankred 254
Drexler, Peter 73, 93, 146, 177
Drüeke, Ludger 14, 167
Drvenkar, Zoran 256

Eiermann, Egon 130
Elsen-Schwedler, Beate 244
Engbarth, Gerhard 256
Enzensberger, Hans Magnus 242
Erhard, Ludwig 70
Erker, Paul 8
Ernst, Max 238, 245
Eyth, Max 64
Feldmann, Gerald D. 10
Fitz, Lisa 208
Fontano, Lucio 239
Ford, Henry 267
Foster, Norman 247
Frantz, Justus 208, 236
Fried, Gerhard 123, 132, 180, 225, 276
Friedmann, Robert 277, 304
Fruhtrunk, Günter 239

Gauguin, Paul 246
Geißler, Theo 253
Genscher, Hans-Dietrich 114
Gläser, Stefan 65
Glass, Philipp 230, 253
Goethe, Johann Wolfgang von 237
Golisch, Stefanie 256
Gorbatschow, Michail 161
Goytisolo, Juan 254

Grass, Günter **245, 251, 254**
Gräter, Dieter **222**
Greger, Max **208**
Grieshaber, HAP **238**
Gschnell, Helmut **90, 94, 104**
Guillaume, Günter **114**
Guimaraes, José de **239, 245**

Haag, Werner **182**
Häckel, Jürgen **145, 151**
Hacker, Dieter **239**
Hammerschmitt, Markus **255**
Hampel, Rudolf **79et seq**
Hartung, Harald **257**
Hauschild, Anne **255**
Hausner, Rudolf **239, 245**
Hayek, Nicolas G. **164**
Hebenstreit, Manfred **239**
Helferrich, Karl **10**
Hempel, Otto **40et seq**
Hendriksen, Klaus **90, 104et seq**
Herold, Artur **40et seq, 43, 831, 83**
Herzog, Roman **232, 258**, Plate 4/4
Heuss, Theodor **10, 21et seq, 64**
Hierdeis, Irmgard **255**
Hildebrandt, Dieter **208**
Hofmann, Richard **49**
Holzer, Mirko **268et seq**
Hrdlicka, Alfred **239, 242, 244et seq**
Huang, Ken **106**
Hügel, Hans **30, 36et sqq, 75, 77et seq, 81et sqq, 85, 87, 99, 121et seq, 125, 129, 192, 202**
Hugel, Pierre **96**
Humpert, Alfons **118**
Hundhausen, Prof. **86et seq**
Hüsch, Hans-Dieter **208**
Hutter, Wolfgang **239**

Immendorf, Jörg **239**

Jacobsen, Robert **229, 238et seq, 245, 248, 253**
Jaeger, Walter **96, 116, 141, 182, 216, 220et sqq, 226et sqq, 232, 270, 276et sqq, 282, 284, 303et seq**
Jakob, Paul **131**
Jawlensky, Alexej von **238**
Jenninger, Philipp **166, 236**
Jensen, Marcus **256**
Jeschke, Matthias **256**
Jetelovà, Magdalena **254**
Johannes Paul II. Plate 3/3
Jong, Annette de **256**
Jungfer, Erika **141et seq**

Just, Volker **256**
Kellermann, Fritz **248**
Kennel, Odile **255**
Kern, Michel **108**
Kern, Stephan **254**
Kieninger, Martina **256**
Klein, Hans Joachim **265et seq, 284**
Kleinknecht, Heinz **77et seq, 80, 116, 220**
Knoblauch, Gerhard **115, 122**
Knoch, Ernst **40**
Kofler, Hubert **157**
Kohl, Helmut **212**
Köpf, Gerhard **254**
Krämer, Dieter **96, 103, 107, 111, 117, 119, 121et sqq, 132, 143et sqq, 160, 165, 178, 216, 220, 276, 280, 282**
the Krätzer family **16**
Krebs, Volker **256et seq, 269**
Kreizberg, Yakov **253**
Kriedemann, Terèzia **255**
Krupp, Georg **24, 119, 176, 231**
Küblbeck, Ursula **66**
Kübler, Michael **198et seq, 209**
Kühlke, Kirsten **256**
Kühn, Gerhard **40**
Künast, Hermine **44, 85, 134**
Küng, Hans **32, 237**
Kurz, Manfred **235**

Lafontaine, Oskar **212**
Laister, Josef **90, 93et seq, 101**
Larsen, Henning **230, 247**
Lastdrager, Hendrik J. **73, 90et seq, 97, 177**
Lavizzari, Alexandra **256**
Léger, Fernand **238**
Leiser, Hermann **38et seq, 42et sqq, 81et seq, 199**
Lenk, Thomas **239**
Lenz, Herrmann **257**
Lenz, Volker **62et seq**
Lepper, Gereon **254**
Liebermann, Max **248**
Lüpertz, Markus **239, 245**

Magnelli, Alberto **245**
Magris, Claudio **257**
Malter, Rebecca **256**
Mandela, Nelson Plate 2/1
Manzoni, Piero **239**
Markart, Mike **266**
Mayer, Johann Friedrich **47**
McDonalds, Richard und Maurice **267**
Merck, Emanuel **10**
Merkel, Angela **212**

INDEX OF PERSONS

Meyer, Henry W. 253
Meyer, Jean-Paul **95et seq**
Michel, Jürg **108**
Miró, Joan **238**
Molland, Ole **97**
Mortensen, Richard **239**
Müller-Wieland, Birgit **256**
Müller, Herta **254**
Müller, Pius **93**
Müller, Siegfried **166, 206, 228et seq, 244, 261**
Munch, Edvard **248**
Münter, Gabriele **239**

Nedwal, Peter **249**
Nestlé, Henry **10**
Neus, Werner **264**
Niermeyer, Sandra **256**
Nolde, Emil **237et seq, 241**

Oakes, Alan **103**
Oetker, August **10**
Ohnemus, Chris **255**
Ohnesorg, Benno **72**
Ören, Aras **254**
Oz, Amos **254**

Pakleppa, Fabienne **256**
Palmer, Christoph **236**
Pelgrim, Hermann-Josef **61, 66, 234, 301**
Penck, A.R. **239**
Pfleiderer, Helmut **118**
Picasso, Pablo **238, 245, 250**
Pierer, Heinrich von **236**
Pohl, Manfred **12**
Poliakoff, Serge **238, 245**
Polt, Gerhard **208**
Preisendörfer, Bruno **255**
Presley, Elvis **35**
Pronk, Hans **108**
Pruckner, Olaf **60**
Puttmann, Anette **255**

Quant, Mary **72**
Quinn, Freddy **35**

Rademacher, Guido **256**
Rainer, Arnulf **239, 245**
Ramírez, Juan **100**
Rantanen, Pentti **90, 98, 101**
Rapp, Hans **37et seq, 79**
Rappold, Manfred **220**
Rau, Werner **123et seq, 135, 164**
Reckewell, Doris **255**
Reichelt, Jutta **256**

Reimert, Karla **255**
Reisser, August **59**
Reisser, Gotthilf **27, 59**
Reisser, Hermann **59**
René, Denise **238, 240**
Reuter, Edzard **305**
Reuter, Ernst **21**
Ribeiro, Joao Ubaldo **254**
Richter, Ilja **208**
Riedel, Christian **54**
Röhrig, Jürgen **130**
Rössler, Gerd **108**
Roth, Ulrich **194**
Roth, Ute **278, 300**
Ruf, Sepp **130, 166, 260**
Rühmkorf, Peter **254**
Rumpf, Friedrich K. **255**
Rygiert, Beate **256**

Sandrini, Engelbert **90, 94**
Sarafin, Lee **103**
Sarmento, Juliao **239**
Scharpf, Johann Georg **249**
Scheel, Walter **72, 114**
Scheibl, Hubert **239**
Schenk - Gonsolin, Sylvie **256**
Schiebenes, Heinz **60**
Schlachter, Beate **255**
Schmalix, Hubert **239**
Schmidt-Dubro, Eckhard **256**
Schmidt, Harald **208**
Schmidt, Helmut **114, 161**
Schmidt, Jochen **256**
Schmidt-Dubro, Eckhard **266**
Schneebelli, Max **92**
Schönherr, Dietmar **253**
Schönherr, Karlheinz **7**
Schröder, Gerhard **212, 230, 234, 236, 242, 247, 269, 271,** Plate 4/3
Schuh, Kurt **258**
Schulte, Ingeborg **255**
Schulteis, Martin **282**
Schütze-Schröder, Friedrun **256**
Sedlak, Silwa **239**
Seebacher, Anton **90, 94**
Seiler, Hellmut **256**
Sérusier, Paul **246**
Siemens, Georg von **10**
Sigrist, Hans **90, 92et seq, 106**
Soccol, Onorino **94**
Sommer, Johann Andreas **249**
the Sommer family of artists **62, 248et seq**
Sommer, Ron **272**
Sorg, Martin H. **182**

Späth, Lothar **66,** Plate 4/1
Specht, Karl **41, 67, 78, 81et sqq, 85, 87, 121, 125et sqq, 131, 170et seq, 191, 213et sqq, 225, 276**
Sperling, Hans-Peter **86, 260**
Starbatty, Joachim **262et seq**
Steck, Otto **217**
Steinbeis, Ferdinand **47**
Steinfest, Heinrich **255**
Stinnes, Hugo **10**
Stöckli, Christian **93**
Streeruwitz, Marlene **254**
Stroh, Frank **66et seq, 292**
Sturm, Gerhard Plate 1/2
Susset, Franz **65**
Swiridoff, Paul **31, 134, 166, 238, 243, 245,259**
Szczypiorski, Andrzeij **254**

Tag, Kurt **132, 141et seq**
Tapiès, Antoni **239**
Tauber, Gerald **127**
Tawada, Yoko **254**
Telgenbüscher, Antje **255**
Teufel, Erwin **231, 232, 236, 242,** Plate 4/2
Theis, Adolf **263**
Theurer, Günter **101et seq, 116, 165**
Thon, Paul **101**
Tietz, Bruno **117et seq, 123, 144, 160, 217et seq, 279**
Tisma, Aleksander **254**
Tomas, Stefan **255**
Trenker, Luis Plate 1/1
Truco, Matté **260**
Trux, Walter **180**
Tuchnowski, Lun **239, 254**
Turrini, Peter **254**

Unkelbach, Harald **132, 144et seq, 219, 277**

Vasarély, Victor **238et seq**
Viana, Gerti **108**
Viana, José Carlos **90, 98et sqq, 104, 108et sqq, 222, 276**
Vigée, Claude **257**

Wader, Hannes **208**
Wagner, Thomas **199, 203, 303**
Walser, Alissa **254**
Walther, Christoph **41et seq, 82et sqq**
Walton, Sam **267**
Warhol, Andy **239**
Weber, C. Sylvia **14, 167, 209, 229et seq, 234, 244, 259**
Weber, Max **9**

Wehler, Hans-Ulrich **9**
Weidner, Karl **133et sqq, 168**
Weizäcker, Richard von **231et seq**
Wilden, Patrick **256**
Willikens, Ben Plate 9/6
Winter, Harald **256**
Winter, Karl Heinz **106**
Wittig, Sigmar **265**
Wölzl, Rainer **239**
Wurmbrand, Alfred **94**
Würth, Adolf **12, 16et sqq, 22et sqq, 30, 36, 45, 59, 89**
Würth, Alma **16, 23, 26et sqq, 30, 36, 38, 118**
Würth, Anne-Sophie **32**
Würth, Bettina **31et sqq, 182, 191, 232 , 276et seq, 304**
Würth, Carmen **30et sqq, 62et seq, 182, 230,238et seq, 252**
Würth, Friedrich **27**
Würth, Klaus-Frieder **16, 26, 28et sqq, 79, 173**
Würth, Marion **31et seq, 182, 186**
Würth, Markus **32**
Würth, Markus **31**
Würth, Nikolaus **33**
Wyss, Peter **92et seq**

Zahno, Daniel **255**
Zimmermann, Tabea **253**
Zürn, Peter **101, 106, 179, 181, 202, 274, 276, 279**
Zylla, Klaus **245**

IMPRINT

Photo Credits
Roland Bauer, Braunsbach: Pages 54, 230, 243, 244, 259, Plate 7.4 | Stefan Boness/ IPON, Berlin: Page 286 | Foto André GmbH, Ismaning: Page 257 | Burghard Hüdig, Stuttgart: Page 232.2 | Marcus Kaufhold, Wiesbaden: Plate 1.2 | Eva Maria Kraiss, Schwäbisch Hall: Pages 66, 234, Plates 6.3, 9.6 | Kunsthalle Würth, Schwäbisch Hall: Plate 9.5 | Museum Würth, Künzelsau: Plates 8.2, 10.1 | Photostudio Haslinger, Vienna: Page 31 | picturesborn, Vienna: Pages 92, 258 | Press- and Information Office of the Federal Government, Picture Library, Berlin: Page 232.3, Plate 4.3 | Christof R. Sage, Filderstadt: Plate 4.2 | Andreas Schmid, Munich: Pages 88, 145, 184, 277, Plates 6.2, 8.1, 13.1, 13.2, 14.1, 14.2, 14.3, 15.4, 15.5, 15.6, 16.1, 16.2 | Kai-Uwe Schneider, Freiburg: Plate 11.4 | Philipp Schönborn, Munich: Plates 7.5, 8.3, 9.4, 10.2, 11.3, 12.1, 12.2 | Servizio Fotografico de „L'Osservatore Romano", Vatican City: Plate 3.3 | Vitesse Kärcher GmbH, Fellbach: Page 228 | Wolfgang Volz, Düsseldorf: Plate 6.1

Page 18/19: with kind permission of the Künzelsau city archives
All other pictures: central archives of Adolf Würth GmbH & Co. KG

Compilation
Norbert Bamberger

Translation
Carla Bassermann, Nürtingen

Editing
First Edition Translations, Cambridge

Grafic Design
ENORM, Agentur für Visuelle Kommunikation, Köln

Printed and bound by
Druckhaus „Thomas Müntzer", Bad Langensalza

© 2005 Swiridoff Verlag, Künzelsau
All rights reserved. No part of this publication may be reproduced, stored in a retrieval system, or transmitted, in any form or by any means, electronic, mechanical, photocopying, recording, or otherwise, without the prior permission of the publishers.

ISBN 3-89929-060-7